THE GUARDIAN: PERSPECTIVES ON
THE MINISTRY OF FINANCE OF ONTARIO

IPAC *The Institute of Public Administration of Canada* **IAPC** *L'Institut d'administration publique du Canada*

The Institute of Public Administration of Canada Series
in Public Management and Governance

Editor: Patrice Dutil

This series is sponsored by the Institute of Public Administration of Canada as part of its commitment to encourage research on issues in Canadian public administration, public sector management, and public policy. It also seeks to foster wider knowledge and understanding among practitioners, academics, and the general public.

For a list of books published in the series, see page 365.

EDITED BY PATRICE DUTIL

The Guardian

Perspectives on the Ministry of Finance of Ontario

IPAC IAPC
The Institute of
Public Administration of Canada

L'Institut d'administration
publique du Canada

UNIVERSITY OF TORONTO PRESS
Toronto Buffalo London

ISBN 978-1-4426-4254-6

Printed on acid-free, 100% post-consumer recycled paper with vegetable-based inks.

Library and Archives Canada Cataloguing in Publication

The guardian : perspectives on the Ministry of Finance of Ontario / edited by Patrice Dutil.

(Institute of Public Administration of Canada series in public management and governance)
Includes bibliographical references.
ISBN 978-1-4426-4254-6

1. Finance, Public – Ontario. 2. Fiscal policy – Ontario. 3. Budget – Ontario. 4. Ontario. Ministry of Finance. I. Dutil, Patrice A., 1960– II. Series: Institute of Public Administration of Canada series in public management and governance

HJ795.O5G82 2011   336.713   C2011-900926-9

Canada School   École de la fonction
of Public Service publique du Canada

Financial support from the Canada School of Public Service for this book is gratefully acknowledged. The views expressed herein are not necessarily those of the Canada School of Public Service or of the Government of Canada.

This book has been published with the help of a grant from the Canadian Federation for the Humanities and Social Sciences, through the Aid to Scholarly Publications Program, using funds provided by the Social Sciences and Humanities Research Council of Canada.

University of Toronto Press acknowledges the financial assistance to its publishing program of the Canada Council for the Arts and the Ontario Arts Council.

Canada Council   Conseil des Arts
for the Arts   du Canada

ONTARIO ARTS COUNCIL
CONSEIL DES ARTS DE L'ONTARIO

University of Toronto Press acknowledges the financial support of the Government of Canada through the Canada Book Fund for its publishing activities.

For Don Stevenson,
Witness, Scholar, Friend

Contents

Acknowledgments   ix

Introduction   3

SECTION 1: STRUCTURES AND CONTEXTS OF THE GUARDIAN

1 The House Frost Built: Institutional Change and the Department of Treasury, 1943–1961   13
KEITH BROWNSEY

2 From 'Treasury' to 'Finance': The Anatomy of a Guardian, 1961–2001   37
PATRICE DUTIL AND DEVYN LEONARD

3 Priority Setters and Guardians: The Relationships between Premiers and Treasurers in Ontario, 1960–2001   74
JP LEWIS

SECTION 2: THE GUARDIAN IN POLICY MAKING

4 Intergovernmental Guardians: Treasury's Role in Setting the National Agenda, 1959–1967   109
P.E. BRYDEN

5 From Pragmatism to Neoliberalism: Ontario's Hesitant Farewell to Dr Keynes   131
BRYAN EVANS AND JOHN SHIELDS

6 Thoughts into Words: The Budget Speech, 1968–2003   162
PATRICE DUTIL, PETER RYAN, AND ANDRÉ GOSSIGNAC

7 The Ontario Ministry of Finance as an Exception in Canadian
Public Administration   206
LUC BERNIER AND JOSEPH FACAL

SECTION 3: THE GUARDIAN AND BUDGET MAKING

8 Dealing with Complexity: Innovation and Resistance in Crafting
the Expenditure Budget, 1961–1985   229
CAROLINE DUFOUR

9 Budget Making in the Ontario Ministry of Finance, 1985–2000   257
KEN OGATA AND GARY SPRAAKMAN

10 'Guardian' as 'Spender': Infrastructure Investment,
1960–2005   287
GERVAN FEARON

11 Guardians in Check: The Impact of Health Care on the Ontario
Budget, 1960–2004   320
PATRICE DUTIL

Conclusion   351
PATRICE DUTIL

Contributors   361

Acknowledgments

No book finds its way into the hands of readers without accumulating a long list of debts, and this one is no exception.

The first note of thanks goes to the Ontario Ministry of Finance for a number of reasons. The first one is financial. The leadership of the Ministry kindly accepted my proposal for a study of their department and my request for financial support when I approached them in 2006. Its support made this study possible, but the money involved here was not the point. What mattered was the symbolism of a ministry entrusting a variety of scholars to draw up a composite sketch of what its evolution over the past forty years looked like. The leaders – and I have to single out Mr Len Roozen, who retired after a long and distinguished career as Assistant Deputy Minister in 2007, for championing this effort – believed that the story of their department needed to be told. Len easily shared his lifelong enthusiasm for his department with me and his zeal for the project had an infectious effect on all of us. Another leader was Carol Layton, the Deputy Minister of Infrastructure Planning and for many years of her distinguished career a staff member in the Ministry of Finance. Carol graciously accepted my calls for help, and, as president of the Institute of Public Administration of Canada in 2004–5 was key in promoting this project inside the Ontario government.

Many individuals in the Ministry were particularly helpful after the job got started. Helen Katz, the ministry librarian, showed the authors and their research assistants where to find material, how to find it, and in many cases found it herself. The project would have taken much longer without her. Many former employees of the ministry were generous with their critiques as we drafted these papers. Ian Macdonald, who in many ways godfathered this project, was a helpful memory to many of us. Tom Sweeting confirmed many hunches and was unsparing in his encouragement. David Redgrave regaled us with long memoranda about the evolution of the Ministry. Terry Russell was never easy to convince about anything, but he did let himself be swayed into thinking that this project was important, and his comments invariably put *us* on guard. His questions and suggestions to get to the sources strengthened the product. Don Stevenson, the dean of the Ministry staff, patiently answered questions and kindly shared his memories and papers with many of us. It is worth emphasizing that the current and past Ministry of Finance staff did not play any further role in producing this volume. What is convincing and what is questionable in this book is entirely the product of its authors.

In the summer of 2006, the scholars gathered to organize the book in Toronto and also participated in a small symposium organized by the Institute of Public Administration of Canada that featured past public servants as well as former Ministers of Finance. Bob Nixon, Floyd Laughren, and Ernie Eves participated enthusiastically and shared their impressions of the ministry based on their experiences. All three of them have been helpful to the scholars and deserve a warm round of thanks from all of us. Naturally, neither the public servants nor the politicians were in agreement with everything that was written in these pages, nor should they be held responsible for its contents.

On a personal note, I am grateful to all the scholars for contributing their precious time, imagination, and energy to this project from the very beginning. I was fortunate in attracting individuals from many parts of Canada to this project and indeed from many generations, each bringing their own interesting methods to bear on this topic. This book is the product of political scientists, public administration scholars, historians, and political economists. Many of them worked in government before becoming academics. Three of them worked in different capacities for the Ontario government and two observed Ontario from various departments in Alberta. One of them observed Ontario from the cabinet table in the government of Quebec. They were a swell team to lead and all had interesting experiences while drafting their chapters. One gave birth to a baby girl; the other had kidney stones. Four contributors completed their PhDs in the course of writing their papers for this book. A few contributors changed jobs; one became a dean! Some of them published other books and most published articles in specialized journals on topics foreign to the Ontario Ministry of Finance. A few of them had to deal with serious family illnesses. In other words, they all had to contend with the ups and downs of life, but came through. I look forward to working with all of them again soon.

In speaking about academics, I want to extend my sincere gratitude to the anonymous evaluators of the manuscript. They accepted the challenge of appraising a manuscript composed of many diverse approaches and produced helpful criticisms that have fortified the product that is in your hands now. Their professionalism in dealing with the ideas, innovations, and tragic mistakes of our work serves as a model for scholarship. True peers, they delivered their response within agreed deadlines and graciously reread the manuscript before it went to press. There may still be parts of the book that irritate them, but that is not their fault, simply ours.

I thank Ryerson University for making a home for me in the Department of Politics and Public Administration and my dear friends and colleagues in the Institute of Public Administration of Canada – my home for some seven years – for supporting the publication of this book. The current board of directors of IPAC, led by its president Ms. Wynne Young, deputy minister in the Government of Saskatchewan; Gabriel Sekaly, the CEO; and Wendy Feldman, Director of Research, deserve a firm handshake and a fond 'thank you' for their continued support of the series. Inevitably, I must acknowledge the late Joseph Galimberti in recognition of his leadership and guidance in the early months when this project was conceived. Joe was an economist by training and always contributed insights and wisdom in conversations on the financial dealings of governments. I know he would have been proud to see this project come to fruition and be the first to point out that IPAC was the brainchild of some of the key executives in the Ontario Treasury in the 1940s. They had the notion that Canada was ready for a learned society, drawing strength from both practitioners and scholars, to better understand the problems faced by the public sector. I am sure Chester Walters, Philip Clark, George Gathercole, and Herbert Frind would be happy to see IPAC involved in documenting the work of their department some sixty years later.

This book is dedicated to Don Stevenson for many reasons. I have known Don since 1987, when as a young policy officer in the Ministry of Intergovernmental Relations, I was introduced to the fascinating (sometimes endless) missives to the Premier and Deputy Minister he wrote from his post in Quebec City, where he served as Ontario's representative. Don incarnated the ideal of the reflective practitioner: a thoughtful public servant who questioned tirelessly the workings of the policy-making machine and worked just as energetically to make it smarter, more self-aware, and better. He took interest in the concerns of young public servants. I've discovered since then that this was not a quality he had suddenly discovered. He bore witness to the evolution of the Department of the Treasury, the development of the Premier's Office, and the deployment of the Ministries of Intergovernmental Affairs and then Municipal Affairs. Don, readers will not be surprised to learn, was present at the very first meeting that launched this book, a gathering that memorably included the estimable J. Stefan Dupré, professor emeritus of the University of Toronto, who contributed his own memories. Don Stevenson has been a lifelong friend of the Institute of Public Administration of Canada, serving as its president in 1978–9, when he was Deputy Minister of Intergovernmental Affairs.

The staff of the University of Toronto Press continues to shine with its attention to editorial detail and production logistics. My thanks go to Daniel Quinlan, my editor at UTP, for his support and energy in helping get this project to its final conclusion. He assumed the IPAC collection on Governance and Public Management in 2009, succeeding the inimitable Virgil Duff, who has guided this collection since 2001 through three editors with his trademark skill and good humour. Quinlan has brought to the task the vigour and rigour of his predecessor, and I can only hope that he will keep alive Duff's fine tradition of holding court at the Artful Dodger pub. Thanks also go to Wayne Herrington who as Associate Managing Editor guided the project through its production phases and, last but not least, John St James, who as copy-editor took literary flowers of different sizes, colours, and shapes and assembled a fine bouquet.

This book has been published with the help of a grant from the Canadian Federation for the Humanities and Social Sciences, through the Aid to Scholarly Publications Program, using funds provided by the Social Sciences and Humanities Research Council of Canada. I gratefully acknowledge this assistance.

Patrice Dutil
May 2010

THE GUARDIAN: PERSPECTIVES ON
THE MINISTRY OF FINANCE OF ONTARIO

Introduction

There is something unreal about the Treasury considered in isolation.
Hugh Heclo and Aaron Wildavsky[1]

Visitors to Toronto often make a visit to Queen's Park, a charming expanse of downtown greenery where joggers hurry past sunbathers in the summer and cross-country skiers desperate for stretches of snow congregate in the winter. In the middle of Queen's Park stands the Ontario legislative building, affectionately nicknamed the 'pink palace' in reference to the rose-coloured granite that dominates its exterior. Surrounding the Legislature is a necklace of illustrious politicians immortalized in bronze and, of course, Queen Victoria, in whose honour the park was named. Visitors will notice a number of military monuments were also erected over the years in the park. An equestrian statue of Edward VII stands in the middle, almost as if it were marching towards the war memorial of the 48th Highlanders, which stands at the park's northern tip. Just south of the Legislature, visitors find a memorial in honour of the dead of the Northwest Rebellion and the new Ontario Veterans Memorial. A monument honouring militia volunteers who died fighting Fenians is located just west of Queen's Park. Just east of Queen's Park is the memorial to fallen police officers, and to the south stands the monument to heroic firefighters.

Naturally, the Province of Ontario has honoured those who have defended it. But visitors will also find among these memorials, practically facing the Legislature, two imposing modern (one is curved!) buildings on the south-east side of Queen's Park Crescent. The 'Frost Buildings' have, for over fifty years, been the seat of the Department of the Treasury, or, as it has been known since 1993, the Ministry of Finance of

Ontario. The Ministry of Finance also takes its place among the 'guardians' of Queen's Park, and of the Province.

Aaron Wildavsky, the man who transformed the way scholars generally looked at budgeting and public finance two generations ago with the publication of *The Politics of the Budget Process*, was the first to call those who worked in budget offices 'guardians' in that their role was to defend the public purse against the demands of the 'spenders' – all the other departments whose existence depended on their success in making demands of the treasury. In their study of budget making in the British government of the 1970s, Wildavsky and Hugh Heclo humorously put it this way: 'Treasury's business is to save money, not to spend it. Spending is the province of the departments. The Treasury man who comes up with ideas for programme expansion, albeit in a good cause, is likely to be reprimanded, as was one principal recently: "you are in the treasury. It is not your business to come up with ideas for spending money. The departments will do that on their own."'[2]

Heclo and Wildavsky had great fun in interviewing former Treasury officials. 'The culture of the Treasury calls for something more active than mere skepticism,' they wrote. 'The Treasury role … is to be energetically critical.'[3] Perhaps their best line was that 'if there is any principle Treasury men learn, it is "to avoid precedent-setting" behaviour.' Joking aside, they presented the employees of the department as a zealous organization that was fiercely dedicated to protecting its Minister and indeed the citadel of the state's finance. And yet they concluded that the Treasury could only be understood in its context: 'The Treasury's supreme talent lies in its sensitivity to others. It rules indirectly by trying to shape other's assumptions, expectations and mental sets.'[4]

Donald Savoie discussed 'the guardians' in the Government of Canada's Department of Finance and in the Treasury Board Secretariat in his *The Politics of Public Spending in Canada*. He scrutinized mostly on the experience of the late 1970s and 1980s, and pointed out that 'finance plays its opposition role to spending proposals in various ways,' but pointed out that in its handling of taxation breaks, Finance had in fact also played a role as a 'spender.' This theme was confirmed when one of Wildavsky's students offered an updated Canadian adaptation of this model. In his *The Politics of Public Money: Spenders, Guardians, Priority Setters, and Financial Watchdogs inside the Canadian Government*, David Good portrayed the Department of Finance in the Government of Canada as significantly empowered 'guardians' after many years of austerity. 'By nature,' he wrote, guardians do not naturally reveal themselves. Protecting the public purse, like minding the chickens coop from the ravages of the wolf, is never an easy task even at the best of times. Better to do it quickly in the darkened hours of night than under full exposure of the midday sun. For guardians, working behind closed doors has been the traditional way in which they have plied their craft, and this continued even in a world of increased transparency and openness in government. When it comes to matters of public money, prudence and probity prevail and no self-respecting guardian ever wants to be seen by his/her colleagues as giving in too early or too much to the seemingly insatiable appetites of spending ministers and scheming officials. It is one thing to be seen as soft by outsiders but quite another to be viewed as a lightweight by colleagues. Acquiring and maintaining a reputation for guardianship among fellow colleagues is what guardians hope to achieve. When it comes to certain expenditure programs they many not know as many of the details as the spenders, but they do know more than anyone else at the centre of government.[5]

Finance Departments are critical to the understanding of public administration because of what they are, and because of what they reveal about government. Yet in Canada they have not been the focus of much more than a passing attention. Robert B. Bryce, a former deputy minister of the Department of Finance in Ottawa, wrote an impressive history of his ministry during the 1930s and was at work on a sequel focusing on the 1940s when he died in 1995. His *Maturing in Hard Times: Canada's Department of Finance through the Great Depression* was published in the Institute of Public Administration of Canada's collection in 1986, and his *Canada and the Cost of World War II: The International Operations of Canada's Department of Finance, 1939–1947* in 2005.[6] Taking full advantage of rich archival material and his own recollections, Bryce's contribution to the study of the development of the finance bureaucracy as it helped the federal government cope with two death-defying crises was immense. No other books have examined the workings of this government department so closely, and no provincial department has been so thoroughly profiled.

This book, therefore, addresses a few gaps in the Canadian public administration literature. It examines for the first time a provincial ministry of finance over a critical fifty-year span, from the early 1950s to the early 2000s. During these two generations, the Ontario ministry was transformed from the small, informal office John Robarts inherited from Leslie Frost to a sophisticated policy machine that was inherited by the Ernie Eves government in 2001. Drawing on different methodologies, it profiles a ministry in action: raising revenue, building capacity, determining budgets, relating to line ministries and other central agencies, and playing a significant role in shaping the Ontario state of today.

The Ministry of Finance, or the 'Treasury' as it was known through most of its years, worked in many fields. It was present at the birth of the province, and quickly expanded. Two years after Confederation, an audit branch was added to the Treasury. Twenty years later, that branch was renamed the Office of the Provincial Auditor, but it would not become an independent office of the Legislative Assembly until 1950. An Office of the Inspector of Finance was created inside the department in 1879, and the Treasury also acted as the Registrar General for a few years before the end of the nineteenth century.

During the early years of the twentieth century, the Treasury was called upon to house a variety of branches, bureaus, sections and divisions. Motion pictures were hardly commonplace, but Ontario created a Board of Censors of Motion Pictures in 1911 inside the Treasury, and that concern would endure inside the department until 1958. The Office of the Comptroller of Revenue was created in 1926 as taxation became a growing concern for the province. At the height of the Second World War, a bureau of Statistics and Research was created to orient decision makers on the first paths to 'evidence-based' policy making.

In his chapter on the evolution of the Department of Treasury as it emerged from the Second World War, Keith Brownsey first examines how the newly elected Progressive Conservative government led by George Drew was determined to use finance to ensure that Ontario never returned to the dark days of the Depression. But the Department of Treasury was small. In 1943 it consisted of accountants who monitored a decentralized spending process and a tax collection division. It was unrecognizable as a key central agency able to manage the creation of a modern state or engage in prolonged conflict with the senior level of government. Focusing on the role Leslie Frost played as the treasurer and then as prime minister of Ontario, Brownsey's chapter argues that the department was forced to grow because of the Conservatives' ambitious program as well as their frequent quarrels with the Government of Canada over key issues such as taxation. Despite their personal reservations about state expansion, the three premiers during this period and their provincial treasurers oversaw the creation of a key central agency of the Government of Ontario. Drew and Frost, especially, understood that without adequate resources the Conservative government could not implement its program or engage in what was a continuous battle with a centralizing federal government.

The section on 'Structures and Contexts' continues with a chapter on the structural evolution of the department. Patrice Dutil and Devyn Leonard chronicle the evolution of the 'treasury' that still looked like a banking operation to a 'finance ministry' that drew heavily on learned economic forecasts and dramatically modernized budgeting techniques. The ministry's experience through thirteen ministers and thirteen deputy ministers over the period from 1961 to 2001 meant that it had to adjust politically every three years on average, and every two years in the 1980s and 1990s. In these years, the ministry staff would touch every issue in government ranging from building infrastructure to healthcare, to regional development and horse racing.

JP Lewis examines how the relationship between finance ministers and premiers has evolved in terms of management issues, political ideology, and policy content. In his study he tests the hypothesis that over time the relationship between finance ministers and premiers in Ontario has become more complex in terms of both politics and policy. The goal of the relationship has always been to be complementary, but it has suffered due to political competitiveness and policy contradictions.

The second section of the book, 'The Guardian in Policy Making,' examines the Department of the Treasury/Ministry of Finance as a policy player beyond the simple issues of raising revenue and limiting expenditures. Penny Bryden examines what became known as 'executive federalism' from Ontario's perspective in the 1960s. Her chapter discusses one of the most hotly contested relations in Confederation – that of Ontario and the Government of Canada and of its impact on the bureaucracy at Queen's Park. In the atmosphere of enthusiasm and optimism that characterized John Robarts's government in Ontario, and with the example of Quebec's successful negotiations with the federal government over pensions, the intergovernmental affairs division of Ontario's Treasury Department began to take shape. Intent on setting the national agenda and having a voice in national policy formation, the team arranged in Ontario was also convinced that the province could play a role in protecting Canadian unity. Motivated thus by the twin goals of flexing its muscles in federal-provincial discussions and ensuring that other provinces – and especially Quebec – were not left out, the Ontario intergovernmental affairs division secured a new role for the province.

Bryan Evans and John Shields cast a different net to capture the evolution of the department in terms of its thinking, situating it as the
fiscal-policy paradigms in Ontario shift from a 'Keynesian' mode in
which the state assumes an important role in the economy to a post-
Keynesian, neo-liberal approach that favours a smaller influence for
government. The transition proved to be difficult, controversial, and
hotly contested in some parts, but it was managed in a manner that
could only be considered 'Ontarian' – part practical, part ideological,
and part necessity.

How did the various ministers of finance see their universe? Speeches
can give clues in terms of broad messages. Patrice Dutil, Peter Ryan,
and André Gossignac used new software to examine the language of
the budget speech each year since 1968. As many authors have already
pointed out, political texts have a widely recognized potential to reveal
important information about the policy positions of their authors.
Furthermore, one can certainly assume that the budget speech delivered by the minister of finance expresses his/her policy preferences as
well as that of senior administrative officers, who carefully crafted the
text. Thus, any serious adjustments should be distinguishable in the
speech. Using content analysis of budget speeches given by ministers
in the years 1968–2002, the authors measure the vision of public finance
their governments had been endorsing. Computer-aided analysis with
budgetary position category schemes and multidimensional scaling
should help us discover what rationale the ministers and their governments had been using to explain and to justify their financial decisions.
Dutil, Ryan, and Gossignac discuss the significant similarities and differences in the speeches and assess the rhetoric used to rationalize fiscal
policies. Their work also serves to position budget speeches in light of
each other and draw intriguing conclusions about the issues that were
emphasized through a period of over thirty years.

In the fourth chapter of this section, Luc Bernier and Joseph Facal cast
a glance at the evolution of the Ontario Ministry of Finance, and measure its policy capacity against the Quebec and federal examples. They
conclude that the development of the Ontario Treasury/Ministry of
Finance was indeed an exception to the trend in Canada and discuss
the reasons for and consequences of that evolution.

The third section of the book, 'The Guardian and Budget Making'
examines more closely the process of budget making, which is a vital
concern for the people who work in Finance. Caroline Dufour examines
the challenges in implementing new policy making methods in Ontario's

budgeting process. The government expenditure budget serves three purposes: control, management, and planning of the funds voted by legislative powers. Since the beginning of the twentieth century, three main styles of expenditure budget have been adopted in public bureaucracies: line-item, performance, and program-based. Scholars have produced numerous studies regarding the impacts of the adoption of these styles of budget. However, there are no studies to explain why and how public administrations choose a style of budget at a specific moment. Ken Ogata and Gary Spraakman continue the story of budget making from 1985 to 2000 by focusing on the reforms that were brought to the process under three different political parties. They probe a number of innovations introduced in this era, focusing on the nature of these innovations, and the rationales for acting or not acting upon these developments represent an important area of study with respect to the diffusion of management and accounting innovations over time and between organizational fields.

Gervan Fearon contributes another look at the 'guardians,' but this time as spenders. Focusing on infrastructure spending, he shows how Ontario approached this critical policy area. From the 1940s to the 1970s, Ontario spent massively in building up roads, schools, colleges, universities, and hospitals to facilitate economic growth. Spending continued in the years following, but at a much slower rate. Fearon discusses the approach of the department under various ministers in his study of how 'guardians' can be very effective 'spenders.'

Patrice Dutil probes the impact of the fastest-growing expense in the Ontario government's finances: health care. Starting with the good intentions of the 1950s and the increasingly strong public pressures for generalized health insurance, the Ontario government has seen its finances take a very different shape in the 1970s, 1980s, and 1990s. Health care now consumes more than 40 per cent of the Ontario budget, and trade-offs have had to be made in order to meet this demand for government dollars. This chapter focuses on the frustration caused by the inexorable rise of this aspect of public finances.

Collectively, these essays present a composite portrait of a dynamic department as it grappled with changing economic circumstances, a political environment dominated by one party for half the years under study, and then a virtual carousel of political change. As the most influential ministry in the most influential province of the Canadian confederation, its story is rich with lessons about the evolution of public administration and policy making in Canada.

NOTES

1 Hugh Heclo and Aaron Wildavsky, *The Private Government of Public Money* (Berkeley and Los Angeles: University of California Press, 1974), 75.
2 Ibid., 42.
3 Ibid., 45.
4 Ibid., 75.
5 David Good, *The Politics of Public Money: Spenders, Guardians, Priority Setters, and Financial Watchdogs inside the Canadian Government* (Toronto: University of Toronto Press, 2007), 56.
6 Robert B. Bryce, *Canada and the Cost of World War II: The International Operations of Canada's Department of Finance, 1939–1947*, edited by Matthew Bellamy (Montreal: McGill-Queen's University Press, 2005). For other studies in the Westminster model, see Samuel Brittan's work, particularly *The Treasury under the Tories, 1951–1964* (London: Secker & Warburg, 1964) and *Steering the Economy: The Role of the Treasury*, rev. ed. (Harmondsworth: Penguin, 1971).

SECTION 1

Structures and Contexts of the Guardian

1 The House Frost Built: Institutional Change and the Department of Treasury, 1943–1961

KEITH BROWNSEY

On an August day in 1954, various provincial dignitaries gathered on Grosvenor Street, just a few steps from Queen's Park in Toronto, to watch the 'Prime Minister of Ontario' touch the cornerstone of what would eventually be the new home of the Treasury department. By his side were William Griesinger, the minister of public works, and Chester Walters, the deputy treasurer. Leslie Frost, often referred to as 'old man Ontario,' had blessed an uncommonly contemporary design for this office block. It was austere and functional, smoothly sheathed in stone and dominated by large windows. The ultra-modern building was in sharp contrast to the Romanesque legislative building across the Queen's Park circle. The new building was symbolic of a new Ontario – a province that looked to the future with a new design, both literally and figuratively. It was fitting that Frost lay the cornerstone. He had been treasurer of the province since early August 1943, when, as a rookie minister in George Drew's government, he began the slow but steady process of transforming the Ontario Department of Treasury.

Guided by Frost's leadership, the Ontario treasury emerged in the 1940s and 1950s as the key force in the administrative apparatus of Ontario. During the eighteen-year period government spending grew five-fold, from $227,691,803 in 1943 to $1.46 billion in 1961. This massive increase in expenditures, however, did not fully reflect the changed role of the Treasury department. Numerous reorganizations and reassignment of functions also reflected new provincial priorities.

With the election of the Progressive Conservative government under George Drew in August 1943, through the interregnum of Tom Kennedy in 1948–9 and the Frost premiership from 1949 to 1961, the Ontario Department of the Treasury underwent a dramatic institutional transformation. It grew from a small administrative agency to become the key department – a virtual central agency long before the term was coined – in the government of Ontario. Treasury brokered numerous funding requests, collected data on economic and social trends, and provided information and advice to the premier and the other cabinet ministers in their debates, discussions, and negotiations with other governments and opposition parties. Five years into his career as treasurer, Leslie Frost was bold enough to claim that the Treasury's mission was to protect Ontario's wealth from 'the clamor of self-interested or short-sighted groups who would surrender the solid resources of the community for some illusory or ephemeral advantage.'[1]

The reasons for the institutional transformation of the Ontario Department of Treasury are a complex mix of personal, political, economic, and social factors. They can be understood in three broad categories. The first factor that led to an institutional change in the Ontario Treasury department was the decision-making style of the Drew and Frost cabinets that necessitated a broader understanding of the economic circumstances of post–Second World War Ontario. The simple accounting of revenue and spending which had occupied the Treasury since Confederation was an insufficient base from which to launch the ambitious reform program Drew had promised in the August 1943 election campaign. In order to achieve its policy goals, the government needed more and better information. This entailed increasing the policy capacity of the provincial bureaucracy, especially that of the Treasury.

A second factor precipitating the dramatic transformation in the Treasury was the relationship of Ontario with the federal government. Drew had been a vocal, partisan and strident critic of the Liberal government of Mackenzie King and its policies, especially its efforts in the war. With the centralization of taxation at the outset of hostilities in 1939–40, the government of Canada appropriated personal, corporate income taxes, and succession duties, leaving the provinces dependent on grants from the federal government. This was an untenable situation for the new Ontario Conservative government. In a series of negotiations over the structure of post-war federal arrangements, the Ontario government depended on the staff of the Treasury department to provide the necessary information with which it could build its case for greater provincial autonomy through an increased tax base.

The third category of factors which helped transform the Treasury was economic. The war-time spending had generated a massive expansion of economic activity.[2] Both the federal and provincial governments wanted the prosperity of the war years to continue, but approached the question from different perspectives. Where the government of Canada committed itself to an approach that focused on maintaining high levels of demand for goods and services, the Ontario Conservatives believed that continued economic prosperity demanded direct state involvement in the economy and an expansion of provincial services from education to transportation. The diverging perspectives became apparent at the various federal-provincial meetings in the 1940s and 1950s, forcing the two levels of government to improve the articulation of their positions. This required the Ontario treasury to compile and analyse unprecedented quantities of economic data – far more than the publicly available estimates of revenue and spending found in the provincial budget.

Frost understood the Treasury department to be at the centre of the Westminster parliamentary system. The oldest department of state, it was created earlier than the cabinet in England and preceded representative and responsible government in Canada. The nineteenth-century British prime minister William Gladstone described the role of the treasury in this period as 'the savings of the candle ends.' Frost held a more expansive view of the treasury, one that allowed for a greater role for the state in social and economic life of the state in post–Second World War Ontario.

The Ontario treasury had been marked by four distinct periods in its history. The first period began with the founding in 1791 of Upper Canada, where the treasury soon became a central focus for the notorious family compact. With the advent of the legislative union with Lower Canada in 1841 and the winning of responsible government, the treasury's affairs were subjected to a more democratic debate on taxation and expenditure. The third major institutional change was triggered by Confederation in 1867. The administrative apparatuses of the new federal government and the provinces were disentangled, while the basic elements of the provincial governments – lieutenant governor, executive council, and legislature – were created.

The Treasury department of Ontario was held responsible for managing and controlling the expenditures of the Government of Ontario and for supervising, controlling, and directing all matters related to the financial affairs of the province. It managed the Consolidated Revenue Fund, examined and controlled departmental accounting methods, and reported on various trends in finance and taxation. Not least, it collected the taxes in the province and helped to develop the provincial budget.

Treasury had a strong 'comptrolling' culture. An audit branch was installed in the department in 1869 (it became the Office of the Provincial Auditor, a division of the department, in 1886). Treasury was respected for its work of inspection and was granted additional audit functions on delicate applications of policy. The department eventually found itself responsible for the Board of Censors of Motion Pictures (established in 1911) and then the Motion Picture Bureau (1917) and the Motion Picture Censorship and Theatre Inspection Branch (in 1938). Even though the Auditor General was established as an independent office of the Legislative Assembly in 1950, the auditor general would long continue to exercise a pre-audit function and to play a role in Treasury's formulation of the budget.[3]

Frost in the Drew Cabinet

In the middle of the 1943 Ontario provincial election, George Drew announced in a radio address what was to become known as the '22 point program.' He declared that a Progressive Conservative government would cooperate with the Dominion government to establish a comprehensive system of health insurance, pensions, and social security. He also affirmed that the 'constitutional rights of the people of Ontario be preserved and that the Government of Ontario exercise full control of its own Provincial affairs.' Agriculture, manufacturing, mining, services, and forestry would, moreover, be supported in their efforts to increase employment at good wages. Bureaucratic restrictions would be removed and taxes lowered to encourage initiative and hard work.[4] The Tory platform proposed a reversal of the laissez-faire policies of the Liberal government. It was a realization that the political agenda had changed and that voters did not want a return to the dark days of the Depression and looked to the government to ensure economic prosperity. With the popularity of the program of economic planning and public ownership of the Co-operative Commonwealth Federation (CCF), the Tories were left with little choice but to move in this direction.

The Progressive Conservative Party of Ontario, with 38 seats, won a minority government. The democratic-socialist CCF, led by E.B. Jolliffe, managed to win 34 seats, while the Liberals under Harry Nixon elected only 16 members. As well, two communist Labour Progressive candidates won in the Toronto ridings of Bellwoods and St Andrew. In this minority situation, Drew formed a tight, disciplined ten-member cabinet, with most of the ministers taking on two portfolios.

Leslie Frost, a forty-eight-year-old lawyer from the central Ontario town of Lindsay, was named provincial treasurer and minister of mines. Born in Orillia, Frost had served in the Canadian infantry in the First World War and was wounded on the front. Promoted to captain, he returned to Canada and studied law at Osgoode Hall. Settling in Lindsay he practised law and became involved in Conservative politics, and was elected to the legislature in 1937 as the MPP for the riding of Victoria. Tory politics was a family vocation. Frost's older brother Cecil was the Conservative party president from 1938 to 1943 and remained active in party politics both provincially and nationally until his death in 1946.

Frost fully supported his premier in emphasizing that the constitutional division of powers between the federal government and the provinces had to be restored when peace came.[5] He assumed his position with clear ambitions for his department: Treasury would play an important part in the skirmishes with the Dominion government and assume a central role in making policy.

In 1943 the Ontario Department of Treasury had a complement of 214 permanent and 18 part-time employees and a budget of $1,578,145. The department operated under an impressive array of twenty-two different pieces of legislation that included the Agricultural Development Finance Act, the Income Tax Act, the Race Track Act, and the Tile Drainage Act.[6] It was organized into five different divisions: the Main Office, Motion Picture Censorship and Theatre Inspection, the Controller of Revenue, and the government Post Office. The Main Office employed 42 permanent and 8 temporary staff, the Office of Motion Picture Censorship had 14 permanent and 4 temporary employees, and the Controller of Revenue Branch had 146 permanent employees and 40 temporary staff members who were hired each spring to aid in the preparation of revenue and spending estimates.

The deputy minister, Chester S. Walters, had been with the Ontario Public Service since 1934, first with Public Works and then with the Treasury. A self-educated accountant from Hamilton, he had excelled as controller of revenue before his promotion to deputy minister.[7] As the new treasurer, one of Leslie Frost's first decisions was to keep Walters as deputy. Although Walters had been closely associated with the Hepburn government and at times acted as a type of deputy premier, overseeing much of the provincial government's activity, he was too valuable for a new minister to dismiss. Walters was, in the words of George Gathercole, an 'organizing genius.' His 'long experience and practical knowledge, to say nothing of his political acumen, were assets to the new ministry too valuable to be discarded at once,' noted Frost's biographer Roger Graham. 'Moreover, he could be counted on as a strong defender of the provincial interest against the King government.'[8] Walters, like his erstwhile patron Mitch Hepburn, had a visceral distrust of the federal Liberals, but he was eager to create strong intergovernmental links between Ottawa and the provinces and among the provinces as well. Eager to see a 'learned society' focused on problems in public sector management, he took advantage of his contacts across the country and, with Philip Clark, the comptroller of revenue, founded the Institute of Public Administration of Canada (IPAC) in 1947 and worked diligently in organizing its first annual conference in Quebec City in 1949.[9] Clifford Clark, the deputy of the Finance department in Ottawa, joined Walters on the governing council of IPAC.

Within weeks of taking office, Frost announced changes. The accounting system would be overhauled and the public accounts would be simplified. To bring more rigour to the government's understanding of the province's business, a new Bureau of Statistics and Research was established. The bureau was 'to keep constantly under review all matters relating to the economy of the province.'[10] Frost and Walters wanted the bureau to monitor Ontario's relations with Ottawa and the other provinces. Its key task was to 'develop statistics relating to finances, not only regarding the province's specific financial operations but on matters of national import such as Dominion-Provincial Relations, inter-Provincial relations and Provincial-Municipal relations also on other extraneous subjects of current interest.'[11] Dividing Ontario into economic zones, the bureau staff conducted surveys and analyses of industry in the regions. The analyses provided the government with more accurate and standardized measures of economic activity in Ontario.[12]

Harold Chater was named the first provincial statistician and director of the Bureau of Statistics and Research. Chater, in turn, had to hire a team. One of his first acts was to approach George Gathercole, a lieutenant in the intelligence division of the Royal Canadian Navy. Gathercole, thirty-four, was an economics graduate from McMaster University and had completed several years of graduate study at the University of Toronto and the London School of Economics. Securing a release from active service, Gathercole began work with the Bureau of Statistics in November 1944.[13] He went on to enjoy a long and distinguished career in the Ontario public service, becoming a deputy minister in the late 1950s and eventually chairman of Ontario Hydro.

Another important innovation of the Drew government in 1943 was the creation of a Department of Planning and Development under Dana Porter. As a coordinating department, it was designed to consider 'the sort of problems that would emerge after the war.' It was to determine the provincial role in post-war reconstruction and to 'work out ways and means for delivering these responsibilities.' Porter stated that 'the province would take some steps to interest the municipalities throughout the province in planning the future development of their own community along methodical and scientific lines.' The department would, the minister claimed, 'retain technical staff to give general advice and guidance in the planning of towns.'[14] This was a first effort at land-use planning in the province of Ontario.

Although much of the Drew government's 22-point program had been supported in the legislature and had proved popular with the public, the opposition parties combined in order to defeat the government in March 1945. This tactic did not favour the opposition, and the election would go down as one of the dirtiest in history. When the votes were counted, Drew and the Progressive Conservatives had won a majority government. The Tories' percentage of the popular vote rose from 35.7 to 44.3 per cent, with 66 seats. Except for the two seats held by the Labour Progressive Party, the Tories were victorious in all the ridings in the Toronto region, taking seats from the Liberals in the rural areas and from the CCF in the urban centres.[15] The CCF was crushed, electing only eight members in the ninety-member House and its share of the popular vote declined by nearly a third from 31.7 to 22.4 per cent. Jolliffe was beaten in his own riding of York South. The Liberals became the Official Opposition with eleven seats and 29.8 per cent of the vote. These eleven seats would be combined with the three Liberal-Labour members who had been elected.

As the war was coming to an end in the spring and summer of 1945, a series of Dominion-provincial conferences were held in an attempt to re-define the division of powers between the two senior levels of government. Strengthened by their respective re-elections, there was little agreement between the Ontario and federal governments. The two governments could not, for example, even agree on the measure of the gross national product (GNP). The key documents in the discussions were the report of the Royal Commission on Dominion Provincial Relations, commonly known as the Rowell-Sirois Report, and the 1941 tax agreements which had ceded income and corporate taxes as well as succession duties to the Dominion government for the duration of the war. The

Rowell-Sirois Report had recommended a realignment of federal and provincial areas of responsibility, with the Dominion gaining considerable responsibility. At the Dominion-Provincial Conference Co-ordinating meeting of 28 January–1 February 1946, Drew opposed federal retention of the areas of personal and corporation income taxes and succession duties. Direct taxes, he explained, were the only area of taxation permitted to the provinces under the British North America Act. He went so far as to argue that the provinces had exclusive jurisdiction in direct taxation, that income and corporate taxes had only been rented to the federal government. The federal minister of finance, J.L. Isley, countered that the Dominion needed to retain control of these taxes in order to maintain the ability 'to stimulate the economy in times of depression.'[16] Finding a new ally in Quebec premier Maurice Duplessis, Drew insisted on the return of these tax fields to the provinces. Drew also claimed that succession duties should be returned immediately to the provinces.

A few months later at the April 1946 Dominion-Provincial Conference, Drew presented a proposal that would allow Ontario to 'rent' the fields of corporate and personal income tax to the federal government for a period of five years in return for a minimum per capita payment if the Dominion government, for its part, would undertake not to re-enter the areas of succession duties, gasoline, amusement, security transfer, electricity, and pari-mutual betting taxes. Drew also stipulated that the federal government had to promise not to engage in any other type of direct taxation other than corporation and personal income taxes. Despite intense negotiations, the provinces and the federal government failed to come to a new tax-rental agreement.

After the 1945 election, the Ontario Tories undertook several administrative reforms. Drew created a new cabinet office, the provincial secretary, and named Roland Michener to the post with the mandate to organize the executive council: it had no office, agenda, or records. Ministers would arrive at cabinet meetings not knowing what topics would be discussed. Michener conferred with Prime Minister King and the secretary to the federal cabinet, Arnold Heeney, on how to set up the office of cabinet secretary. Some, of course, liked the old way better. Colonel T.L. Kennedy, the minister of agriculture, for example, did not want a cabinet secretary. He was suspicious of an outsider sitting in on what he believed were privileged conversations. Eventually the objections were overcome and Lorne R. McDonald was appointed the first cabinet secretary in Ontario.

Michener also sought to introduce the merit system in the civil service. He established a Civil Service Appeals Board and made it policy that except for deputy ministers and a few other senior officials, personnel in the civil service were to be recruited on merit. Having been summarily dismissed from a government position in 1934 by Hepburn, Drew was sympathetic to these changes that protected both individuals and the integrity of the provincial public service,[17] but ensured that there was still an understanding that government members of the legislature had the ability to suggest that certain individuals be hired in various positions. These were typically seasonal and occasional positions such as parks employees and highways maintenance crews.[18]

Treasury was now working with new rules. By 1945 the department had grown to 244 permanent and 119 temporary staff, for a total of 363 employees. Most of the increase in staffing had occurred in the Revenue division, which now consisted of 144 permanent and 77 temporary employees. The Bureau of Statistics also added to the higher number of staff, with nine permanent and eight temporary employees. Two divisions were added to Treasury, the new Travel and Publicity Bureau and the King's Printer, and they accounted for thirty-one employees.[19]

In a 1948 speech, Frost described the development of the Department of Treasury over the previous five years. While the department had grown in size and responsibility, a more fundamental shift had occurred. The Treasury was, Frost believed, at the centre of the economic and political system in Ontario. Through the Treasury the people of Ontario had 'instituted public undertakings that entail a yearly expenditure of vast sums of money and they have reaped the harvest of health, wealth and happiness.' As 'the economic heart of society,' the Treasury brought in money through taxation and pumped out money through public expenditure. Without this spending, Ontario would, Frost claimed, 'soon degenerate into a sickly and emaciated condition.' Always mindful of his political role, Frost went on to say that the Conservative government had 'guarded and managed the public treasury to the advantage of every citizen, and to the present and future benefit of the community.'[20]

In the 1948 election, the Conservatives were returned with a reduced majority and Drew himself was defeated in his riding of High Park by the CCF. Two other cabinet ministers, Roland Michener and William Wallace, also went down to defeat. The early election call, controversy concerning amendments to the Liquor Control Act, the fight with the federal government over taxation and social programs, and the failure to deliver on the remaining promises in the '22 point' program had prompted voters to reassess their commitment to the Conservative party. Drew resigned as leader of the Ontario Progressive Conservative Party on 20 September 1948 and recommended that Thomas L. Kennedy be appointed as temporary party leader and premier.[21] In order to quell opposition within the party – mainly from the rural and eastern parts of the province – Kennedy agreed to stay as premier only until a full leadership convention could be called the following spring.

The Conservatives faced a society in transition. By 1951 the province's population would have grown by almost 20 per cent from the last census in 1941, from 3.7 to 4.6 million residents. Manufacturing nearly doubled from 1942 to 1950, increasing from $1.7 billion in production to $3 billion, while the resource industries and the service sector continued to expand rapidly. Employment in the service or non-manual sector of the economy began to rival that of the manufacturing and agricultural sectors. In response to concern that the economic prosperity would not continue, the Drew government had overseen a massive increase in government spending and state activity. Record numbers of teachers, nurses, civil servants, and others in the state sector were hired. Even business had come to depend on government to ensure the continued growth of the economy.[22]

A convention would be held in April 1949 to pick a new leader and premier.[23] Leslie Blackwell, the attorney general, declared himself a candidate, as did Highways minister George Doucett, Dana Porter, the provincial secretary and education minister, and former MPP Kelso Roberts. Leslie Frost, recently appointed government House leader, was unquestionably the front runner. The spring session of the legislature in 1949 had established him as the successor to Drew. At the leadership convention, he pledged to translate 'the principles, the ideals and objectives of the Progressive Conservative Party into action.' He called upon the delegates to join with him in carrying 'the blessings of good government to every home, mansion or cottage in this province.' Arguing that it was important for Ontario to maintain its high rate of economic growth, he called for a rationalized Dominion–provincial relationship.[24] Frost was chosen as party leader and prime minister of Ontario by the Progressive Conservative convention. In a signal of continuity with the Drew government, the next day he announced that his cabinet would essentially be composed of the same men who had dominated it over the previous six years. One change Frost did make was to relinquish the mines portfolio. He would, however, remain treasurer.

Frost: In Control

Frost had an informal and personal style of politics and this attitude spilled over into his government as well. But he understood that this way of doing things would not last. More formal approaches to governance were required and he was prepared to implement what he saw as necessary changes. During his years as premier and treasurer, the Department of Treasury grew substantially. By 1948 the Treasury had undergone some organizational changes. The Travel and Publicity Bureau and the King's Printer were reassigned to other departments, but Treasury assumed responsibility for the Ontario Savings Office. An Ottawa office, staffed with one employee, had been created to act as a conduit to the Government of Canada. Not including the Savings Office,[25] the Treasury now had 283 permanent and 70 temporary employees for a total of 353 individuals. This was a 52 per cent increase from 1943.

After being in office for two years, Frost called a provincial election for 22 November 1951 and campaigned with a strong focus on economic development. The Conservatives vowed to expand hydro-electric coverage, seeking federal help to develop the Niagara River for hydro electricity and pledging provincial cooperation on the St Lawrence Seaway project. He also promised to establish a labour relations code to create a less rancorous industrial climate and promised women 'equal pay for equal work' and free textbooks for the province's public schools. The Conservatives were rewarded with a comfortable majority, and Frost began his new term unhindered by the leadership and factional battles of the past. He ignored divisive issues such as separate-school funding and devoted his energies to creating a favourable investment climate for business. His inclinations had a bureaucratic translation. To shape policy, he created an Office of the Provincial Economist in 1951 within the Department of Treasury, and named George Gathercole to the post.[26] Frost came to depend on Gathercole for advice on a wide range of issues.

The Frost government supported a program of rapid industrialization and expansion in productive capacity.[27] It pursued this goal through extensive highway construction and other public works as well as by reducing the provincial debt and running budget surpluses. 'Pervading the atmosphere from the Premier down was a philosophy that growth had to be prepared for in advance, remembered Don Stevenson, a senior official in the Department of Economics.

> The Premier's guideline was that at least 60 per cent of capital expendi-
> tures should be paid for from current revenues [and] he always made the
> final decision on the budget. The amount that would be in the highway
> capital account had to be financed by ordinary revenue [which tended to
> show a surplus in the 1950s, unlike capital budgets] … This sleight of hand
> allowing the province to declare a surplus when it really was borrowing
> more used to bother my puritanical ideals about a transparent govern-
> ment. I was very happy in the late 1960s when Ian Macdonald argued
> successfully that capital and ordinary accounts should be combined to get
> a true accounting of the budget's impact on the economy. In retrospect,
> however, I think Frost's practice enabled the public and the critics to ac-
> cept a level of valuable infrastructure spending that we have since let fall
> to unsustainable levels.[28]

These policies dovetailed nicely with the federal government's promotion of major capital undertakings such as the St Lawrence Seaway,
the Trans-Canada Highway, and a gas pipeline from Alberta to central
Canada.[29] The arrival of Louis St-Laurent on the federal scene had
worked as a balm in soothing federal–Ontario relations. Even the vexa-
tious federal-provincial question of taxation was settled (at least tem-
porarily) in 1952 with the signing of a new tax rental agreement between
Ontario and Ottawa.[30]

Although efforts had been made by Michener and other in the 1940s
to establish a merit-based civil service, free of political control, the interests of the Conservative party were often seen as synonymous with
those of the province. Appointed by Drew in 1945 as his executive assistant, Colonel Ernest J. Young, for example, often used the public service to further the interests of the Conservative party. When Frost
succeeded Drew in 1949, Young retained his key role as gatekeeper to
the premier's office. He handled most of the routine affairs for the premier *and* the party and made little distinction between the two. He arranged meetings between party organizers and civil servants and
generally kept the backbench MPPs in touch with the policy makers in
the bureaucracy. Moreover, he summarized reports and submissions for
Frost, adding his own comments on the appropriate course of action. In
this sense Young combined the roles of party activist and civil servant.
Stevenson describes the relationship between the public service and the
government as collegial. Having moved from the Department of
External Affairs in Ottawa to the Department of Economics in Ontario,
Stephenson explained the different styles of the two organizations:

External Affairs was full of Rhodes Scholars writing elegant dispatches within an intricate system of document classification but which in the Diefenbaker years had little impact on policy or action. It was a real culture shock coming to the Treasury building. The communications were largely oral rather than written; the tone was pragmatic and certainly not academic. There was often a very short distance between proposal and action, but action on most issues depended on the premier's acute sense of political timing.[31]

Another notable example of the cross-over between the bureaucracy and the party was chief economist George Gathercole. He and a group of analysts in the Department of Treasury routinely advised Frost and party organizer A.D. McKenzie on the worthiness of various proposals ranging from human rights legislation to regional development and hospital insurance. The lack of separation allowed McKenzie and Frost to dispense patronage in such a fashion that it increased their influence within the party and aided the Tory cause in the province. With the Ontario government at its disposal, the Progressive Conservative leadership was in an extraordinarily strong position. Their opponents – inside and outside the party – had no comparable rewards to offer their supporters. The senior ranks of the civil service had become a key feature of the Conservative hold on power.

Indeed, Frost allowed caucus little role in policy making. While he always listened to the views of others, he was considered autocratic and abusive in caucus, cabinet, and the legislature.[32] Conservative MPPs were presented with legislation and expected to support it without question. Adding to Frost's influence in both the party and government was his position as provincial treasurer. From April 1949 until January 1955 he held both positions, and this dual role placed him in unquestionable direct control of the government's decision making apparatus. With the help of A.D. McKenzie, Frost was able to dominate almost all aspects of Ontario political life.

Frost called his second election as premier for 9 June 1955. Speaking to five hundred delegates at the Western Ontario Progressive Conservative Association meeting in London, he presented his party's fourteen-point election platform. He claimed that Ontario was the model of prosperity and reminded voters that his government had even managed to reduce taxes. Work on the St Lawrence Seaway had just started, and the prospect of jobs for hundreds of construction workers would certainly help Conservative electoral fortunes.[33] There was, moreover, the promise of inexpensive natural gas from the west if a planned trans-Canada pipe-line could be completed from Alberta to Ontario. As well, with Frost's close friend Fred Gardiner as the first chair of the new Metropolitan Council, the creation of a Toronto area regional municipality had proved popular. Highway construction was under way across the province and Ontario housing starts were leading the country. The hospital system was rapidly expanding. The government made significant strides in protecting the civil rights of the province's native population and racial minorities following years of discrimination and neglect. The Conservatives believed their record would win them the continued support of voters.[34]

Despite questions of inappropriate behaviour in the Highways department, Frost led the Ontario Progressive Conservative Party to a second overwhelming majority. With 48.5 per cent of the popular vote, the Tories were returned with 83 out of a possible 98 seats. The percentage of seats won was only slightly lower in 1955 than in 1951, falling from a high of 87.9 per cent in 1951 to 84.6 per cent. The Liberals improved slightly in both seats and votes. They won three more seats, for a total of eleven, and gained 2 per cent in the popular vote for 33.3 per cent.[35] The CCF elected their leader Donald MacDonald in York South, but fell from 19.1 per cent to 16.5 per cent of the vote. The lone Labour-Progressive member from the Toronto riding of St Andrew, Joe Salsberg, was defeated by a Toronto city alderman and Progressive Conservative candidate, Alan Grossman. The Labour-Progressive Party no longer held a seat in the provincial legislature.[36]

A New Treasurer, Or Two

While there was a steady growth in the size of the Treasury – its expenditures had nearly doubled from $2.8 million in 1951 to $5.55 million in 1955 – there had been few modifications of the departmental organization (a small Tabulating Branch was created in 1954)[37] or turnover of senior personnel. Chester Walters continued as deputy treasurer and Hugh Brown stayed as assistant deputy treasurer. On the third floor of the Treasury building, George Gathercole developed the Office of the Provincial Economist.

The Conservative government faced several difficult economic issues. The first was the dislocation caused by the development of the St Lawrence Seaway. The flooding of low-lying areas along the St Lawrence River displaced a number of small communities. The expense involved with relocating cemeteries and compensating individuals and businesses, and the general disruptions of daily life in the region caused problems for the party and government. It was only after considerable care was taken to offset the real and perceived injustices – and with significant financial support from the federal government – that the problems associated with the seaway project were resolved.

The other major issue facing the government was energy related. In May 1954, Trans-Canada Pipelines Limited had secured a permit from the government of Alberta to sell 4.35 trillion cubic feet of natural gas. Later that year Trans-Canada Pipelines received permission from the federal Board of Transport Commissioners to construct a pipeline to Montreal. Unsuccessful in arranging financing for the western Canadian section of the line, the company had applied to the federal government for assistance. In November 1955, the federal government recommended to Parliament the creation of a Crown Corporation to assist in the construction of a Canadian pipeline. As well, Frost agreed that Ontario would participate in the financing to the extent of one-third of the cost of the northern Ontario section.

Frost had given clear instructions to his cabinet that no provincial minister was to be involved with any aspect of the Trans-Canada project, yet it was revealed that several had bought or been given stock in the company building the line through Northern Ontario (Northern Ontario Natural Gas or NONG). Although no evidence of bribery or corruption was uncovered, three cabinet ministers – Philip Kelly, the minister of mines; public works minister William Griesinger; and the minister of lands and forests, C.E. Mapledoram – resigned. It was also learned that the new Liberal leader, John Wintermeyer, and A.D. McKenzie, the Conservative party president and Frost confidant, had purchased stock in the company. Indeed, McKenzie had been named general counsel to the gas company. The Conservative Party of Ontario was intimately connected with the Northern Ontario Natural Gas Company and the scandal swirling around it.

The issues surrounding the construction of the St Lawrence Seaway and the question of inappropriate behaviour by several cabinet members and Conservative party officials appear to have been the incentive Frost needed to reorganize the Treasury Department. In 1955 he resigned as provincial treasurer. The province's finances had become so complex and so massive that Frost believed Ontario needed a full-time treasurer. As his replacement, Frost appointed his close friend Dana Porter. Although he was no longer the province's treasurer, Frost retained considerable influence over Ontario's finances and economic direction as premier and a member of the Treasury Board.

Frost's resignation as treasurer in 1955 was the beginning of a period of institutional transformation of the department. The long-serving deputy treasurer, Chester Walter, retired and was replaced by H.E. Brown, who had served as assistant treasurer since the early 1940s. A new Department of Economics and Bureau of Statistics and Research was created out of the Office of the Chief Economist at the Treasury, and Gathercole was named deputy minister. The economics division had grown fast, from a total salary expenditure of $33,106 in the 1952–3[38] to $206,340 in 1957.[39] Quickly expanding, the new department often hired qualified immigrants from various parts of Europe, which gave the department a distinctive culture within the government of Ontario.[40] While the new department remained the responsibility of the provincial treasurer, its budget was small, with total expenditures amounting to $232,939 in the 1957–8 fiscal year[41] (an amount that paled in comparison with the $5.3 million in ordinary expenditures for the Treasury department during the same period).[42]

With Gathercole, a key member of Frost's inner circle of advisers, as deputy minister, the Department of Economics was given the most critical and sensitive policy files of the government, crafting messages on a host of issues and writing speeches for the premier. Don Stevenson, who joined the Department of Economics in 1959, remembered that 'the range of activity ... covered the waterfront of the province's main policy concerns given the absence of a strong cabinet and premier's office and the fact that most departments were deliverers of services without much broader research or policy planning capacity. The department of economics did most of the writing of the budget, the throne speech, and most other speeches by the Premier, was responsible for preparing the province's position on federal-provincial fiscal and economic issues and overall provincial-municipal financial matters.'[43] The chief academic adviser to the department was Malcolm Taylor of the University of Toronto (Taylor was also the first editor of *Canadian Public Administration*, the learned journal of the Institute of Public Administration of Canada, launched in 1958), who had a singular influence in shaping Ontario's approach to hospital insurance and, later, medicare. To give a sense of the range of issues: Don Stevenson remembers being 'involved in a study for Fred Gardiner recommending that Metro Toronto should have four rather than 13 lower tier governments, on how to simplify the process for approving and building social housing, as secretary to the body that wrote the Pension Benefits Act, on a study for the Premier on university expansion needs in the 1960s and on a system to subsidize hospital insurance premiums for lower income people.'[44] 'Although formally the Minister responsible for the Department of Economics was the provincial treasurer, Jim Allan, the real decision maker was Premier Frost ... Frost used the Department of Economics as later premiers would use the premier's office and cabinet offices. Gathercole at the time was Frost's closest advisor in the civil service, even spending holidays with the Frosts on occasion.'[45]

In early 1958 Dana Porter was appointed as the chief justice of Ontario. Unable to settle on a replacement, Frost returned to the position of treasurer and minister of economics for three months until James Allen was appointed. Allen would remain as treasurer until November 1966.[46] There were few changes in the Treasury over the next few years. In the 1958–9 fiscal year, for example, the Treasury consisted of the Main Office, the Office of Comptroller of Revenue, interdepartmental mail delivery, the Ontario Racing Commission, the Tabulating Branch, and a new Mortgage Housing Branch. The Hydro-Electric Power Commission of Ontario and the Savings Office also reported through the Treasury. In 1959 the Public Service Commission was transferred to the Treasury. The Provincial Treasurer was thus responsible for the overall operation of the Ontario Public Service. This was a major consolidation of authority in one department, but it let Frost and Allen keep a close watch on the growth of the public sector and provincial spending.

On 4 May 1959, ten years to the day he first took the oath of office as premier of Ontario, Leslie Frost called an election.[47] While other issues, such as education and housing, played a role in the campaign, the election was seen as a test of Frost's handling of the scandal surrounding the North Ontario Natural Gas pipeline.[48] Neither the highways scandal nor the cabinet resignations over the northern Ontario pipeline seem to have diminished the control Frost and McKenzie exercised over party and government. Because of this tight control – and a weak opposition – Frost was able to deflect controversy. The economic achievements of the government bolstered Frost's quip that the opposition parties promised to do everything but it was the Conservatives that got things done.[49] The results of the 11 June 1959 contest left little doubt about the popularity of the Conservative government. The Tories won 71 of the 98 seats. Although their percentage of the popular vote declined only 2 per cent, from 48.5 to 46.3 per cent, the party lost eleven seats.

In the late 1950s and early 1960s, the Treasury continued to grow. In 1959 the Public Service Superannuation Board – the pension board – was moved to Treasury. The departmental budget continued to increase. Over the 1960–1 fiscal year, the ordinary expenditure for the Treasury department had reached $12.7 million. This was an almost ten-fold increase from the 1943 Treasury expenditures of just under $1.3 million. Even factoring in the rates of inflation for the eighteen years between 1943 and 1961, this was a massive increase in departmental spending on personnel and other related costs that offers an indication of the ever-growing role the Treasury played in the administrative apparatus of the Ontario state.[50]

When Alex McKenzie died suddenly in May 1960, Frost lost his closest confidant.[51] Frost had grown accustomed to his daily meetings with McKenzie in the dining room of the Royal York Hotel and had come to depend on his advice. No one individual was capable of filling the role McKenzie had played. For the first time since 1943 the positions of chairman of organization and party president were split. (While McKenzie's successors, Hugh Latimer as organizer and Elmer Bell as party president, were capable of running the Progressive Conservative party of Ontario, Frost did not rely on them in the same way he had on McKenzie.) For Frost, the loss of McKenzie seemed to have taken the fun out of the game. In 1960, in the words of biographer Roger Graham, the Conservative leader was 'sixty-five years old and did not want to run the risk of leaving the party in a leaderless state, as had happened when Sir John A. Macdonald and, more recently, Maurice Duplessis died.'[52] Moreover, there was pressure from his wife, Gertrude, to retire. She felt that he should leave politics while they could still enjoy some years together. It was a promise that she insisted he keep.[53] Many of the old guard were now considering retirement, had retired, or were in failing health. The only two members of Frost's inner circle who were still active in the government or the party were his secretary and deputy minister, W.M. McIntyre, the deputy minister of economics, George Gathercole, and the deputy treasurer, Hugh Brown. None of them was actively involved in the Conservative party. There seemed to be little choice left to Frost but to prepare his political departure. Stressing the need for an orderly succession, Frost submitted his resignation to the president of the Ontario Progressive Conservative Association, Elmer Bell, on 31 July 1961, and a leadership convention was scheduled quickly for three weeks later. The Frost era in Ontario and at the Treasury had come to an end.

Conclusion

The period 1943 to 1961 saw a dramatic growth in Ontario's public sector. This growth occurred across all departments, but it was particularly evident in the institutional transformation of the provincial treasury. There were several factors which led to the institutional transformation of the Ontario Department of Treasury. First was the election of a Progressive Conservative government in August 1943 under George Drew. Drew and his cabinet brought a new, managerial perspective to governing, recognizing that the unstructured, personal style of the previous Liberal government was no longer appropriate for a quickly growing Ontario economy. If they were going to implement their 22-point election program, they understood that a more structured style of decision making was required. As the Ontario government initiated new programs and sought to maintain high levels of economic growth and employment, the Department of Treasury emerged a central institution in this new managerial regime. As provincial treasurer, Leslie Frost was instrumental in helping to establish the Treasury as the key department, a central agency of the Ontario state.

A second factor which led to the transformation of the Ontario treasury was the ongoing battles between the provincial governments – especially Ontario and Quebec – and Ottawa. Through the end of the Second World War to the early 1950s, Ontario fought vigorously to regain control over personal and corporate income taxes and succession duties and to reassert the roles assigned to it under the British North America Act 1867. A third factor in the rise of the Ontario treasury was the growth in the provincial economy. Not only was there a pervading fear of a return to the Depression era of the 1930s, but there were new demands for increased services. Drew and Frost, and later Porter and Allen, understood the necessity of increasing the capacity of the Treasury to respond to the new challenges of a rapidly growing economy. Moreover, the reform agenda – the 22-point program announced in the radio broadcast in July 1943 – that Drew brought to office required an administrative capacity that did not exist under the former Liberal government.

A fourth factor was also responsible for the transformation of the Ontario Department of Treasury. The commanding figure throughout the entire 1943–61 period was Leslie Frost. As provincial treasurer and later as premier, he dominated the politics and administration of Ontario. Appointed treasurer in 1943, he initiated a process of restructuring and reform. But Frost was a cautious reformer. A veteran of the Great

War and a small-town lawyer, he brought a conservative world view to the Treasury. Although he established the Bureau of Statistics and Research within the first few months in office, Frost made few other personnel and organizational changes. He kept, for example, the deputy minister of the Treasury, Chester Walters, and other senior departmental staff. This was an unusual move in the very partisan environment of mid-1940s Ontario politics. Even the creation of the position of provincial economist in the early 1950s reflected Frost's halting approach to institutional reform. In appointing George Gathercole to the position Frost looked no further than his Bureau of Statistics. With several minor exceptions made for administrative convenience – the removal of the Motion Picture Censorship Board, the King's Printer, and the Travel and Publicity Bureau from the Treasury in the early and mid-1950s – very little organizational change occurred until the creation of the Department of Economics in 1956. While the new department was an important milestone in the organizational transformation of Ontario's administrative structure, the deputy minister of the new department, George Gathercole, had been with the Treasury for twelve years.

As deputy in the new Department of Economics, Gathercole, however, recruited a small but able team of policy advisers who could help cabinet make critical decisions on its most important file. The Department of Economics (renamed the Department of Economics and Intergovernmental Relations in 1961) was, for all intents and purposes, the cabinet office and the premier's office rolled into one. As a priority-setter for the provincial government,[54] the Department of Economics was used by Frost and the cabinet as a type of central agency to weigh and order priorities. It was the department that did the thinking on various initiatives, from hospital insurance, regional development, and relations with Ottawa to relations between the provincial government and the municipalities.

Frost made the Department of Treasury and later the Department of Economics central to the functions of the Ontario state – an administrative structure that would continue to provide the foundation of later reforms. It was his administrative style of cautious reform and ardent desire for 'getting the facts' that dominated the thinking of the two departments and gave them shape, initiating a process of slow institutional change that responded to the changing economic, social, and political environment of 1940s and 1950s Ontario. Under Frost the Treasury played the tradition role of watchdog in that it closely monitored revenue and spending as well as housing the Office of the Auditor General and the Motion Picture Censorship and Theatre Inspection

Branch. Even after the Auditor General was made an officer of the Legislature, Frost sought the AG's advice in preparing budgets.

It was fitting, therefore, that the cornerstone of the Treasury building that Frost laid in 1954 would be engraved with his name, but also that of William Griesinger, the minister of public works, and Chester Walters, the deputy treasurer. It was a unique testament – carved in stone – to the relationship that existed between the bureaucracy and the government in the Frost years.

NOTES

1 Leslie M. Frost, 'The Province of Ontario and Its Treasury, 1943–1948,' speech, n.d. Archives of Ontario (henceforth AO), RG6-15, File Treasury no. 12 (c), Bureau of Statistics and Research.
2 Samuel H. Beer, *Treasury Control: The Co-ordination of Financial and Economic Policy in Great Britain* (Oxford: Oxford University Press, 1956), 1.
3 Reflecting on budget making in the last years of the Frost government, Don Stevenson wrote that 'the small group of senior civil servants who were making the key budgetary decisions then included Hugh Brown, Chester Walters, Philip Clark, and George Gathercole. To my amazement and in direct contradiction to what I thought were basic principles of public finance, much of the more political input to the budget discussions came from the Provincial Auditor, Harvey Cotnam.' Don Stevenson note, July 2006.
4 'Drew Offers 50 P.C. Cut in Ontario School Tax. 22 Point Platform Proposed,' *Globe and Mail*, 9 July 1943, 1.
5 K.J. Rea, *The Prosperous Years: The Economic History Of Ontario 1939–1975* (Toronto, Buffalo, London: University of Toronto Press, in cooperation with the Ontario Historical Studies Series, 1985), 11.
6 Memorandum, E.J. Young to Hon. Leslie M. Frost, 'Acts Under the Jurisdiction of the Treasury Department,' n.d., AO, RG6-15, Box 37, B272167, File: Treasury no. 1, Main Office, 18 February 1935 to 12 August 1952.
7 John T. Saywell, *'Just call me Mitch': The Life of Mitchell F. Hepburn* (Toronto: University of Toronto Press, 1992), 171, 197.
8 Roger Graham, *'Old Man Ontario': Leslie M. Frost* (Toronto: University of Toronto Press, 1990), 97
9 Ibid., chap. 1.
10 'The Province of Ontario and Its Treasury 1943–48,' AO, Ontario Ministry of Finance, RG6-15, Box 43, File: Treasury no. 12 (c), Bureau of Statistics and Research.

11 H.J. Chater, 'The Work and Problems of the Ontario Bureau of Statistics and Research,' AO, Ontario Ministry of Finance, RG6-15, Box 43, File: Treasury no. 12 (c), Bureau of Statistics and Research.

12 'The Province of Ontario and Its Treasury 1943–48,' AO, Ontario Ministry of Finance, RG6-15, Box 43, File: Treasury no. 12 (c), Bureau of Statistics and Research.

13 Harold Chater to Leslie Frost, letter, 29 May 1944, AO, RG 6-15, Ontario Ministry of Finance, Box no. 44, File: Treasury no. 12, Bureau of Statistics.

14 Hon. Dana Porter, 'Notes of Speech of the Honourable Dana Porter, K.C. at the Annual Meeting of the Kitchener Women's Progressive Conservative Association,' Press release, 6 February 1946. AO, RG3-19, Box 1B396818, File: 226-G, Press release – Office Copy, Feb.–April 1946.

15 Dennis Wrong, 'Ontario Provincial Elections, 1934–1955: A Preliminary Survey of Voting,' *Canadian Journal of Economic and Political Science* 23 (August 1957): 398.

16 'The Dominion-Provincial Conference Co-ordinating Committee meeting January 28 to February 1, 1946.' Archives of Ontario, RG6-16, B2900787, Dominion-Provincial Conference Miscellaneous Working Papers 1.

17 Roland Michener, interview with author, Toronto, 6 June 1988.

18 Fred Cass, interview with author, 19 May 1988, Chesterville, Ont.

19 Public Accounts, *Department of Provincial Treasurer, Fiscal Year, 1944–45*, AO, Government Documents, Ontario Public Accounts 1944/45, R1–R13.

20 Frost, 'The Province of Ontario and Its Treasury.'

21 George A. Drew, 20 September 1948, Press Release, AO, RG3-19, Box 1, B396878, File 226-G, Press Release – Office Copy, 1948.

22 Ontario, Department of Economics, *1956 Economic Survey of Ontario* (Toronto: Queen's Printer, 1956), 0-40, 0-41.

23 Leslie M. Frost Papers, Trent University Archives, Trent University, 77-024, Box 5, folder 1.

24 Leslie M. Frost, 'Speech at Convention,' Leslie M. Frost Papers, 77-024, Box 5, file 1, Trent University Archives.

25 The number of permanent and temporary employees in the 22 branches of the Provincial Savings Office are not listed in the Public Accounts for 1947–8.

26 Public Accounts of Ontario, Part P, Department of Provincial Treasurer, Fiscal Year, 1953–4, p. 9. AO, Government Documents, Ontario Public Accounts, 1953–4, pp. 1–11.

27 For a full discussion of the federal government's economic policies during the late 1940s and 1950s, see Robert M. Campbell, *Grand Illusions: The*

Politics of the Keynesian Experience in Canada, 1945–1975 (Peterborough, ON: Broadview Press, 1987).
28 Don Stevenson notes, July 2006.
29 Rea, *The Prosperous Years*, 23.
30 Graham, *Old Man Ontario*, 192–7.
31 Note from Don Stevenson, July 2006.
32 Robert Macaulay, interview with author, Toronto, 14 June 1988.
33 William Kinmond, 'Ontario Election on June 9. Announcement Cheered. 14-Point Platform Presented by Frost,' *Globe and Mail*, 2 May 1955, 1.
34 Ibid.
35 This figure includes the Liberal-Labour member Albert Wren from Kenora.
36 Office of the Chief Election Officer, *Electoral History of Ontario. Candidates and Results* (Toronto, 1982), J9–10.
37 Public Accounts of Ontario, Part P, Department of Provincial Treasurer, Fiscal Year, 1953–4, p. 1. AO, Government Documents, PA, Ontario Public Accounts 1953–4.
38 Public Accounts of Ontario, Part P, Department of Provincial Treasurer, Fiscal Year, 1952–3, p. 9.
39 Public Accounts of Ontario, Part C, Department of Economics, Fiscal Year 1957–8, C1, AO, Ontario Public Accounts, 1957/58, C1–C3, VI–VII.
40 Note from Don Stevenson, July 2006.
41 Ibid.
42 Public Accounts of Ontario, Part V, Department of Provincial Treasurer, Fiscal Year 1957–8, p. V4. AO, Government Documents PA, Ontario Public Accounts 1957–8.
43 Don Stevenson, note, July 2006, p. 6.
44 Ibid.
45 Ibid, p. 5.
46 Ontario, Executive Council Office, 'Treasurers for the Province of Ontario,' Public Archives of Ontario, RG-6-114, B290852, Public Service Ministers and Deputy Ministers, 1967.
47 Jack Marks, 'Calls June 11 Elections, Frost Issues Blueprint. Nominations May 28. Premier Cites Record of Decade in Office,' *Globe and Mail*, 5 May 1959, 1.
48 E.A. Ingraham, 'Unveils 15 Planks in Liberal Platform,' *Globe and Mail*, 12 May 1959, 1.
49 Marks, 'Calls June 11 Elections,' 1.
50 For a discussion of the inflationary pressures during the 1940s and 1950s see Campbell, *Grand Illusions*, chaps 3 and 4.

51 Leslie Frost to H.W. (*sic*) Robbins, 13 June 1960, H.R. Robbins Papers, Box 4, folder 13, Trent University Archives, B-75-014.
52 Graham, *Old Man Ontario*, 399.
53 Robert Beal, conversation with author, Peterborough, 18 March 1991.
54 See David A. Good, *The Politics of Public Money* (Toronto: University of Toronto Press, 2007).

2 From 'Treasury' to 'Finance': The Anatomy of a Guardian, 1961–2001*

PATRICE DUTIL AND DEVYN LEONARD

Established at Confederation as the 'Treasury' of Ontario, the department of finance had its organizational development shaped by the demands of governments of all stripes and of over thirty 'treasurers' or 'ministers.' The concern was to ensure that that the bureaucracy was organized to deliver on the government's concerns, plans, and visions. The evolution of Leslie Frost's 'Treasury' to the 'Ministry of Finance' of the early twenty-first century reveals how the administration's mandate was perceived and how the government of Ontario's general bureaucracy was understood to function. During the forty years under study in this book, there was significant growth and retrenchment in the size and scope of the ministry as changes were incessantly made to its leadership and to its divisional and branch structures. Nevertheless, its mission to 'guard revenue' and shape the budget has been a constant. Indeed, the study of Ontario's Ministry of Finance reveals what decision makers considered vitally necessary for the budget to be produced confidently. The 'guardians' actually took on many different roles.

This chapter examines the evolution of the department's organization chart to shed light on its organizational change and structural evolution: it focuses on establishing the connection between the organizational structure of the bureaucracy and the policy and decision-making goals and abilities of government as a whole. The Department of Treasury/Ministry of Finance's structure created roles and rules, as the adage goes, for 'who does what, how, and with who else.'[1] One of the first theorists of administration, Luther Gulick, noted the bureaucratic structure's

---

* All figures referred to in this chapter are available at http://www.utppublishing
.com/The-Guardian-Perspectives-on-the-Ministry-of-Finance-of-Ontario.html.

impact on public policy making. He argued that the organizational coordination, particularly of internal structures, played a critical role.[2] The structure of Ontario's Ministry of Finance certainly tells the story of the evolution of the various roles played by a 'guardian.' Starting from a simple 'treasury' that submitted a budget speech and then chased numbers in order to assemble a real budget months later, the department assumed a number of roles Aaron Wildavsky would recognize. It certainly was a 'guardian' of the public purse in ensuring that government moneys were not spent unaccountably. However, over the years, the 'guardian' became the home of organizations as widely diverse as the Ontario Horse Racing Commission and the Commission for French Language Services. In the 1970s, as the department oversaw regional policy development, it played a big hand in determining spending priorities. For many years, it assumed the function of collecting tax moneys, and then lost that role. The story of the evolution of this department reveals it as a 'guardian' in constant evolution, never static.

Scholars and public-sector professionals easily recognize that the organizational structure of a bureaucracy can influence policy making through several dimensions. One recently noted that the size of an organization, its horizontal and vertical specialization, and the organization's coordination – that is, either collegial or hierarchical – can determine its success. The number of people involved in an organization provides an indication of its structural capacity to be involved in policymaking, while horizontal and vertical specialization refers to an organization's relative or hierarchical interconnectedness with other areas of concern.[3] It can be indicative of the way in which decisions are reached within the organization itself: collegial coordination necessarily involves argument and deal-brokering, while hierarchical coordination reveals a command-and-control structure.[4]

This chapter probes the body of the department, not its mind. The descriptions are founded on data gathered from the government's telephone books every three or four years. Telephone books were the most reliable and standard information available on ministry structure and hierarchies until the 1990s, when the department itself systematically created its own organization charts. (The department had produced only a few such charts sporadically until then.) The organization charts created from the data chart the evolving structure of the department and illustrate the hierarchical relationships between different bureaucratic and personal roles. The evolution of the posts of ministers, deputy ministers, assistant deputy ministers, directors, and, where possible,

Table 2.1

Treasurers / Ministers of Finance	Deputy Treasurers / Deputy Ministers of Finance
Hon. James Allan (Prog. Cons.) (Apr. 1958–Nov. 1966)	Hugh E. Brown (Apr. 1953–Dec. 1967)
Hon. Charles MacNaughton (Prog. Cons.) (Nov. 1966–Mar. 1971)	Harold Walker (Dec. 1967–July 1968)
Hon. William Darcy McKeough (Prog. Cons.) (Mar. 1971–Sept. 1972)	H. Ian Macdonald (Dec. 1967–Apr. 1974)
Hon. Charles MacNaughton (Prog. Cons.) (Sept. 1972–Jan. 1973)	
Hon. John White (Prog. Cons.) (Jan. 1973–June1975)	A. Rendall Dick (Apr. 1974–Sept. 1981)
Hon. William Darcy McKeough (Prog.Cons.) (June 1975–Aug. 1978)	
Hon. Frank S. Miller (Prog. Cons.) (Aug. 1978–July 1983)	Thomas I. Campbell (Sept. 1981–Aug. 1984)
Hon. Larry Grossman (Prog.Cons.) (July 1983–June 1985)	Brock A. Smith (Aug. 1984–Oct. 1987)
Hon. Bette Stephenson (Prog.Cons.) (May 1985–June 1985)	Mary Mogford (Oct. 1987–July 1989)
Hon. Robert F. Nixon (Liberal) (June 1985–Oct. 1990)	Bryan Davies (Sept. 1989–Jan. 1992)
Hon. Floyd Laughren (New Democrat) (Oct. 1990–June 1995)	Eleanor Clitheroe (May 1992–Nov. 1993) Jay Kaufman (Nov. 1993–June 1995)
Hon. Ernie Eves (Prog. Cons.) (June 1995–Feb. 2001)	Micheal Gourley (June 1995–June 1998) Bryne Purchase (Oct. 1998–Aug. 2000)
Hon. Jim Flaherty (Prog. Cons.) (Feb. 2001–Apr. 2002)	Robert Christie (Aug. 2000–Feb. 2004)

managers are explored. That being said, there are limitations to using phone books. Many interviews with former executives in the department revealed that reporting relationships were not always as clear-cut as phone books would indicate and that on several occasions, sections of the department were inadvertently omitted or incompletely presented.[5] We are confident, nevertheless, that the evolution presented in this chapter captures the developing shape and mission of the department of the treasury over the years.

The 1960s Treasury Department: An Era of Growth

In the years following the Second World War, the government was a relatively stable institution overseen politically by the Progressive Conservative Party of Ontario under Premiers George Drew and Leslie Frost. Premier Frost resigned in 1961, following the tabling of Ontario's first billion-dollar budget, and John Robarts took over as premier. In Ontario, the public service already had over 34,000 employees and a budget of $738 million.[6] The province witnessed a period of significant economic expansion, and the ministry saw a corresponding expansion of its role.

The 1961 Treasury

As Leslie Frost retired, the Treasury department employed a staff of 1224 deployed over four different areas (see figure 2.1). In terms of structure and titles, it far more resembled a banking institution than a vital agency of government. The minister was known as the 'Treasurer' and, Hugh E. Brown, the deputy minister, was accordingly referred to as the 'Deputy Treasurer.' The deputy treasurer supervised an impressively flat organization dedicated to unequivocal guardian functions. Reporting to him were a comptroller of finances, comptroller of accounts, comptroller of revenue, director of the Securities Branch, head cashier, director of the Savings Office, and two executive officers (including one responsible for the 'tabulating' branch). Where there was guardianship, the Treasury was also in the business of loaning money. Also answerable to the deputy treasurer were the directors of the Housing Mortgage Branch and the commissioner of Agricultural Loans and Settlers' Loans. The management of the department was thus distributed across four discernible levels: deputy treasurer, comptrollers/directors, assistant comptrollers/ directors, and inspectors/accountants.

Ensuring revenue was as important as overseeing expenditures. The comptroller of revenue supervised a number of professionals with a mix of general and specialized interests. Hierarchically, the chain of command was relatively clear, but its features attested to the wide range of specific fields in which the ministry operated. Discrete areas of the provincial economy were readily identified as key sources of revenue in the organization chart (gasoline, corporation tax, securities, and hospitals). Remarkably, the task of creating the provincial budget, a vital aspect of the ministry's responsibilities, does not appear to be the concern of any specific division, branch, or office. The budget was drafted in two distinct phases, but drew especially on the particular expertise of the comptroller of finances. A team drawn from the deputy treasurer's office (involving the comptrollers of Finance and of Revenue especially) and key individuals around George Gathercole, the deputy minister of the Department of Economics and Intergovernmental Affairs (DEIA) worked with the premier personally to craft the budget speech. Once delivered, the work of putting together the 'real budget' would begin – a process that typically took eight to twelve weeks. That same team would also conduct research into specific economic issues, then draft the Speech from the Throne, the budget speech, and the budget itself.

Don Stevenson, who was hired by Gathercole in 1959, later observed that 'while nominally the minister responsible for the Department was the Provincial Treasurer, in fact the Department acted as a research and policy advisory body to the Premier.'[7] He stated elsewhere that 'within the civil service, the Deputy Minister of Economics – George Gathercole – was his closest confidant.'[8] 'Most departments were vertical service delivery agencies reporting directly up through their minister to Cabinet or the Premier with relatively little interdepartmental interaction prior to decision-making. Leslie Frost was in total control and his "yes" or "no" was clearly the final decision-making process.'[9] Frost, after all, had himself been treasurer since 1943 and had kept the portfolio for a number of years even while he was premier. His staff as premier of the province was very small, so he relied extensively on the executives in the Economics department in the way a modern-day premier would rely on Cabinet Office. Clearly, DEIA was key to the economic policy making of the government. In the late 1950s, it acted as a secretariat for the Continuing Committee on Fiscal and Economic Matters, helped in the negotiation of the 1957 Fiscal Arrangement Agreement with the federal government, and played a key role in defining provincial policy on pensions (both in terms of portability and in advocating the Ontario position on the Pension Benefits Act). It prepared the Ontario brief to the Royal Commission on Canada's Economic Prospects, chaired by Walter Gordon, as well as the Federal Royal Commission on Transportation, the Porter Commission on Banking and Finance, and the Bladen Commission on the Automotive Industry. The DEIA's reach extended to the municipal area. It was actively involved in creating the metropolitan level of government in the Toronto area, and negotiated the creation of hospital insurance in the 1950s.[10]

The 1964 Treasury

With John Robarts as premier, the Government of Ontario expanded and responded to his driving ambitions to improve the government's ability to conduct policy work.[11] Hugh Brown, who had been deputy treasurer since April 1953, continued in the job until the end of 1967. His fourteen years as deputy would not be replicated. In his last years, Brown oversaw an expansion of the department, adding as a fifth tier of personnel the assistant deputy minister to help him steer the more demanding portfolios. Mid-level management was thus born in the department, but more importantly, the ministry was restructured into three divisions (see figure 2.2). The evolution of the divisional organizational structure provided a clear chain of command and leadership within the ministry, establishing a kind of one-stop shop for all things related to the provincial economy or provincial finance, including pension funds and taxpaying. The two main divisions were Revenue, overseen by the comptroller and the assistant comptroller of revenue, and Accounts Division, under the purview of the comptroller and the assistant comptroller of accounts. These divisions were further divided into branches, illustrating the beginnings of a division/branch structure. In the Accounts Division, the new/reorganized branches included the Government Accounts Branch, Securities Branch, Loan Accounting Branch, and a Pension Funds Branch. They were all overseen by directors answerable to the comptroller of accounts. In the Revenue Division, a Retail Sales Tax Branch and a Security Transfer Tax Branch, each also overseen by a director, joined the branches mentioned in 1961. Retail sales tax was a new tax field that helped to provide the revenue to pay for publicly provided services for the growing province. In all, the number of full-time employees in the department had grown to 1284 in 1964.

The department also assumed responsibility for a number of new agencies. It housed the Director of the Savings Office and the Chairman of the Public Service Superannuation Board, both of which were concerned with servicing the members of the Ontario public service. The chairman and treasurer of the Ontario Municipal Improvement Corporation would also now report through the treasurer.

The most significant change in these first years of the Robarts administration was the disappearance of a 'Finance' office and the appearance of the Treasury Board. It appeared in the Treasury Department's organizational structure in 1964, with its 'Secretary of the Board' answerable to the treasurer (who was also the chairman of the Treasury Board). The

Treasury Board, a committee of cabinet, was charged with evaluating the government's financial plans and making recommendations based on their knowledge and research – an area that still needed a good deal of development. The creation of the Treasury Board would trigger the slow development and partial application of a program planning and budgeting system (see chapter 7).

Robarts renamed the DEIT the Department of Economics and Development in 1963 to show that the government aimed to understand and respond to increasingly difficult obstacles to economic growth. The new department would have responsibilities for trade, regional development, and housing. It was also a favour to Bob Macaulay, who had swung the leadership to Robarts in 1961 and who wanted, in return, to be influential in economic policy. The Department of Economics and Development soon took on the task of preparing Ontario government interventions on federal initiatives, medical insurance, the creation of the Ontario Economic Council, and the preparation of a regular Ontario economic review. Its creation shed light on how Treasury was perceived: not so much as a policy shop, but more as an operational division concerned with the government's cash flow.

The 1967–8 Transformation of Treasury

As the Robarts government found its stride, the Treasury department adopted a structure in the mid-1960s that accommodated a horizontal expansion. The department assumed the administrative support for six new agencies, boards, and commissions created to manage capital expenditures, pensions, and horseracing (in the form of the Ontario Racing Commission). The structure was also expanded to include a reborn Finance Division in addition to the Revenue Division, Accounts Division, and Administrative Division (see figure 2.3). Some divisions gained new branches, and an exchange of branches remodelled the ministry. The Administrative Division oversaw functions relating to the ministry's daily operations, including the increasingly important function of 'data' processing, as well as the personnel branch. While directors led the Administrative Services and Personnel branches, a manager led the Data Processing Branch. The Accounts Division now included a new Group Insurance Section led by a supervisor. The new Finance Division included the Securities Branch and the Province of Ontario Savings Office. Revenue continued to be the largest division, with six branches under the comptroller of revenue.

The Finance division's rebirth announced that more changes were coming. As Ontario celebrated the Canadian centennial, and Brown was preparing to retire, Robarts asked H. Ian Macdonald, the chief economist in the Department of Economics and Development, to assume the position of deputy treasurer in December 1967. Macdonald was thirty-eight years old when he assumed the job. Born in Toronto, he had studied commerce at the University of Toronto and pursued his studies as a Rhodes Scholar at Oxford University, where he took a Master of Arts degree in 1954 and a Bachelor of Philosophy (Economics) degree in 1955. He returned to teach economics at the University of Toronto in 1955, and had worked there for a decade when he was recruited personally by John Robarts to join the Ontario Public Service as chief economist. Macdonald's promotion to deputy treasurer announced a radical break with the past in terms of economic and fiscal policy making in Ontario. The new department was conceived as a policy powerhouse: a place where a comprehensive approach to the Ontario economy could be engineered so as to take optimal advantage of all the levers at the disposal of the provincial state. Budget making would be more rigorous; and with the absorption into Treasury of the critical regional development functions of the Department of Economics and Development, as well as the Federal-Provincial Affairs Secretariat (FPAS), led by Ed Greathed, Treasury acquired the capacity to manage policy on many fronts.[12] The 'guardians' were now responsible for more than producing a budget or raising revenue. They now had leave to deliver a range of services to a number of industries and citizens.

From the fall of 1967, Macdonald built his team. In the words of David Redgrave, a long-time executive in the department, 'Macdonald established a university atmosphere with a policy-directed research culture.'[13] He hired Terry Russell, thirty-six, who was teaching economics at McGill University, to work on the budget, and recruited Duncan Allan, also thirty-six, to bring more verve to economic policy. In the summer of 1968 the Treasury department and the Department of Economics and Development formally merged to form the Department of Treasury and Economics (DTE). The departments had easily worked together on overlapping issues since the creation of the Office of the Provincial Economist in 1954 and its mutation to a full department in 1956 as the Department of Economics. 'This union represents a significant step in public administration,'[14] wrote Macdonald. He further argued:

The creation of the Department of Treasury and Economics represents a challenge to the conventional wisdom and a conscious belief by the

Ontario Government that economic policy and economic planning are not only inherent parts of fiscal and financial policy, but, indeed, also the very basis for forecasting, planning and setting fiscal goals. The role of a sensitive and creative finance department is not simply one of managing money, balancing the books, or raising revenues to finance the inevitable – important as those tasks may be. It is a matter of determining what part public expenditure should play in creating an atmosphere in which economic development can take place and in which economic growth will flourish. It is a matter of assessing the potential of the economy and determining how the extent, locale, and timing of public expenditures and the provision of social capital will assist in the development of the economy, upon which all social progress must rest. In other words, it is a matter of determining objectives of expenditures, setting priorities, and planning the road between actions and ends.[15]

DTE was shaped by four divisions: Policy Planning, Finance, Government Accounts, and Economic and Statistical Services. It would continue to provide the Secretariat of the Treasury Board and boasted a Computer Services Centre that would service its needs as well as those of four other departments.

Don Stevenson was named the executive director (or assistant deputy minister) of the Policy Planning Division. Stevenson was responsible for the Taxation and Fiscal Policy Branch, the Economic Policy Branch, the Regional Development Branch, and the Federal-Provincial Affairs Secretariat (FPAS): a staff of over two hundred people.[16] For Macdonald, the Economic Planning Branch's responsibilities were to 'frame, prescribe and recommend broad economic policies, goals, and alternatives for adoption by the government; recommend various courses of action in terms of public policy alternatives, either to advance the growth or retard the stagnation of particular sectors in the provincial economy; and test and evaluate individual policy recommendations for conformity with overall provincial policy objectives and goals.'[17] Embedded in the mix of priorities was the increasingly demanding file of federal–provincial relations.[18]

The formal insertion of federal-provincial affairs in the Treasury was a direct product of John Robarts's conviction that the provincial government's capacity to deal with Ottawa on federal questions urgently needed to be strengthened, along with areas of provincial jurisdiction – education, culture, health – that seemed under threat of federal encroachment. The secretariat supported the Ontario Advisory Committee on Confederation, and contributed considerable policy work in support

of Robarts's announcement in August 1967 that the province would create French-language secondary schools in the public education system.
Federal–provincial relations were to move from a theoretical pursuit to a
more concerted, hard-nosed approach. 'The rationale was that if the
Premier's Office were to be kept small, the other central agency of government with a vital interest in intergovernmental relations was surely
the Treasury, since almost all intergovernmental problems come around
to a question of finance sooner or later,' explained Don Stevenson. 'It
was also felt that outside of the Premier only the Treasurer had the kind
of leverage with other ministries that was sufficient for making policy
guidelines for intergovernmental relations stick.'[19] FPAS would have
two duties. First, to spearhead policy development in the area of federal-
provincial relations, and second, to improve the coordination of intergovernmental relations within the government.

The Finance Division's prime mandate was to bring rigour to budget
making and to manage the public debt of the province. Divided into two
branches, the Finance Management Branch and the Securities Branch, the
division was responsible 'for cash and investment management of ordinary and capital funds approaching $4 billion per annum and for all the
debt transactions emanating from an increasingly broad and complex
character,' wrote Ian Macdonald.[20] The division maintained the government's presence in the bond market, including the floating of new issues,
servicing the debt, and the management of the various crown corporations concerned with capital expenditures. It also had to maintain 'a continuing liaison on financial and debt matters with the Hydro-Electric
Power Commission of Ontario.' Macdonald noted that the Finance
Division and the Taxation and Fiscal Policy Branch were 'blood brothers
in the budgetary process and in the realm of public finance.' 'It will be
interesting to observe, over time,' he wrote, 'the development of a common language among government bankers and economists.'[21]

The third division was Government Accounts. It was responsible for
the maintenance of the government's accounting and financial systems,
including its pension and insurance plans. Finally, the fourth division
was devoted to the provision of 'Economic and Statistical Services.' It essentially would continue the work done under the Department of
Economics and focus on improving the understanding of the Ontario
economy. The work was divided between the Economic Analysis Branch
– the 'scientific arm of our body of economists,' as Macdonald called it –
the Ontario Statistical Centre, and the Systems and Programming Branch,
which brought together the computer systems analysts.

The largest change to the structure of the ministry was the addition of a number of boards and commissions to the scope of its mandate, perhaps most notably those associated with education and university funding. These were the Ontario Education Capital Aid Corporation (OECAC), the Ontario Universities Capital Aid Corporation (OUCAC), the Pension Commission of Ontario, and the Ontario Racing Commission, as well as the Ontario Municipal Improvement Corporation and the Public Service Superannuation Board, started in 1964. The establishment of the OECAC and the OUCAC inside the ministry left the financing of educational capital aid to the Finance ministry, thus increasing further the scope of its responsibilities and duties.

Finally, the Treasury Board Secretariat was expanded under the auspices of the Treasury of Ontario. A number of new directorates showed the growing importance and influence of the Ontario TBS: Program Analysis, Staff Relations, Advisory Services, Organization and Methods, Automatic Data Processing Standards, and Actuarial Services. The consistent growth of area-specific directors in the Treasury Board since 1964 was indicative of the board's development as a management and oversight tool for the government of the day.

Clearly, the ministry expanded dramatically in the 1960s under Robarts. From a relatively small nucleus emerged the deployment of an organizational structure complete with divisions and branches that maintained active conversations and negotiations with all the government departments; it was now a central agency. The organizational charts bear witness to the modernization effort within the wider departmental structure that may have been used to deal with the ministry's growth in terms of both employees and economy. At the same time, the political field was not experiencing much by way of change: the Conservatives had been in power since 1943, and comfortably dominated the political landscape. With the help of the senior staff, the Conservatives had transformed the public administration system of the province. Government could be more activist because its department of treasury and economics was more present, more informed, and more 'learned' on the widest range of policy issues.

The department tasked with preparing the budget was merged with the department that planned government tax and fiscal policy. It would 'pull together the budget, recommend taxation, federal-provincial and provincial municipal financing approaches, and ensure that at least aggregate expenditure and fiscal policies were consistent with a deliberate government impact on economic development.'[22] What was important was that it was the economists, led by Macdonald, who landed on top. These were men who had trained in the Canadian 'political economy' school; they were not steeped in the econometrics of their successors, but as budgeters were now also responsible for economic research, regional development, statistics, and intergovernmental affairs. As the capacity for research and analysis grew, the department transformed its ability to budget for the province, deepened its studies, and published reports. Budget making was transformed as staff prepared studies that justified the budget as it was tabled, instead of after the fact. The Budget Papers of 1968 announced that a new approach, 'program budgeting,' would be used to 'allow orderly changes in expenditure patterns over the course of several budgets.' The budget in effect became the 'driver' of the entire department, according to Terry Russell; and its success was the metric by which the ministry staff measured their performance. 'We took command of the budget system,' Russell remembered.[23] The minister was briefed comprehensively (the briefing books grew more massive with each passing year). As an indicator of the new approach, the 1969 Budget Papers featured a report on 'The Ontario Economy' as well as a discussion of the impact of reforms in taxation on government structure.

The economy of Ontario was growing throughout this period, and there was a need for more people, more divisional structure, and more branches to fulfil the increased mandate of the ministry. There was a demand for more public services,[24] and the ministry had to organize the province's finances to pay for an increase in services. For example, the establishment of the Retail Sales Tax branch signalled the entry of the province into a new taxation field to pay for provincial programs. The 'deal' between the public and the government reflected the growth of the Keynesian welfare state: the government would provide for a certain standard of living in exchange for increased tax revenues. This required more staff whenever the scope of what the government wished to do widened and attested to the increase in boards and corporations placed under the ministry's purview during these years. Not surprisingly, the rapid growth threatened to impede clarity in mandates.

To remedy this situation in part, the department was split in 1968 as the Revenue Division became its own ministry, taking with it no fewer than two-thirds of the employees. The Treasury of the 1960s, as Donald Stevenson put it in 1972,

was primarily a revenue collecting agency. To a considerable extent, budgetary policy could be defined as the decision-making necessary to provide the revenue to finance the expenditure requests of the various departments and agencies, once the Treasury Board had reviewed them to cut down exorbitant demands. Economic forecasting and attempts at the development of overall provincial economic policies were carried out in the Department of Economics and Development, but there was no integral connection between this activity and the budget-making process. As in so many other provincial governments, economics research was directed more to support of an industrial promotion and development program than to the overall economic impact of government programs.[25]

By 1970, Revenue had 1325 employees, while Treasury and Economics had 536.

Looking for ideas on how to improve government performance, Robarts commissioned a Committee on Government Productivity (COGP), composed of public-sector executives and businessmen, in late December 1969. It would soon have an impact on Treasury and Economics.

The 1970s Treasury of Ontario and Ministry of Economics: Organizational Trials

Bill Davis succeeded Robarts as premier in 1971, and led the Progressive Conservatives through two minority governments from 1975–80 and a majority government from 1981–5. These years were fraught with economic difficulties, from the oil crisis and resulting inflationary increases in the early to mid-1970s, to recession in the later years of the decade. The Treasury of Ontario witnessed a number of changes in its organizational structure in the 1970s as it tried to adapt.

The COGP submitted its conclusions in March 1973, and its thinking affected the way ministry staff would be deployed in the 1970s. Don Stevenson hailed it as 'our version of the Glassco Commission,' referring to the federal study team that had made important organizational recommendations in 1964, especially on the structure of the Treasury Board.[26] One of the major recommendations of the COGP was that the Ontario government implement 'an organizational structure which distinguishes between responsibility for policy formulation and planning on one hand and program delivery on the other.'[27] Treasury's executives would not wait for the COGP to come to its conclusions. The first attempts at instituting an organizational structure that would facilitate performance were illustrated by the charts of 1970 (figures 2.4–2.7). They would emphasize the differences, by division, branch, and job title, of employees who focused on policy rather than operations. The chart of 1973 (figure 2.9) accentuated the differences even more. This was the department's apogee, its golden age. Its executive had worked fairly consistently together for six years and Treasury and Economics played a key role in all aspects of policy making. Ontario's Finance department had ideas on many if not most policy areas, and had a particular objective: delivering good policy and making sure Ottawa's economic and fiscal policies did not threaten Ontario's prosperity. The *Toronto Star* dedicated an important, and unusual, article to it in May 1973. Focusing on Ian MacDonald, Terry Russell, and Duncan Allan, the piece presented them as 'aggressive, efficient, anxious to keep their minister in the spotlight and themselves out of it.'

The *Toronto Star* article blew the cover off the senior staff in the ministry and let some of the good humour that reigned in the ministry come to light. Ian Macdonald was described as 'quiet and extremely cautious,' while Terry Russell and Duncan Allan were portrayed as 'irreverent' in the 'the most tedious situations.'

'Terry and the Pirates' as one provincial politician calls them, have come up with songs and skits mocking the federal government at conference cocktail parties. They once had a string of 'Simon says' jokes at the expense of Simon Reisman, the deputy finance minister in Ottawa.

They take great delight in keeping one of their attractive female economists near the head of the Ontario delegation at conferences, particularly when she can challenge an uneasy federal official on the details of a double rolling log regression system.

They shocked a federal delegation which had come down to Queen's Park for a meeting on a hot afternoon last summer by bringing in a case of beer instead of coffee for an afternoon break.[28]

Clearly, the team Macdonald had created in 1967 had gelled into an envied policy generator for its ministers, mostly Charles MacNaughton and, for an eighteen-month period in the early 1970s, Darcy McKeough.[29] In an atmosphere described by journalist Eric Malling as 'open, young and competitive,'[30] they provided sound financial data and credible and well-researched policy positions that enabled Ontario to challenge the Ottawa machine and to assert provincial demands in intergovernmental meetings. This attested to the effectiveness of the organizational structure that had been created over the 1960s and early 1970s.

The 1970 Treasury of Ontario and Ministry of Economics

By 1970, the organizational chart of the ministry was noticeably larger than it was in 1967, despite the removal of the revenue division into its own ministry (figures 2.4 and 2.5). The position of associate deputy minister would disappear from the chart and would not return for another two decades.

There were still four divisions in the ministry: Policy Planning, Finance, Economic and Statistical Services, and Government Accounts. Executive directors oversaw both the Policy Planning and Economic and Statistical Services divisions, while the Finance and Government Accounts divisions were under the comptroller of finances and the comptroller of accounts, respectively. Reporting to the executive directors and comptrollers were the directors of various branches and a few accountants.

The proliferation of branches demonstrated the further expansion of the ministry's scope, and explained each division's primary roles in both policymaking and financial management. The Policy Planning Division, for instance, featured branches for Economic Planning, Taxation and Fiscal Policy, and Regional Development, and the Federal-Provincial Affairs Secretariat. The establishment of a Regional Development office along with a Federal-Provincial Affairs Secretariat within the ministry indicated a change in both the ministry's scope and in the priorities of government. Regional development, or the use of province-mandated plans to improve the economies of certain regions,[31] was a significant issue during the first years of the Davis government, as municipalities were facing increased pressures from accelerated growth.[32] The study of localized economic issues therefore became a responsibility of the Regional Development Office of the ministry that changed its nature as a pure 'guardian' of the public purse.[33] 'Our ministry is almost unique,' said Don Stevenson, the ADM of the Policy Division of the department in 1972, 'in combining most of the ... broad policy responsibilities with the central budgetary function of government.' The fit was indeed odd:

> Finance departments traditionally have been tagged with the label of being 'the NO men,' fighting increases in expenditures and new programs. Many of the program areas the Ministry is involved in are those where increasing expenditures will be required in the coming years. We hope that having both functions will put this government in a much better position to allocate expenditure to the highest priority areas, even in a period

of severe expenditure restraint. The dilemma is great and in the next few months may represent the toughest set of policy questions we have to face.[34]

Growth in staff matched the extension of the ministry's scope: 594 people worked in the ministry in 1973. The increased numbers of mid-level managers, including chiefs/managers/senior budget advisers/senior economists/supervisors, illustrated employee growth at this time (see figures 2.6 and 2.7). There were no fewer than four chiefs answerable to the director of the Ontario Statistical Centre, and the director of the Economic Planning Branch received reports from three chiefs, each responsible for different policy planning areas and also for the economists in their own areas. The Government Accounts Branch was split in two. A supervisor managed a staff of several accountants, an administrator, as well as a manager of the Loan Accounting Section and an assistant to the manager in Government Accounting. This was a distinct contrast to the Accounts Division of 1967, in which the comptroller of accounts was responsible for two directors and a supervisor.

Another area of growth through the 1960s was in support for the Treasury Board. Gone were the multiple directors for different areas of the 'Management Board of Cabinet' that replaced the 'Treasury Board.' The new Management Board was now formally headed by a chairman and a board of members drawn from the Cabinet. It was supported by a deputy minister, the secretary of Treasury Board, and a very small staff.

The Ministry of Revenue, 1970

The bureaucracy associated with Revenue was formally recognized as a separate department with its own minister in 1968. (The Treasury of Ontario and the Ministry of Economics and Ministry of Revenue would be reunited in the 1990s under the title of the Ministry of Finance, and split again in 2005.) The deputy minister supervised three branches, each led by a director: Revenue Research, Legal Services, and the Operational Audit.

Most of Revenue was moved to Oshawa, east of Toronto, in a building designed to its own specifications in order to house its computers. It was split into two divisions: Revenue and Administrative (see figures 2.4 and 2.5). Each division was overseen by an executive director. The divisions were further broken down into branches. In the Revenue Division, these were the Corporations Tax and Logging Tax Branch, the

Gasoline Tax Branch, the Retail Sales Tax Branch, the Succession Duty Branch, and district offices. These echoed the former Revenue Division branches of the 1960s. In the Administrative Division, branches included Accounts, Office Services, Personnel, Systems and Programming, and Library. Led by directors – and in the case of the Gasoline Tax and Retail Sales Tax branches, a director and assistant directors – the mid-level management of these branches belonged to supervisors, chiefs, specialists, and coordinators. Specialists were another somewhat new introduction to the ministry organizational structure, and most often were given the title of tax specialists.

The 1972 Treasury of Ontario and Ministry of Economics and Intergovernmental Affairs

In early 1973, John White succeeded the retiring Charles MacNaughton and assumed the direction of a ministry restructured along the lines proposed by the COGP and the Smith Committee on Taxation, which had proposed new arrangements between the regional level and the provincial government on tax reform. Both argued that finance and regional/community planning could reinforce each other and ensure that municipal concerns were in the forefront of budgetary considerations. White would bear the new title of 'Treasurer and Minister of Minister of Economics and Intergovernmental Affairs,' because in April 1972, the department was renamed the Treasury of Ontario and Ministry of Economics and Intergovernmental Affairs (TEIGA) (see figure 2.9). The new titled formally recognized the importance of the federal-provincial dossier and reflected the fact that Treasury had absorbed the Department of Municipal Affairs – a first in provincial administration. From a hierarchical perspective, the reorganization was notable for the introduction of large, overarching 'Super Divisional' structures led by assistant deputy ministers.

TEIGA, still under the leadership of Ian Macdonald, had grown to close to six hundred staff, many of whom were now recognized formally for the first time as 'policy advisers,' following the recommendations of the final report of the COGP.[35] Reporting directly to the deputy ministry's office were the director of the Ministry Central Office, as well as the directors of Systems and Programming, the Legal Services Branch, Organization Development, the Office of Information, a Policy Liaison, and a head librarian. Macdonald had changed his office dramatically since 1970. The establishment of the Office of Information was indicative of a wider change in ministry, and even governmental, scope as ministry staff were now responsible for delivering information directly to the public. Macdonald had organized an enviably strong group of personnel, but also looked outside government ranks for policy advice. He chaired a regular breakfast with a small group of outside economists from both the private sector and academia, and both the minister, Darcy McKeough, and the premier, Bill Davis, attended assiduously.

The 'Super Divisions' also changed. ADMs led the Finance Division (Terry Russell), Urban and Regional Affairs Division (C.P. Honey), and Economic Policy and Intergovernmental Affairs Division (Don Stevenson). Executive directors led the Administrative Services Division, Central Statistical Services, and Local Government Services Division and reported to the deputy. Executive directors also worked in the 'super' divisions led by ADMs.

Urban and Regional Affairs, the Super Division that stemmed from the original Regional Development Branch seen in 1970, was further divided into the Urban and Regional Planning and Local Government Services divisions.[36] Indicative of the Regional Development Branch's scope were its responsibilities to manage the Haldimand-Norfolk Project (a proposed new town adjacent to Stelco and Ontario Hydro projects) and the North Pickering Community Development Project (to manage land and create a new town near the proposed second international airport for Toronto). It also housed a Local Planning Policy shop and a Local Government Organization office. In the expansion of the branch into a division, regional finance gained prominence within the ministry, which reflected the government's prioritizing of regional issues.[37]

The organizational structure became more complicated. The Finance Super Division, led by Terry Russell, included the Fiscal Policy and Treasury divisions. The Fiscal Policy Division itself contained the Municipal Finance, Taxation and Fiscal Policy, and Intergovernmental Finance and Grants Policy branches, while Treasury Division included the Financial Management, Securities, and Financial Information and Accounting Policy branches.

The process of budgeting had adapted to a more sophisticated calendar. Since the late 1960s, the new Treasury Board had received five-year expenditure forecasts from each ministry. Ministries were asked to provide two lists, those for expenditures required to maintain existing programs, and a separate list for improvements to programs, or to fund additional programs. Reports were analysed by staff from the Treasury Board and the Department of Treasury and Economics. By the end of

June, decision items would be considered by the Cabinet Committee on Policy and Priorities in light of anticipated budgetary targets and the province's fiscal situation. The decisions would be turned back to the individual departments with the request to prepare a detailed plan for the upcoming fiscal year. The Cabinet Committee on Policy and Priorities (renamed the Policy and Priorities Board in 1972) would hold special retreats in August to set expenditure levels and again in November to consider a refinement of the items that could appear in the budget that would be presented to the legislature in the spring.

The department had also turned itself into a think tank as it published 'staff papers' on a variety of topics starting in the 1970s. The 'Ontario Studies in Tax Reform' collection, featured papers on subjects as varied as 'Effects of Ontario's Personal Income Tax Proposals' and 'Analysis of Income and Property Taxes in Guelph' and 'The Dynamic Impact of Indexing the Personal Income Tax.' Other staff papers included publications on 'Ontario Proposals for Tax Reform in Canada,' 'Intergovernmental Policy Co-ordination and Finance,' 'Financing the Canada Pension Plan,' and 'Intergovernmental Liaison on Fiscal and Economic Matters.' The department also distinguished itself as an 'early adopter' of new technologies. Xerox word processors, electronic calculators, mainframe computers, and, later, on-line and desktop computers were the constant focus of experimentation in Finance's offices. As technology developed, so did the econometric ability of the department. 'These models provided the annual and quarterly GNP and GPP forecasts, revenue and expenditure forecasts, and special program models for federal-provincial and inter-provincial negotiations such as GITAN [General Income Tax Analyzer] and PENSIM [an actuarial model of pensions],' noted David Redgrave. 'Other models were developed for municipal tax reform, detailed health sector expenditures, the inter-provincial fiscal impact of energy prices increases.'[38]

Two agencies reported to the ministry: the Ontario Economic Council and the Ontario Land Corporation were both overseen by the chairmen of their respective boards. The government was interested in investigating the COGP's suggestion of 'early experimentation with widening the use of government contracts for service with the private sector.'[39] It went on to mention spurring competition between the public and private sectors for services, and certain issues that the public service might face in coming years, including economic hardship.[40] 'I think the 1970s will be a period of real experimentation in private sector involvement in government decision-making on economic policy,' said Don Stevenson at the time. 'Ontario has just established a joint committee on economic policy reporting to the premier. The federal government is establishing an institute of public policy. Royal Commissions are going out of fashion and are being replaced by mixed bodies like the Committee on Government Productivity ... or Advisory Committees on Housing or Energy. All of this implies that the era of public-private sector confrontation is coming to an end and that the dilemmas of the future will be met together.'[41]

The 1976 Treasury of Ontario and Ministry of Economics and Intergovernmental Affairs

Rendall Dick succeeded Ian Macdonald in the summer of 1974, and Darcy McKeough returned as treasurer in June 1975. Within two years, the department would undergo another metamorphosis. By 1976, Ontario was facing economic difficulties and a plan of restraint in government spending was instituted: the overarching Super Divisional structure was eliminated. Instead, three ADMs (including a senior ADM) would report to the deputy, but all areas of the ministry would report to them. There was only one assistant deputy minister left with supervision of the Ministry Office, the coordinator of ministry policy, the executive coordinator of special projects, and the women's coordinator. These were all new positions, with the exception of the director of the Ministry Office. The women's coordinator was a somewhat anomalous position that came with little explanation except to signal that the ministry was seriously committed to encouraging employment equity.

The department wanted more flexibility and an improvement of the quality and quantity of the outputs of the ministry and its associated agencies, boards, and commissions. To this end, 'the removal from the diagram of formal lines between branches and the use of dotted lines between divisions is designed to illustrate the intention to use multi-disciplined task and project groups to achieve the desired outputs, particularly in the area of policy development, program delivery and program management.'[42] A briefing note of the period noted that the changes had to be made to 'accommodate this Ministry's role in the shift in the government's emphasis toward the area of economic development of the province, particularly to overcoming regional inequities and the provision of jobs, and away from the community development and micro planning which are now largely in the Ministry of Housing.'[43]

With the disappearance of the Super Divisions, the ranks of ordinary divisions now included: Administration, Central Statistical Services, the Office of Economic Policy (OEP), Local Government, and Project Implementation. Each division was led by an executive director instead of an ADM, and a director oversaw most branches. In OEP, the Policy Planning, Economic Analysis, Securities, and Financial Information and Accounting Policy branches were listed along with Regional Development Branch. The Local Government Division was composed of Local Government Organization, the Advisory Services Branch, the Provincial Municipal Affairs Secretariat, the Subsidies Branch, as well as a number of Regional Offices overseen by directors and area managers (see figure 2.11). Finally, the Project Implementation Division appeared to have been broken up into units that dealt with very specific projects or issues, including the Parkway Belt, Program Coordination, and Economic Development.

Don Stevenson, the ADM for planning, reflected on the harsh realities: 'If Ontario is any example, public administration is going to have to devote more and more of its attention to problems of phasing out or reducing government programs. There is a determination in the Ontario Government now to attack the bureaucratic monster greater than I have ever seen in twenty years of government services and that I have not seen exhibited in the federal government to quite the same degree.'[44] His ministry would have to tighten its belt. In 1976, the ministry had grown to 656 employees. Within three years, it would shed 33.6 per cent of its staff. In 1979, 435 people worked for the Treasury.

The 1979 Treasury of Ontario and Ministry of Economics

McKeough was replaced by Frank Miller in August 1978, but his departure was not the only loss in the department. A few dozen staff migrated to the new Ministry of Intergovernmental Affairs that was created to show that Ontario wished to monitor and respond to constitutional proposals. Premier Davis named Tom Wells as minister and Don Stevenson as deputy, with the mandate to look after interprovincial, federal–provincial, and municipal relations. This arrangement would continue until 1980, when the thickening constitutional dossier consumed most of that small ministry's capacity. (A Ministry of Municipal Affairs and Housing was then created, with Tom Wells as minister. Wells was also House Leader in a minority legislature and had only a limited amount of time to meet with mayors.)

Interestingly, the office of the deputy minister, still under Rendall Dick, was given more strength. An ADM was now responsible for the operations of the deputy minister's office that now housed only Legal Services and the deputy minister's staff, including the director and policy coordinator of his office. The ministry also shed most of its agencies, with the Ontario Economic Council as the only survivor.

Small changes were also brought to the divisional structure, with the Treasury and the Fiscal Policy divisions supplanting the Local Government and Project Implementation divisions. Local Government concerns were shared between two other branches within the Fiscal Policy Division: Municipal Finance and Intergovernmental Finance and Grants Policy. This was another indication of shifting government priorities: the health of the economy was declining, and the government may have been more concerned with exercising fiscal restraint[45] than with devoting a ministry division and its corresponding resources to smaller-scale regional development instead of provincial development. Treasury and Economics still held the lead on overall intergovernmental finance policy, despite the creation of the new Intergovernmental Affairs Ministry.

The developments of the late 1970s positioned the ministry as a central agency (reminiscent of the Department of Economics under Frost), with a number of different portfolios within its terms of reference. The Project Implementation Division had become a branch in the Office of Economic Policy.

The branches within the divisions had altered slightly as well, although discrete areas were still discernible through the branch titles. Within the Administration Services Division, four of the branches of 1976 remained (figure 2.12). However, Cartography and Drafting Services and Records and Forms Management Services were added, while the Communications Group appeared to have taken the place of the Office of Information Services. The branches in the new Treasury Division, reminiscent of the Treasury Division of the 1960s, included Securities, Research Policy and Information, Financial Reporting, Central Accounting and Reporting, and Finance Management. The Fiscal Policy Division comprised the Taxation and Fiscal Policy Branch, as well as the previously mentioned Municipal Finance and Intergovernmental Finance and Grants Policy branches (see figure 2.13).

At this time, the main change on the management side was that in addition to managers and supervisors, senior budget or senior policy advisers and financial analysts had been added to mid-level management. Senior budget advisers were found primarily in the Fiscal Policy

Division's Taxation and Fiscal Policy Branch in specific budget areas with teams of economists.

The 1970s in Perspective

The 1970s were a period of widespread changes within the Treasury of Ontario and Ministry of Economics, and sometimes Intergovernmental Affairs, that arced through the decade. Treasury retained its principal functions: to recommend fiscal, economic, regional, and taxation policies to the government; to implement expenditure management policies; to provide advice to ensure consistency among these policies and other government programs; to develop the provincial budget and manage the province's finances; to administer the province's major tax statutes and tax assistance programs; to provide information and analysis on Ontario's international activities and on its relationships with the federal and other provincial governments; and to provide analysis and reform of local governments.

Through four different ministers, the department experienced a period of build-up as policymaking inside the ministry became a governing concern. The capacity to generate policy proposals was fully expressed in the structure that was created in 1973, but did not last long. The government rethought its priorities,[46] tinkered often with the structure of its ministries, sought the advice of 'outsiders' in the form of the Ontario Economic Council, and froze hiring. The idea of internalizing spending responsibilities in the Ministry of Finance did not gel. It simply could not adopt the 'No' stance in front of dozens of ministries while favouring expenditures in regional and local portfolios.

The Super Division structures of 1973, including Finance and Urban and Regional Affairs, were rescinded and replaced with more traditional division/branch structures by 1976. The freeze and even the resulting downsizing, particularly in the senior ranks, illustrated the return to a pre-1973 organizational structure in 1976. Even though fewer people worked in the ministry, the organizational chart would be refined again as became apparent at the close of the decade.

The decade demonstrated how far the department had moved beyond its strict 'guardian' duties and assumed a variety of roles as 'coordinator,' 'watchdog,' and even priority setter in a number of areas. This was attributable to a number of factors. First among them was the confidence that was placed in Ian Macdonald and his successor, Rendall Dick. Both men were exceptional, deeply experienced administrators who clearly were not inclined to say 'no' when political masters asked them to take on different portfolios. Both were seen personally as extraordinarily competent and intelligent policy advisers and as highly capable managers who were adept at attracting and retaining a professional staff that was equally eager to take on more work. (It is worth noting that future deputies Bryan Davies, Eleanor Clitheroe, Michael Gourley, Bryne Purchase, and Robert Christie were all hired by either Macdonald or Dick.) They took on a remarkable range of issues, and as the department charts attest, often ensured that the reports on the cutting-edge issues they were asked to oversee came to them directly, unfiltered. The senior staff welcomed the opportunity to delve into issues that went beyond revenue and budgeting and relished the opportunity to get involved in issues that elsewhere would have been given to line ministries. The involvement of 'treasury' or 'finance' staff in this variety of issues contributed to their image as somewhat arrogant, but this was hardly surprising. They knew they had the ear of the most influential minister of the government, and of the premier himself. Such assurance could hardly fail to affect relations with public servants in other departments. Not surprisingly, treasury also became a training ground for individuals who eventually became deputy ministers in line departments in their own right. Some were elected to office, both federally and provincially.

The 1980s Treasury: Changes in Government, Similarities in Structure

The 1980s were a decade of change in Ontario's government, as five different people served as treasurer. For the public servants, the decade that started with the rather conservative Frank Miller, experienced a quick see-saw between Larry Grossman and Bette Stephenson, followed by five years under the Liberal Robert Nixon and then the New Democrat Floyd Laughren. The bureaucracy's leadership also changed hands three times. Rendall Dick was replaced by Thomas Campbell in September 1981 and he held the position of deputy treasurer until August 1984. Brock Smith assumed the post, and would hold it for more than three years, until October 1987. The first woman to occupy the position, Mary Mogford, replaced him and was succeeded by Bryan Davies in September 1989. Davies would pilot the department through the first years of the NDP government. The end of the Progressive Conservative government that had lasted for forty-two years was a momentous turn in Ontario politics and government, and particularly within the Ontario public service as it was called upon to adapt and answer to a new political master.

While the organizational structure of the ministry in the 1980s remained similar to that of the later 1970s, there were reductions in some areas with expansions in others. The ministry shed more employees in the 1980s, going from 435 in 1979 to 365 in 1989, a drop of 16 per cent. The ministry shifted emphasis: there was a manifest increase in the deployment of mid-level managers towards the end of the 1980s, while senior bureaucrats (directors, ADMs, etc.) seemed to be vanishing. Constraint of government expenditures in the face of an economic downturn may help to explain the slow disappearance of senior bureaucratic roles in the organizational structure throughout this decade. In fact, government operating costs were frozen in 1984 and the treasurer, Larry Grossman, spoke about increasing the role of the private sector in providing some of the services for which the government had traditionally been responsible.[47]

The growth at the ministry in this decade was indeed limited. There were significant changes in the organizational structure, including a move from multiple branches to consolidated branches, the elimination of several divisions, the rise in the use of units to make up for the lack of branches, and also in the number of management-type positions as well as general staff. In many ways, it appears that after the major changes introduced in 1973 and then removed by 1976, the ministry established its preferred organizational structure and state, and stayed fairly true to that form until the reorganization that brought Revenue back into the ministry's fold in the 1990s.

The 1982 Treasury of Ontario and Ministry of Economics

In 1981, the Bill Davis Progressive Conservatives won a majority in the general election, their first in six years. With the economy caught in a recession, however, fiscal restraint was again the order of the day and changes would be minimal in these years. One major difference between 1979 and 1982 (figure 2.14) was the reintroduction of assistant deputy ministers acting as divisional leaders. This gesture recognized the quality of the work performed by these senior public servants.

A few sections were renamed or combined. The Central Statistical Services, for instance, brought together all the data-gathering parts of the department. The Fiscal Policy Division was renamed the Office of the Budget and Intergovernmental Finance. Led primarily by directors and senior budget advisers, the branches included those found previously in the Fiscal Policy Division: Fiscal Policy Planning, Taxation Policy, and Intergovernmental Finance Policy.[48] More importantly, Crown corporations were now part of this division, thus adding responsibility for corporations owned by the government to the Treasurer of Ontario and Minister of Economics (see figure 2.15).

The Board of Industrial Leadership and Development (BILD), an oversight group created to identify public infrastructure projects, was also added to the ministry. Political in nature, it was supported by its own secretariat. BILD was an attempt to spur economic growth and development within the province in order to combat both unemployment and stagflation,[49] although it was sometimes accused of being nothing more than a pre-election gimmick. Its addition to the ministry reflected the ministry's responsibility for the province's economy, which included finding a solution for the issues the economy faced in a stubborn recession.

The 1986 Ministry: The Robert Nixon Years

The change in government brought about by the 1985 election of the Liberals brought change to the department's organizational structure. The same four major divisions existed: the Office of the Budget and Intergovernmental Finance, the OEP, the Office of the Treasury, and the Administration Division, but the number of branches was reduced. The OEP was reorganized into two major branches: Economic Policy and Sectoral and Regional Policy. Department executives aimed to shape the ministry to have fewer divisions and fewer branches, and thus fewer directors, but many smaller units within the overarching organizational structures. This was especially apparent in the Office of the Budget and Intergovernmental Finance, which had only three branches but thirteen units led by either managers or senior policy/budget advisers. Employment levels, however, were steady, with 389 full-time employees in 1986 and 365 three years later.[50] The Liberals thus echoed the themes enunciated in 1976: a reduction in the number of director-level positions, but an increase in senior management/senior policy/senior budget employees.

The 1989 Ministry

There was a further unification of the divisional structure at the ministry in the late 1980s under Mary Mogford. At that point, only two divisions existed: the Office of the Treasury and the Administration Division. Three other important branches existed outside of any division: Sectoral and Regional Policy, Demographics and Social Economics, and Economic Forecasting, two of which were found in OEP in 1986 (see figures 2.17 and 2.18).

The Office of the Budget and Intergovernmental Finance seemed to have all but disappeared from the phone book by 1989, but the job of writing the province's budget continued to be the focus of a dedicated office. The change to the large-branch, small-unit structure was limited, however. The organization chart for 1989 still placed a significant number of units under the authority of a single director. Lindquist and White have highlighted the 'Tomorrow Project' of 1989–90 as an important aspect of the Liberal government's public administration agenda, although it was almost entirely driven by the bureaucracy. They indicated that the restructuring of the ministry played a significant role in the project:

> The initial phase of the Tomorrow Project involved three discrete projects. First was a rethinking and restructuring of the key central agencies, Cabinet Office, the Ministry of Treasury and Economics, and Management Board Secretariat ... The central agency project was chosen as an early priority in order to gain credibility for the whole exercise and to demonstrate that the centre would not be immune to change.[51]

This reorganization exercise was apparent in the organization chart for 1989 (see figure 2.19), with its elimination of divisional structures and some ADMs.

Conclusion: the 1980s

Despite the changes that occurred in Ontario politics at this time, the organizational make-up and scope of the Treasury of Ontario and Ministry of Economics remained essentially faithful to its late-1970s incarnation, but with some important changes. A layer of executives was practically eliminated, branches were consolidated, and a few divisions were merged.

While the Liberal government transition in 1985 was fairly smooth,[52] gaining the respect and commitment of the bureaucracy was a significant challenge. This was illustrated perhaps best by the lack of senior public servants in the 1989 organization chart (see figure 2.19). All told, however, the Liberal governments did not choose to refocus the scope of the ministry, which continued to provide for both service delivery and policy implementation, as was illustrated with the increased number of policy specialists.

The 1990s and 2001 Ministry of Finance – A Process of Reintegration

The Treasury Department of Ontario would experience two very different men as minister in the new decade, Floyd Laughren and Ernie Eves, and the department's organization would be dominated by two themes. First were the reintegration of Revenue and Treasury in 1993 and the renaming of the department as the Ministry of Finance.[53] The second would be a dramatic cut in personnel brought on in the latter part of the decade.[54] As in the 1980s, the tenure of ADMs would average no more than two years, as Bryan Davies, Eleanor Clitheroe, Jay Kaufman, Michael Gourley, Bryne Purchase, and Robert Christie occupied the position.

The 1993 Ministry

The recombination of Finance and Revenue in 1993 created a ministry of 5003 employees. In addition to the minister and deputy minister of finance, there was also an associate deputy minister, a position brought back from the 1960s. The associate deputy minister was responsible for the Revenue side of the combined organization, while the deputy minister of finance retained oversight of the Treasury/Economics side. The divisional structure was reinstituted, and the title of assistant deputy minister was brought back for each division. The minister at the time was also the chair of Treasury Board, and had oversight of a number of boards and commissions, notably the Fair Tax Commission, the Ontario Share & Deposit Insurance Corporation, and the Ontario Insurance Commission. (It is worth noting that Ontario ended its nomenclature of 'Management Board of Cabinet' – in usage since 1971 – in 1991.) These commissions greatly increased the scope of the ministry at the time, specifically into policy areas that held political significance to the governing party.

Under the Treasury side of the Ministry of Finance (MoF), there were four main divisions: the Public Sector Labour Market and Productivity Commission, Financial Services, the reinstituted Office of Economic Policy, and Taxation and Intergovernmental Finance Policy. The most notable of these was the Public Sector Labour Market and Productivity Commission, which held the Job Security Fund branch and the Office of the Social Contract Adjudicator. These reflected changes in both the priorities of government and the responsibilities of the ministry. Responsibility for the administration of the Job Security Fund provided for in the Social Contract Act of 1995 fell to the ministry.[55] This was unfamiliar territory.

The Revenue side of the MoF was significantly larger than the Treasury side in terms of branches and their associated directors. Revenue had four main divisions: Tax Administration, Corporate Services, Property Assessment, and Deposit Institutions. The associate deputy minister had direct oversight of the Corporate Planning Branch, the Employment Equity Office, and the Restructuring Project Office, with the latter two having been instituted by the NDP. Branches on the Revenue side closely resembled those in Revenue's 1970 organization chart. Corporations Tax and Services now had its own division, marking the rise in importance of corporate tax revenues to the province since 1970. Property assessment was now a MoF responsibility and would remain as such until the end of the 1990s, when the responsibility was given to the Ontario Property Assessment Corporation, later the Municipal Property Assessment Corporation (MPAC), a municipally owned, not-for-profit corporation.

There was a clear demarcation between the Treasury and Revenue sides of the newly created Ministry of Finance in 1993. Despite some areas, such as the Taxation Policy Branch of Taxation and Intergovernmental Finance Policy Division on the Treasury side, where an overlap may have existed with operations on the Revenue side, there appeared to be very little attempt in 1993 to connect these two aspects of the ministry.

The 1996 Ministry

The election of the Mike Harris Progressive Conservatives in 1995 had little immediate impact. The segregation of the 'finance' and 'revenue' functions was still evident; indeed, there still was not a single deputy minister for the entire department, but instead two differently titled deputies: a deputy minister of finance, and a deputy minister of revenue and financial institutions. Despite the change in government, the minister still maintained oversight of several NDP-instituted commissions and offices at this point, including the Office of Social Contract Adjudication and the Ontario Insurance Commission.

There were now three main divisions on the Finance side of the organization. These were Fiscal and Financial Policy, the OEP, and the Office of the Budget and Taxation (OBT). The OBT appeared to have been both a reinstatement of the Office of the Budget and Intergovernmental Finance, last seen in 1982, and a promotion of the Budget Secretariat Branch, seen in 1993. OBT now contained three branches: Intergovernmental Finance, Taxation Policy, and Tax Design and Legislation. While the creation of the OBT did not indicate an expansion of the responsibilities of the MoF, it did establish a budget-activity-specific office within the MoF sphere. ADMs led all the divisions, thus solidifying the position within the organizational structure of the MoF from this point until the end of the period studied here.

The divisional oversight of ADMs was also apparent on the Revenue side of the MoF. The Revenue divisional structure remained the same as under the 1993 reorganization, as did the majority of the branches. The deputy minister of revenue and financial institutions has had direct oversight of the Financial Services Policy and Audit Services branches.

The organization chart of the MoF in 1996 illustrated the separation between the former Treasury and the former Revenue. It was somewhat of a transitory chart, however, for changes were made as the new minister and deputy ministers asserted their authority.

The 1998 Ministry

As in the early 1970s, authority was again concentrated in the hands of the deputy minister, who had direct responsibility for Priority Projects, the Stadium Corporation of Ontario, the Office of Legal Services, the Audit Services Branch, and the Communications and Corporate Affairs Branch. The organization at the close of the century did not feature the same kind of visual demarcation between the former Treasury and Ministry of Revenue noticed in the 1996 chart (see figure 2.20), thus perhaps illustrating the further-developed integration of the ministry at this time. Here again, the telephone books demonstrated a relationship that was more apparent than real. As Len Roozen put it, 'from my earliest involvement in the early 1970s until my departure in 2007, staff in the Finance and Revenue functions were for the most part geographically separated, rarely interacted except by necessity, and felt little kinship or commonality.'[56]

The divisional structure remained much the same, with the addition of Financial Services Policy and the IFIS (Integrated Financial System) Project Division. The IFIS Project was a large-scale project meant to modernize and unify financial information systems in order to make business more effective and efficient within the Government of Ontario. Creating efficiencies in government was a priority outlined in the Common Sense

Revolution, and IFIS was one of the leading projects in this priority area. It further expanded the scope of the ministry's responsibilities into significant information technology areas, which in turn affected every ministry and government agency at the time.

With the dissolution of many NDP-instituted commissions and offices, the structure of the Ministry of Finance was stabilized to a degree not seen since the early 1970s. Important changes were made, however, in staffing. By 2001, the Ministry of Finance was down to 3552, a 29 per cent drop in FTEs since the unification of Treasury and Revenue in 1993.

2001: A Finance Odyssey

In 2001, forty years after the Frost era and its very small organizational structure, the Ministry of Finance had a significantly different organization chart that reflected the emergence of certain government priorities. The minister of finance was directly responsible for seven corporations, authorities, and commissions, including the Ontario SuperBuild Corporation and Ontario Electricity Financial Corporation, both of which were PC priorities. The SuperBuild Corporation centred on large-scale investments in infrastructure and general building, and had two vice-presidents: one responsible for Public-Private Partnerships, the other for Infrastructure Strategies and Communications. These areas also reflected neoliberal priorities such as gaining more private involvement in traditionally public areas. The Ontario Electricity Financial Corporation was primarily focused on the possibility of privatizing all or parts of Ontario Hydro. The deputy minister of finance's responsibilities also reflected the Harris government's priorities, in that he was placed in charge of the Ontario Electricity Restructuring Secretariat and the Coordinated Strategic Research Division.

The divisional structure again remained similar, but with a few notable additions. These included the Chief Information Officer's office, the Provincial Local Finance Secretariat, and the Corporate and Quality Service Division. The Chief Information Officer dealt primarily with information and information technology, which was of course a significant priority for the whole world in 2001. The Provincial Local Finance Secretariat enveloped the Property Taxation Branch, the Provincial Local Funding Unit, and the Stakeholder Management Unit. Property Assessment had since been taken over by the not-for-profit corporation MPAC, so the Property Taxation Branch was a branch centred mostly on property tax legislation and policy. The Corporate and Quality

68   Patrice Dutil and Devyn Leonard

Service Division contained Communications & Corporate Affairs, Human Resources, Corporate Planning & Finance, and the Revenue Operations & Client Services Branch. The entire division reflected an attempt to make the Ministry of Finance more client-oriented and service-centred. This was not a MoF-specific initiative – it was government-wide and highly enforced – reflecting the goal of providing better customer service.[57]

Conclusion: The 1990s

The 1990s were a period of wide-ranging reorganization and reintegration for the Ministry of Finance. It is important to note that the mergers of ministries under the NDP government reflected its interest in restructuring government comprehensively, and the urgency of restructuring to downsize and to engender cost savings during a deep recession without the complete loss of publicly provided services.[58] At an organizational structure level, the Ontario Ministry of Finance remained essentially the same in 2001 as it had been in 1993. However, concerns for cost savings, decreases in government spending, and heightened involvement of the private sector in traditionally public service delivery were all illustrated by shifts in the organizational structure, either to include certain Progressive Conservative political priorities or to eliminate NDP priority areas upon the arrival of the PCs.

The Common Sense Revolution directive of reducing the bureaucracy was upheld. Employment in the Ontario public service fell over 32 per cent, from 81,300 in 1995–6 to 54,952 in 1999–2000.[59] The downsizing affected the Ministry of Finance also. It boasted over 5000 employees in 1993, but by 2001 had 3552, including people working for the Ontario Financing Authority and Ontario SuperBuild Corporation. The reduction in numbers included the 1999 municipalization of the property assessment system through MPAC, and the elimination of the Deposit Institutions division between 1996 and 1998; the ministry was slowly getting out of the service provision business.

From the Treasury to Finance: Some Conclusions

The structural changes in the Ministry of Finance during the forty-year span of this study reflected both internal and external pressures. From the 1960s, and continuing through the late 1980s, the ministry was structured in a way that echoed the overarching government concern with the public-service provision of services and a faith that government had to play the dominant role in shaping public policy. This was perhaps best illustrated by the creation of various boards, commissions, and corporations within the structure of the ministry. In the late 1960s, as demands for services were increasing – with the resulting move by government to pay for these services through the establishment of a Retail Sales Tax – a new branch was created. Change was a constant and even ambitious transformations hardly stood the test of time.

This chapter has described how the traditional role of 'guardian' was transformed to mean very different things. As the department grew and was increasingly recognized for its policy savvy and its ability to deliver operational services, the guardianship assumed many other functions. It became a watchdog for financial services, a regulator (the horse racing commission, for example), and a policy coordinator in a vast number of areas. It was also a spender – not just in terms of tax breaks but also in terms of directing expenses in areas of regional and municipal development. The guardian was thus very much a central agency, yet kept its personality distinct by maintaining its 'guardian' persona. The study of organizational charts is helpful in documenting the many roles of the ministry. It is, by its nature, a dry exercise that, in the words of one executive who witnessed many of the transformations, 'can never illustrate the unwavering teamwork, flexibility, commitment, dedication, and loyalty of Finance staff to the public policy work they do and to their political masters, regardless of ideology.'[60] The period between 1961 and 2001 transformed the ministry many times over as senior management and cabinet sought to respond to ambitions and emergencies alike. As Ontario experimented with Keynesian ideas, the Robarts and Davis governments reorganized and expanded the ministry's structures to the point where it was actively involved in program spending in the area of regional and local development. As neoliberal notions of smaller government took effect in the 1990s under the Harris government, the ministry's organization was downscaled.

The structural capacity displayed by ministry staff to mobilize behind certain key government policies or issues was evident in the structural charts. However, connecting the bureaucratic structure of the ministry with its ability to directly influence policy was not the intent of this chapter: it focused instead on documenting the evolution of the structure of the Ministry of Finance to demonstrate how structure and overarching policy goals or ambitions have been related. In essence, what this chapter has illustrated is not ministerial influence on government,

but the effect of various attempts to recreate the ministry in a way that
better reflected overarching ideas that the ministry be something more,
or something less, or just something *different* than it had been. The ministry's structure changed significantly throughout the 1990s: it grew
smaller and more reflective of the ambitions of the PC government with
the addition of private-public corporations and commissions.

The structural changes illustrated in this study of the Ontario
Ministry of Finance reflect wider changes in the scope of the ministry,
the administration of the province, and the priorities of government.
Through an examination of these structural changes, a snapshot of government emerges, which can then be compared and contrasted to political and economic change, and also to changes in the preferred
bureaucratic administration of the province. Shifts in priorities and in
accepted paradigms have become clear, thus allowing for a better understanding of the wider issues facing government during the forty-
year span of this study.

NOTES

1 W.R. Scott, *Organizations: Rational, Natural and Open Systems* (Upper Saddle
   River, NJ: Prentice-Hall, 1981).
2 Luther Gulick, 'Notes on the Theory of Organization,' in *Papers on the Science of Administration*, ed. Luther Gulick and L. Urwick (New York: Institute
   of Public Administration, 1937), 7–15. For a more modern treatment, see
   William F. West, 'Searching for a Theory of Bureaucratic Structure,' *Journal
   of Public Administration Research and Theory* 7.4 (1997), 592.
3 Morten Egeberg, 'How Bureaucratic Structure Matters: An Organizational
   Perspective,' in *Handbook of Public Administration*, ed. B. Guy Peters and Jon
   Pierre (San Francisco, CA: Sage Publications, 2003), 117–18.
4 Ibid.
5 Interview with Don Stevenson, 5 February 2009.
6 Office of the Auditor General of Ontario, 'Our History,' 12 December 2005,
   accessed 20 August 2008, at http://www.auditor.on.ca/en/about_history
   _en.htm.
7 Donald W. Stevenson Papers, 'Notes for possible use at Niagara Institute
   Seminar, November 17, 1977,' 3.
8 Ibid., 'Points for use in remarks to seminar of Queen's Institute of Intergovernmental Affairs, 9 April 1984 – Reminiscences of participation in intergovernmental issues since the early sixties,' 1.

9 Ibid., 'Notes for Panel – Feb 29, 1984,' 1.
10 Ibid., 3.
11 For more context on Robarts's approach, see A.K. McDougall, *John P. Robarts: His Life and Government* (Toronto: University of Toronto Press, 1986), esp. chap. 10.
12 That office had been created in March 1966 as the government ramped up its abilities to organize and host the 'Confederation of Tomorrow' conference that had been spearheaded by the premier.
13 David Redgrave to P. Dutil, 12 February 2009.
14 Ibid., 2.
15 H. Ian Macdonald, 'The Solemnization of an Institutional Marriage (or, The Joining of the "Treasury" with "Economics"),' *Ontario Economic Review*, Spring 1969, 3.
16 See Donald W. Stevenson Papers, 'Points for possible use on March 29 1989 at retirement party,' 1.
17 Ibid., 4.
18 Donald W. Stevenson Papers, 'Notes on Don Stevenson's career,' n.d., 4.
19 Ibid., 'Notes for possible use at Niagara Institute Seminar,' 3.
20 Macdonald, 'The Solemnization,' 8.
21 Ibid.
22 Donald W. Stevenson Papers, 'Notes for paper to be given to the Regina Group, Institute of Public Administration of Canada, 11 February 1972,' 6.
23 Terry Russell to P. Dutil, 12 February 2009.
24 Desmond Morton, '*Sic Permanet*: Ontario People and Their Politics,' in *The Government and Politics of Ontario*, ed. Graham White (Toronto: University of Toronto Press, 1997), 5.
25 Donald W. Stevenson Papers, 'Notes for paper to be given to the Regina Group,' 3.
26 Ibid., 4. A good eyewitness analysis is James D. Fleck, 'Restructuring the Ontario Government,' *Canadian Public Administration* 16.1 (March 1973), 55–68.
27 Committee on Government Productivity, Ontario Government, *Report Number Ten: A Summary* (Toronto, Ontario: Queen's Printer for Ontario, 1973), 5.
28 Eric Malling, 'The Brainy Team of Economists at Queen's Park Has 'em Jumping in Ottawa' *Toronto Star*, 13 May 1973, 25.
29 David Redgrave to P. Dutil, 12 February 2009.
30 Malling, 'The Brainy Team.'
31 N.H. Richardson, 'Insubstantial Pageant: The Rise and Fall of Provincial Planning in Ontario,' *Canadian Public Administration* 24.4 (1981), 564.

32 Michael J. Prince, 'The Bland Stops Here: Ontario Budgeting in the Davis Era, 1971–1985,' in *Budgeting in the Provinces: Leadership and the Premiers*, ed. Allan M. Maslove (Toronto: The Institute of Public Administration of Canada, 1989), 95. See also H. Ian Macdonald, 'Government Reorganization and Treasury Economics and Intergovernmental Affairs,' *Ontario Economic Review* 11.2 (March/April 1973).
33 See Richardson, 'Insubstantial Pageant,' 566.
34 Donald W. Stevenson Papers, 'Notes for possible use at the National Defence College Briefing, September 18, 1972.'
35 Committee on Government Productivity, 5.
36 See Richardson, 'Insubstantial Pageant,' 567.
37 Prince, 'The Bland Stops Here,' 95.
38 Redgrave to P. Dutil, 12 February 2009.
39 Committee on Government Productivity, 10.
40 Ibid., 8.
41 Donald W. Stevenson, 'Notes for speech to the Ontario Association of Land Economists, September 23, 1972,' 14.
42 Donald W. Stevenson Papers, 'Ministry of Treasury, Economics and Intergovernmental Affairs, 1976,' 2.
43 Ibid., 1.
44 Donald W. Stevenson Papers, 'Notes for Remarks by DW Stevenson at the Founding Meeting of the Southwestern Ontario Regional Group of IPAC,' London, 9 February 1976, 5.
45 Prince, 'The Bland Stops Here,' 100.
46 Ibid., 96.
47 *Ministry of Treasury and Economics. Ontario Budget 1984* (Toronto: Queen's Printer for Ontario, 1984). See also Bryan M. Evans, 'From Pragmatism to Neoliberalism: The Politics of the Remaking of the Ontario Administrative State, 1970–2002,' PhD dissertation (York University, 2008), 177.
48 Prince, 'The Bland Stops Here,' 101.
49 Ibid.
50 See also Graham White, 'Change in the Ontario State 1952–2002 – Paper prepared for the Role of Government Panel,' October 2002. Accessed on 29 August 2008 at http://www.law-lib.utoronto.ca/investing/reports/rp8.pdf , p. 21.
51 Evert A. Lindquist and Graham White, 'Streams, Springs and Stones: Ontario Public Service Reform in the 1980s and the 1990s,' *Canadian Public Administration* 37.2 (1994), 267–301.
52 David R. Cameron and Graham White, *Cycling into Saigon: The Conservative Transition in Ontario* (Vancouver: UBC Press, 2000), 24.

53 White, 'Change in the Ontario State,' 22–3.

54 Ontario Progressive Conservative Party, *The Common Sense Revolution* (Ontario: Progressive Conservative Party, 1994). See also Sidney Noel, *Revolution at Queen's Park* (Toronto: Lorimer, 1997).

55 Bob Hebdon and Peter Warrian, 'Coercive Bargaining: Public Sector Restructuring Under the Ontario Social Contract, 1993–1996,' *Industrial and Labor Relations Review* 52.2 (1999), 199.

56 Len Roozen to P. Dutil, 31 December 2008.

57 Christopher D. Foster and Francis J. Plowden, *The State under Stress: Can the Hollow State Be Good Government?* (Buckingham, Eng., and Philadelphia: Open University Press, 1996), 47–9.

58 Evans, 'From Pragmatism to Neoliberalism,' 216–17.

59 Ibid., 265.

60 Len Roozen to P. Dutil, 31 December 2008.

3 Priority Setters and Guardians: The Relationships between Premiers and Treasurers in Ontario, 1960–2001

JP LEWIS

In his study of the budget process in the Government of Canada, David Good accented the growing role of a group he called the 'priority setters.' Good argued that the growing involvement of the prime minister and his staff in setting the broad direction of the budget was an important departure. In part, this was because the 'priority setting' has evolved into a year-long affair, not just the concern of a critical few weeks in early winter, as it had once been. Good's work in this regard was original also in highlighting 'the most important of all relationships,' that of the prime minister and the minister of finance. 'The prime minister cannot do it without the minister of finance and the minister of finance cannot do it without the prime minister. There is no relationship that is more critical to the functioning of government and to the determinants of the budget.'[1]

The same could be said about the Ontario experience with the relationships between the head of the ministry of finance and the head of the government. The relationship at Queen's Park has proved to be more stable than in Ottawa over the past forty years, however. The personal context, and not the context of the relationship between first minister and finance minister, caused stress in many federal instances. Lester Pearson was often at pain in his relations with his first minister of finance, Walter Gordon. Pierre Trudeau's relations with John Turner were hardly better from the start and did not improve with time: Turner resigned from Trudeau's cabinet owing to personality conflicts. The friendly personal relations between Allan MacEachen and Trudeau were strained by the strife caused by the budgets of 1981.[2] Even Jean Chrétien was acutely frustrated, if not humiliated, by Trudeau's unilateral announcement of spending cuts in the summer of 1978 without informing Chrétien. Chrétien's own relationship with Paul Martin, his minister of finance, would end with the prime minister leaving office in favour of the latter.

The story of the relationship between the political leaders in the ministry of finance and the premier's office between 1960 and 2000 in Ontario was remarkably peaceful. Leslie Frost acted as his own minister of finance and seemed to manage the relationship with ease. John Robarts's relations with his ministers were productive and constructive. Bill Davis's fourteen years in office (which included minority government) featured a striking variety of finance ministers. No minister of finance served more than six years.

The 'hot potato' years of Liberal–New Democrat–Progressive Conservative governments from 1985 to 2001 ensured three distinct reigns for finance ministers. The last three finance ministers of this period – Robert Nixon, Floyd Laughren, and even Ernie Eves (who eventually changed his mind) – shared a common trait: none had ambitions for the premier's job, thus ensuring a peaceful relationship between the priority setters and the ministers of finance. Indeed, many who have worked with various finance ministers and premiers saw the relationship as successful. [3] Although those who have been part of the relationship have admitted that it is 'always ... interesting,'[4] I would argue that there was more to the systematic evolution of this critical relationship than coincidence or mere good luck. There were moments of strain in the relationship over the forty years in question, but the success of the rapport between the 'priority setters' and the 'guardians' of the ministry of finance owed more to career timing, professional trust, the political environment, and an adherence to the managerial philosophy of government. These four factors of political friendship – timing, trust, environment, and adherence to management philosophy – will act as the analytical framework for evaluating the relationships under study here. To reach this evaluation, a thorough descriptive review of the historical narrative of these relationships needs to be completed; the bulk of this chapter will attempt that goal.

Premiers, Minister of Finance, and Cabinet

In his exploration of political executives, Graham White argued that 'most writing and commentary on Canadian cabinets has focused on the structures and processes of cabinet decision-making and on the policy and political role of cabinet within our governmental system ... Yet, if cabinet is primarily an institution it is also an aggregation of individuals who are important in their own right.'[5]

White pointed to a difficult challenge in that so much of cabinet business is protected by secrecy laws or encompasses work completed and relationships built behind closed doors and out of the public spotlight. Cabinet ministers have been studied, but mostly in isolation from each other. W.A. Matheson, who wrote the first book on Canadian cabinets, defined the members of cabinet as 'a group of individuals whose personality, background, and temperament all affect the quality of the decisions of government.'[6] Matheson discussed the various backgrounds of ministers in different cabinets, but did not offer a rigorous historical treatment of ministerial rapport. Herman Bakvis's research on the connection between geographical representation and powerful cabinet ministers, J. Stefan Dupré and Christopher Dunn's studies on the change from departmental to institutional cabinets, and Peter Aucoin's work on the hierarchical structural transformations of cabinet have all helped define the cabinet canon, but did not examine the particular relationship shared by the premiers and the ministers of finance.[7]

In his *Governing from the Centre: The Concentration of Power in Canadian Politics*, Donald Savoie argued that the 'Canadian centre of government has evolved a great deal during the past thirty years.'[8] His hypothesis was that 'power in the federal government has shifted away from line ministers and their departments towards the centre, and also, within the centre itself, power has shifted to the prime minister and his senior advisers at both the political and public service levels and away from cabinet and cabinet committees.'[9] Savoie's general ideas were seminal to the analysis of current cabinets. The shift of power to the centre of government greatly affects cabinet, as it takes influence away from ministers and places it in the hands of the prime minister or premier and his or her inner circle while also giving some ministers more leverage than others. In the past, ministers of vertical departments would attempt to focus on a region and a delivery of service. With the strengthening of the centre, ministers of horizontal departments such as finance and justice have grown in importance, as they represent the central agencies that increasingly control the government. The centralization thesis is important to keep in mind when reviewing the years presented in this case and the growing importance of the treasurer's office in Ontario.

A Brief History of Good Relations

For almost half of his thirteen years as premier, Leslie Frost also served as the province's treasurer. Eventually, he surrendered the treasury to his closest and most trusted colleague, Dana Porter. Frost let it be known that he would still be a part of the budget process, but as Roger

Graham contends, 'the province's finances had become so large, the department's operations so complex, that they required a minister free to give them his undivided attention.'[10] Still, in Frost's time as leader the scope of government, the scale of operations, and the scrutiny of the media were more easily managed. As Graham White argued, 'Frost could personally oversee all the important political and administrative decisions to a degree no longer possible today.'[11] Even after he shed his official title as provincial treasurer, the man known as 'Old Man Ontario' continued to play a key role in the department. A former treasurer official who worked under Frost noted: 'It was very clear that Frost, since he had been treasurer, was part of every detail that was going on at government accounts ... more so than the treasurer himself ... Frost knew all the people who worked in the treasury ... Under Frost there was very little formal structure: he would deal directly with civil servants.'[12] In discussing the previous arrangement of serving as both premier and treasurer, Frost noted: 'I wanted a periscope to see where we were going and there isn't any better economics branch in Canada including the Federal Government. The branch has its fingers on the pulse of the province.'[13] The premier could also bask in a boom period of state activity while treasurer as his government initiated such major projects as the Trans-Canada Highway, the establishment of the Ontario Water Resources Commission, and the St Lawrence Seaway. Rand Dyck referred to this collection of major infrastructure projects as 'the concrete initiatives.'[14]

Frost's treasurer for the dawn of the 1960s was James Allan (also known as the 'dairyman from Dunnville'), who first joined the Ontario provincial cabinet in 1955 as minister of highways.[15] During his time as treasurer under Frost, Allan never forgot who was still in charge of Ontario's purse strings. Allan was known to leave the major decisions in the budget to the premier, understanding that Frost was still the 'master' who should not be challenged.[16] Even though he may not have left a major imprint as treasurer, working as he did in the shadow of Frost, Allan was viewed by many to be the next Ontario Progressive Conservative leader when rumours circulated in 1960 that Frost was hoping to retire.[17] Unfortunately, Allan was already sixty-five years old – older than Frost – at a time when many in the party thought the time had come to pass the torch to a younger generation. Regardless of his age, Allan enjoyed much political strength. He was considered to be well liked and widely respected within the party and throughout the province.[18] Frost cast a long shadow over the 1961 convention, and

Table 3.1 Ontario premiers and treasurers, 1960–2001

Premier	Party	Treasurer	Start	Finish
Leslie Frost	Progressive Conservative	James Allan	28 April 1958	15 December 1961
John Robarts	Progressive Conservative	James Allan	15 December 1961	24 November 1966
		Charles MacNaugton	24 November 1966	1 March 1971
Bill Davis	Progressive Conservative	Darcy McKeough	1 March 1971	7 September 1972
		Charles MacNaugton	7 September 1972	15 January 1973
		John White	15 January 1973	18 June 1975
		Darcy McKeough	18 June 1975	16 August 1978
		Frank Miller	18 August 1978	6 July 1983
		Larry Grossman	6 July 1983	1 May 1985
Frank Miller	Progressive Conservative	Bette Stephenson	17 May 1985	26 June 1985
David Peterson	Liberal	Robert Nixon	26 June 1985	1 October 1990
Bob Rae	New Democrat	Floyd Laughren	1 October 1990	26 June 1995
Mike Harris	Progressive Conservative	Ernie Eves	26 June 1995	8 February 2001

many believed that Allan, who appeared to be the protégé of Frost, would lead as a stopgap until a new guard was selected. Frost suggested that his successor did not need to be a young man.[19] Allan did enter the race after much hesitation and even though he was considered an energetic politician with a strong rural base, his late entry into the leadership contest damaged his chances of victory.[20]

The 1961 leadership contest also included an old friend of Allan's, John Robarts. The two were good acquaintances, both being from outside Toronto and of similar views on the future of the party and the province. Robarts showed solid strength at the convention, and when Allan and most of his delegates moved to Robarts on the fifth ballot, the political relationship between the two men was cast.[21] Robarts would keep Allan on as treasurer. In the tradition of Ontario political leadership, some viewed Robarts as a 'good man to mind the store,'[22] but he demonstrated flexibility in government and was able to remain Ontario's premier through ten years of major social and cultural turmoil.[23] As A.K. McDougall contends,

John Robarts began his career in the rural-dominated, personal government of Leslie Frost, with its eight-week sessions and the simple departmentalized structure of government and the civil service. When Robarts left power, Ontario had an administratively centralized, management-oriented governing system capable of processing the volume of work and conflicting demands generated by modern, technologically based urban society.[24]

Although Allan acted as a key figure in Robarts's early years as premier, those who worked under him believe the treasurer had lost his leadership aspirations after 1961, and was content to remain treasurer until his retirement five years later.[25] In 1966, Robarts tapped Charles MacNaughton as treasurer. The two were close political allies, as McNaughton had managed Robarts's leadership campaign in 1961.[26] Living in Exeter, MacNaughton's home was very close to Robarts's well-known cottage in Grand Bend.[27] His son, John MacNaughton, became a part of the 'London Mafia' that carried considerable clout with the Progressive Conservative party and across provincial politics.[28] The arrival of MacNaughton represented continuity with another close friend of Robarts in the position, but also triggered change in the direction of the provincial treasury. During the MacNaughton era budgets began to evolve from their simple accounting formats into documents based in long-term planning and fiscal policy.[29] MacNaughton had gained familiarity with the treasurer's portfolio as minister of highways and had experienced many cases of 'horizontal communications' when dealing with the Metropolitan Toronto transportation policy as a 'close adviser and protégé' of Prime Minister Robarts (the title of 'premier' was introduced by Bill Davis).

By 1968, as a result of many reforms introduced by Robarts, MacNaughton was further empowered as treasurer by assuming a new role on the Policy Development Committee. It effectively made him 'Robarts' lieutenant in a more hierarchical cabinet.'[30] A year later, he made his most important budget announcements with the introduction of a provincial personal income tax.[31] With the retirement of John Robarts in 1971, MacNaughton thought briefly about contending for the leadership, but at age fifty-nine decided that 'by contemporary standards' he was too old. He invested his energies instead in running the campaign of education minister William Davis.[32] MacNaughton had been fond of Davis for over a decade. As he recalled, 'I first met him in 1959 when we were back-bench seatmates. Even then, at 29, he worked like hell. I used to kid him about his industriousness but he'd come back day after day with a big notebook full of stuff from his constituents.'[33]

As the torch had passed from Frost to Robarts, the Ontario PC dynasty was now in the hands of a new forty-two-year-old premier, Bill Davis, a man who would famously offer the political advice that 'bland works.' His group of five treasurers between 1971 and 1984 would include three with leadership ambitions ranging from what could be called 'ambivalently covert' to the 'progressively overt.' Working under the 'bland' model, Davis continually attempted to keep political drama within his party to a minimum so as to maintain as much discipline as possible, particularly during two minority governments (1975–7 and 1977–81). Like Robarts before him, Davis was described as a 'chief executive officer or chairman of the board' who felt comfortable giving his treasurers a generous degree of autonomy. Moreover, the treasurer's position was enhanced with added responsibilities for intergovernmental affairs.[34] This leadership philosophy did not end with the treasury post, but existed with other cabinet ministers.[35] As insider Hugh Segal wrote, 'Every minister sensed that he or she had a direct line of appeal to cabinet and to the Premier personally in the event the whole process did not produce a result that was responsive to his or her own view of political or departmental priorities.'[36] In this sense, Davis was more like Frost than Robarts – very comfortable in immersing himself in the details of political management.

In June 1971 Davis replaced the retiring MacNaughton with Darcy McKeough, an avowed right-wing conservative who delighted, in his early backbench days, in yelling 'Socialist Bilge!' at the New Democratic Party across the aisle.[37] Davis and McKeough were a study in contrasts, but were allies nonetheless and agreed on most policy areas where government should take a lead. After being promoted to cabinet by Robarts, McKeough distinguished himself as minister of municipal affairs and eagerly contested the party leadership in the 1971 convention. McKeough's actions in the leadership race would seal his fate and cabinet position for the next decade. On the day of the vote, McKeough moved to Davis after the third ballot.[38] As McKeough recalled, 'I put him there ... I went to him on the last ballot ... [I was] the kingmaker.'[39] McKeough was in a group of leadership contestants who would all receive posts as so-called super-ministers in the new cabinet. The foursome included McKeough in finance, Allan Lawrence in justice, Bert Lawrence in natural resources, and Robert Welch in social development.[40] In effect, the Policy and Priorities Board of Cabinet was made up of the five candidates for leader, as well as the winner's campaign manager. The centralization of power in Ontario politics was growing and the media was beginning to identify a trend in the increasing strength of both the treasurer and the premier.[41]

McKeough's rise came to an abrupt stop in August 1972 over accusations of conflict of interest. The controversy was based on revelations that McKeough's ministry of municipal affairs had approved subdivision plans in Chatham during the Robarts years in which both he and his family had financial interests.[42] McKeough resigned over the scandal, dealing a serious blow to the young Davis government that triggered intense discussions concerning ministers and conflicts of interest.[43] The fallout from the resignation created a fair amount of bitterness. Some McKeough supporters believed that Davis had been much more severe with McKeough compared to his treatment of other cabinet colleagues.[44] A senior civil servant working in the Davis government speculated that 'more investigation may suggest that the Real Estate resignation was orchestrated to put him (McKeough) in his place.'[45] Either way, the combination of ministerial responsibility and public pressure, especially exerted by opposition parties, had forced McKeough to step down and re-navigate his route up the Ontario political ladder. (McKeough would be out of cabinet for less than a year: he returned as minister of energy in July 1973.)

Former treasurer Charles MacNaughton stepped in as interim treasurer until Davis could reshuffle his cabinet team. A few months later, he turned to the minister of trade and industry, John White, and named him treasurer. White had been chair of the special committee of the legislature that had reviewed the recommendations of the 1967 Report of the Smith Committee on Taxation. White's committee report was a 'masterpiece' according to Don Stevenson and garnered the unanimous support of the legislature for major policy issues including the province's role in regional government. With no known leadership ambitions and a rather personal approach to government, White's brief tenure in the treasury was memorable for those who worked under him. As one former mandarin remembered,

White was very different ... [but] I enjoyed working for him ... [He] wrote the key decisions of his budget on the back of a cigarette pack ... [He] took four or five of us out to lunch the first day and said, you guys have been working too hard, I've seen you working in the evenings, you've been producing too much paper, I don't work that hard, if you understand me we will get along fine.[46]

White was a leading Red Tory to the point where some New Democrats considered him even to the left of them on the political spectrum.[47]

White, however, did not make a good impression with his first budget. In the 1973 budget he proposed a 7 per cent tax on fuel and electricity in order to dampen demand for energy following the OPEC oil embargo. The idea was met with outrage from not just the Opposition and the public, but also Conservative backbenchers. More than a dozen Tory members vowed to publicly oppose the tax.[48] Fraser Kelly of the *Toronto Star* described the energy tax scheme as 'a political boner of the first magnitude.'[49] The Progressive Conservative caucus forced Davis to back down from the plan, but not before White would provide Ontario citizens with such cheeky advice as 'They should turn down their thermostats and buy sweaters.'[50] It was a serious setback to have the major plank in a first budget withdrawn, but White, sticking to his unique view of politics and life, responded with an erudite answer: 'I've been a Jeffersonian Democrat in my 14 years in the Legislature. To acknowledge that the energy tax proposal was intolerable was not a defeat for me. It was a victory for democracy,' he told reporters.[51]

His 1973 budget debacle aside, White showed progressive traits and enjoyed supporters both inside and outside the party. He was the first treasurer to discuss the province's budget with cabinet when he met with his colleagues in February 1973. Allan Grossman, who was minister of revenue at the time, wondered 'if anyone will ever realize that this is the first time a Provincial Treasurer has agreed to discuss the [budget] with cabinet ... As far as I could determine, it had never happened before over all the years I had been in government.'[52] Stephen Lewis, Ontario New Democratic Party leader at the time, noted that White's 'fiscal views are decades ahead of the other ministers.'[53] White left the treasurer's post in late 1974 after telling Bill Davis that he would resign from politics before the next election.[54]

In January 1975 Davis reappointed Darcy McKeough as Ontario's treasurer and minister of economics and intergovernmental affairs.[55] Just as he had in his first stint as the province's treasurer, McKeough quickly resumed a dominant position in government. As a former assistant deputy minister notes, 'McKeough and Davis worked well until McKeough started to become so powerful ... Remember, McKeough had the equivalent of the ministry of housing, the ministry of intergovernmental affairs, the ministry of finance, the ministry of revenue ... He was hugely powerful.'[56] Regardless of the ascent of McKeough, Davis remained grounded. The premier was seen by insiders to handle

McKeough's leadership aspirations, outlined daily in newspapers, very professionally.[57] For his part, McKeough contends that 'leadership aspirations did not play a major role in the dynamics of the relationship'[58]

With his re-entry into the political limelight, McKeough returned to his role as the potential leader of the Progressive Conservative Party in Ontario (or in Ottawa, for that matter). McKeough, who had gotten along very well with John Robarts, was shaped in the traditional mould of the former premier. Associates of the treasurer were impressed by 'his ability to gobble up work with relish, to put in a 14 to 16 hour work day, topped off with several very dry martinis, and show up for another similar day at 8 the next morning, as bright-eyed and sharp-witted as ever.'[59] As Davis's number two, McKeough appeared to be on his way to the premier's office, but as time wore on, he began to lose more and more cabinet battles. The pressures of managing budgets while only holding on to a minority in the legislature were excruciating. Subtle political signals were beginning to stream back and forth between Queen's Park and the Frost Building. In 1977, Davis named Bob Welch as deputy premier, a move that some believed was a indication to McKeough that Davis would be staying on as premier for a few more years.[60] The issue of Ontario Health Insurance Premiums in 1978 would provoke his downfall (for more details, see chapter 10).

McKeough proposed an increase in the Ontario Health Insurance Plan premium of 37.5 per cent. A former treasury official commented on the culmination of financial headaches greeting McKeough in recent years: '[With the] OPEC crisis ... the revenue stream dried up ... McKeough's projects [regional governments] began to be seen as political losers ... The treasurer started to worry about saving, rather than spending.'[61] Davis, not mounting much of a defence for his treasurer, sought a compromise with the Opposition in the legislature and eventually cut the premium number in half. [62] When asked about the security of McKeough's job, Davis responded, 'I will say that the treasurer's job is as secure as anyone's in political life can be secure.'[63] Within two months McKeough left Queen's Park, saying that he had no federal or municipal political plans.

Speculation on McKeough's resignation was rabid at the time. Pat Crowe wrote that 'McKeough quit after a series of setbacks that chipped away at his image as a colossus in the government. But his decision, in the end, was triggered by word from Davis that he would be staying on as premier through the next election.'[64] Jonathan Manthorpe described the situation as desperate for McKeough: 'One thing is obvious.

McKeough is close to being isolated. He had few political friends among his fellow Tories and it is up to Davis whether McKeough survives.'[65] A later report suggested that McKeough had told Davis in July that he found himself 'out of step' with a majority of the cabinet ministers who were attempting to greater democratize the work of economic policy-making.[66] The Opposition parties were swift to react to McKeough's departure. Liberal finance critic David Peterson noted that his resignation was 'a serious blow to the government of Ontario and to the Conservative party. He single-handedly represented the government's image of management competence'; while NDP finance critic Floyd Laughren confirmed the impression: 'His resignation will deal a severe blow to the Davis government.'[67]

Sources close to McKeough suggested the reasons for resigning were more personal than political.[68] During this time McKeough began to dine regularly with former federal finance minister and leader aspirant John Turner.[69] The coincidence would not be lost on political observers. After McKeough's second and final departure from the role of treasurer, the *Globe and Mail*'s Hugh Winsor wrote about the parallels between McKeough and Turner:

> Both were considered heirs apparent and yet both quit, leaving a cloud of ambiguity swirling around their departures, including the possibility they will be back some day. Both seem to have left because the way to the top job appeared to be blocked, at least temporarily, and both sought solace in the world of big business. There may also be some significance in their timing. Mr. McKeough said that his 45th birthday played a big part in his decision to seek a new career. Mr. Turner was 46 when he made the switch.[70]

McKeough was replaced with Frank Miller who, while more conservative than his predecessor, was much more friendly with other ministers.[71] On his first day as treasurer, Miller told the senior staff that he had read the theories of John Kenneth Galbraith and Milton Friedman and that the staff should know that he was firmly in the 'Friedman camp.'[72] An engineer by training and self-styled small businessman by vocation, Miller had been elected to Queen's Park in 1971, eventually earning his stripes as a minister of health. He worked on rural hospital closings and the consolidation of urban services. The public reaction to the attempted hospital closures was anything but pleasant, and Miller's miserable winter of 1975–6 ended with a heart attack in March 1976.[73] With his tartan jackets and Muskoka folksiness, Frank Miller was a contradiction of sorts. One former reporter described him as the 'sort of fellow you would like to have as a neighbour.'[74] But others believed that Miller's right-wing views, trumpeted by the press, gave him a compassionless persona that was difficult to shake.[75] Murray Gaunt, Liberal MPP, noted that Miller was 'amiable, likeable and much more inclined to try to win you over rather than kick you into submission.'[76] The friendly accolades should not overshadow Miller's strong leadership ambitions and competitive political side. A Davis loyalist, his tenure was nonetheless marked by an important disagreement with Davis's energy policy, two near resignations, and endless backroom battles with eventual leadership candidate Larry Grossman.

'Project Phoenix' was Bill Davis's 1981 plan to purchase 25 per cent of Suncor shares for $650 million. Suncor owned 553 Sunoco gas stations, and the acquisition idea was driven by the growing nationalism of the time and Ontario's desire to create leverage for itself in the oil and gas market.[77] Miller was 'completely and wholly opposed' to the purchase.[78] A former senior ministry official contends that at the time, 'the Treasury wasn't informed of the Suncor purchase plan until the 11th hour and when it was informed of it, the minister on down thought it was a crazy idea and a waste of money.'[79] At the end of 1981 Miller seriously considered resigning from cabinet. In December, Miller had written Davis a resignation letter, informing him that he would leave the following month. On 20 January Davis met Miller in the premier's office and the boss convinced his treasurer to stay on.[80] One official close to the situation remembers that 'on certain policy issues Miller would take a strong stand on Davis but he always pulled back and the reason he pulled back was he desperately wanted to be premier. It was always his game plan to be premier and he knew he could never piss off the party.'[81]

The provincial economy, combined with budget blunders, almost derailed Miller's political career. First, Miller held the province's purse strings through miserable economic conditions: during his time as treasurer unemployment exploded in the province from 299,000 in August 1978 to 519,000 in the spring of 1983.[82] Second, two mishandled budgets launched calls for his resignation. The 1982 budget included a 7 per cent sales tax on such previously exempted items as 'puppy dogs, take-out foods and tampons.'[83] The 1983 budget's trouble was due not to its contents but rather to its security: a keen reporter pieced together some of the budget figures from rummaging through a green garbage bag outside the printer's office.[84] Miller contemplated resignation, but decided not to go through with it.

The intriguing dynamics in the Davis cabinet did not pit potential successors and the premier. Conflict was more obvious between certain cabinet ministers than between the treasurer and the premier. The battles, for instance, between Miller and industry minister Larry Grossman were frequent and notorious. While Grossman 'wore his ambition on his sleeve a little bit more than Miller,' both spent much effort attempting to outmanoeuvre the other in succeeding Davis.[85]

The Grossman–Miller relationship was described as a 'mutual antipathy going back many years.'[86] Those close to both believed it could be traced back to when Miller was health minister and Grossman, a backbencher, fought plans to close a hospital in his riding.[87] Grossman would threaten Miller that he would resign with the knowledge that this would hurt the Tories' prospects in Toronto ridings.[88] In 1983, when Miller and Grossman exchanged the finance and industry portfolios, both believed they were getting the better end of the deal. A former deputy minister believes that 'Miller went over to industry because he thought that would be a great place to launch a leadership campaign … Grossman went to the treasury thinking this was his chance to prove that he was a great manager and economic mind.'[89]

Grossman replaced Miller as treasurer and expected little involvement from the premier's office as Davis undertook his final victory lap. Many were impressed by Grossman's accomplishments in the industry and health portfolio. As industry minister, he was successful in opening a number of technology centres throughout the province and as health minister he was central in negotiating a new deal with the province's 15,000 doctors.[90] During these last years, Davis encouraged ministers to prepare to replace him and continue the Tory dynasty.[91] Frank Miller would come out as the winner in 1984.

Miller was something of an odd replacement for Davis, as the Tories had relied in the last two leadership changes on a transfer to a new generation. Miller, by contrast, was two years older than Davis.[92] Larry Grossman was particularly disappointed, having campaigned for the job of party leader informally.[93] One-time aid John Gustafson suggested that Grossman had been coveting the job since 'probably about the age of five.'[94] Grossman was viewed as a young, confident, and keen politician, and his own thoughts supported this belief. Grossman once remarked that at one point in 1981, when Bill Davis had announced his intention to step down, 'I looked around the cabinet table and said to myself "I'm the best of this bunch. I'm going to try for the leadership. Why not, everyone wants to be president of the company."'[95] Grossman pleaded with Davis to stay on as premier: he realized he needed at least another year as treasurer to prove himself to the Progressive Conservatives, who believed he was a 'free-spending Red Tory.'[96] Grossman promised a tired and worn-out Davis that he and other key ministers would carry the government for a period of time after the next election. [97]

Grossman would eventually come within seventy-seven votes of winning the party's leadership,[98] but Frank Miller won the dramatic leadership race. After spending a few days contemplating his future and weighing attractive offers from the private sector, Grossman decided to stay on as treasurer in Miller's cabinet. Frank Miller moved Grossman from the treasury, but still gave him a major amount of responsibility, appointing him education minister, government house leader, and provincial secretary for social development.[99] The shuffle included the appointment of Dr Bette Stephenson as the first female treasurer in the province's history. It was an important step in cabinet representation, but it lasted only a few weeks.

Miller called an election, but the campaign soured, and the Tories earned only a minority. After the New Democratic Party formed an agreement with the Liberal Party, Lieutenant Governor John Black Aird asked Liberal leader David Peterson to form the government. Only four months into his premiership Miller was forced to the Opposition with the loss of a confidence motion, and by August 1985 he had resigned as party leader. On his way out of politics, Miller cited the Tories' inner political battles: 'I sensed that, in the final analysis, there would be pretenders to the throne, working hard not for party unity, but for themselves. I could not afford that in the hierarchy, and therefore, I had to make way for someone who could unify the party.'[100] Some even blamed Miller's quick downfall as premier to the possibility that he was still fighting Grossman.[101]

Bette Stephenson, a former president of the Canadian Medical Association, certainly holds the record for shortest tenure at treasurer during the 1960 to 2000 era. The first female to hold the position was appointed on 17 May 1985, only to have the government fall a month later, on 18 June.[102] The Miller-Stephenson partnership could have been a very successful one as the two were close friends whose children, Miller's son and Stephenson's daughter, had married.[103] A month in politics can be a lifetime, but in this case the Miller minority government did not leave much of a historical trail. The entry of David Peterson started fifteen years of three premiers from three different parties. While this appears to be a model of electoral volatility, the period did represent a time of treasurer stability, beginning with Robert Nixon.

Peterson had received the advice from former Premier Bill Davis that the 'crucial seats' in cabinet were the attorney general and treasurer.[104] With this advice in mind, Peterson selected a party veteran and former party leader from 1967 to 1976 as his treasurer. Alongside education minister Sean Conway and attorney general Ian Scott, Nixon was one of three 'super-ministers' in Peterson's cabinet.[105] Robert Nixon was a well-liked and well-respected parliamentarian with legislative exper-tise and small-town charm. He was first elected on 18 June 1962 to the same riding his father, former premier Harry Nixon, had represented, Brant-Oxford-Norfolk.[106] Nixon's farming roots were never forgotten. One of his favourite hangouts was Earl's Garage in his Brant riding. At times, when defending a policy decision, Nixon would claim that 'the boys at Earl's told me to do it.'[107] Nixon was a safe pick for Peterson as his leadership aspirations had long passed and his connection to the party was strong. As New Democratic former house leader Eli Martel said of Nixon, 'He's the backbone of the Liberal Party.'[108] A senior bu-reaucrat remembers that 'Nixon was the dean of cabinet ... Peterson always asked his view openly at cabinet ... He was the key player on Planning and Priorities [committee].'[109]

Nixon was able to deliver a handful of economic good news before the belt-tightening of the 1990s. In his 1987 provincial budget, he cut taxes by $246 million, reduced the annual deficit by $381 million, re-moved provincial sales tax on meals of less than four dollars, and gave money to farmers, roads, and public transportation.[110] In May 1989, he replaced OHIP premiums with employer payroll taxes.[111] But Nixon also felt opposition during his tenure due to a number of other tax poli-cies: he raised or introduced taxes on everything from land transfers to gasoline and cigarettes to tires.[112] Regardless of the political and eco-nomic strains, from most accounts Nixon and Peterson enjoyed a strong and open working relationship.

A former assistant deputy and deputy minister notes that 'Peterson discussed a lot of things more openly and thoroughly ... Budget used to be taken to cabinet just to be endorsed, not discussed and in terms of his treasurer, Nixon engaged his premier a lot more than other treasur-ers engaged their premiers ... They [Nixon and Peterson] sometimes had philosophical differences, but they were very open.'[113]

One political split Nixon and Peterson experienced was over a na-tional issue, the Meech Lake Accord. Even though Peterson demon-strated strong and active support of the constitutional deal, a number of cabinet ministers including Nixon supported Meech Lake critic Jean

Chrétien in his bid for the federal Liberal leadership.[114] Another occasion of dispute between Nixon and Peterson came during the unsuccessful 1990 provincial election campaign. As the Liberals fell in the polls, strategists suggested a 2 per cent cut in the provincial sales tax. At first, Nixon opposed the plan of action: 'You've got to be out of your [expletive] minds.'[115] Eventually, he relented, supporting the proposal. As Gagnon and Rath contend, 'Staff on the premier's bus realized Peterson had not made up his mind about doing the cut and appeared "uncomfortable" with the plan until he heard from Nixon.'[116]

In the aftermath of the surprising 1990 Ontario election, the New Democratic Party formed the government. Similar to Peterson in selecting a party stalwart to the post, new premier Bob Rae picked Floyd Laughren as treasurer. As a former deputy minister recalled, Laughren was 'very similar to Nixon, brought a real understanding of politics to Queen's Park ... [and] had an understanding of what the professional civil service was there to do, which was different from most of the NDP cabinet.'[117] On Laughren, Rae wrote in his 1996 memoir,

> My choice for deputy premier and treasurer was Floyd Laughren, and this proved to be wise. Floyd was elected in 1971, having working as an economics lecturer at Cambrian College in Sudbury. He was well liked in the caucus, and well regarded by the other members of the legislature while in opposition. He had a steady hand and always displayed a marvelous sense of humour. We had not always seen eye to eye on all issues – in the seventies Floyd had been a voice on the left of the party – but since my becoming leader he had been a tremendous source of quiet support. He had an enormously difficult job in the government, and he never wavered or flinched.[118]

Winning his first election in 1971 in the Nickel Belt constituency just outside of Sudbury, Floyd Laughren quickly became well respected in the NDP. Laughren and other leftists in the party routinely criticized leader Stephen Lewis and the party's attempts to 'soft-pedal socialism,' and proposed such policies as the nationalization of Inco Limited.[119] Laughren was known as an individual of integrity for his honesty and forthrightness.[120] Those who knew him during his 'radical economics instructor' years at Cambrian College were surprised by his conversion into a pragmatic treasurer under Rae. Thomas Walkom cites two factors for the transformation of the man his children called 'Pink Floyd': 'the nature of the economy the government faced upon taking power; and the perennial failure of the NDP, both federally and provincially, to develop a coherent and practical approach for dealing with that economy.'[121] Floyd Laughren almost never made it to the treasurer's post. After the 1987 election disappointment and the experience of propping up the Liberal government, many NDP MPPs including Laughren contemplated leaving politics.[122]

Floyd Laughren's time as Ontario finance minister was filled with difficult politics and economic troubles. In October 1990 he announced that the province would be running a $2.5 billion deficit in the 1990–1 fiscal year as opposed to the $23 million surplus that had been declared by the Liberals in the spring budget. He would present three consecutive budgets whereby the government borrowed more than $10 billion, including the 1992–3 fiscal year, when Ontario had net financing requirements of $15.5 billion.[123] When Bob Rae announced an election on 8 June 1995 the province's debt had more than doubled since 1990, going from $39.3 billion to $89.6 billion.[124] The most notable budget out of a collection of notorious ones was the party's first. The newly elected NDP government was hit with grim economic times. The early 1990s recession was considered the worst since the 1930s, as 330,000 jobs disappeared by the spring of 1992.[125] To make things worse, this was on the heels of Nixon's claim that the Liberal government's last budget was the first balanced budget in twenty years.[126] The 1991 budget, however economically unavoidable, was a political disaster for the New Democratic Party, which, following the announcements, dropped by 20 to 25 percentage points in opinion polls.[127] In support of their 1991 budget Laughren argued, 'I think it is important for people to understand that we had a choice to make this year – to fight the deficit or fight the recession ... We are proud to be fighting the recession.'[128]

While Rae and Laughren got along for the most part, certain decisions that the premier made without the treasurer's knowledge are telling of the premier's power regardless of successful working relationships. In 1993 Rae transformed cabinet by creating three super ministries (one being Finance, which Laughren would head). Laughren had no idea, even as treasurer and deputy premier, that the restructuring was imminent.[129] The struggles of government would highlight philosophical differences between Rae and Laughren. In terms of transforming welfare, Rae mused, 'My own view about welfare ... is that simply paying people to sit at home is not smart,' but Laughren disagreed: 'There are not enough jobs out there for everybody now so it would be silly to be punitive at a time when there aren't enough jobs for everybody who wants to work.'[130] In spite of the incredible economic and political challenges Laughren and Rae faced, it is a testament to their relationship that more disagreements between the two men did not emerge. The New Democrat experiment was ended in 1995 as Ontario returned the PCs to government after a ten-year absence.

The relationship between Mike Harris and Ernie Eves may have been the strongest of any premier-treasurer partnership between 1960 and 2000. Eves and Harris had been cottage country MPPs since 1981 (Parry Sound and Nipissing, respectively).[131] The two were elected at the same time, and Harris belonged to Eves's riding association in Parry Sound. Both also had an interest in golf and occasionally played a round together.[132] Friendship was central to Eves's and Harris's premier-treasurer relationship. Eves noted: 'We've become good friends ... We first met in the 1970s ... We both shared a lot of common interests and quite frankly, I think we think along the same lines.'[133] Regardless of their personal connection, Eves believed their friendship was not the sole reason he was finance minister: 'I'd like to think that I'm not here because I'm Mike's friend.'[134] One reporter noted the similarities: 'He [Eves] is the other northerner ... He thinks like Harris, acts like Harris, and understands where Harris is coming from ... He even looks a little like Harris.'[135] Harris surprised some when he selected Eves to fill not one but three high-profile positions: finance minister, deputy premier, and house leader. John Ibbitson wrote,

> There may never have been a Canadian head of government more inti-mately allied to a finance minister than Mike Harris is to Ernie Eves. They are more than political allies. They are close and trusted friends. They had known each other since Harris's days on the Nipissing school board. They golfed together; they and their wives vacationed together. Eves still calls the premier Mikey. It was Eves who, more than any other, had convinced Harris to run for the leadership of the party. Harris, on becoming premier, made his friend not only Finance minister, but House Leader – Harris's old job – and deputy premier as well. As one confidant put it, 'When word got out that Mike and Ernie were having dinner together, all policy work stopped. Because whatever they decided over dinner was going to be-come policy.'[136]

Eves once said about the connection between him and Harris,

> We think alike ... We do the same things ... I think it's because we both have small-town, small-c conservative upbringings, both, one way or an-other, have been exposed to small business, both understand what it

means to make a payroll, regardless of how big or how small, and we both had parents that had to work very hard to be successful.'[137]

Eves and Harris were not simply pals, but in some sense a very successful and formidable legislative duo. Sharing a pro-business, small-government philosophy, the two were able to focus on their attempts to reform Ontario. The government was not without its critics. Many related the Harris Tories to the Thatcher Conservatives in Britain of the 1980s. One left-leaning writer claimed the Harris philosophy was 'a potent neo-conservative brew of neo-liberal economics and "authoritarian populist" social policy ... They have the same fundamental objective, the redistribution of income from the "worse-off" to the "better off" sections of society.'[138] Harris's economic philosophy did not appear out of thin air. During the 1990 provincial election campaign Harris presented himself as the 'tax fighter.'[139] Eves demonstrated his compatibility with the 'tax fighter' by cutting provincial income taxes by 30 per cent in the first budget.[140] Similarly to Nixon's deficit reduction record, Eves took a deficit that stood at the equivalent of 3.3 per cent of the gross domestic product in 1995 and reduced it to zero by the 2000–1 fiscal year.[141] All these economic achievements were not produced by political philosophy alone; political friendship and trust also played a major role for Eves and Harris. As Eves recalls, 'I met with him daily ... We had a huge legislative agenda ... I always had his ear.'[142]

The Four Factors for Political Friendship

While it is difficult to summarize forty years of premier–minister of finance relations in a few pages, it is important to emphasize positive and negative aspects between the chief elected officer in the province and the position that is almost always considered 'number two.' Why have Ontario premier–treasurer relationships been relatively harmonious? Peace has endured due to four key factors: career timing, professional trust, the political environment, and, most important for this jurisdiction's governance culture, an adherence to the managerial philosophy of government.

Career timing may simply be blind luck and have nothing to do with intentions, but it still has played a major role in keeping the peace between the leaders in the Frost Building and the premier's office. Out of the ten individuals who held the treasurer's post from 1960 to 2000 only three (McKeough, Miller, Grossman) held overt leadership aspirations

Table 3.2 Leadership threat level

Treasurer	Situation	Aspiration level
James Allan	Had previously run for leadership and lost to Robarts; age a factor	Low
Charles McNaughton	Served close to Robarts's retirement; contemplated running in 1971 but age a factor	Medium
Darcy McKeough	Lost to Davis in 1971, but was under 40; rumours swirled throughout post linking him to leadership	High
John White	Set retirement date at 50 years old; openly stated treasurer was career peak	Low
Frank Miller	Openly sought leadership but fought battles with Grossman not Davis	High
Larry Grossman	See above	High
Bette Stephenson	Only in post one month	Not applicable
Robert Nixon	Had already served as leader from 1967–76	Low
Floyd Laughren	Party veteran; almost retired from politics in 1987	Low
Ernie Eves	Considered to be successor, but never a threat to Harris	Low

and only one (McKeough) appeared to have aspirations that may have interfered with the relationship. But even McKeough's intentions are a point of contention. While senior public servants who worked in the Frost Building at the time believe McKeough greatly desired to be leader, McKeough himself denies it.[143] Table 3.2 attempts to rank the leadership aspirations of each treasurer.

Indeed, one could argue that much of the tension within Ontario government has not taken place between the premier's office and the Ministry of Finance, but between such departments as the Management Board Secretariat and the Ministry of Finance. In fact, under the Progressive Conservative government in the late 1990s, the executive management reforms, including changes to the Treasury Board and the cabinet system, were aimed at lessening tensions between the Ministry of Finance and the Management Board Secretariat.[144]

The actors were aware of the impact of leadership aspirations. Ernie Eves contended, 'You don't want to be looking over your shoulder to see if what the finance minister is doing is right for the government or doing what is right for their own political aspirations,' and concerning himself and Harris, 'I wasn't pushing him at all.'[145] Eves elaborates further: 'I never had any thought of becoming premier and I think Mike knew that and I think that made the relationship a lot easier.'[146] In terms of a situation that did have tension, a former deputy minister observed on the Miller–Grossman–Davis relationship that 'it wasn't so much Davis they were attacking it was one another ... They knew if they did this publicly they would lose the support of the caucus and the Conservative party voters that they had to rely on to get the leadership.'[147]

Along with trusting that your number two in cabinet is not attempting a coup, a general level of everyday trust must exist to ensure a productive professional relationship. Floyd Laughren commented that 'trust is the key – trust that neither one will blind-side the other and that if disagreements do occur they will be aired privately and not in the press or in caucus ... It is important that each one gives the other advance warnings of events and policies.'[148] Eves also believed that 'trust is the ultimate thing' and that there 'needs to be mutual respect, the finance minister has to be seen to be supportive of the agenda of the government and the leader, they have to be able to stand their ground, they have to have a relationship with the leader that they can oppose.'[149] Even in the case of McKeough and Davis, where some tension existed, the trust level was high: 'They weren't best friends but there wasn't antagonism ... Davis gave McKeough a lot of responsibility.'[150]

Trust can stem from strong personal feelings of respect and admiration. David Peterson once admitted, 'There's no man, outside of my own family, for whom I have more affection, than Robert Nixon.'[151] This trust was on display when Peterson appointed Nixon to a crisis team to respond to the explosive Patti Starr affair.[152] Nixon 'always felt like he had quite a bit of confidence in me. I was a senior of him in age and had been the leader for a decade so I was pretty well established.'[153] It is not only in times of crisis that a premier can find trust in his treasurer, but also in expected but important events. The only entire Eves budget Harris ever saw was his first one. Eves states, 'I remember somebody commenting from his office sometime. The great thing about having me there is that Mike knew he didn't have to worry about it.'[154]

As in the case of leadership aspirations and career timing, the state of the political environment is somewhat out of the hands of the premier or treasurer; they may not have created it, but they certainly are a part of it. The most important development between the premier and treasurer in terms of the political environment affecting the relationship has been the evolving professionalism of the public service and the growing sophistication of decision making in the Ontario government. Queen's Park has evolved dramatically from a time when Leslie Frost would speak to frontline public servants directly and keep only a few staffers in his office. The relationship between finance minister and premier has also been affected by an evolution of the Ontario cabinet system from a simple decision-making organization to one institutionally dependent on an ever-increasing complex committee system.[155] Michael J. Prince describes the grand political and public administration organization that took form during the 1970s when Bill Davis 'was premier at the apex of an elaborate and formalized cabinet system atop a vast public service in a complex, industrial community.'[156] As one former senior public servant recounts of the treasury in the 1960s, 'Things were a little smaller, a little more informal, a little easier and less under the eye and scrutiny of the media.'[157] Along with increasing complexity in relations between the treasury and the premier's office there has developed an overall growing centralization of government procedure. While this appears to refute the presence of trust, it may also demonstrate a stronger relationship due to proximity. Some believe that there has been a return to the Frost era in the sense that 'the general trend has been more hands-on of premiers concerning the mandate of finance ministers.'[158] A veteran treasury official recalls: 'In the past the treasurer would bring a close to finished product and the premier would nibble at the edges of it, now finance ministers are working hand in hand with the premier and [there is] more presence of people from the premier's office.'[159] Before the 1960–2000 period, Canadian provincial and federal cabinets were considered 'unaided,' having few institutional resources or professional staff. Ted Glenn argues that Ontario's cabinet was first minister–dominated and largely unaided until 1972.[160] At this point the simplicity of Leslie Frost's approach to governance disappeared. A growing complexity in governance was emerging throughout the Government of Ontario.

Another major aspect contributing to the political environment in which a treasurer would find him- or herself, was the changing nature of the role. From the stand-alone treasurer to one with responsibilities that would eventually include those of minister of economics, minister of municipal affairs, and minister of intergovernmental affairs, the

position has at times lived up to its 'super minister' billing. The added
responsibility coincided with the additional portfolios taking on unprecedented importance, whether it was Charles McNaughton supporting John Robarts in his Confederation of Tomorrow initiatives or
Darcy McKeough working his way through regional government experiments throughout the province. With a greater role created by the
premier and political circumstances, the treasurer became a solidified
'number two,' especially when anointed deputy premier.

The changing environment and context of the treasurer's role has
been tempered by the tradition of a managerial style of government
that had been established by decades of stability and consistency under
Progressive Conservative rule. Bill Davis's belief in a bland style of
government only continued the philosophy of managing the province's
purse under Drew, Frost, and Robarts. Sid Noel contends that 'prior to
1985, the old Tory party's pragmatic mix of progressivism and conservatism was generally seen as one of the key reasons for its extraordinary hold on political power.'[161] Brian Tanguay describes the Tory
dynasty in Ontario from 1943 to 1985 in the following manner:

> Chief among [the various factors contributing to the success] were the
> province's continuing economic prosperity during this period, despite the
> normal peaks and troughs of the business cycle; the ability of the Tories to
> revitalize themselves every ten years or so with the selection of a new
> leader; their successful appeal to a broad coalition of moderate voters,
> along with an intimidatingly efficient party organization, the vaunted 'Big
> Blue Machine'; and, of course, the fact that opposition votes were split
> between two parties roughly equal in strength.[162]

The managerial style that would appear to set the tone for the premier–
treasurer relationship was rooted in respect for tradition and organization
that the Progressive Conservative dynasty would colour with a hint of
populism. Leslie Frost believed that 'government is business, the people's
business ... It has to be a partnership between the two philosophies of
economic advance and human betterment.'[163] Davis once remarked that
Ontarians were only concerned with how their provincial government
could 'manage the store.'[164] In 1961 Robarts declared, 'I'm a management
man myself ... This is the era of the management man ... I'm a complete
product of my times.'[165] Sid Noel defines five key norms to Ontario's past
that are tied closely to the effectiveness of the Ministry of Finance. In the
list of norms, Noel included the concept of 'managerial efficiency':

Managerial efficiency in government, variously conceived and interpreted, has always been one of the core norms of Ontario's operative political culture. In the eighteenth century the prevailing notion of efficiency
was, like so much else, drawn from the military; Governor Simcoe's ideal
administration, for example, was one modelled on a well-run regiment:
firm and fair in its authority, clear in its objectives, and paternalistic in its
concern for the welfare of all ranks.[166]

Along with sharing a common view of the province, the individuals
who filled the roles of treasurer and premier had respect for their positions. Robert Nixon says: 'I think it's productive and more safer and at
another level, much more pleasant [when the premier/treasurer get
along] but everyone's aware who the boss is and that is the premier.'[167]
Robarts and Davis were both viewed by one former senior bureaucrat
as premiers who respected the function of the treasurer.[168] Darcy
McKeough finds not only respect but also confidence as a significant
aspect of the relationship, 'the most important trait is confidence of the
premier in his minister in terms of political judgment and economics.'[169]
Even during the Miller-Grossman battles, the conflict was contained by
greater concerns. As a former deputy minister remembers, 'These guys
always tempered their own ambitions ... They would stick the shiv in a
little bit to one another, they wouldn't turn it and eviscerate one another because they knew that wouldn't be good for the province.'[170]
Without institutional and tradition restraints, instability would wreak
havoc on the cabinet relationship. On the heels of the Suncor dispute
with his premier, Bill Davis, Frank Miller suggested that if he had to
step down each time he disagreed with a cabinet decision, he – or any
other minister – would be faced with resignation 'at least once a week.'[171]

Conclusion

David Peterson once said that 'to run a government, you need three
guys – a premier, a treasurer and an attorney general.'[172] This chapter
has explored the close proximity at which the treasurer and the premier
work and the relative harmony the partnership has enjoyed in Ontario
during the period between 1960 and 2000. Further work could be completed in attempting to identify other portfolios that have significant
important relationships with the premier, but it would be difficult to
find any rapport as important as that which exists between the treasurer and the premier. While Ontario's financial policies are driven by

numbers, this chapter has focused on the importance of words and relationships in an elite governance setting.

The positive climate surrounding Ontario treasurers normally continued after their Queen's Park career ended. Many of the province's finance ministers were greeted with a soft landing at the end of their career in Ontario politics, on some occasions staying within arm's length of government. To name a few: Floyd Laughren was appointed chair of the Ontario Energy Board by Mike Harris, Robert Nixon was appointed chairman of Atomic Energy of Canada by Jean Chrétien.[173] Charles MacNaughton would eventually be named head of the Ontario Racing Commission and James Allan would land the position of chairman of the Niagara Parks Commission.[174] The bipartisan flavour of Laughren and Nixon's appointments demonstrates the level of respect these individuals created for themselves.

In the time since 2000, the treasurer–premier relationship experienced some turmoil before eventual restoration. After Eves resigned, Jim Flaherty became finance minister under Harris and quickly provided an example of the opposite of the Eves-Harris peace bond by having a minor public spat. Harris's desire to give tax breaks to the province's professional sports teams was not met with agreement from Flaherty, who was out of the country at the time Harris was lobbying his ministers for support. Flaherty later publicly stated, 'I did not support a change in the policy … I would not have signed it had it been presented to me.'[175] Once becoming leader and premier, Eves had some treasurer-premier friction of his own. Concerning the budget-making process, a Queen's Park insider noted that the budget was written in the premier's office: 'He [Eves] put in what he wanted and passed it over to Janet [Ecker] to announce.'[176]

While Eves and Harris may have experienced challenges in adapting to new partners in their respective positions, the more recent Liberal government has provided another example of a strong treasurer–premier relationship. As happened in the McKeough-Davis years, Liberal finance minister Greg Sorbara resigned due to a family real-estate controversy, only to be reappointed to the position seven months later when a judge cleared his name. In the days following the judge's ruling, but before Sorbara's reappointment, Dalton McGuinty confessed, 'I'm going to take a few days to consider where we're going from here, but it's no secret I would be pleased to be able to return Greg to cabinet.'[177] Similarly to Nixon and Laughren, Sorbara was a party veteran who had served in David Peterson's cabinet and acted as Ontario Liberal party president from 1999 to 2001.

Bill Davis's 'bland works' political philosophy was misleading. First of all, there was probably nothing bland about the late nights at John Robarts's cottage in Grand Bend between him and MacNaughton, or the colourful language and temper of Robert Nixon or the confident bravado shared by Mike Harris and Ernie Eves. Second, none of these individuals were close personal friends, although in relative political terms they appeared to be high on each others' lists. From the mentoring roles of Allan, Nixon, and Laughren to the aggressive paths set by MacNaughton, McKeough, and Eves, the Ontario treasurers between 1960 and 2000 represented a diverse group, but all had a common bond: a solid relationship with their premier. Even in contexts where leadership aspirations did stir emotions, the role and responsibility of the treasurer to the party and the province routinely took precedence. The Ontario experience presents a pattern of political harmony that is key to understanding the recent history of the Ontario Ministry of Finance.

NOTES

1 David A. Good, *The Politics of Public Money* (Toronto: University of Toronto Press, 2007), 98.
2 For more on each episode consult Walter Gordon, *A Political Memoir* (Halifax: Goodread Biographies, 1977), 331; Lawrence Martin, *Chrétien: Volume 1. The Will to Win* (Toronto: Lester Publishing Ltd, 1995), 264–5; and Pierre Trudeau, *Memoirs* (Toronto: McClelland & Stewart Inc., 1993), 296–8.
3 Interview with former public servant (1972–2006), 15 May 2007.
4 Interview with Ernie Eves, 20 March 2007.
5 Graham White, 'Shorter Measures: The Changing Ministerial Career in Canada,' *Canadian Public Administration* 41.3 (Fall 1998), 370.
6 W.A. Matheson, *The Prime Minister and the Cabinet* (Toronto: Methuen, 1976), 20.
7 Peter Aucoin, 'Independent Foundations, Public Money and Public Accountability: Whither Ministerial as Democratic Governance?' *Canadian Public Administration* 46.1 (Spring 2003); Herman Bakvis, *Regional Ministers: Power and Influence in the Canadian Cabinet* (Toronto: University of Toronto Press, 1991); Christopher Dunn, *The Institutionalized Cabinet: Governing the Western Provinces* (Montreal: McGill-Queen's University Press, 1995);

J. Stefan Dupré, 'Reflections on the Workability of Executive Federalism,' in Richard Simeon, ed., *Intergovernmental Relations* (Toronto: University of Toronto Press, 1985).

8 Donald J. Savoie, *Governing from the Centre: The Concentration of Power in Canadian Politics* (Toronto: University of Toronto Press, 1999), 3.

9 Ibid.

10 Roger Graham, *Old Man Ontario: Leslie M. Frost* (Toronto: University of Toronto Press, 1990), 309.

11 Graham White, 'Governing from Queen's Park: The Ontario Premiership,' in *Prime Ministers and Premiers: Political Leadership and Public Policy in Canada*, ed. Leslie Pal and David Taras (Scarborough: Prentice-Hall Canada Inc., 1988), 158.

12 Interview with Don Stevenson, 20 June 2007.

13 'Premier Shuffles 8 Cabinet Posts' *Globe and Mail*, 18 August 1955, 2.

14 Rand Dyck, *Provincial Politics in Canada: Towards the Turn of the Century* (Scarborough: Prentice-Hall Canada Inc., 1996), 339.

15 A.K. McDougall, *John P. Robarts: His Life and Government* (Toronto: University of Toronto, 1986), 63.

16 Interview with Don Stevenson, 20 June 2007.

17 'Frost Tired of Retiring Rumors,' *Toronto Daily Star*, 15 February 1960, 6.

18 William McGuffin. 'Dark Horses Thunder after Frost's Job,' *Toronto Daily Star*, 4 August 1961, 7.

19 'P.C.'s Plan "Biggest Show" to Pick Frost Successor,' *Toronto Daily Star*, 18 August 1961, 27.

20 McDougall, *John P. Robarts*, 63.

21 Ibid., 71.

22 'Here's My Personal Choice for the P.C. Leadership,' *Toronto Daily Star*, 23 October 1961, 7.

23 Robert Bothwell, *A Short History of Ontario* (Edmonton: Hurtig Publishers Ltd., 1986), 185.

24 McDougall, *John P. Robarts*, 71.

25 Interview Don Stevenson, 20 June 2007.

26 Michael Lavoie, 'Davis Started Campaign for Premier 2 Years Ago,' *Toronto Daily Star*, 13 February 1971, 9.

27 McDougall, *John P. Robarts*, 182.

28 'Ex-minister Had Clout in Ontario Tory Circles – Charles MacNaughton,' *Globe and Mail*, 19 November 1987, A23.

29 Interview with former senior bureaucrat involved in ten budgets (1965–75), 12 July 2007.

30 McDougall, *John P. Robarts*, 213.

31 John Ibbitson, *Loyal No More: Ontario's Struggle for a Separate Destiny* (Toronto: HarperCollins, 2001), 96.

32 'Davis 1st to Declare for Tory Leadership,' *Toronto Daily Star*, 21 December 1970, 4.

33 Trent Frayne, 'The Bill Davis Story: A Careful Climb to the Top,' *Toronto Daily Star*, 13 February 1971, 14.

34 Dyck, *Provincial Politics in Canada*, 342.

35 Michael J. Prince, 'The Bland Stops Here: Ontario Budgeting in the Davis Era, 1971–1985,' in Allan M. Maslove, ed., *Budgeting in the Provinces: Leadership and the Premiers* (Toronto: Institute of Public Administration of Canada, 1989), 113.

36 Hugh Segal, 'The Evolving Ontario Cabinet: Shaping the Structure to Suit the Times,' in *The Politics and Government of Ontario*, 3rd ed., ed. Donald C. MacDonald (Scarborough: Nelson, 1985), 70.

37 Margaret Daly, 'A Plan for Public Services: Let Private Enterprise Do It,' *Toronto Star*, 17 July 1972, 21.

38 Jonathan Manthorpe, *The Power and the Tories: Ontario Politics – 1943 to the Present* (Toronto: Macmillan of Canada, 1974), 123.

39 Interview with Darcy McKeough, 20 June 2007.

40 'Ontario's New "Super Ministers,"' *Toronto Daily Star*, 6 January 1972, 26.

41 Walter Pitman, 'Premier Davis' Power Is Growing,' *Toronto Star*, 7 July 1972, 9.

42 Jonathan Manthorpe, 'McKeough Shows the Many Scars of Lost Battles,' *Toronto Star*, 16 August 1978, A1.

43 James W. Snow, *Mr. Jim: The Personal Recollections of James W. Snow* (Hornby: James W. Snow, 1990), 151.

44 Claire Hoy, *Bill Davis* (Toronto: Methuen, 1985), 103.

45 Interview with former assistant deputy minister, deputy minister (1973–92), 15 May 2007.

46 Interview with Don Stevenson, 20 June 2007.

47 Manthorpe, 'McKeough Shows the Many Scars of Lost Battles,' 279.

48 'Dozen PCs Joining Protest against Sales Tax on Energy,' *Toronto Star*, 21 April 1973, 96.

49 Fraser Kelly, 'Bill Davis' Bad Luck Is Bad Politics Too,' *Toronto Star*, 30 April 1973, 8.

50 Hoy, *Bill Davis*, 109.

51 Rosemary Speirs, 'White Calls His Defeat "a Victory for Democracy,"' *Toronto Star*, 25 April 1973, 9.

52 Peter Oliver, *Unlikely Tory: The Life and Politics of Allan Grossman* (Toronto: Lester & Orpen Dennys Ltd, 1985), 257.

53 Jim Robinson. 'Ontario's Red Tory Rides High as Boss of All Our Tax Money,' *Toronto Star*, 12 January 1974, B7.
54 Hoy, *Bill Davis*, 118.
55 David Allen, 'Davis Brings McKeough Back in No. 2 Spot,' *Toronto Star*, 14 January 1975, A1.
56 Interview with former ADM, deputy minister (1973–92), 15 May 2007.
57 Interview with former senior bureaucrat involved in ten budgets (1965–75), 12 July 2007.
58 Interview with Darcy McKeough, 20 June 2007.
59 Andrew Szende, 'McKeough's Job Tough – but He Likes That,' *Toronto Star*, 15 January 1975, B3.
60 Eric Dowd, 'Confusion as to Who's the Premier,' *North Bay Nugget*, 24 November 2005, A6.
61 Interview with former senior public servant (1960–85), 20 June 2007.
62 Prince, 'The Bland Stops Here,' 98.
63 Jonathan Manthorpe, 'OHIP Fight Could Be End for McKeough,' *Toronto Star*, 21 April 1978, A1.
64 Pat Crowe, 'Why Some Tories Hope McKeough Stays Away,' *Toronto Star*, 23 August 1980, B4.
65 Manthorpe, 'OHIP Fight Could Be End for McKeough,' A1.
66 Jonathan Manthorpe, 'Gap Remains after Darcy's Departure,' *Toronto Star*, 15 December 1978, A10.
67 Rick Haliechuk, 'Treasurer Questions Balancing Budget,' *Toronto Star*, 17 August 1978, A20.
68 Rick Haliechuk, 'McKeough Quits Treasurer's Job and Legislature,' *Toronto Star*, 16 April 1978, A1.
69 Jonathan Manthorpe, 'Would-be Premiers Play a Waiting Game,' *Toronto Star*, 19 October 1976, D1.
70 Hugh Winsor, 'Intriguing Political Parallels,' *Globe and Mail*, 29 August 1978, P7.
71 Prince, 'The Bland Stops Here,' 99.
72 Don Stevenson to P. Dutil, 12 February 2009.
73 Pat Crowe, 'Ontario's New Treasury Boss Seen as Likeable Right-winger,' *Toronto Star*, 17 August 1978, A10.
74 Walter Gowing, 'Frank Miller "Good Guy" Who Deserved Better,' *Cambridge Reporter*, 1 August 2000, A2.
75 Edwin A. Goodman, *Life of the Party: The Memoirs of Eddie Goodman* (Toronto: Key Porter Books, 1988), 266.
76 Crowe, 'Ontario's New Treasury Boss,' A10.

77 Rosemary Speirs, *Out of the Blue: The Fall of the Tory Dynasty Ontario* (Toronto: Macmillan of Canada, 1986), 13.

78 Ken MacGray, 'Senior Cabinet Minister Opposed Province's Deal with Suncor,' *Toronto Star*, 15 October 1981, A1.

79 Interview with former ADM, deputy minister (1973–92), 15 May 2007.

80 Hoy, *Bill Davis*, 345

81 Interview with former ADM, deputy minister (1973–92), 15 May 2007.

82 Martin Cohn, 'Self-styled Hustler Miller Puts "Tough" Ideology behind Him,' *Toronto Star*, 24 October 1984, A21.

83 Ibid.

84 Ibid.

85 Interview with former ADM, deputy minister (1973–92), 15 May 2007.

86 Speirs, *Out of the Blue*, 85.

87 Ibid.

88 Ibid.

89 Interview with former ADM, deputy minister (1973–92), 15 May 2007.

90 Editorial: 'Shuffling the Key Players,' *Toronto Star*, 7 July 1983, A20.

91 Prince, 'The Bland Stops Here,' 103.

92 Robert MacDermid and Greg Albo, 'Divided Province, Growing Protests: Ontario Moves Right,' in *The Provincial State in Canada: Politics in the Provinces*, ed. Keith Brownsey and Michael Howlett (Peterborough: Broadview Press, 2001), 176.

93 Hoy, *Bill Davis*, 397.

94 Martin Cohn, 'The Man Who Would Be Premier,' *Toronto Star*, 14 August 1983, D1.

95 Val Sears, 'Four Stake Their Claim to Power,' *Toronto Star*, 24 January 1985, B4.

96 Speirs, *Out of the Blue*, 28.

97 Ibid.

98 '33 Ministers in Ontario's Big Cabinet,' *Toronto Star*, 9 February 1985, B4.

99 Alan Christie and Denise Harrington, 'Grossman Said the Key Player as Miller Picks His New Cabinet,' *Toronto Star*, 17 May 1985, A1.

100 Bill Walker and Robin Harvery, 'Miller Quits – It's "Foolish" to Stay as Tory Leader,' *Toronto Star*, 21 August 1985, A12.

101 Ibid.

102 Alan Christie, '72–52 Vote Signals End to Ontario Tory Rule,' *Toronto Star*, 19 June 1985, A1.

103 George Gamester, 'This Radar Cop's Heard All Your Excuses,' *Toronto Star*, 11 May 1981, A3.

104 Georgette Gagnon and Dan Rath, *Not without Cause: David Peterson's Fall from Grace* (Toronto: HarperCollins, 1991), 27.
105 Dyck, *Provincial Politics in Canada*, 349.
106 'Liberals Fete Nixon for 25 Years at Park,' *Toronto Star*, 15 January 1987, A21.
107 Jon Wells, 'Look What's Happened to Baby Jane,' *Hamilton Spectator*, 8 August 1999, D1.
108 Alan Christie, 'Robert Nixon Bakes Budgets and White Bread,' *Toronto Star*, 8 December 1985, F1.
109 Interview with former ADM, deputy minister (1973–92), 15 May 2007.
110 'Bob Nixon's Happy Meal,' *Brantford Expositor*, 16 April 2004, A9.
111 Joan Brekenridge, 'The Ontario Budget: Payroll Levy to Replace OHIP Premiums,' *Toronto Star*, 18 May 1989, A15.
112 Ibbitson, *Loyal No More*, 118.
113 Interview with former ADM, deputy minister (1973–92), 15 May 2007.
114 Matt Maychak, 'Key Ontarians Back Chrétien,' *Toronto Star*, 5 February 1990, A10.
115 Gagnon and Rath, *Not without Cause*, 334.
116 Ibid., 335.
117 Interview with former ADM, deputy minister (1973–92), 15 May 2007.
118 Bob Rae, *From Protest to Power: Personal Reflections on a Life in Politics* (Toronto: Viking, 1996), 133.
119 Thomas Walkom, *Rae Days* (Toronto: Key Porter Books, 1994), 85.
120 Patrick Monahan, *Storming the Pink Palace. The NDP in Power: A Cautionary Tale* (Toronto: Lester Publishing, 1995), 140.
121 Walkom, *Rae Days*, 86.
122 Ibid., 45.
123 *Globe and Mail*, 'Ontario Election 1995 Chronology: Highlights of NDP's 4½ years, 9 June 1995,' A9.
124 Ibid.
125 Chuck Rachlis and David Wolfe, 'An Insiders' View of the NDP Government of Ontario: The Politics of Permanent Opposition Meets the Economics of Permanent Recession,' in *The Government and Politics of Ontario*, 5th ed., ed. Graham White (Toronto: University of Toronto Press, 1997), 336.
126 Ibid., 336.
127 Ibid., 344.
128 Ibid., 343.
129 Ibid., 312.
130 George Ehring and Wayne Roberts, *Giving Away a Miracle: Lost Dreams, Broken Promises and the Ontario NDP* (Oakville: Mosaic Press, 1993), 320.

131 Peter Woolstencroft, 'Reclaiming the "Pink Palace": The Progressive Conservative Party Comes in from the Cold,' in *Government and Politics of Ontario*, ed. White, 385.
132 Interview with Ernie Eves, 20 March 2007.
133 Christina Blizzard, *Right Turn: How the Tories Took Ontario* (Toronto: Dundurn Press, 1995), 131.
134 Ibid.
135 Ibid., 128.
136 John Ibbitson, *Promised Land: Inside the Mike Harris Revolution* (Scarborough: Prentice-Hall, 1997), 137.
137 Ibid., 138.
138 Paul Leduc Browne, 'Déjà Vu: Thatcherism in Ontario,' in *Open for Business, Closed for People: Mike Harris's Ontario*, ed. Diana S. Ralph, Andre Regimbald, and Neree St-Amand (Halifax: Fernwood Publishing, 1997), 37.
139 David R. Cameron and Graham White, *Cycling into Saigon: The Conservative Transition in Ontario* (Vancouver: UBC Press, 2000), 79.
140 MacDermid and Albo, 'Divided Province, Growing Protests,' 192.
141 Bruce Little, 'Boom Hasn't Spurred Harris to Tackle Ontario's Deficit,' *Globe and Mail*, 17 May 1999, A4.
142 Interview with Ernie Eves, 20 March 2007.
143 Interview with Darcy McKeough, 20 June 2007.
144 David A. Wolfe, 'Queen's Park Policy-Making Systems,' in *Revolution at Queen's Park: Essays on Governing Ontario* (Toronto: James Lorimer & Co., 1997, 162.
145 Interview with Ernie Eves, 20 March 2007.
146 Ibid.
147 Interview with former ADM, deputy minister (1973–92), 15 May 2007.
148 Interview with Floyd Laughren, 23 June 2007.
149 Interview with former public servant (1972–2006), 15 May 2007.
150 Interview with former senior public servant (1960–85), 20 June 2007.
151 William Walker, 'Nixon Grins through Tribute Marking 25 Years in Politics,' *Toronto Star*, 17 January 1987, A6.
152 Thomas Walkom, 'Liberals Need to Lick Starr-inflicted Wounds,' *Toronto Star*, 15 July 1989, D1.
153 Interview with Robert Nixon, 11 April 2007.
154 Interview with Ernie Eves, 20 March 2007.
155 Richard A. Loreto, 'The Structure of the Ontario Political System,' in *The Government and Politics of Ontario*, 3rd ed., ed. Donald C. MacDonald (Scarborough: Nelson Canada, 1985), 20.

156 Prince, 'The Bland Stops Here,' 88.
157 Interview with former senior bureaucrat involved in ten budgets (1965–75), 12 July 2007.
158 Interview with former public servant (1972–2006), 15 May 2007.
159 Ibid.
160 Ted Glenn, 'Politics, Personality, and History in Ontario Administrative Style,' in *Executive Styles in Canada: Cabinet Structures and Leadership Practices in Canadian Government*, ed. Luc Bernier, Keith Brownsey, and Michael Howlett (Toronto: University of Toronto Press, 2005), 156.
161 Sid Noel, 'Ontario's Tory Revolution,' in *Revolution at Queen's Park: Essays on Governing Ontario*, ed. Sid Noel (Toronto: James Lorimer & Co., 1997), 13.
162 Brian Tanguay, '"Not in Ontario!" From the Social Contract to the Common Sense Revolution,' in *Revolution at Queen's Park*, ed. Noel, 19.
163 Randall White, *Ontario since 1985* (Toronto: Eastend Books, 1998), 184.
164 Desmond Morton, '*Sic Permanet*: Ontario People and Their Politics,' in *The Government and Politics of Ontario*, ed. White, 7.
165 Hoy, *Bill Davis*, 47.
166 Sid Noel, 'The Ontario Political Culture: An Interpretation,' in *The Government and Politics of Ontario*, ed. White, 60.
167 Interview with Robert Nixon, 11 April 2007.
168 Interview with former senior bureaucrat involved in ten budgets (1965–75), 12 July 2007.
169 Interview with Darcy McKeough, 20 June 2007.
170 Interview with former ADM, deputy minister (1973–92), 15 May 2007.
171 Ken MacGray, 'Miller Won't Quit over Suncor,' *Toronto Star*, 16 October 1981, A15.
172 Sandra Martin, 'Ian Scott, Lawyer and Politician: 1934–2006,' *Globe and Mail*, 11 October 2006, S9.
173 Eric Dowd, 'Politics Can Be Lucrative Career,' *Guelph Mercury*, 21 March 2001, A8.
174 Hoy, *Bill Davis*, 183.
175 Robert Benzie, 'Allies Say Harris Never Discussed Teams' Tax Breaks,' *National Post*, 10 October 2002; Caroline Mallan, 'Harris Blamed for Sports Tax Break,' *Toronto Star*, 10 October 2002.
176 Graham White, *Cabinets and First Ministers* (Vancouver: UBC Press, 2005), 76.
177 Robert Benzie and Les Whittington, 'Sorbara to Return to Cabinet,' *Toronto Star*, 20 May 2006, A4.

SECTION 2

The Guardian in Policy Making

4 Intergovernmental Guardians: Treasury's Role in Setting the National Agenda, 1959–1967

P.E. BRYDEN

There was a time, more than half a century ago now, when Canada's civil service was among the best in the world, argued J.L. Granatstein in his important study *The Ottawa Men*.[1] Armed with educations from Oxford or the London School of Economics and a profound commitment to the Protestant work ethic, possessing the liberal inclinations that wrapped their icy logic in a thick veil of compassion for the under-privileged, this group of able men led Canada's financial and external affairs departments through the Second World War and beyond. Their dominance was brief but significant: Canada established its reputation for peace-keeping and international problem-solving in this period abroad, and laid the foundations for the modern welfare state at home. Ottawa has changed a great deal since the middle of the twentieth century, and the civil service no longer enjoys either the security or the power that it did in the days of O.D. Skelton, Arnold Heeney, and Louis Rasminsky, but the legacy of those towering figures remains.

Considerable attention has been paid to the federal bureaucracy, documenting both its heyday and its decline.[2] Other jurisdictions have also attracted scholarly attention, with the extraordinary civil servants in Tommy Douglas's Saskatchewan administration garnering particular interest that highlights both their prairie dominance and documents their important dispersal across the country.[3] The growth of the administration state in Quebec, particularly during the Quiet Revolution, has also been the focus of academic attention.[4] Despite its considerable size and its centrality to an understanding of Canadian political evolution, however, far less attention has been paid to the development of the civil service in Ontario. This can in part be explained by noting that during the years in which the provincial bureaucracies grew most dramatically following the Second World War, Ontario emphasized sound, managerial government rather than innovative administration; the absence of a clear bureaucratic revolution has perhaps allowed scholars to overlook the important changes that actually were going on in the provincial capital.

The financial departments within any government are usually the most important: in studies of the Ottawa civil service, Deputy Minister of Finance R.B. Bryce figures prominently just as his counterpart in Saskatchewan – and then assistant deputy minister in Ottawa – A.W. Johnson plays an important role in our understanding of provincial bureaucratic development. The same is true in Ontario, where the office of prime minister itself was tightly tied to the administration of the Treasury Department and the Department of Economics. Leslie Frost, premier from 1949 until 1961, served as provincial treasurer as well for many years, and when he was replaced as leader by John Robarts the status of the department had been well established. The other jewel in the federal administrative crown is usually the department of external affairs: Granatstein divided his focus between financial and foreign policy departments, and Canada's administrative reputation was in large part built on the expertise of the external affairs mandarins of mid-century such as Skelton, Loring Christie, Hume Wrong, and Lester Pearson. For a brief period in Ontario in the post-war era, finance and the provincial version of foreign affairs were married in one section – the intergovernmental affairs division of the Department of Economics and Development. Ontario's capacity to manage intergovernmental relations developed slowly in the late 1950s and early 1960s. Embarrassing failures in the mid-1960s over pensions policy, however, pushed federal–provincial relations to the top of the agenda. From that point on, Robarts endeavoured to establish a powerful administrative section by luring a coterie of able young staff members to work in the division. Backed by their skill and enthusiasm, Ontario was able to play a determinative role in the formation of national social, economic, and especially constitutional policy in the 1960s. With able people playing a key role on the national stage, the intergovernmental affairs division flourished as the bureaucratic epicentre of the Ontario government in the 1960s.

Becoming Guardians: Background to Mega-intergovernmental Management

In the years following the Second World War, successive Ontario premiers had sought to establish a workable relationship with the federal government. With the enormous centralization of power that occurred as a result of wartime and, after the end of appeals to the provincially-minded Judicial Committee of the Privy Council in 1949, no longer capable of enjoying the same recourse to the courts when questions of jurisdiction arose, all Canadian provinces struggled to define the extent of their powers in the post-war world. Direct taxes, the provinces' only source of income, had been being shared between the two levels of government since the implementation of the Wartime Tax Rental Agreements in 1942, and the sharing continued, in one form or another, throughout the remainder of the century. The British North America Act, which remained a piece of British legislation and was, therefore, amendable only in Britain, had been being discussed since the 1920s, but the heightened environment of nationalism and independence in Canada in the 1940s and 1950s ensured that there would be further attempts to agree on a domestic amending formula. All foundered on intergovernmental disagreement and, ultimately, the need to turn attention to more prosaic issues such as defence or budgeting. And finally, the experience of a decade-long depression in the 1930s had left deep scars on Canadian policy-makers, so as the country entered a period of unprecedented prosperity, proposals for social-security measures entered the public discussion, troubled only, but significantly, by the fact that most measures were squarely within provincial jurisdiction, while most of the money was in Ottawa. The intertwined issues of tax-sharing, constitutional amendment, and social-policy formation plagued the intergovernmental agenda for the better part of five decades following the Second World War. By the time John Robarts was chosen to lead the Conservative Party of Ontario – and therefore lead the province as well – much energy had been spent on discussing intergovernmental issues, but little, if anything, had been decided upon.

The early years of Robarts's administration, during which he solidified his hold on power by tightly controlling cabinet, dealing early on with organized crime, and establishing a sound economic strategy for the province, were characterized by difficult relations with the federal wing of the Conservative Party.[5] Prime Minister John Diefenbaker had done little to address the concerns of Ontario, and Robarts was loath to offer much assistance in the election of 1962. When Diefenbaker was forced to call another election the next year, his luck ran out, and the Liberals under Lester Pearson emerged with a minority government. The Liberals had been biding their time in Opposition since 1957 and had accumulated a long grocery list of plans and commitments, many of which Pearson promised to embark upon during his first two months in office. It would be, he claimed, '60 days of decision.' That many of the programs envisioned by the Liberals were, in fact, within provincial jurisdiction, did little to dampen the enthusiasm of Pearson, his cabinet, or his advisers.

One of the programs that was of particular interest to Robarts's government was a plan to introduce a national contributory pension scheme. In Ontario, the Committee on Portable Pensions had tabled its report in the summer of 1961, a draft bill had been prepared and debated, a revised bill was submitted to the legislature in the spring of 1962, and one final round of public hearings had begun in September 1962.[6] Diefenbaker had looked to Ontario for guidance on the pension issue, and other provinces had made complimentary noises when Robarts informed them of the work that was being done in his province.[7] Although the Liberal plan for pensions differed from that proposed in Ontario in that it envisioned a publicly administered scheme, rather than one that utilized private insurance companies, Robarts had good reason to imagine that the work that Ontario had already put into the pension plan would stand him in good stead during the intergovernmental negotiations that were required. The Ontario Pension Benefit Act was already in place, although not yet in effect, and early appraisals were very positive. Representatives of the insurance industry were said to be 'strongly in favour of it over the Liberal proposals'; in the press 'the editorial comment particularly has been surprisingly unanimous and favourable'; politicians in other provinces were continuing to seek assistance from Ontario in preparing their own provincial pension schemes.[8]

But the early reports were unquestionably premature. The first meeting on the subject, in July 1963, failed to produce any kind of agreement, sending not only Ottawa back to the drawing board, but also ensuring that more work would be done in Toronto. Officials in the Treasury Department were responsible for conducting the background work in preparation for these ministerial and first ministers conferences, but most of the work had already been done during the four years in which the Ontario plan had been studied, interrogated, and introduced. The Ontario representatives at intergovernmental meetings merely had to press the position that had already been determined, which is what happened for the better part of a year, until the acrimony that had been building for just as long finally erupted during the first ministers meeting in the spring of 1964. On the second day of the conference Quebec premier Lesage, who had been indicating all along his intention to opt out of the federal pension scheme, dropped his bomb-shell and announced the details of the Quebec Pension Plan legislation that was about to be submitted to the legislature: the Quebec plan would be compulsory for all employees and self-employed persons; its benefits would begin at age sixty-five; contributions were to be based on that portion of a person's income between $1000 and $6000, making them more generous than the federal proposal, and were graduated within that range; and survivor benefits were included, as was legisla-tion for the preservation of rights existing under private pension schemes. It thus contained all the features that Ottawa had been desir-ous of maintaining, plus those that were important in Ontario. But the best was yet to come: the reserves built up under the plan were at the complete disposal of the provincial government.[9] Joey Smallwood, the outspoken premier of Newfoundland, summed up the surprise and enthusiasm of the assembled first ministers when he asked whether it would be possible for a province to join either the Quebec Pension Plan or the Canada Pension Plan.[10] According to federal adviser Tom Kent, there was 'just no question at that moment the Canada Pension Plan was dead.'[11] Nor was there any question that the Ontario Pension Benefits legislation was dead.

Federal and Quebec officials worked furiously over the next couple of weeks to find some way to salvage the appearance of a national plan while simultaneously establishing a scheme that mirrored the great ad-vantages of the Quebec plan. Ultimately, they were able to do so, but there was little question that Ontario's officials had been sidelined. Robarts was 'kept in the picture'[12] through prime ministerial phone calls, but he was definitely not central to an agreement on pensions. Although discussions over the details of contracting-out, terms of pay-outs, and opportunities for amendment continued through much of 1964 and beyond, it was clear from the first of April onward that Ontario had been outmanoeuvred by Quebec. From that moment, Robarts resolved to 'build a base of new competence in the Ontario govern-ment' as a means to combat the forces in Quebec and 'the "Tom Kent Liberalism" prevailing in the nation's capital.'[13] Adopting the Quebec plan, by and large, for the rest of Canada was a 'veritable landmark in federal–provincial financial relations.' As a subsequent chief economist for Ontario recalled, 'A province suddenly moved to centre stage on a very complex national issue, and the so-called mysteries of govern-mental finance – previously the exclusive domain of federal civil ser-vants – could be understood by a province with the will to do so.'[14] Ontario definitely had the will.

The Treasury Department, and in particular that component of it that was devoted to intergovernmental-affairs issues, would be under extraordinary pressure throughout the 1960s. Pearson's agenda included not only pensions, but also the touchy subject of national health insurance, another clear invasion of provincial jurisdiction. Moreover, there was always the question of tax-sharing; since the Wartime Tax Rentals Agreements of 1942, the two levels of government had both been occupying the direct-tax fields on the basis of continuous five-year agreements, which always seemed to be in the process of negotiation. And then there was the constitution, which had sporadically been opened up for discussion in the post-war years in an effort to fix the rules before trying to fix the entangled jurisdiction. To this point, all efforts had ended in failure, but hope had not completely faded. Social policies, tax agreements, and a constitutional amending formula were all destined for discussion in the 1960s; by 1964, it was clear that Quebec had an enviable bureaucracy that had given Lesage the upper hand in the pension negotiations. Vowing to build the same kind of strength in Ontario, Robarts set out to staff his civil service with young, able, energetic men and women, many relatively recent university graduates, and then to give them the space to be innovative.[15]

The structure of federal–provincial relations thus underwent a transition. In 1963 and 1964, the weight of intergovernmental affairs fell on the shoulders of either the premier or the treasurer – in this case, either Robarts or Treasurer James Allan. A couple of public servants, including Donald Stevenson, 'were involved in the preparation of Ontario submissions' to intergovernmental conferences, but the coordination and correspondence usually fell to the Prime Minister's Office. In the spring of 1966, however, that loose, informal structure changed, and Robarts established a Federal-Provincial Affairs Secretariat. Working closely with the new Office of the Chief Economist, the secretariat took 'a much more active part in recent conferences.'[16] It was a formidable team that congregated within the Treasury Department, and it soon had developed an equally striking strategy with which to address intergovernmental issues. Rather than getting mired in the details of each shared-cost program, or tax-sharing agreement, or proposal to invade provincial jurisdiction, the Ontario team gradually came to take a longer view, to look at the big picture, and, ultimately, to encourage dialogue between the eleven participants in federal–provincial relations in Canada. It was a shift to mega-, rather than micro-, intergovernmental management.

There were a number of innovations in the mid-1960s that made that approach more feasible than it had been in the past, including the formation of the Tax Structure Committee (TSC) and the Advisory Committee on Confederation. The former was charged with evaluating the entire intergovernmental system of taxation in Canada, and held out high hopes for the Ontario public servants, who expected it would be broadly based and provide 'a declaration of what Canada's needs are from 1967 on.'[17] In early presentations made before the TSC, Ontario representatives made the decision to avoid miring the discussion in debates about figures and projections, and instead offered 'Ontario's view of the nature of the economic problems of Confederation, and of how we may approach these problems.' The problems themselves were an old story: most of the costly responsibilities fell within provincial jurisdiction, whereas the federal government collected most the revenue. The solution, however, was interesting. Not only did there have to be 'better matching of revenue resources with constitutional responsibilities,' but there needed to be clear cooperation between the two levels of government. The Ontario bureaucracy was careful to lay out the role it saw for Ottawa: 'We look to the Federal Government for leadership,' Treasurer James Allan was instructed to state. 'We would emphasize ... that the requirements of the national economy must be met, and that we require national leadership in an endeavour to meet these requirements.'[18] While the Tax Structure Committee ultimately failed to achieve a satisfactory reconceptualization of the intergovernmental fiscal environment in Canada, it was nevertheless an impetus to Robarts's Ontario to begin taking a foundational approach to these mega-intergovernmental issues.

Another innovation that pointed Ontario's intergovernmental affairs officials towards a broad conception of both the problems with, and the solutions to, the current division of powers was the formation of an Advisory Committee on Confederation. Early in 1965, the group was established in response to governmental 'concern with the position of Ontario within the framework of confederation.' The terms of reference noted that 'the relationship between the provinces and between provinces and the federal government has undergone great changes since Confederation,' and that Robarts's government sought 'continuous advice' on issues that affected 'its part in maintaining and strengthening Canadian unity.'[19] To this end, the committee would offer advice on specifically constitutional issues, but also on 'matters in relation to and arising out of the position of Ontario in Confederation.'[20] It was a broad mandate, in keeping with the new vision of the government. The group itself, drawn largely from academia as a reflection of Robarts's desire to establish something of a 'brains trust,' was not part of the intergovernmental affairs group of the Treasury Department, but nevertheless had an important effect on the thinking of the civil servants.[21]

John Robarts himself did not usually attend meetings of the group, which were held once a month in Toronto, but he often joined them at the end of their day of discussion for drinks and dinner. Its format reflected Robarts's style: while the group might be exclusively male, it was relatively young and hard-working and potentially experimental in its thinking. And despite its seemingly informal structure, in some ways, it had the potential to be even more influential than the more traditional advisory body of the royal commission. Commission reports could be ignored, but an advisory body that met monthly for over two years would have to be ignored in a more concerted and systematic manner. And there is little evidence that Robarts sought to ignore their advice; rather, he seemed to enjoy his regular meetings with the professors.[22]

The chair of the committee was the new chief economist in the Department of Economics and Development, H. Ian Macdonald, a young economist lured from the University of Toronto. The secretary was Donald Stevenson, another young man who had worked in the Ontario government since the late 1950s and had developed a reputation as a keen observer of intergovernmental affairs in general, and Quebec in particular. Both men were close to the premier and able to bring Robarts's concerns to the group. At an early meeting, as the advisers struggled to figure out how best to undertake their work, Macdonald indicated the premier's thinking on the matter: Robarts felt that 'this is the time in the reconstruction of Confederation, that the Prime Minister of Ontario should be in a position where from day to day he does not have to take a position or take a stand without the best advice, without the best counsel, without the best guidance he can muster.'[23] The group must have been pleased with the endorsement of the premier of Ontario – although some, no doubt, wondered why others in the room had been included – as they set about 'interpreting the concern of Ontario,' which the Ontario government viewed the same 'as the concern of the country as a whole.'[24]

Guarding the Future: The Confederation of Tomorrow Conference

In the years following Ontario's embarrassment in the negotiations over pensions, the new strategy of focusing on mega-intergovernmental affairs was employed, with varying degrees of success, in discussions over health insurance, tax-sharing agreements, and the process of opting-out. Nowhere was Ontario's new approach more effective, however, than in discussions about the constitution, a topic that clearly lent itself to a broad, foundational approach. In the spring of 1966, the Advisory Committee had suggested that as 'interest in the problems of Confederation ... [reaches] a climax in 1967,' it might be appropriate for the Government of Ontario to sponsor a 'conference on the future of Canadian federalism' in that year.[25] Roberts did not act immediately on the suggestion, but it perhaps remained in the back of his mind when he, seemingly out of the blue, proposed the Confederation of Tomorrow Conference at the end of a very disappointing meeting of the Tax Structure Committee.[26] The conference, held in the fall of 1967, showcased the skill of Ontario's intergovernmental affairs bureaucracy and the effectiveness of the approach that had been being perfected over the previous three years.

Roberts's comments at the federal-provincial conference had perhaps been made in haste, and perhaps had been thrown out to antagonize the federal government, but there was no question that he was serious. In addition to making his intentions known to a group of Montreal businessmen later that fall, he also announced the conference in the Ontario legislature in January 1967. There, he clarified that the intention was neither to examine fiscal issues nor to 'set about the drafting of a new Constitution,' but rather was 'to examine Confederation as it is today; to take stock after 100 years; to examine the areas of agreement and the areas of disagreement; and to explore what can be done to ensure a strong and united Canada.'[27] As the *Globe and Mail* editorialized, 'Somebody had to start the discussion, and it is fitting that Ontario, a founding province, should do so.'[28]

The prime minister was less certain. Pearson wrote Roberts immediately to express 'some points of concern,' most of which revolved around the appropriateness of a province calling what appeared to be a federal-provincial conference. Pearson's recollection of Roberts's October 1966 announcement of his conference intentions was that he was planning to discuss the 'working of Confederation' at one of the annual premiers conferences. To discover through the Ontario Throne Speech that Roberts was inviting all the first ministers – including the prime minister – to a meeting to discuss the future of Confederation was something of a surprise. 'I think I am right,' Pearson wrote, 'in saying that there is no precedent for a Federal-Provincial Conference being called by a provincial government.' While not wanting to stymie Robarts's initiative, Pearson nevertheless wondered if it might not be possible for Ontario to simply propose an item 'for possible inclusion on the agenda' of the next first ministers conference.[29] Robarts tried 'to allay any feelings of disquiet and alarm' by assuring the prime minister that he had no intention of holding a traditional federal-provincial conference. What he envisioned was 'a meeting of minds, in a relaxed atmosphere, where representatives of all our people could enter upon a great discussion of all the elements involved, and bring about an intelligent and fruitful approach to the points of view put forward for examination. Within the framework, it should be possible to come to certain conclusions and to endeavour to determine what can be done.'[30] It would have been difficult for Pearson to miss the implication that the approach taken at recent, acrimonious, intergovernmental meetings was far from 'intelligent and fruitful.' Although Pearson tried to derail the conference by offering one of his own, the die was already cast.[31]

Quebec premier Daniel Johnson was the first to voice his enthusiasm for the scheme. Like the *Globe and Mail*, he appreciated that it was the premier of one of the original provinces that proposed such a conference, congratulated Robarts for taking 'an enlightened step,' and pledged his province's full participation.[32] His intergovernmental affairs deputy minister Claude Morin echoed that sentiment, and 'expressed the hope fervently' that this would be the first of a series of conferences. His argument was that 'the Quebec people would feel compelled to present a complete statement of their desires at any one-shot conference which might result in a complete breakdown of any constructive work.'[33] It was a somewhat ominous judgment that reminded the Ontario public servants of the many complexities they faced in planning and orchestrating this conference. With enthusiasm and expectations high, and the cost of failure perhaps even higher, the Federal-Provincial Affairs Secretariat began its preparations for the fall gathering.

Without any precedent to guide them, the civil servants were free to design the conference in a variety of different ways. It could be small, like a first ministers conference, or could include 'larger delegations of senior civil servants and outside advisers.' The advantage of the former was that there was more chance 'for meaningful discussion,' while the latter was appealing in terms of the optics it would present for the press. Should it be at a university or a hotel? With formal opening statements or 'more of a seminar-style discussion'? An agenda that included 'little more than statements of the problems' or, as Morin suggested, 'planned on the assumption that there would be a series of conferences'?[34] These were difficult questions, and the answers to each would have an effect on the success of the conference both as an event and as a first step in solving the problems of Confederation.

Each of the provincial premiers also had to be approached delicately, a job that fell to the secretariat. While Quebec's Johnson had already expressed his enthusiasm for the conference, the formal letter of invitation nevertheless had to be carefully constructed. Ed Greathed of the secretariat suggested that 'the position of this province in Confederation and the whole question of English–French relations are obvious tacks' to take in the invitation. That approach obviously would be less appropriate in Alberta and Saskatchewan, where 'both Mr. Manning and Mr. Thatcher have been skeptical of any "deux nations" theory.' For those letters, Greathed suggested that it might be best to emphasize 'our awareness of their relative geographical isolation and the advantages of having their specific ideas on how to achieve a more equitable relationship between their provinces and central Canada.' Premier Roblin of Manitoba might be solicited through emphasis on 'the outlook he shares with Mr. Robarts about French-Canadians' outside Quebec. In drafting the letters to the Maritime premiers, Greathed proposed underlining their 'place *vis a vis* the rest of Canada.'[35] In suggesting these different approaches, Greathed was utilizing a skill that would continue to be important to the Federal-Provincial Affairs Secretariat – an intimate knowledge of the goals and aspirations of each of the other provinces.

By the end of the summer, the secretariat had effectively laid out all the questions that would need to be addressed in preparation for the conference, and had set up a planning committee to try to work out some of the answers. For much of September, the group wrestled with where to hold the conference, choosing someone other than Robarts to act as chair of the gathering, determining the extent of press coverage that was both appropriate and desirable, and finalizing the letters of invitation to all the premiers. They also repeatedly noted the need to travel to the other provincial capitals to conduct some initial reconnaissance so that the host province could anticipate some of the actions of the others once the conference itself opened.[36] This kind of intelligence was a crucial component of the work of the secretariat, and was a key to revitalizing the Ontario bureaucracy. Familiarity with the approaches that other provincial delegations would use was one way to control the outcome of the conference and, having been sidelined during other intergovernmental opportunities, having some control was considered a positive change.

To that end, members of the secretariat – often with people from other departments in tow – fanned out across the country to both lay the groundwork for a successful conference and gather as much intelligence as possible about what was going on in other provincial capitals. Ian Macdonald and Ed Greathed conducted the western tour, with Deputy Attorney General Keith Reynolds joining the group in Winnipeg because his counterpart in Manitoba 'seemed interested' in the Confederation of Tomorrow Conference, whereas 'most of the others would not be actively involved.'[37] The Conservatives in Manitoba were heading towards a leadership convention, guaranteeing that Premier Roblin would no longer be in office by the time of the conference, and this fact no doubt dampened their enthusiasm for the plan the Ontario visitors were trying to sell. As the clerk of the executive council informed Greathed and Reynolds quite clearly, 'Little, if any, thought about the CTC has been given by anyone in the Manitoba Government.'[38]

The meetings unfolded quite differently the further west the Ontario secretariat went. In Saskatchewan, Ian Macdonald and Greathed met with civil servants and had no opportunity to discuss any of the proposals with Premier Ross Thatcher. The public servants were concerned about the proposed discussion of 'linguistic and cultural duality' that 'implied the existence of that duality,' something that Saskatchewan was not yet ready to concede, and were curious about the options that had been provided as possible forms of Canadian federalism. In general, though, it appeared that Thatcher had not shown them the formal letter of invitation, and they were thus 'surprised' by much of what the Ontarians had planned. That the conference would be open to the press, for example, was especially surprising.[39] In Alberta, in contrast, it was clear that Premier Ernest Manning had 'given considerable thought' to the form and function of the conference, and willingly spent more than an hour with Macdonald and Greathed. It was, apparently, 'a fascinating interview during which the Premier did most of the talking.'[40] He expounded on the need to recognize that Canada included a large number of people who were neither English or French, his distaste for any 'special status' for Quebec, his objection to an entrenched bill of rights, and his scepticism about establishing any more formal intergovernmental institutions. He was, unlike his colleagues in Saskatchewan, 'strongly in favour of an "open" conference suggesting that it was time for these issues to be discussed candidly and publicly.'[41] Manning's enthusiasm for the open nature of the conference might have caused the Ontario Finance staff some concern: while they were pleased with the amount of thought he had given to the invitation, it was 'equally evident that he has reached a number of firm positions on these issues and that he is fully prepared to discuss these with zest and candour next month.'[42]

The east coast tour got off to a bad start. Fog kept the Ontario delegates out of Halifax, so they missed their meeting with Nova Scotia officials. Both the weather and the attitudes seemed to have cleared up somewhat by the time they reached St John's, where 'the attitude in Newfoundland toward the Confederation of Tomorrow Conference appears to have undergone a complete change for the better.' Colourful premier Joey Smallwood would definitely be attending, although he might be content to 'sit back and listen.' In Prince Edward Island, the officials were 'sympathetic to the Conference' and prepared to participate in it fully, despite some reservations about its 'public aspect.'[43] The New Brunswick meeting was also plagued with some bad luck, and the Ontario delegation was down to only one person by the time of the Fredericton discussion. Perhaps talking only to one person – chair of the planning sub-committee S.W. Clarkson – emboldened the five New Brunswick officials, all of whom were 'very critical of the whole concept of the Conference.' They echoed Ottawa's line, arguing that a province ought not to have called the conference in the first place, invoking imagery of 'parents, children and who had the authority' that Clarkson 'did not fully understand.' They expressed concern about official languages, an issue that Premier Robichaud was confronting at that moment during his campaign for re-election, and about the hearings being public. They also suggested that each provincial delegation should include the leaders of Opposition parties, which appealed to Clarkson in some ways. He thought it might be a way for 'those provinces that are fearful of publicity' to determine a way to 'speak with one voice at the Conference and everything can then be said openly.'[44]

Thanks to weather and scheduling problems, separate junkets were made to Victoria, Halifax, and Quebec City. In British Columbia, Keith Reynolds was met by officials who had not seen the letter of invitation to Premier W.A.C. Bennett and 'appeared to be disinterested in the Conference.' By the end of the fact-finding mission, they were warming to the idea, but were hardly bubbling with enthusiasm.[45] In Nova Scotia, the officials with whom Ed Greathed met were well informed about the objectives of the conference and were prepared to discuss details of the physical arrangements and the agenda.[46] The most important visit, however, was to Quebec City, and only the most senior and experienced of the Ontario officials were entrusted with the mission. Ian Macdonald and Don Stevenson met with three of their counterparts just a month before the Confederation of Tomorrow Conference was scheduled to open. Clearly, 'the Quebec people believe that the ... Conference offers the best opportunity for the province to outline in a comprehensive fashion its views on Confederation.' To that end, Johnson had apparently already prepared a forty-page opening statement, and the officials 'hoped that the proposed agenda might be adjusted somewhat to allow for a longer presentation by Mr Johnson.' It was a minor point of friction in an otherwise smooth meeting between officials, and suggested that the secretariat had thus far done an effective job of laying the groundwork.[47]

In addition to the Federal-Provincial Affairs Secretariat, the Advisory Committee on Confederation also had an important role to play in the preparations for the full conference. They were consulted on the content of Robarts's introductory statement, and were kept apprised of the progress of the cross-Canada consultations and the agenda's development.[48] They also weighed in on the role that Robarts should be playing at the conference, where it was looking more and more likely that he would have to be not only host but chair. While John Meisel thought that 'Robarts would have to use the Socratic approach,' Donald Creighton thought that there might be conflict between encouraging compromise from the chair but adopting an alternative position as one of the provinces, and Paul Fox thought that 'Ontario was obliged to act as an intermediary to some extent.'[49] Getting the professors to agree on a position was difficult, although their skill at laying out the various alternatives was impressive.

As the opening day of the conference loomed closer, members of all the various groups involved in the planning process began to give increasing consideration to the possible implications of hosting such an event, suggesting that people were beginning to acknowledge the wide-ranging significance that the Confederation of Tomorrow Conference might hold. First, there was concern about whether the die was now cast for a provincially-sponsored discussion of constitutional issues. Robarts himself thought that Johnson might host the next 'Confederation of Tomorrow Conference,' and Eugene Forsey 'hoped that a federal initiative for future meetings might not be excluded,' although others worried that that would mean that 'Ontario would lose control.'[50] The planners seemed to be divided on whether to relinquish the idea of an informal discussion of mutual goals, but it was clear that all involved recognized that Ontario was taking a clear leadership role in opening this discussion. As John Meisel noted, giving voice to a frequently thought but rarely articulated idea, 'in speaking for Ontario, the Hon. Mr. Robarts would be speaking for Canada.' The premier, wisely, 'wondered about getting into such a position,'[51] and later Paul Fox thought it better to offer 'Ontario as a "link" in Canadian federalism.'[52] Nevertheless, the debates that the officials and the participants were engaging in suggested a clear recognition of the importance of what was about to happen.

In opening the conference on 27 November, Robarts identified the gathering as 'an historic occasion.' He then proceeded to identify the provenance of the conference, and his hope that it would be an informal discussion of a number of matters upon which the provinces both agreed and disagreed. And then, speaking as the premier of Ontario, he offered his own introductory remarks, which were both disarmingly simple and clearly reflected the orientation of the Ontario officials within and associated with the Federal-Provincial Affairs Secretariat: 'Canada is a federal state, not a unitary state ... [The] provinces were created, and exist, in recognition of regional differences ... [There] is only one government in Canada which can represent the interests of all Canadians ... We in Ontario have no intention of undermining the place of primacy of the federal government.'[53] Thus, while Ontario obviously had a position on the issues under discussion, the goal was to conduct those conversations implicitly recognizing the role of the federal government, not to diminish it.

Over the course of the three days of meetings, both formal ones under the blazing lights of television cameras and informal ones in the corridors and bars of the brand new Toronto-Dominion Centre (designed by Mies van der Rohe), the premiers both talked and listened and seemed to come away with a better understanding of the problems confronting Canada, if not the solutions. There were some tense moments, but the convivial atmosphere seemed to require that dialogue continue and that hard lines relax.[54] As Don Stevenson commented a few days after the close of the conference, it had been 'noteworthy because of the spirit of compromise that was evoked.'[55] The conference was an enormous success. Federal constitutional adviser Carl Goldenberg personally congratulated Robarts for his 'expert handling' of the event. 'There is general agreement,' he wrote, 'that you deserve the credit for the feeling that with goodwill and continued effort Confederation may yet be saved.'[56] The newspaper accounts were also glowing, with the *Globe and*

Mail identifying 'an emerging will to unity,' and complimenting the premiers for acting, 'at last, as if they had a show on the road.'[57]

Relinquishing Guardianship

But the organizers never imagined that the provinces would have the last say on constitutional issues: as Robarts declared after the fact, 'We believe that our decision to call the Confederation of Tomorrow Conference made it possible for the federal government, if it chose to, to resume its primary role in these matters, and I think that events have proved us to be correct.'[58] Long before the opening of the Confederation of Tomorrow Conference, Pearson had announced that the federal government would be convening a full federal-provincial conference on the constitution that would begin in February 1968. There was considerable evidence that the federal officials had been impressed with the results of Ontario's efforts. The assistant deputy minister of finance in Ottawa, Al Johnson, was able to identify a number of very positive outcomes of the meeting, many of them of interest to Ottawa as the federal government considered its ongoing role in the constitutional amendment process. As Johnson reported, 'there was an awakening to the seriousness of the problem,' and the premiers, far from focusing on individual concerns, had 'managed to identify a number of national goals' relating to the economy, equalization, and language rights. He also noted that 'a willingness developed to open up the whole constitutional issue for discussion' and that some provinces, at least, had noted the 'need for the federal presence.'[59] He understood that the Ontario initiative had not foreclosed the opportunity for Ottawa to resume its rightful place at the helm of constitutional discussions.

This left Ontario in something of a quandary. On the one hand, the conference could not have been a greater success. But now the Federal-Provincial Affairs Secretariat was left wondering where to proceed next. A Continuing Committee on Confederation had been struck at the conclusion of the conference, with representatives including the premiers of Nova Scotia, Alberta, Quebec, and Ontario. Although 'all governments, federal and provincial, will be consulted by the Committee,' its existence nevertheless gave the distinct impression that the provinces were now running the show. This was not exactly what the Ontario Finance officials envisioned. Perhaps, Ed Greathed argued, another member should be added to the committee – a representative of the federal government.[60] And in contemplating the work of the committee, it quickly became apparent that 'only Ontario and Quebec (and the federal government if it becomes a member of the Committee) have the organizations and staffs necessary to conduct the research,' a situation that itself raised a number of concerns about representativeness and fairness of workload.[61] Finally, there was the question of how the group intended to approach the three topics that had been identified for consideration – 'constitutional change, regional disparities and linguistic practices and rights. There will be a temptation to focus on the constitutional change question,' wrote Greathed, but he thought 'this bias should be resisted.'[62] Within barely more than a week of the closing of this most successful of conferences, then, Ontario was wrestling with the problem of where to go next.

So, too, was Ottawa. The conference that had been announced in May 1967 for February 1968 was originally intended simply 'to reach an agreement on the enactment of the provisions of the Canadian Bill of Rights in each province as an ordinary statute.' Over time, it transformed into an increasingly major undertaking, and by the fall of 1967 was being described as a conference to discuss not only entrenching a Bill of Rights in the constitution, but also opening the agenda 'to any and all suggestions of the participating provinces with regard to constitutional problems.'[63] Ontario's Finance officials struggled with what to make of such an 'open-ended and unstructured' conference, worrying that if Ottawa made a series of concrete proposals, then the provinces would be forced into a position, once again, of simply reacting to a federal initiative. And that, warned Gary Posen, might then leave Ontario as nothing more than 'a bystander in an Ottawa-Quebec struggle.'[64]

But whatever happened next was largely beyond Ontario's control; Ottawa had resumed its position in the constitutional dialogue. The conference of February 1968 was crucial on a number of different levels. Despite efforts to keep the tone conciliatory, the conference included a rancorous exchange between Justice Minister Pierre Trudeau and Quebec Premier Johnson that helped propel the former into the prime minister's office two months later and marked the beginning of a long series of constitutional conferences. Posen's concerns were well founded, for as Robarts said at the time, 'That's the end of Ontario's role as a helpful middle man. From here on in, it is going to be a battle between two varieties of French-speaking Quebeckers.'[65] Ontario's role certainly changed, but in many ways that had been the goal of the Ontario officials from the outset. From the earliest efforts to build a civil service that would be prepared for the unexpected in intergovernmental relations, to the extensive work of the Federal-Provincial Affairs Secretariat to build bridges between provinces and between policy portfolios, to the extraordinary success in spearheading mega-constitutional change in Canada, the Ontario government had been striving to secure a coherent, equitable intergovernmental relationship across all governments in Canada. Giving the federal government a nudge in that direction in 1967 was enough to start the whole process. The constitutional conference of 1968 finally ended in failure in Victoria in 1971, resumed in the late 1970s, to culminate in the patriation of the constitution in 1982, and began anew in the search for inclusiveness with the Meech Lake Accord of 1987 and the Charlottetown Accord of 1992. In some ways, our constitutional dialogue continues even today, although the voices are quiet and feel peripheral. That it has not broken down, and continues to be a dialogue and not a debate, finds its genesis in the work of a remarkable generation of public servants working in the Ministry of Finance of the government of Ontario.

NOTES

1 J.L. Granatstein, *The Ottawa Men: The Civil Service Mandarins, 1935–1957* (Toronto: Oxford University Press, 1982).
2 On the latter, see Donald Savoie, *Breaking the Bargain: Public Servants, Ministers, and Parliament* (Toronto: University of Toronto Press, 2003).
3 See papers by Don Tansley, Ken Rasmussen, Murray Knutilla, and Gregory P. Marchildon at http://www.uregina.ca/gspp/marchildon/symposium/douglas_symposium; A.W. Johnson, *Dream No Little Dream: A Biography of the Douglas Government of Saskatchewan, 1944–1961* (Toronto: University of Toronto Press, 2004); and Lisa Pasolli, 'Bureaucratizing the Atlantic Revolution: The Saskatchewan Mafia and the Modernization of the New Brunswick Civil Service, 1960–1970,' MA thesis, University of New Brunswick, 2007.
4 Claude Morin, *Quebec versus Ottawa: The Struggle for Self-Government, 1960–72* (Toronto: University of Toronto Press, 1976).
5 See A.K. McDougall, *Robarts: His Life and Government* (Toronto: University of Toronto Press, 1986), 75–92 and Steve Paikin, *Public Triumph, Private Tragedy: The Double Life of John P. Robarts* (Toronto: Viking Canada, 2005), 33–57.
6 Archives of Ontario (AO), Office of the Premier: Robarts general correspondence, RG 3-26, box 287, file: Premier's Conference, Victoria BC, 1962 – Portable Pensions. 'Notes on Portable Pensions for the Use of the Hon. John P. Robarts ... Aug. 6th and 7th, 1962.'

7 AO, RG 3-26, vol. 403, file: Pensions – Portable, Mar.–May 1962, Robert
   Clark to Robarts, 26 April 1962; AO, RG 3-42, box 13, file: Provincial Premiers Conference, Aug. 1962, pp. 127–39.

8 AO, George Gathercole Papers, MU 5332, Acc. 12401, file: Portable Pensions, correspondence, 1963. Gathercole to Robarts, 8 May 1963; Gathercole
   to John Connolly, 1 May 1963.

9 Library and Archives Canada (LAC), Department of National Health and
   Welfare Papers, RG 29, vol. 2114, file: 23-3-6. Draft minutes, 'Canada Pension Plan, Federal Provincial Conference, Quebec, April 1, 1964,' pp. 3–4.

10 Ibid., 4.

11 LAC, Peter Stursberg Papers, vol. 33 file: Tom Kent, 1977, interview.

12 LAC, Walter Gordon Papers, vol. 16, file: Pearson, Rt. Hon. L.B. – Correspondence and memos. Gordon to Pearson, 15 April 1964.

13 McDougall, *John P. Robarts*, 133; Wayne Austin Hunt, 'The Federal-Provincial
   Conference of First Ministers, 1960–1976,' unpublished PhD dissertation
   (University of Toronto, 1982), Hunt's interview with Robarts, 25 September
   1978.

14 AO, Cabinet Office Papers, RG 75-21-0-20, box 3, file H.I. Macdonald. 'The
   Role of Ontario in the Formation of National Policy,' 8 March 1974.

15 Interviews with Gary Posen, 23 January 2007; H. Ian Macdonald, 25 January 2007.

16 AO, Department of Finance, Policy Division Subject Files, RG 6-44, UF 34,
   file: Federal-Provincial Relations, Enquiries. Stevenson to Richard Simeon,
   16 March 1967.

17 AO, RG 3-26, box 490, file: Federal-Provincial Conference, Ottawa, 13–16
   October 1964. Economics Branch, Department of Economics and Development, 'Notes for the Federal-Provincial Tax Structure Committee,' 29 July
   1964.

18 Ibid., box 393, file: Federal-Provincial Tax-Sharing Agreements, '61–'65.
   'Submission by the Treasurer of Ontario to the Second Federal-Provincial
   Conference of Finance and Treasury Ministers on Economic Problems,'
   9 December 1965.

19 AO, Gathercole Papers, MU 5311, file: correspondence, 1965–71. Ontario
   Advisory Committee on Confederation, terms of reference, 5 January 1965.

20 Ibid.

21 The original committee members were Alexander Brady (Political Economy, University of Toronto); John Conway (Humanities, York University);
   Donald Creighton (History, University of Toronto); Richard Dillon (Engineering, University of Western Ontario); Eugene Forsey (Political Science,
   Carleton); Paul Fox (Political Economy, University of Toronto); George

Gathercole (Vice-Chair, Ontario Hydro); Bora Laskin (Law, University of Toronto); W.R. Lederman (Law, Queen's University); C.R. Magone (Lawyer); Lucien Matté (President, University of Sudbury); John Meisel (Political Studies, Queen's University); R.C. McIvor (Economics, McMaster University); Edward McWhinney (Law, University of Toronto); Harvey Perry (Canadian Tax Foundation); Roger Seguin (lawyer); T.H.B. Symons (President, Trent University). See AO, Gathercole Papers, MU 5311, file: correspondence, 1965–71: Ontario Advisory Committee on Confederation, terms of reference, 5 January 1965.

22 Interview, H. Ian Macdonald, 25 January 2007.

23 AO, Gathercole Papers, MU 5325. Verbatim report of the proceedings of the Ontario Advisory Committee on Confederation meeting, 19 March 1965, 6.

24 Ibid.

25 AO, RG 3-26, vol. 466, file: Ont. Advisory Committee on Confederation, Jan 67– Jun 67. Macdonald to Robarts, 13 May 1966.

26 Simeon, *Federal-Provincial Diplomacy: The Making of Recent Policy in Canada* (Toronto: University of Toronto Press, 1972), 84.

27 Private collection, *Canadian Annual Review* (CAR) files, 'Statement by the Hon. John Robarts …,' 25 January 1967; Throne Speech, 25 January 1967.

28 'Government by Evolution,' *Globe and Mail*, 26 January 1967.

29 AO, Gathercole Papers, MU 5311, file: Correspondence, 1965–71. Pearson to Robarts, 26 January 1967.

30 Ibid., Robarts to Pearson, 1 February 1967.

31 AO, Subject files of the executive assistant to H. Ian Macdonald, RG 9-79, box 2, file: Confederation of Tomorrow Conference. Pearson to Robarts, 28 February 1967, and Pearson to all other premiers, 28 February 1967. Premier Johnson of Quebec did not, apparently, 'like Mr. Pearson's suggestion of a short informal meeting without advisers,' and the idea fell apart almost as soon as it was floated. AO, RG 3-26, box 517, file: Provinces, Quebec, 1966–67, Macdonald to Robarts, 20 March 1967.

32 AO, RG 9-79, box 2, file: Confederation of Tomorrow Conference. Johnson to Robarts, 16 March 1967.

33 AO, RG 3-26, box 517, file: Provinces, Quebec, 1966–67. Macdonald to Robarts, 20 March 1967.

34 AO, RG 9-79, box 2, file: Confederation of Tomorrow Conference. Stevenson memo, 'Confederation of Tomorrow Conference,' 3 April 1967.

35 Ibid., Greathed to Stevenson, 17 August 1967.

36 Ibid., Minutes of the first plenary session of the planning committee …, 25 August 1967; Progress report of the agenda sub-committee, 5 September

1967; Minutes of the second plenary meeting ..., 8 September 1967; 2nd
progress report of the agenda sub-committee, 11 September 1967; Minutes
of the 3rd plenary meeting ..., 11 September 1967; Minutes of the 4th plenary meeting ..., 26 September 1967.
37 Ibid., Stevenson to file, 13 September 1967.
38 AO, RG 3-26, box 444, file: Confederation of Tomorrow Conference, Background papers, 1967. Notes on meeting held in Winnipeg, 10 October 1967.
39 Ibid., Notes on meeting with officials in Regina, 12 October 1967.
40 AO, RG 9-79, box 2, file: Confederation of Tomorrow Conference. Notes on
a meeting with Premier E.C. Manning, 13 October 1967.
41 Ibid.
42 Ibid.
43 AO, RG 3-26, box 444, file: Confederation of Tomorrow Conference, Ontario Government, Sept.–Oct. 1967. Posen to Stevenson, 16 October 1967.
44 Ibid., Clarkson to file, 16 October 1967.
45 AO, RG 9-79, box 2, file: Confederation of Tomorrow Conference. Minutes
of the seventh plenary meeting of the planning committee ..., 24 October
1967.
46 AO, RG 3-26, box 444, file: Confederation of Tomorrow Conference, Ontario Government, Sept.–Oct. 1967. Notes on a meeting held with officials
in Halifax, 27 October 1967.
47 AO, RG 9-79, box 2, file: Confederation of Tomorrow Conference. Team
Visit to Quebec, 26 October 1967.
48 AO, Gathercole Papers, MU 5311, file: Notices and Agendas, 1967. Minutes
of the meeting of the fiscal and economic sub-committee ..., 24 October
1967; Minutes of the plenary session of the Ontario Advisory Committee
on Confederation, 24 October 1967.
49 AO, Gathercole Papers, MU 5311, file: Notices and Agendas, 1967. Minutes
of the plenary session of the Ontario Advisory Committee on Confederation, 24 October 1967.
50 AO, RG 3-26, box 444, file: Confederation of Tomorrow Conference, Ontario Government, Nov.–Dec. 1967. Meeting of the Confederation Committee, 10 November 1967.
51 Ibid.
52 Ibid., box 445, file: Confederation of Tomorrow Conference – Correspondence – Requests – Ontario Government – Jan. 1967. Fox to Macdonald,
17 November 1967.
53 CAR Papers, Statement by the Honourable John P. Robarts, Prime Minister
of Ontario, to the Confederation of Tomorrow Conference, 27 November
1967.

54 P.E. Bryden, 'The Ontario-Quebec Axis: Postwar Strategies in Intergovern-
    mental Negotiations,' in *Ontario Since Confederation: A Reader*, ed. Edgar-
    André Montigny and Lori Chambers (Toronto: University of Toronto Press,
    2000).
55 AO, RG 3-26, box 444, file: Confederation of Tomorrow Conference, On-
    tario Government, Nov.–Dec. 1967. Donald Stevenson, Follow-up on the
    Constitutional Questions Raised at the Confederation of Tomorrow Con-
    ference, 4 December 1967.
56 AO, John Robarts Papers, Series F-15-4-3, box 2, MU 7998, file: Golden-
    berg, Carl, 1967–69, Goldenberg to Robarts, 4 December 1967.
57 Quoted in *Canadian Annual Review for 1967*, ed. John Saywell (Toronto:
    University of Toronto Press, 1968), 91.
58 *Ontario Legislative Debates*, 27 February 1968, 263.
59 LAC, Department of Finance Papers, RG 19, vol. 4720, file: 5517-04(68/1)-
    1. A.W. Johnson, Summary of a talk on the Confederation of Tomorrow
    Conference, 4 December 1967.
60 AO, Department of Finance Papers, Deputy Minister's General Corres-
    pondence, RG 6-14, box 118, file: Continuing Committee on Confederation.
    Greathed to Stevenson, 8 December 1967.
61 Ibid.
62 Ibid.
63 Ibid., box 113, file: Constitutional: Federal-Provincial Conference, Feb.
    1968. Gary Posen to Greathed, 13 December 1967.
64 Ibid., Posen and Bob Metcalfe, 'How Ontario might approach the federal-
    provincial conference called for the beginning of February,' circa mid-
    December 1967.
65 Private collection, Donald W. Stevenson Papers, 'Notes for use by Don
    Stevenson at the Federal-Provincial Conference simulation, University of
    Waterloo, December 12, 1988.'

5 From Pragmatism to Neoliberalism: Ontario's Hesitant Farewell to Dr Keynes

BRYAN EVANS AND JOHN SHIELDS

John Maynard Keynes came to Ontario on a number of occasions as he helped the British government navigate the deep waters of wartime financing. His destination was Ottawa, where he cajoled and convinced the Mackenzie King government that Canada had a duty and a stake in ensuring the financial health of the United Kingdom. Keynes even celebrated the 250th anniversary of the Bank of England with a sumptuous dinner at the Chateau Laurier in July 1944. The records do not show that he ever stayed in Toronto or met with Ontario government officials, but the influence of his thought certainly left a legacy.[1] Ontario's Ministry of Finance – the key bureaucratic institution charged with navigating the politics-economics interface for government and society – operated in a rapidly transforming macroeconomic context from the post–Second World War period until the turn of the new millennium. The MOF was both affected by these changes and involved in the government policy response to them. As in most Western economies, the Ministry's approach was in no small part concerned with the application of economic principles associated with Keynes: that government could assume a more important part in the economy without harming the presence of the business sector and that government had a duty in actively redistributing resources so as to minimize risk and expand opportunity. The key objective was to stabilize the business cycle and to ensure steady social and economic progress through public investments.

Ontario's post-war experience was an on-again, off-again invitation to apply the ideas of Keynes. And this was particularly evident as the post-war 'Golden Age' of prosperity began to wane in the early 1970s. This chapter documents the importance of the rise, consolidation, and decline of the Keynesian policy paradigm and its eclipse by new political forces and, by extension, policy agendas. The opening and closing of the invitation are documented by how evolving political party commitments and ideological orientations, the changes in political administrations over this period, and their influence over economic and fiscal policy shaped the intellectual response of the Government of Ontario towards the economy. In this sense 'economic realities' were inevitably 'politically mediated.' Documents such as budgets, which MOF officials play key roles in developing, sent 'signal[s] to officials where their own and where other governments intend[ed] to go.'[2]

Ontario's post-war embrace of Keynesian policy approaches was driven by a pragmatic sensibility to urbanization, industrialization, and the demands of a politically mobilized working class. It was also marked by a generalized societal demand that economic stability and growth be central to any government's policy agenda. This pragmatic Keynesianism began to unravel as controlling inflation displaced unemployment as the primary policy challenge in the early 1970s. The incremental building of a broadly, perhaps even loosely, Keynesian-informed paradigm began to unravel as what would come to be called neoliberal perspectives in matters of economic policy and public administration ascended towards orthodoxy. The turn to neoliberalism was also incremental through the 1970s, 1980s, and early 1990s.

The term neoliberalism is used here rather than neoconservatism to capture the reality that what was called for was not a 'conservative' order, but a new one. Friedrich Hayek, the intellectual paragon of market liberalism, used to explain that he could not be a 'conservative' because he preferred 'drastic' and 'fundamental' change to stop the march of the welfare state.[3] The neoliberal alternative was composed of a policy mix of 'privatization, market liberalization and deregulation ... to roll back the frontiers of the state, and to maximize the opportunities for entrepreneurship, competition and profit.'[4] Neoliberalism consequently emerged as an alternative to the post-war order by proposing 'the restructuring of capitalism ... to provide a means by which capital could begin to disengage from many of the positions and commitments which had been taken up during the Keynesian era.'[5] For these reasons, the term 'neoliberalism' has tended to supplant 'neoconservatism' in characterizing the substantive changes in the role of the state towards social and economic management since the 1980s.

Keynes's Tories: The 'Red' Tory Dynasty, 1945–1985

The Conservative party of the 1940s onward was both transformer and sustainer of the modest post-war Keynesian 'revolution' in Ontario. During the four decades after the Second World War it dominated the political landscape of Ontario and undertook the project of building the post-war redistributive welfare state and managing the macroeconomic crisis of the mid-1970s. Keynes, in other words, had an open invitation. The decade of the 1970s was formative, as it was during this period that the leadership of Ontario's Progressive Conservatives found itself having to rethink this model and begin to consider, and even implement, policies of a neoliberal orientation. In the context of social struggles and economic change, the political terrain of Ontario would shift, and eventually so too would the state's administrative machinery.

The PCs under George Drew, Leslie Frost, John Robarts, and Bill Davis took full advantage of an Ontario that delivered prosperity and political stability in this 'postwar golden age of capitalism.' Through this period, average real growth stood at nearly 5 per cent per year, and real per capita income tripled between 1939 and 1975. Hundreds of thousands of semi-skilled jobs were created in Ontario's burgeoning manufacturing sector. Such prolonged prosperity provided the foundation for the Ontario Conservatives' electoral success for from 1945 to 1971 as Ontario's contented voters rewarded the party with unbroken legislative majorities.[6]

The robust economy allowed the province to expand the range and scope of public services and goods. Provincial government expenditures, expressed as a percentage of Gross Provincial Product, grew from a minuscule 3.08 per cent in 1947 to 16.28 per cent in 1985,[7] the year the Tories fell from power. Between 1945 and the early 1970s provincial government spending increased in real terms from $73 to $324 per capita.[8] David Foot's analysis of the period has demonstrated that the expansion of the public sector was driven by population growth and rising levels of per capita income. This provided the foundations, in terms of both public finance and political impetus, to stimulate the growth of public services. Rapid urbanization, in particular, had a discernible effect on the growth in public expenditures in health care and income maintenance.[9]

From 1945 to the early 1970s total government expenditures in Ontario for such core public goods as education, health, and welfare tripled, increasing from 4 per cent of GPP to more than 13 per cent. Economists of the 1950s and early 1960s concluded that Ontario's improving productivity was a function of 'better health, improved training, and attainment of higher levels of education ... Thus arose the notion that investments in 'human capital' were possibly important sources of economic growth.'[10]

The size of the core public administration also grew. The number of functional departments composing the Ontario government rose from 20 in 1950 to 25 by 1968 and again increasing to 27 by 1973.[11] Employment in the Ontario public service expanded dramatically from 11,368 persons in 1947 to 75,770 in 1970, and by 1985 the number of direct Ontario public-service staff had grown to 80,885.[12] Notwithstanding this expansion of the Ontario public sector, the Conservatives' approach to governance was guided by 'cautious reform,'[13] described as 'a mixture of progressive, centrist policies, good management, and sophisticated electoral strategies, [in which] the machine became well-nigh invincible in its determination to provide Ontarians with solid Tory government.'[14]

Under George Drew's premiership (1943–8) the primary macro-policy objective was 'to assist the industrial development of Ontario' by encouraging 'the exploitation of provincial resources and [the promotion of] energy and highway construction in order to create a favourable investment climate' and to better respond to the demands for social reform emanating from the growing industrial working class.[15] Drew's successor Leslie Frost (1949–61) – who also retained the position of treasurer until 1959 – is credited with establishing the infrastructural foundation of the modern Ontario state. For Frost, education, health, and welfare were three policy fields bundled up under the rubric of 'human betterment.' Their support was predicated upon economic growth and so took a decidedly secondary place to economic development.[16] Indicative of Frost's disposition towards planning, as both premier *and* treasurer, was his belief that 'the budget must do more than lay out anticipated revenues and expenditures for the coming year; it should express the broad objectives of government over a longer term, especially economic growth.'[17] This did not mean there were not significant investments by the province into health, education, and welfare, as expenditures in these policy fields grew from $12.6 million, $15.7 million, and $11.7 million respectively with his first budget in 1944 to $227.6 million, $94.9 million, and $50.7 million in his last year as premier in 1961.[18] The Ontario government's expenditures as a share of the total economy grew from 2.76 per cent to 4.87 per cent during the Frost years.[19]

Frost was dedicated to the notion that economic development could only be achieved through the private sector, but also responded to the notion that the Ontario state had to play a significant role in establishing the infrastructure necessary for capital accumulation. During his administration, provincial spending increased from approximately $300 million annually to over $1 billion. Under his leadership, the size of the civil service would quadruple, from about 7000 employees in 1945 to over 30,000 employees in 1960.[20]

With respect to policy and public expenditure, spending in health, education, and welfare between 1946 and 1971 grew from 3.8 per cent of GPP to 13.1 per cent, representing a 345 per cent increase. In the 1950s Ontario's real expenditures doubled, setting off a significant and apparently unstoppable momentum. They doubled again in each of the subsequent five-year periods.[21] This marked the emergence of what the economist Vernon Lang called the Ontario 'service state' in 1974.[22]

If the Frost administration was identified with economic development, the John Robarts era (1961–71) could be seen as even more concerned with the minimization of the impacts of the business cycle by focusing efforts on the fights against recession and temporary unemployment. The cautious budgetary policies of the early Frost years were replaced by a remarkably bold policy which used the provincial budget as a major instrument to 'manipulate the short-run performance of the provincial economy.'[23] This approach constituted classic Keynesian budgeting practices.

The Robarts era of welfare-state building, assisted in no small part by federal cost-sharing initiatives, was dramatic. The province was now involved in the provision of public housing, legal aid, single-payer medical insurance, and, owing to the advent of the Canada Assistance Plan, a significantly improved level of funding for income maintenance and post-secondary education as well as homes for the aged. Through the 1960s and into the early 1970s Ontario's public expenditures reflected this expansion in state activities, growing from $1.053 billion in 1961–2 to $6.113 billion in 1971–2; the number of Ontario Public Service employees grew over this period from 36,468 to 65,000.[24] Robarts had concluded that Ontario's public service did not possess the 'technical, fiscal, and planning resources necessary' to effectively influence the allocation of public resources.[25] Subsequently, he directed that the Ontario state acquire the necessary technocratic, but especially economic, expertise.

As the signs of an economic slowdown became pronounced and the challenges of growth and complexity manifested themselves in the

early 1970s, it became necessary 'to re-examine the budgetary and decision-making processes at Queen's Park.'[26] The Government of Ontario
focused on its own machinery, creating the Committee on Government
Productivity (COGP) in 1970 to re-examine how the state interacted
with the general economy and to propose new decision-making structures which would provide for greater political control.

The COGP marked the emergence of an awareness of the limits to
public-sector growth, but also incarnated a public administration
'Enlightenment' whereby the incremental rise of technocracy in the
Ontario administrative state had finally established itself as a dominant
force and thereby brought rational planning and the scientific method
to prominence. One internal discussion paper set the context as one
where 'projections of government costs and revenue into the immediate future indicate that costs are rising much faster than revenues. This
implies that government managers should become more financially
conscious for cost factors will loom larger in decisions on proposed
new activities.'[27]

In the words of a later budget paper, the first half of the decade was
noteworthy because 'fiscal policy was guided by conventional Keynesian doctrine ... Expansion of the public sector relative to the size of
the economy during this period was seen to be beneficial and sustainable.'[28] The second half of the 1970s witnessed a reaction to the policy
approach as 'the use of spending and substantial budget deficits to
stimulate the economy during an inflationary period became strongly
suspect.'[29] Consequently, 'the introduction of Ontario's public sector restraint program in 1975 marked the beginning of a new approach to
fiscal policy for the Province.'[30] The numbers in this regard told the
story eloquently: growth in provincial public expenditures slowed significantly from 24.4 per cent in fiscal year 1970/71 to only 6.4 per cent
by 1978/79.[31]

The Ontario budgets of 1969, 1970, and 1971 were increasingly concerned with the containment of inflation and public-sector growth. In
Treasurer Charles McNaughton's last budget of 1970, he noted that 'our
immediate legacy from the 1960s is an economy and a public sector in
Canada that are fundamentally out of balance,' the evidence for which
he cited as 'persistent inflation,' rising expectations, excessive public-
sector growth, and a fiscal mismatch between levels of government.
The solution offered was a continuation of the previous budget's policy
of expenditure control. Also of note in the 1970 budget was an ac-
knowledgment of the increasing proportion of the budget dedicated

to transfer payments to the broader public sector (schools, hospitals, and municipalities) and a recognition that these expenditures were more difficult for the Ontario government to control directly.[32]

While the slowdown in social investment during this period was significant, it was hardly draconian. The Ontario welfare state was still under construction. The post-war tacit 'social compact' between business, labour, and society still resonated in the corridors of the Ontario treasury, as the central thrust of the 1972 budget was concerned with 'regaining full employment.'[33] While the trends were emerging with respect to the financing of social policy, this budget was significant for explicitly linking control of public expenditures with the 'modernization of government' – that is, the implementation of various recommendations made in the third report of the COGP, which would set the stage for the Ministry of Treasury, Economics and Intergovernmental Affairs to play an expanded role in coordination, planning, and the control of expenditures.[34]

This was in stark contrast to the counter-cyclical budget of 1971, wherein the focus was the problem of unemployment.[35] It is worth noting that the provincial unemployment rate in 1971, which Treasurer Darcy McKeough characterized as 'intolerable,' was 4.9 per cent.[36] Janus-like, the 1971 budget looked in two rather different economic policy directions simultaneously, as if the Ontario treasury of the day was uncertain as to which way to move. It was committed to an expansionary policy aimed at regaining full employment while seeking to control public spending, particularly in education and the core public service. The budget of 1971 was in most respects, then, the last gasp of a cohesive Keynesian perspective on economic policy within the Ontario state. Reflecting certain recommendations of the COGP, the budget set out a plan to reorganize and rationalize the Ontario Public Service.[37]

Indeed, the paradigm shift became obvious in the 1974 budget: the Treasurer was unequivocal in expressing 'the most important problem facing us today is inflation.'[38] McKeough's budgets of the mid-1970s would be informed by this shift in focus. His new approach was now to 'bring growing deficits under control by a "freeze" on the size of the civil service and a general halt to spending increases … McKeough believed that the rapid growth of transfer payments and other spending, coupled with the escalation of public sector compensation, had resulted in the misallocation of wealth in Ontario.'[39]

The overarching fiscal policy goal was that 'the expenditures of the Ontario Government as a percentage of the Gross Provincial Product should decline.'[40] The treasurer's conviction was that 'one of the root causes of the current inflation problem in Canada is excessive government spending and unnecessary growth in the size and complexity of the public sector.'[41] If one can point to a defining moment in post-war politics and the history of public policy and management in Ontario when the state 'changed its mind' (to use Michael Pusey's words), the 1975 budget would be a turning point: the government was showing Dr Keynes the door.[42] The long post-war boom had come to an end in the mid-1970s. Between 1980 and 1994, average family incomes in Canada increased by only half of one per cent, while 'families are working more hours collectively, earning lower real incomes, and losing a higher proportion of their declining real incomes to taxes.'[43] In this context, the political turbulence that emerged first in 1975 can be understood as indicative of a changing socio-economic landscape.

Budget Paper 'C' of the 1977 budget, 'Towards a Balanced Budget,' was unequivocal in making expenditure control central, stating that 'deliberate expenditure control in the government sector is of central importance to Ontario's long-range fiscal and economic planning. It contributed to the economic stability of the province by restoring a more appropriate public-private sector balance.'[44] With the aid of a Special Program Review, designed to help find ways to curtail government growth, the budgets of 1976 and 1977 revealed that Ontario indeed had turned a corner. Between 1975–6 and 1982–3, Ontario government expenditures as a percentage of GPP fell year after year.[45]

The establishment of the Ontario Business Advisory Council in 1977 was important for helping to solidify the shift in government thinking towards a post-Keynesian world. At the advisory committee's inaugural meeting on 15 April 1977, Premier Bill Davis noted that the key to policy should be to focus on the efficient and effective use of resources, stating, 'We must go for growth or the redistribution game is over.'[46] The minutes of the committee meetings reveal the schizophrenic nature of economic policy thinking at that moment when the state was just beginning to 'change its mind' in Ontario as neoliberal ideas challenged offices that were still largely dominated by Keynesian thinking. New questions were posed: 'How much government do we require and are we willing to pay for this amount? Or if the politicians, bureaucrats and special interest groups give us "too much" government, how can the uncoordinated majority restrain government growth?'[47] Moreover, with respect to the size of government, the Council suggested a 'return [of] the ratio of non-market to market activity to some base period, say

1965.'[48] One treasury document prepared for a May 1979 meeting of the Advisory Council posed the question of post-Keynesian policy adjustment as follows:

> In the 1970s it has become apparent that fiscal policy by way of general demand stimulation may have limited impact on structural economic problems. Specific, targeted programs can address the problems of certain industries and labour force groups without creating undesirable inflationary side effects which may be inherent in unfocused, across-the-board fiscal policy initiatives.[49]

Premier Bill Davis led the Progressive Conservatives to minority governments in the general elections of 1975 and 1977, suggesting that the grand post-war coalition that had kept the Tories in office since 1943 was coming unglued as a result of the policy of continuous restraint.[50] Given the structural changes to the economy and the challenges this posed for government policy, however, alternative choices appeared to be limited.

The early 1980s witnessed an increasingly aggressive assault on public-sector expenditures as Ontario followed the lead of the federal government's '6 and 5' restraint legislation, designed to contain wage increases in the public sector specifically to 6 per cent in the first year and 5 per cent in the second year of the program.[51] Still, given historical perspective, the rhetoric of restraint was more militant than the actual practice.[52] The final Davis era budget of 1984 continued to constrain public-sector compensation by limiting growth in transfer payments to 5 per cent and freezing the Ontario government's direct operating costs.[53] Treasurer Larry Grossman questioned the entire apparatus of public-services delivery and posed the issue of a greater role for the market in the production and delivery of public goods and services: 'We must now consider the fundamental relationship between the public and private sectors. We must invite more private sector sharing of what has come to be considered as public sector responsibilities ... Given finite taxpayers' dollars we must provide greater latitude.'[54] The constraint program helped reduce inflation from 10.8 per cent in 1981–2 to 6.6 per cent in 1982–3, and then to below 5 per cent in 1983–4.[55]

The provincial state had thus managed to find an acceptable means to bridge the transition from the Keynesian-informed public administration to a new neoliberal order. The party which had successfully led the Keynesian paradigm shift though the 1940s, 1950s and 1960s was

140   Bryan Evans and John Shields

unable to find the political basis for a new 'social contract.' In 1985 the Conservatives fell from political power, opening the door to a more competitive period of electoral contest, in which all three major political parties were able to form governments.

The Liberal and New Democratic Interregnum, 1985–95: Dr Keynes, Please Come Back?

Haddow and Klassen have characterized the Liberal administrations of the 1985–90 period as having 'moved the province significantly to the left.' This was reflected in increases in taxation and public expenditures, and in labour-market policy reforms which touched upon training, occupational health and safety, and workers' compensation. This political shift would also be seen in the creation of a new institution – the Premier's Council – as a mechanism for social bargaining across sectors and classes which made recommendations to create policy-making mechanisms approximating those found in the European 'co-ordinated market economies.'[56]

The decade was a mixed post-Keynesian moment. The Liberal tax-and-spend approach certainly was consistent with some Keynesian principles. The New Democrats would also continue this strategy for the first two years of their mandate. But both Liberals and New Democrats sought to forge a new policy paradigm informed by 'progressive competitiveness,' which explicitly rejected a low-wage economic strategy, maintaining a commitment to Keynesian-era consumption and legitimation strategies, but with an added strong emphasis on investments in human capital to address supply-side labour market blockages.[57]

In the 1985 election, the Liberal Party was able to secure enough seats in the Ontario Legislature to broker a minority government with the formal support of the NDP. The basis for this support was set out in the so-called 'NDP-Liberal Accord,' which set out an ambitious reform program based on campaign themes shared by both parties. Legislative stability was ensured as the agreement stipulated it was to survive for a two-year term 'from the day that the Leader of the Liberal party assumes the office of premier.'[58] As a total agenda, 'the proposed reforms ushered in the most progressive period of change in Ontario history.'[59]

Between 1985 and 1989, the broader Ontario public-sector workforce grew by 131,300 workers, or 15.2 per cent, while the Ontario Public Service expanded by nearly 6000 staff, or 8.8 per cent.[60] These workforce increases accompanied a dramatic increase in provincial public expenditures over same period of nearly 50 per cent.[61] Notwithstanding the expansion of the public sector, the Liberals did little to fundamentally change the Ontario state.[62] They created the Premier's Council to 'steer Ontario into the forefront of economic leadership and technological innovation. The high level council will be chaired by the Premier and include as active participants several cabinet ministers and leaders from business, labour, and post-secondary education.'[63] This institutional innovation may be understood as a mechanism to help guide the Ontario government through change in difficult times.

The Premier's Council observed weakness within the strength of the 1980s boom, noting that 'there are clear signs amid this boom that many of our industries have significant competitive weaknesses in international markets,' and that 'our scientific and technical capability, our education and training performance, and our government policies and programs as presently constituted will not be adequate to the new economic challenges we face.'[64] As one observer of the 'shift' noted, the 'post-Keynesians perceived that simple manipulation of aggregate demand by fiscal and monetary policy could no longer create the conditions for profitable capital accumulation.'[65]

This turn towards progressive competitiveness was not unique to Ontario, but in fact marked an emerging consensus across the Organization for Economic Cooperation and Development countries that 'human resources development policy designed and delivered through corporatist institutions was the essential ingredient in restructuring strategies that would enable high-wage, high-taxation jurisdictions to maintain their standards of living in a global economy.'[66] The ambitious policy agenda, stemming both from the Accord and beyond, was an indication of the emerging sense that the Ontario state had to lead an adaptation to a new reality of globalized hyper-competition and must change itself in order to have the capacity to lead that change.

The Ontario of the late 1980s was a very different place, and more than 'renewal' was necessary. To some of the public servants of the Ontario state, a different kind of organization was required.[67] Despite the robust economy, warning signals that the 1980s boom was closing came early on in the Liberals' second term. Only five weeks after Election Day, on 19 October 1987, with the Liberals winning a clear majority government, the Dow Jones industrial average fell 508 points in New York, with an estimated loss of $503 billion. The Toronto Stock Exchange plummeted 407.2 points, erasing $37 billion from the value of Canadian stocks.[68]

The NDP came to office in 1990 by capturing the smallest plurality of votes for a majority government in Ontario history, only to bear witness to the deepest recession since the 1930s. The budget of 1990, the last Peterson Liberal budget, projected a small surplus of $30 million.[69] But on 10 September 1990, just four days after the election, the new government was briefed by Ministry of Finance officials that this surplus had evaporated and had been replaced with a $2 billion deficit.[70] The descent into recession was signalled by a recalculated deficit of $3 billion for 1990. By the time of the NDP's first budget of 1991, that deficit had grown to $9.7 billion.[71]

NDP policy continuity with the Peterson era was demonstrated in that the new government sought to

> supplement the Premier's Council and Liberals' version with more progressive elements. They called for more attention to employment rates and structures and to incorporation of social policy concerns, while empowering workers in the workplace and facilitating bi- and tri-partite partnerships for things like sectorial training and adjustment. This stance might best be characterized as a search for social partnerships, in which everyone's shared interest in the wellbeing of the Ontario economy was assumed.[72]

These sets of policy initiatives aimed at adapting Ontario through a process of restructuring by promoting 'a highly qualified labour force, strategic investments by firms in higher-value-added activities, and investment by government in the necessary social and physical infrastructure'[73] soon came to be captured within the rubric of 'economic renewal.' For Ontario's New Democrats, this marked a break with their Keynesian legacy, yet the turn in policy direction had in fact begun before the 1990 election and represented a political reorientation for the party. Hence, for the NDP, redistribution of income and wealth was no longer the role of the state; rather, the state had to work to improve 'social productivity.'[74]

The first social democratic–inspired Speech from the Throne in Ontario picked up on themes that had first been expressed by the previous Liberal government. Continuity prevailed at a policy level. Not only did the new government commit to various social- and labour-policy reforms, it continued with the theme of improving Ontario's competitive position within a globalizing economy through investments in human capital, alluding to neo-corporatist arrangements as the mechanisms through which Ontario would succeed. The speech

contextualized Ontario's challenge as one in which 'global trading relationships, the ways of organizing and conducting our work, the kinds
of knowledge and skills our workers require – all these things are being
transformed. [The] government recognizes that Ontario must compete
in a worldwide marketplace'; the means to address this economic reality lay in 'the need for a new relationship and respect among all the
forces in the Ontario economy – labour, business, community organizations, government – so we can begin to work better together to achieve
our common goals. New ways of co-operating will be needed.'[75]

Within this broadly post-Keynesian perspective, a clear role for the
state in economic management was understood and characterized as
'market reinforcing rather than market replacing,'[76] where partnerships
were central to a more robust role for the state in 'supporting and promoting adjustment to the new realities of a global economic system ...
Much of this activity lies in facilitating technological adaptation, promoting human capital development through increased emphasis on
training, and orchestrating partnership between business, labour and
government to pursue competitiveness.'[77]

The first NDP budget of 1991 sent two messages respecting economic
change and fiscal policy. Janus-like, the budget looked back towards a
Keynesian past and, forward to a future of progressive competitiveness. Finance Minister Floyd Laughren told the Legislature: 'We believe
that government can and should be active in supporting positive economic change and in ensuring that the costs of adjustment are shared
fairly'; and furthermore, it was 'important for people to understand
that we had a choice to make this year – to fight the deficit or fight the
recession. We are proud to be fighting the recession.'[78] The progressive
competitiveness theme was most clearly expressed in Budget paper 'E,'
wherein the government's economic policy goal was identified broadly
as follows: 'Ontario must promote equitable structural change through
comprehensive economic and social strategy aimed at sustainable prosperity.'[79] The intent, in part, was to promote the development of high-
value-added, high-wage jobs through strategic partnerships.'[80]

The Keynesian theme of the 1991 budget was best epitomized, and
remembered, by the $9.7 billion deficit it projected and the finance min-
ister's contention that 'allowing the deficit to rise to this level this year
is not only justifiable, it is the most responsible choice we could make.'[81]
In pre-budget planning, the official Treasury view was that Ontario was
confronting a typical short-term cyclical downturn, which should be
addressed through some fiscal stimulation. The result, however, was

a budget Keynesian enough to anger business but not stimulative enough to do much good. After tax increases and previously announced programs were counted in, the budget called for about $350 million in net new spending on a budget of $53 billion – enough only to spark about 15,000 new jobs in the economy, in a province where 250,000 jobs had been lost over the past year.[82]

In 1992 Ontario had become the largest non-sovereign borrower in the world.[83] In part, this contributed to a growing sense that the fiscal situation in Ontario was rapidly moving towards an unmanageable state. Over the next two years, 1992 and 1993, the government adopted the view that controlling the deficit was its central policy concern. Following his government's first budget in April of 1991, Rae acknowledged that the post-war arrangements were history. He wrote in his biography: 'The period from 1945 on had been a time of unparalleled growth, and a culture of continuing gains and steady improvements took strong hold in those parts of the economy where trade unions had strength. The blissful security and forward motion of this world began to crumble in the mid-1970s with the oil crisis.'[84]

With the 1992 budget it became clear that the NDP government had overcome its Keynesian impulse and now held that the deficit must be brought under control. In that year the government began decelerating public expenditures in an attempt to arrest the growth of the deficit, and so the budget of that year noted: 'Not since 1953 has the Government of Ontario had a spending increase lower than this year's 4.9 per cent.'[85] Even before the budget the minister of finance announced that transfer payments to the broader public sector, composed of school boards, universities, municipalities, and hospitals, would be limited to 1 per cent in 1992 and 2 per cent in each of 1993 and 1994.[86]

Still, the budgetary shortfall for 1992–3 would total $9.9 billion. For Premier Bob Rae, this was a turning point:

> The province's bottom line was in lousy shape by the fall of 1992. As we started our work on the budget for the next year (1993), I became convinced that something new and bold needed to be tried. I began sharing my ideas with a few close colleagues … And so it was in the New Year of 1993 that I began discussing in cabinet the need for us to do something dramatic to deal with the growing gap between revenues and spending.[87]

The first budget was in one sense inspired by a Depression-era Keynesianism. Peter Warrian, who served as assistant deputy minister of finance and chief economist for the Rae government between 1992 and 1994, said of the NDP's approach to fiscal and economic policy in its first two years in office:

> The NDP can have three different kinds of budgets – you can have a Franklin Delano Roosevelt 'build sewers, roads and infrastructure' New Deal budget; you could have a restructuring budget which says 'hey, this is about restructuring and innovation so here we go with innovation and labour market policy'; or you could have a social welfare budget where you just increase social spending. Well, the government said it had the first, didn't act on the second, and actually implemented the third.[88]

Michael Mendelson, who held several ADM-level appointments under Premier David Peterson and was later appointed to Cabinet Office as a deputy minister within a week of Bob Rae's historic electoral victory, saw the early 1990s very much as Rae did – a reordering of the post-war era. The economic stress of the time marked a qualitative shift and emerged as the restructuring aftershock flowing from the mid-seventies. As Mendelson noted:

> Adjusting to that change was very, very difficult in many ways. It was a sea change in the world. It wasn't just in Ontario, it was everywhere in the western world. It was really in my view the residue from 1974. We never came to grips with it … Essentially the fiscal side of government never came to grips with the world that came about in 1974.[89]

That moment came in February 1993, when Ontario government financial officials projected a deficit of $17 billion.[90]

In a memo to Finance Minister Laughren entitled 'Walking on the edge of the cliff,' Warrian warned that Ontario was heading towards a fiscal crisis,[91] defined as a debt that could not be financed. Jay Kaufman, who served as secretary of Treasury Board under the NDP, recalled the period of 1990 to 1993 as one in which the fiscal terrain under the government's feet kept on shifting and the province 'hit what we described as the "debt wall."'[92] Frances Lankin, a NDP minister, echoed Warrian's contention that the misreading of the significance of the recession was, in her view, a grave error: 'We took the position that we were going to fight the recession, not the deficit … I guess the next thing to say is we were wrong … Over the course of the next year … things were starting to spiral … out of control if we didn't do something different … So that began the process of us looking to whether there were areas where we could control expenditures.'[93]

Beginning in early 1993, a fiscal-control strategy began to unfold that came to be known as the 'three-legged stool,'[94] referring its three component parts: wage cuts embodied in the Social Contract Act, expenditure cuts, and tax increases. The objective was to control the deficit by both reducing expenditures by $6 billion and increasing revenue by $2 billion. Consequently, the NDP government asserted, 'We cannot simply "grow" our way out of deficit problems as we have done in the past … Without prompt and decisive action, the predicted slow recovery in revenues will cause the accumulated debt to grow steadily upwards, possibly approaching $120 billion in 1996.'[95]

The process to reduce costs but maintain productivity in the Ontario public sector was called the 'Social Contract,' and according to Premier Rae the objective of this process was 'to get public sector management and their unions to address the need for savings, and to achieve these savings without big reductions in service to the public or unemployment among public sector workers'[96] through cuts to public sector wages and salaries. The New Right argument that the state sector had become too large and expensive came to be accepted by the NDP as government negotiators argued that salaries and wages were the largest component of public expenditures, consuming 50 cents of the 71 cents that the government spent on public services such as health care, education, and social services.[97]

With the Social Contract implemented, the government began turning its mind to a more fundamental restructuring of the public sector. The Ministry of Finance held a retreat for its ADMs in September centred around a strategic planning discussion paper, which proposed that the economic stress of the 1990s would force a restructuring of program delivery based on a possible separation of policy from delivery functions – in other words, creating an administrative arrangement that would more favourably consider alternative delivery options. The paper stated that a broader range of delivery options might become available, and specifically, a greater role for public-private partnerships would emerge. In part, the paper observed, this could be seen to mark a shift away from a direct program-delivery role for government, with new delivery mechanisms would driven by the need to improve efficiency and effectiveness.[98]

The impasse of the social democrats – the Ontario NDP could neither prosecute the advance of their original reform agenda nor turn to an aggressive form of neoliberalism – appeared to be Ontario's 'There is no alternative' moment. The inability of the NDP to politically and economically manoeuvre fundamentally and fatally undermined the political base of the party.

Goodbye Dr Keynes?: The Conservatives and the Common Sense Revolution, 1995–2003

The election of 1995 saw the Progressive Conservatives, led by Premier Mike Harris, come to power. The Conservatives embraced an aggressive form of neoliberalism embodied in their party platform the 'Common Sense Revolution' (CRS). If Keynes had been waiting in the vestibule during the last years of the Rae government, he was shown the door by the returning PC party. With the Common Sense Revolution (June 1995 to April 2002 – the two terms when Mike Harris led the government) managerialism and New Right thinking conveniently converged. At that point the Ontario state moved to restructure not only its institutional framework but its logic, its 'official state orthodoxy,' and its modes of control.[99]

For its part, the CSR was an unequivocal statement of policy direction. It proffered the most explicit program for a break with the Keynesian past that Ontario had seen – it proposed nothing less than a revolution. Perhaps it may more aptly be described as a 'counter-revolution,' as its program sought a sharper and more hastened rupture with the Keynesian era than what neoliberalism in slow motion had so far delivered. Regardless of the characterization, for Ontario it was the beginning of the province's 'bold embrace' of neoliberalism.[100]

A central goal of neoliberalism was to transform the public service, and this was to be accomplished through the use of managerialism. The ideology of managerialism as carried into the public sector through the New Public Management (NPM) movement is inextricably linked with a concern for improving public-sector productivity. From a historical perspective, the concern with public-sector productivity is itself largely a product of the fiscal crisis of the welfare state beginning in the 1970s and continuing through the 1980s, which made the shrinking of the state and the cutting of public expenditures an intractable political problem.[101] One cannot consider the significance of NPM without reference to issues of productivity and budget constraint.

If Ontario's enlistment into the neoliberal political project was comparatively halting from 1975 to 1985 and resumed again in 1993 (the year of the NDP's expenditure cuts), the election of the Common Sense Revolutionaries may be seen as the occasion of a quick march forward.

The conservative CSR manifesto framed the problems and solutions to those problems for the electorate in a starkly unprecedented way. Courchene and Telmer wrote: 'There can be no doubt that the CSR is a revolution. Within months of taking office the Conservatives had overthrown much of the status quo across a wide range of fronts.'[102] The political genius of the CSR was that its politics sought to ally New Right populism with the broadly felt insecurity of the time. One of the key architects of the Common Sense Revolution, Leslie Noble, said of the popular mood voiced at various policy development meetings the party had been staging that ordinary Ontarians

> felt they were being hacked to death. They were working harder and harder, but still falling farther behind. The government was this rigged game between big business, big government, and big bureaucracy and people who were sitting on the sidelines were paying for it and not getting much value back. They really felt that the system was broken and needed some fundamental revolutionary change. We didn't happen upon that word by accident.[103]

There was little that connected the Progressive Conservative parties of 1985 and 1995, even though both Mike Harris and Ernie Eves, the new minister of finance, had served in Frank Miller's cabinet.[104] The transformation of the Ontario Progressive Conservative Party from a pragmatic, centrist 'electoral coalition of free-enterprise oriented interests and state-centred interests'[105] into a populist and ideological party of the New Right began with the electoral meltdown in the 1987 election. A small group of young and ideological activists emerged and fundamentally reshaped the party.[106]

The sweeping public-policy reforms proposed by the CSR manifesto were concerned not just with narrow technical legislative tinkering but more fundamentally with changing the logic of the Ontario state through changes in modes of delivery, management culture, and means of control. Towards such ends, the program stated: 'The Common Sense Revolution will have a significant impact on the way in which government and its employees do business on a day to day basis, because it will demand that government does business like a business – in other words, in an efficient and productive manner that focuses on results and puts the customer first.'[107] While the CSR offered a broad policy agenda to Ontario voters, it directly stated that 'there is nothing wrong with Ontario that a new vision, a new direction and turn-around management can't fix.'[108] Its proposed strategy for improving competitiveness was a restructuring of the role of the provincial state which primarily amounted to an attack on the cost structure of the Ontario public sector. Guy Giorno, the premier's principal secretary, viewed the commitments to a balanced budget as anchors to the other policy proposals:

> I actually believe that ... the commitment to balance the budget and the steps taken to ensure that the budget was balanced was the primary driver of the government's agenda in '95–'99 ... I guess the agenda within the agenda, the factor which meant that absolutely everybody rolled in the same direction, was the balanced budget ... Would we have been able to implement the CSR if there wasn't this driving force to balance the budget?[109]

The shrinking of public expenditures, linked as they were to a range of regulatory and transfer-payment arrangements, required a comprehensive range of 'reform' proposals. These entailed cuts to personal income tax, deregulation or 'cutting red tape' on business activities, the rescinding of NDP-era labour protections and freezing of the minimum wage to discipline and make Ontario workers more flexible, encouraging contracting out – especially within the public service and broader public sector – shrinking public service employment, a commitment to a balanced budget, and deep cuts in social assistance rates.[110]

The Ontario state was primarily involved in financing the third-party delivery of public goods rather than being an 'owner' of capital assets and a direct producer. However, this is not to say that privatization did not occur. Outsourcing (contracting out) is one form of privatization and the CSR stated clearly that 'many of the things that government does can be done cheaper, faster, and better if the private sector is involved.'[111] The first round of Conservative spending cuts announced on 21 July 1995 and in Finance Minister Ernie Eves's 'Fiscal and Economic Statement' of 29 November 1995 were directed at what David Lindsay, Harris's chief of staff, referred to as the 'low-hanging fruit.'[112] These cuts totalled $1.9 billion, the two largest of which were a 21 per cent cut in social assistance rates and spending reductions for each ministry. In addition, the minister of finance established the Ontario Financial Review Commission (OFRC),[113] which was charged with presenting 'a new framework for better use of resources throughout the public sector.'[114] In November 1995 Eves announced further cuts in 1996–7 totalling $4.5–$5.5 billion, stating: 'The only way to stop the growth of interest costs is to stop government overspending. That will require a complete rethinking of government in Ontario. With a focus on more efficient delivery of services Ontarians need most and on better value for tax dollars.'[115]

What was of interest here was the budget structure itself. For example, in 1996–7 a full 66 per cent of total provincial expenditures went to the education, health, and social services sector. When combined with the 16 per cent paid to public debt interest, it meant that 82 per cent of provincial expenditures were either non-discretionary or were largely allocated to transfer partners.[116] For a government programmatically committed to a balanced budget and tax cuts, there was no room to manoeuvre. Constraint in the broader public sector, essentially the delivery of the Ontario state's most popular and expensive public goods and services, was thus politically much more contested than the core public service cuts. The cuts of July and November 1995 reduced expenditures by $4.9 billion and were to be fully implemented by the fiscal year 1997–8.[117]

Sustaining the direction of the CSR became more difficult, however, as the financial picture for the government and the province improved. Lindsay, for example, noted that 'money started to flow into the provincial Treasury in excess of our budget expectations ... At that point the dynamics started to shift. And to continue to make the argument that downsizing and cutbacks were necessary was harder and harder. The premier's rhetoric ... to continue with the downsizing and reduction plan continued but in fact expenditures kept growing.'[118] The budgetary process is 'vitally important because it acts as the government's nervous system. It sends out signals to every department and agency and to all public servants about what is important to the government,'[119] and as with all matters of politics and policy, the politics of public expenditure reflects the choices of government through the process of allocation of resources. What happened in Ontario in the 1990s, where the provincial state shrinks in terms of employment but expenditures continued to rise, appears contradictory. The case of Ontario's CRS was more limited and muted than that of Britain's experience with Thatcherism, a revolution that was 'much more associated with the administering of the public sector rather than the financing of public services.'[120] This managerialist approach included a cultural/ideological dimension, but also the more realistic aim to contain, but not necessarily shrink, public expenditures. As with Thatcherism, it can be said of the CSR that 'it is difficult to avoid the conclusion that the welfare state is being attacked by the new conservatism at least as much for ideological as for economic reasons.'[121]

Neoliberal policies achieved only a qualified success. The control on overall public spending was limited and the state was not 'rolled back' in any linear way. Instead, the state's capacities were changed, as were its relationships to the market and other social actors and constituencies.[122] Provincial expenditures, for instance, which had dropped in 1992/3, then recovered, and then dropped again in 1996/7, began to expand the following year. More important, Ontario public expenditures as a proportion of the total economy were dramatically shrinking. In 1995/6, Ontario government expenditures were equal to 19.23 per cent of the GPP but by 2000/1 this had dropped to 14.8 per cent of the GPP.[123] The public sector and core Ontario Public Service workforce numbers correspond to this shrinking of the provincial state. Between 1995 and 1999, the first and most aggressive term of the CSR, employment in the Ontario Public Service fell from 81,300 in 1995–6 to 54,952 in 1999–2000. As for the Ontario public sector workforce,[124] it reached a historic high in 1992 of 1,042,000 employees and then began to decline in 1993 through to 1997, when it bottomed out at 938,500 (a decline of nearly 10 per cent) before beginning to grow and recover to one million.[125] For the Ontario Public Service this meant a return, in terms of real numbers, to dimensions not seen since 1967–8.[126] For the broader public sector, the workforce shrank, less dramatically, by nearly 100,000 positions between 1993 and 1997. Again, it is the proportion vis-à-vis the overall workforce which tells a more nuanced story, where the proportion of public sector workers in the Ontario workforce fell from 21 per cent in 1992 to 16.57 per cent in 2001.[127]

The general conclusion for Ontario is that the 'reinvestment' in public services which began to occur after the first two years of the Common Sense Revolution obscures a very important detail: the public sector and the core administrative state shrank as measured against the economy and total workforce as a whole. In Ontario's case, the growth in public expenditures in 2000 over 1990 was 39.7 per cent. What the overall growth in public expenditures hid is the dramatic reversal in provincial expenditures as a proportion of the Ontario GPP, which reached a high of 18.9 per cent in 1992–3, but by 2000–1 had fallen to 14.5 per cent, a decline of 23.3 per cent.[128]

As Guy Giorno observed,[129] it was critical to align the senior management ranks of the Ontario public service with the objectives of the CSR but it was also now evident that Ontario's 'commanding heights' were in the transfer payment sector, the broader public-sector organizations responsible for the delivery of popular and expensive social programs. Together with management performance contracting and pay linked to performance (as the OFRC itself recommended), ministry business plans that would have to be run through the Ministry of Finance were a means of constructing this alignment. Through the invocation of New Public Management methods, and under the watchful eye of the Ministry of Finance, the problem, as neoliberals saw it, of self-interested bureaucracies could be controlled. With a sustained demand that the focus be on balanced budgets and fiscal prudence, the goal was to commit to institutional 'memory' the belief that 'the huge and persistent ... deficit [was] a symbol of everything wrong with our system of government.'[130]

After 2002, with a new Conservative premier and subsequent Liberal governments, the aggressive form of neoliberal governance embodied in the CRS waned. Nonetheless, this period made the return to past Keynesian-inspired practices impossible. A new era of fiscal political economy in which the MOF would operate was firmly fixed in place.

Conclusion

The history of the evolution of Ontario's public policy agenda and macro-economic environment between 1945 and 2002 was marked by profound change. The modern Ontario welfare state was built and a Keynesian policy framework promoted an activist state that would spend extensively in the areas of economy and society up until the economic crisis of the 1970s. After this time a process of fundamental rethinking began and the province's welfare-state architecture came to be restructured and made subject to an ongoing process of constraint influenced by the growing dominance of neoliberal ideas that displaced the Keynesian paradigm. The Ministry of Finance, and its predecessor ministries, were centrally involved and influenced by these transformations.

The journey of Ontario's Progressive Conservative Party from the 'no zeal' pragmatism of the 1940s that characterized its conversion to the idea and praxis of the welfare state to the conviction politics of the CSR in the 1990s is an illustration of the role of ideas, political parties, and public administrative institutions as agents and instruments in trans- forming the state. The party that led, at least at the provincial level, the welfare-state construction project was the same party seeking to dismantle that project in later years. In both instances it was necessary for the party to be ideologically reconstructed, and the Conservative embrace of the CSR marked this transition. The impasse of social democracy and post-Keynesian approaches in Ontario was best captured by the NDP's reversion to fiscal constraint, the strategy first hesitantly attempted by the Davis administration in the 1970s, as the means for addressing the economic crisis. In this respect, the CSR continued and deepened this neoliberal-inspired constraint and also sought to embed a 'culture' of public expenditure control within the Ontario administrative state.

The problems confronting the Common Sense Revolution could be summed up in two points. First, the CSR met with the 'path dependency'[131] of the previous forty years of welfare-state building, the most important components being such widely popular public services as education and health care (social services are less clear because of the income maintenance component). The program of neoliberalism, aimed at an enduring reduction in public expenditures, could not avoid the structural reality that 70 per cent of public expenditures supported the production and delivery of these services. Any enduring reduction in these expenditures would have political consequences. This leads to the second point: in the context of an improving economy and consequently improving revenues, it became increasingly difficult to sustain the roll-back of public sector spending. Again, this does not mean that constraint in public expenditures was not without success. As noted above, the size of provincial expenditures relative to the economy indeed shrank to levels not seen since the 1960s.

The Ontario Ministry of Finance and associate economic ministries over this period were compelled to play many different roles. These ranged from overseeing and financing extensive state investments in the province's economic infrastructure – while also constructing a vast array of health, social, and educational investments that provided the foundations for Ontario's welfare state – to being the public-sector debt and deficit fighter. The ministries have taken up these various roles in response to changes in the political and economic environment. Beginning with the stagflation of the 1970s and continuing into the 1980s, through to the deep recession of the early 1990s, the era of permanent fiscal crisis was ushered in. This was the context in which the Ontario state slowly changed its mind.

The return of the Liberals to government in 2003, despite the themes of their campaign, was not a rupture with the Common Sense Revolution, but rather marked a period of normalization. In the election campaign the Liberals promised both change and continuity with respect to the policies of the CSR. Reinvesting in social policy was central to their platform, but equally so were commitments not to raise taxes and to balance budgets. The blend of fiscal conservatism and modest social progressivism appeared to hearken back to Red Tory Ontario. However, the Liberal politics of 'One Ontario' masked a project to consolidate the neoliberal policy framework constructed over the previous decade by retaining its central features and reforming those aspects which proved politically and economically unsustainable. The central place of post-Keynesian policy prescriptions, especially those respecting human capital formation and innovation, most effectively capture Ontario's permanent break with Dr Keynes and the post-war order with which he and his ideas are so closely associated.

NOTES

1 See Robert B. Bryce, *Canada and the Cost of World War II: The International Operations of Canada's Department of Finance, 1939–1947*, ed. Matthew J. Bellamy (Montreal: McGill-Queen's University Press, 2005), chap. 8 and p. 193. On Keynes's influence in Ottawa at this time, see J.L. Granatstein, *The Ottawa Men: The Civil Service Mandarins, 1925–1957* (Toronto: Oxford University Press, 1982).
2 Timothy Lewis, *In the Long Run We're All Dead: The Canadian Turn to Fiscal Restraint* (Vancouver: UBC Press, 2003), 7, 19.
3 Friedrich Hayek, *The Constitution of Liberty* (London: Routledge and Kegan Paul, 1960), 398.
4 Simon Lee and Stephen McBride, 'Introduction,' *Neo-liberalism, State Power and Global Governance* (Dordrecht: Springer, 2007), 5.
5 Andrew Gamble, 'Neo-liberalism,' *Capital and Class* 75 (2001), 127–34.
6 Bob MacDermid and Greg Albo, 'Divided Province, Growing Protests: Ontario Moves Right,' in *The Provincial State in Canada: Politics in the Provinces and Territories*, ed. Keith Brownsey and Michael Howlett (Peterborough, ON: Broadview Press, 2001), 166.
7 Department of Treasury and Economics, *Ontario Economic Review* (Toronto: Queen's Printer, 1971), 4–9; and Ministry of Treasury and Economics, Sectoral and Regional Policy Branch, Statistics Section, *Ontario Statistics* (Toronto: Queen's Printer, 1986), 67.
8 D.R. Richmond, *The Economic Transformation of Ontario, 1945–1973* (Toronto: Ontario Economic Council, 1974), 43.
9 David Foot, *Provincial Public Finance in Ontario: An Empirical Analysis of the last Twenty-five Years* (Toronto: Ontario Economic Council / University of Toronto Press, 1977), 190–2.

10 K.J. Rea, *The Prosperous Years: The Economic History of Ontario 1939–1975* (Toronto: University of Toronto Press, 1985), 101–2.

11 Foot, *Provincial Public Finance in Ontario*, 20–1.

12 Ontario Civil Service Commission, *Annual Report*, 1948/49 (Toronto: King/ Queen's Printer, 1949), 5; and Ministry of Treasury and Economics, *1985 Ontario Budget* (Toronto: Queen's Printer, 1985), 660.

13 Rosemary Speirs, *Out of the Blue: The Fall of the Tory Dynasty in Ontario* (Toronto: Macmillan of Canada, 1986), xx.

14 Eddie Goodman, cited in Robert Williams, 'Ontario's Party Systems: Under New Management,' in *Party Politics in Canada*, ed. Hugh G. Thorburn, 6th ed. (Scarborough, ON: Prentice-Hall, 1991), 489.

15 Keith Brownsey and Michael Howlett, 'Class Structure and Political Alliances in an Industrialized Society,' in *The Provincial State: Politics in Canada's Provinces and Territories*, ed. Keith Brownsey and Michael Howlett (Toronto: Copp Clark Pitman Ltd, 1992), 147.

16 John Graham, 'What's Wrong with Government Now? A Survey of Viewpoints,' discussion paper, Committee on Government Productivity (November 1970), 231.

17 Ibid., 98.

18 Ontario Treasury Department, *Budget Address* (Toronto: King's Printer, 1944), 18; and Ontario Treasury Department, *Budget Address* (Toronto: Queen's Printer, 1961), 8.

19 Department of Treasury and Economics, *Ontario Economic Review* (Toronto: Queen's Printer, 1971), 4–9.

20 Brownsey and Howlett, 'Class Structure and Political Alliances,' 156.

21 Foot, *Provincial Public Finance in Ontario*, 15.

22 Vernon Lang, *The Service State Emerges in Ontario 1945–1973* (Toronto: Ontario Economic Council, 1974), 52.

23 Rea, *The Prosperous Years*, 227.

24 Graham White, 'Change in the Ontario State 1952–2002,' paper prepared for the panel on the role of government (October 2002), 17, 36.

25 A.K. McDougall, *John P. Robarts: His Life and Government* (Toronto: University of Toronto Press, 1986), 128.

26 Rea, *The Prosperous Years*, 229.

27 Archives of Ontario (AO), Committee on Government Productivity, 'Agencies, Boards and Commissions: A Discussion Paper,' 25 February 1972. File: Boards and Commissions, RG 18-527, box Y82, pp. 31–2.

28 Ministry of Treasury and Economics, *Ontario Budget 1981* (Toronto: Queen's Printer), 4.

29 Ibid, 4–5.

30 Ibid., 5.

31 Ministry of Treasury and Economics, *Ontario Budget 1978* (Toronto: Queen's Printer, 1978), 30; *Ontario Budget* (Toronto: Queen's Printer, 1979), 8; and *Ontario Budget* (Toronto: Queen's Printer, 1981), 4.
32 Treasury Department, *Ontario Budget* (Toronto: Queen's Printer, 1970), 5, 20.
33 Ministry of Treasury and Economics, *Ontario Budget* (Toronto: Queen's Printer, 1972), 18.
34 Ibid., 22–4.
35 Department of Treasury and Economics, *Ontario Budget* (Toronto: Queen's Printer, 1971), 9.
36 Ibid., 10.
37 Ibid., 16.
38 Ministry of Treasury and Economics, *Ontario Budget* (Toronto: Queen's Printer, 1974), 1.
39 Brownsey and Howlett, 'Class Structure and Political Alliances,' 159.
40 Special Program Review Committee (SPRC) – Ministry of Treasury, Economics, and Intergovernmental Affairs, *Report of the Special Review Committee* (Toronto: Queen's Printer, 1975), 20, 36.
41 Ministry of Treasury and Economics, *Ontario Budget* (Toronto: Queen's Printer, 1975), 16.
42 Michael Pusey, *Economic Rationalism in Canberra: A Nation Building State Changes Its Mind* (Cambridge: Cambridge University Press, 2003), 2.
43 Chuck Rachlis and David Wolfe, 'An Insiders' View of the NDP Government of Ontario: The Politics of Permanent Opposition Meets the Economics of Permanent Recession,' in *The Government and Politics of Ontario*, 5th ed., ed. Graham White (Toronto: University of Toronto Press, 1997), 331, 333.
44 Ministry of Treasury, Economics and Intergovernmental Affairs, 'Budget Paper "C,"' in *Ontario Budget* (Toronto: Queen's Printer, 1977), 3.
45 Ontario budgets, 1975–85.
46 AO, RG 7-1, box 10, Records of the Premier's office: Premier's advisory committee on the economic future, 1977–79, 15 April 1977.
47 AO, RG 7-1, box 10, David Barrows, 'Government and the Economy,' Ministry of Industry and Tourism Staff Paper, n.d., p. 8.
48 Ibid.
49 AO, RG 32-1, box 18, File 610-22, Ontario Business Advisory Council, Minutes of meeting, 7 May 1979, p. 11.
50 Brownsey and Howlett, 'Class Structure and Political Alliances,' 160.
51 Leo Panitch and Donald Swartz, *From Consent to Coercion: The Assault on Trade Union Freedoms*, 3rd ed. (Aurora, ON: Garamond Press, 2003), 35.
52 Brownsey and Howlett, 'Class Structure and Political Alliances,' 160.

53 Ministry of Treasury and Economics, *Ontario Budget* (Toronto: Queen's Printer, 1984), 16.
54 Ibid., 1.
55 Ontario budgets, 1980–5.
56 Rodney Haddow and Thomas Klassen, *Partisanship, Globalization, and Canadian Labour Market Policy: Four Provinces in Comparative Perspective* (Toronto: University of Toronto Press, 2006), 95.
57 Stephen McBride, 'Policy from What? Neoliberal and Human-capital Theoretical Foundations of Recent Canadian Labour-market Policy,' in *Restructuring and Resistance: Canadian Public Policy in an Age of Global Capitalism*, ed. Mike Burke, Colin Mooers, and John Shields (Halifax: Fernwood Publishing, 2000), 162.
58 Bob Rae and David Peterson, *An Agenda for Reform: Proposals for Minority Parliament* (Toronto: New Democratic Party, 1985), 1.
59 Robert Ehring and Wayne Roberts, *Giving away a Miracle: Lost Dreams, Broken Promises and the Ontario NDP* (Oakville, ON: Mosaic Press, 1993), 151.
60 Statistics Canada includes in public-service employment all those who work directly for government and employment funded directly by government such as in schools, universities, hospitals, and crown corporations. See Statistics Canada, 'Public Sector Employment, *The Daily* 28 November 1997, at http://www.statcan.ca/Daily/English/071128/d071128c.htm.
61 Ministry of Treasury and Economics, *Ontario Budget* (Toronto: Queen's Printer, 1989), table C8; Ministry of Finance, *Ontario Budget* (Toronto: Queen's Printer, 1997), table B6.
62 White, 'Change in the Ontario State,' 20.
63 Ontario Hansard, Speech from the Throne, 22 April 1986.
64 Premier's Council of Ontario, 'Competing in the New Global Economy (1)' (Toronto: The Premier's Council, 1988), 35.
65 Stephen McBride, *Not Working: State, Unemployment, and Neo-conservatism in Canada* (Toronto: University of Toronto Press, 1992), 25.
66 Neil Bradford and M. Stevens, 'Whither Corporatism? Political Struggles and Policy Formation in the Ontario Training and Adjustment Board,' in *The Training Trap: Ideology, Training and the Labour Market*, ed. Thomas Dunk, Stephen McBride, and Randle W. Nelson (Winnipeg: Fernwood Publishing, 1996), 145.
67 Cabinet Office, *Framework for Action 2000. Working Together: An Integrated Organization* (Toronto, 2000), 14.
68 Georgette Gagnon, *Not without Cause: David Peterson's Fall from Grace* (Toronto: HarperCollins Publishing, 1992), 45.

69 Ministry of Treasury and Economics, *Ontario Budget* (Toronto: Queen's Printer, 1990), 41.
70 Rachlis and Wolfe, 'An Insider's View of the NDP Government,' 336.
71 Ministry of Treasury and Economics, *Ontario Budget* (Toronto: Queen's Printer, 1990), 3.
72 Jane Jenson and Paule Rianne Mahon, 'From "Premier Bob" to "Rae Days": The Impasse of the Ontario New Democrats,' in *Late Twentieth Century Social Democracy*, ed. Jean-Pierre Beaud and Jean-Guy Prevost (Sainte-Foy, QC: Presses de l'Université du Québec, 1995), 157–8.
73 Rachlis and Wolfe, 'An Insider's View of the NDP Government,' 349.
74 Riel Miller, Interview with author, 24 November 2004, Toronto, Ontario. Miller served as an economic policy adviser to the NDP's finance minister, Floyd Laughren.
75 Ontario Hansard, Speech from the throne, 20 November 1990.
76 Michael Howlett and M. Ramesh, 'The Limits of Post-Keynesianism: Lessons from the Canadian Experience,' *Political Science* 45.2 (1993): 172–85.
77 Stephen McBride, 'The Continuing Crisis of Social Democracy: Ontario's Social Contract in Perspective,' *Studies in Political Economy* 50 (Summer 1995), 75.
78 Ministry of Treasury and Economics, *Ontario Budget* (Toronto: Queen's Printer, 1991), 1, 3.
79 Ministry of Treasury and Economics, 'Budget Paper "E"' (Toronto: Queen's Printer, 1991), 86.
80 Ibid., 87.
81 Ministry of Treasury and Economics, *Ontario Budget* (Toronto: Queen's Printer, 1991), 3.
82 Thomas Walkom, *Rae Days: The Rise and Follies of the NDP* (Toronto: Key Porter Books, 1994), 103.
83 David Wolfe, interview with Bryan Evans, 5 January 2005, Toronto.
84 Rae, *From Protest to Power: Personal Reflections on a Life in Politics* (Toronto: Viking Press, 1996), 210–11.
85 Ministry of Treasury and Economics, *Ontario Budget* (Toronto: Queen's Printer, 1992), 3.
86 Rachlis and Wolfe, 'An Insider's View of the NDP Government,' 352–3. Later that November, the finance minister modified this constraint by making the 1993 transfer a one-time occurrence, meaning it would not go into the base budget, and so effectively it amounted to a 2% permanent cut. The transfer payment for 1994 was entirely rescinded (see Rachlis and Wolf, ibid., 353).
87 Rae, *From Protest to Power*, 202–3.

88 Peter Warrian, interview with Bryan Evans, 31 October 1995, Toronto.
89 Michael Mendelson, interview with Bryan Evans, 2 December 2004, Toronto.
90 Rae, *From Protest to Power*, 204.
91 Walkom, *Rae Days*, 117.
92 Jay Kaufman, interview with Bryan Evans, 22 December 2004, Toronto.
93 Frances Lankin, interview with Bryan Evans, 19 January 2005, Toronto.
94 Simon Rosenbloom, interview with Bryan Evans, 27 June 2005, Toronto; and Walkom, *Rae Days*, 137.
95 Government of Ontario, *Jobs and Services: A Social Contract for the Ontario Public* (Toronto: Queen's Printer, 1993), 4, 5.
96 Rae, *From Protest to Power*, 204.
97 Government of Ontario, *Jobs and Services*, 9.
98 AO, RG 6-47, box 3, Records of Ontario Ministry of Finance, Strategic planning discussion paper, prepared for Ontario Ministry of Finance ADMs' retreat (13–14 September 1993) by Johnston, Smith, Fromkin and McCulloch Inc.
99 See Bryan Evans, 'How the State Changes Its Mind: A Gramscian Account of Ontario's managerial Cultural Change,' *Philosophy and Management* 5.2 (2005), 25–46.
100 MacDermid and Albo, 'Divided Province, Growing Protests,' 163.
101 John Shields and B. Mitchell Evans, *Shrinking the State: Globalization and Public Administration 'Reform'* (Halifax: Fernwood Publishing, 1998), chaps 3 and 4.
102 Thomas Courchene and Colin Telmer, *From Heartland to North American Region State: The Social, Fiscal and Federal Evolution of Ontario*, Monograph Series on Public Policy (Toronto: University of Toronto, Centre for Public Management, 1998), 169.
103 Leslie Noble, interview with Bryan Evans, 25 August 2004, Toronto.
104 Peter Woolstencroft, 'More than a Guard Change: Politics in the New Ontario,' in *Revolution at Queen's Park: Essays on Governing Ontario*, ed. Sid Noel (Toronto: James Lorimer and Co., 1997), 366.
105 Ibid., 366; see also John Wilson, 'The Red Tory Province: Reflections on the Character of the Ontario Political Culture,' in *The Government and Politics of Ontario*, 2nd ed., ed. Donald C. MacDonald (Toronto: Van Nostrand Reinhold Ltd, 1980), 208–26.
106 John Ibbitson, *Promised Land: Inside the Mike Harris Revolution* (Scarborough, ON: Prentice Hall Canada, 1997), 39.
107 Ontario Progressive Conservative Party, *The Common Sense Revolution* (Toronto: Ontario Progressive Conservative Party, 1994), 16.

108 Ibid., 2.
109 Guy Giorno, interview with Bryan Evans, 26 January 2005, Toronto.
110 MacDermid and Albo, 'Divided Province, Growing Protests,' 189.
111 Ontario PC Party, *The Common Sense Revolution*, 16.
112 David Lindsay, interview with Bryan Evans, 8 December 2004, Toronto.
113 Ministry of Finance, 'Government Outlines Spending Cuts, Audits, Accounting Review,' news release, 21 July 1995, at http://www.fin.gov.on.ca/english/media/1995/pressj21.html.
114 Ontario Financial Review Commission (OFRC), *Beyond the Numbers: A New Financial Management and Accountability Framework for Ontario* (Toronto: Queen's Printer, 1995), 1.
115 Ministry of Finance, 'Fiscal and Economic Statement,' news release, 29 November 1995, at http://www.fin.gov.on.ca/english/media/1995/news.html.
116 Ministry of Finance, *Ontario Budget* (Toronto: Queen's Printer, 1996), 73.
117 Ministry of Finance, 'Fiscal and Economic Statement,' news release, 29 November 1995, at http://www.fin.gov.on.ca/english/media/1995/news.html.
118 David Lindsay, interview with Bryan Evans, 8 December 2004, Toronto.
119 Donald J. Savoie, *The Politics of Public Spending in Canada* (Toronto: University of Toronto Press, 1990), 3.
120 Maurice Mullard, *The Politics of Public Expenditure*, 2nd ed. (London: Routledge, 1993), 9.
121 Ian Gough, 'Thatcherism and the Welfare State,' in *The Politics of Thatcherism*, ed. Stuart Hall and Martin Jacques (London: Lawrence and Wishart, 1983), 153.
122 John Clarke, Sharon Gewirtz, and Eugene McLaughlin, 'Reinventing the Welfare State,' in *New Managerialism, New Welfare?* ed. John Clarke, Sharon Gewirtz, and Eugene McLaughlin (London: Sage Publications, 2000), 5.
123 Ministry of Finance, *Ontario Budget – Investing in the Future* (Toronto: Queen's Printer, 1997), 67; *Ontario Budget – The Right Choices, Securing Our Future* (Toronto: Queen's Printer, 2003), 69.
124 This includes local government, provincial, federal government in Ontario, publicly owned agencies, crown corporations, and government-funded institutions such as hospitals, school boards, and colleges and universities.
125 Data obtained from Statistics Canada, *Labour Force Historical Review, 2001 (R)*, rev. ed., CD1; Statistics Canada catalogue no. 71F0004XCB (CD–ROM).
126 Ontario Civil Service Commission, *Annual Report* (Toronto: Queen's Printer, 1968), 35.   ·

127 Statistics Canada, *Labour Force Historical Review 2001 (R)*, rev. ed., table CD1T07, 'Employment by class of worker, public and private sector, sex, industry, Canada, province, annual average.'
128 Ministry of Finance, 2003, *Ontario Budget*, 'Ten Year Review of Selected Financial and Economic Statistics,' table B6, 56–7; Ministry of Finance, 2001, *Ontario Budget*, 'Ten Year Review of Selected Financial and Economic Statistics,' table B5, 68–9.
129 Guy Giorno, interview with Bryan Evans, 6 July 2004, Toronto.
130 Donald Kettl, *Deficit Politics: Public Budgeting in Its Institutional and Historical Context* (New York: Macmillan Publishing, 1992), 1.
131 The concept of path dependency essentially means that 'history matters,' in the sense that preceding decisions and events continue to influence, shape, and constrain contemporary decisions and events.

6 Thoughts into Words: The Budget Speech, 1968–2003

PATRICE DUTIL,[1] PETER RYAN, AND ANDRÉ GOSSIGNAC

The budget speech has consistently been the prime focus of the Ontario Treasury/Ministry of Finance. Today, dedicated staffs work year-round in preparing it and its new offspring, the 'Fall Update.' Countless hours are spent examining scenarios, pondering economic models, and injecting formulas with endless generations of data. Weeks are devoted to drafting the speech itself as the Frost buildings suddenly feature armed policemen mandated to ensure that the document's secrecy is not violated. The media and community experts are invited to special 'lock-ups' on the afternoon of the budget, and given a detailed briefing on the features of the document (which is delivered after the stock markets have closed). The media has come to play an important role in explaining the budget to the population, and so naturally a deal great deal of attention is paid to how the budget is worded to offer a mix of vision, caution, and reassurance. As the operations of government have grown more complex, and as the attendant technologies have grown more sophisticated, preparing the speech has necessarily become increasingly time consuming.

It was not always like this. In the early 1960s, the budget speech was assembled in a few weeks. Economic conditions were rapidly diagnosed, the political burden of taxation quickly assessed, and the treasurer would stand in the legislative assembly proud to produce as clean a document as could be rendered. As Finance deepened its capacity to link the budget with the economy in 1968, staff took more time to digest far greater masses of data.[2] The neighbourhood pub, Malloney's, grew legendary as the watering hole where the Finance staff conceived and wrote the budget (it was sometimes referred to as the Frost 'East' building).

There were significant changes in the responsibility for drafting the budget. Naturally, almost every budget boasted that it was the product of 'a careful review and assessment of all our policies and programs' and ensured 'enhanced economic prosperity and stability for the citizens of Ontario' (to borrow the 1971 speech's expressions). Regardless of how high the anticipated deficit was, the expenditure plans were always 'both appropriate and realistic' (1981), or 'realistic and credible' (1996). The budget packages inevitably maintained a 'commitment to productivity and efficiency' (1984), were presented as 'fair, balanced and necessary' (1993), and made 'strategic long-term investments in our people and our future' (1985), with 'a strategic focus on sustainable prosperity' (1991). Many treasurers vaunted their vision of government 'pioneer[ing] a pathway for the people' and saw their budget as 'a deliberate instrument of social and economic guidance' (1968).

Treasurers or ministers of finance use different words to convey different meanings. This chapter uses a combination of methods to understand better the messages conveyed by the budget speech of the treasurers/ministers of finance and their staff. The first part of the chapter discusses the evolution of the speeches in terms of their key themes based on a traditional content review. The second part lifts the skin of the speeches to get a better sense of what could be called their structural word-carpentry. It enquires about which words from 1968 to 2003 were chosen to convey thought and how word usage changed over time.

Concordance (or word counting) software commonly employed in the emerging field of 'digital humanities' was used. Digital humanities, as a discipline, has been dominated by literature and linguistic scholars since its inception in the mid-1980s. In their publications and journals such as the *Digital Humanities Quarterly* and *Literary and Linguistic Computing*, software is used to dissect word patterns and style, and even to help attribution in instances where the author of a piece is not evident. Linguists have used digital humanities to examine the origins of words and the evolution of dialects. They have applied these technologies to a wide range of languages ranging from Latin to Finnish.

The budget speeches from 1968 (the earliest digitized speeches) to 2003 are examined for their originality in terms of the policy themes they promoted and the words they used in combination to express the ideas they advanced. Digital humanities methods are relatively new for understanding politics, although 'key word' and 'issue units' analysis of agenda-setting language has become common in critiquing policy and government documents. Word counting methods are used here for the first time in understanding the styles of budget speeches, and so our aims are modest.³ From the composite image emerges a certain style of budget speech that can be defined as typically Ontarian. More than that, a pattern of kinships emerges from this study that points to distinct approaches and concerns of the governments with respect to the Ontario economy and to the fiscal position of the province. An examination of the speeches by a combination of traditional content review and the use of word pattern–recognition software shows that budget speeches have been affected by changing economic and fiscal circumstances, and that the rhetorical frameworks used by ministers of finance were also changed over time.⁴ The stylistic conventions common to the budget speeches were found to be generally respected, although those of the 1996–2001 period were distinctive in the manner in which a certain cult of the personality was promoted.

The MacNaughton, McKeough, Miller, Grossman Speeches (1968–1984)

The first three budgets delivered in this phase of the Robarts government were presented by Charles MacNaughton. His budget address of 1968 was in fact among the shortest speeches of all at 6764 words (Darcy McKeough's 1975 speech was shorter at 6375 words and Robert Nixon's speech of 1990 was all of 4038 words). His speech lamented the impact of inflation, rising interest rates, and tighter capital-market conditions along with slower growth and higher unemployment on governmental finances. In this context, MacNaughton fostered an 'investment budget' in his post-election budget of 1968. He offered more spending for education, housing, health, and local aid, on the one hand, as well as a 'more rational approach to economic management.' Although the government had already introduced a number of tax increases amounting to $300 million, it was still facing a deficit of $357 million. Government at this time perceived its role as playing a 'purposeful part in the economies and social development of the province and people,' with goals of ensuring progress and raising productivity, reducing price pressures, and increasing overall growth and employment.

A year later, the treasurer's budget speech was preoccupied with the distortions and shortages in the capital markets, as well as with 'the persistent and eroding force of inflation.' The budget, specifically designed as a 'Fiscal Framework for the Future,' would lay the foundations for a modernization of the public finance system in Ontario.

Education, health, housing, and services were again priority areas, but with less emphasis in a text dominated by the question of support to municipalities. Spending restraint was going to be exercised 'to the utmost,' but there still remained a $179 million deficit. This was also a tax budget that broadened the base of the retail sales tax and raised the tax rate on some products.

In 1970, the Ontario treasurer opened his budget speech with a dire assessment of the economic and fiscal situation: the economy was struggling under persistent inflation, tight money, and increasing unemployment, while the public sector was growing inexorably. The federal government began drawing more and more financial resources from Ontario for its expansionary fiscal policies, and this action became a focus of attention in the budget speech. The challenge was reframed by MacNaughton as the 'restoration of balance and stability in the economy and in the federal system,' and the reform of the existing tax system became the foremost priority.

Darcy McKeough became the new treasurer in 1971, and presented the pre-electoral budget of the new government led by Bill Davis. He presented the economic condition of the province as highly uncertain, especially in the face of weakening revenues and centralizing fiscal tendencies in Ottawa. McKeough boasted about 'act[ing] positively to protect the interests of our people' and creating 'a more dynamic, productive and progressively Conservative future.' McKeough underscored the need of increasing expansionary policies of the government, including an increase in the deficit and full-employment policies. It seemed that the new government was even more set in the Keynesian paradigm than its predecessor to the point of reversing certain trends visible in MacNaughton's last years. It was also the result of the electoral budget cycle: in addition to committing to new spending, the government undertook a number of tax and fee reductions. The objective of maintaining firm control over public spending was there, but the government was once again embarking on a route of important budgetary deficits in the order of $400 million. McKeough's speech also signalled an emphasis on the preservation and conservation of the environment, and to create a fulfilling quality of life for Ontario's citizens.

McKeough's 1972 speech argued that 'expansionary and progressive' fiscal policies were necessary to restore full employment and to foster maximum expansion in private-sector activity and investment, and in reordering priorities to meet 'urgent social needs.' The budget proposed an increase in the deficit to stimulate economic recovery. The financial aid to local government was once again increased and the reform of provincial-municipal finance was again accorded a high priority. Employment remained the overriding goal of the economic policy (health and education were noted at length as well). The expansionary policies would stay 'within the limits of moderation,' but the final effect was a large deficit of almost $600 million (a 13.4 per cent increase), although the government reversed the previous year's tax reductions by raising taxes and fees in selective areas by $134 million. In this aspect, this was a truly post-electoral budget.

In 1973, with John White as the new treasurer, the budget presented the now traditional dual preoccupation of moving towards full employment and of exercising maximum restraint on spending while providing resources for priority programs. Sharing provincial resources with local governments was to be given the highest priority. The tax burdens would be redistributed on the fairest possible basis, this subject being present all the way through the text. In order to accomplish this, the budget included increases of certain provincial taxes (retail sales tax, paid-up capital tax), while permitting offsetting decreases of property taxes and significant increases in tax credits. But the major goal of the new tax structure was an additional $333 million in revenues, which helped to shrink the deficit to about $400 million.

White's second budget was billed as 'a bold attack to meet the challenge of inflation.' In a speech that remarkably mentioned 'education' only once, inflation became an obsession. 'The government of Ontario is willing to use every practical measure within its constitutional jurisdiction to combat inflation,' he said, 'in the expectation that other responsible organizations in the public and private sectors will do the same. This is our promise and this is our challenge.' Several new measures were introduced that aimed at offsetting the effects of inflation on low-income families and other groups on relatively fixed incomes: a guaranteed annual income program for the elderly and the disabled, free prescription drugs for elderly persons with low incomes and for all individuals on social assistance, enriched tax credits including a doubling of the property tax credit, and a broadening of exemptions from the retail sales tax. Another set of proposals was intended to stimulate small Canadian businesses, with investment-related incentives designed to encourage the growth of active, Canadian-controlled private corporations. More resources would be directed to local governments. Finally, the budgetary deficit amounted to $625 million.

In preparation for the elections of 1975, Darcy McKeough returned as treasurer and delivered the budget speech that year. Inflation remained a major economic problem, although productivity was mentioned as well. The minister announced several actions that would help stimulate consumer spending and the economy: the reduction of the basic retail sales tax rate from 7 to 5 per cent for a period of eight months, selective income tax cuts including new exemptions, enriched guaranteed annual income payments and new health benefits, extension of the free prescription drug program to all pensioners, more tax credits for small businesses, new programs supporting the farming community, and a doubling of grants for housing including a grant for first home purchases (housing was a key theme of the speech). All of this came with the price of a $544 million deficit absorbed using cash reserves and capital markets. At the same time, the treasurer underscored the need of limiting government spending: 'I am convinced,' he said, 'that one of the root causes of the current inflation problem in Canada is excessive government spending and unnecessary growth in the size and complexity of the public sector. This has shifted an increasing share of our total resources out of private production uses in the economy and has eroded the taxpayer's hard-earned income.' The government's plan for expenditure control concentrated on its own operational expenditures, requiring departments to review their staffing, asking them to absorb the cost increases resulting from inflation, trying to eliminate programs that are no longer useful, and postponing certain provincial building projects.

The fight against inflation was the 'no. 1 objective for economic policy' in the post-electoral budget of 1976 (the Bill Davis government was now in the minority). According to McKeough, the Ontario economy did not require government stimulation at this time, and the thrust of provincial policy would be on private-sector expansion to generate growth and employment. Fiscal restraint was one of the key words of the speech; cash requirements would be largely reduced, which was going to happen through tax increases totalling $330 million. Simultaneously, the health premiums were raised by almost 50 per cent. Containing the growth of provincial spending to 10 per cent was contrasted with the 16 per cent growth of the federal government, and the fact that the new budget did not contain any new public borrowing. After losing the majority, the minister focused his ire on the government in Ottawa:

We need nothing short of a fresh start on developing a national economic policy for Canada. This must include a recognition that it is the free market economy, not bureaucratic regulation, upon which our present standard of living was achieved. It is the free market economy upon which our future economic growth must rely ... If governments continue to expand faster than the private sector, I see no hope for either controlling inflation or solving other national economic problems. Too many of the talents of the nation are already locked up in government offices ... It is imperative that governments reduce their borrowing as well as their spending. Governments cannot live on credit indefinitely any more than families can ... Moreover, stable growth of the economy depends on increased investment by big and small businesses alike. No business can finance its essential expansion if governments crowd the financial markets and take all the money.

Although spending in the fiscal year 1976–7 came in $11 million below the original estimates (the first time since 1947), Darcy McKeough's fifth budget continued to emphasize fiscal restraint. While the government did estimate that it was presenting a package that included a $1 billion deficit, it said that there was no need for increased taxation, and the government embraced the goal of balancing the Ontario budget by 1980–1. Restraint, employment, investment, and efficiency were the key areas of government action. Another change was the extension of the government's fiscal planning horizon beyond the traditional single year.

In spite of these declarations, the province experienced an additional revenue shortfall in 1977–8, setting back the goal of a balanced budget. In his sixth (and last) budget, McKeough estimated that the cash requirements would decline to $1.55 billion, $200 million short of the target set earlier. The fiscal actions of the budget aimed to selectively stimulate the economy by expanding employment for Ontario's youth, cutting taxes to help the tourism and hospitality industry, and improving the situation in the mining industry. The spending growth rate for 1978–9 decreased to 7 per cent for the fourth year in a row, and 'balanced and equitable' tax increases would raise an additional $374 million. The control of health costs continued to be a high priority as well, with a dramatic 30 per cent increase in Ontario Health Insurance Plan (OHIP) premiums.

The 1979 budget presented by Frank Miller specified the need to create more jobs as the most important issue, especially for young people entering the labour force. Battling inflation was another priority. The budget proposed incentives for economic growth and small-business development. Growth and prosperity were only possible through the actions of the private sector; the treasurer, reaffirming the values of his predecessor, stated: 'The private sector flourishes best with a minimum of government regulation.' Continuing, he highlighted his anti-regulation stance: 'In fact, one of the main reasons prompting me to enter politics was my perception as a small businessman of the need to encourage government to lighten the burden of regulation and interference on the business community in Ontario.' The legislature was assured that government would allocate most of its resources to areas of high social priority: health, education, and social service.

Ensuring the financial viability of the health-care system was held as important, necessitating another increase in OHIP premiums. Since the existence of the premiums itself was a subject of political debate, Miller decisively reiterated the belief that the OHIP premiums would be maintained, constituting a 'visible and useful financing link' between individuals and their health-care system. On the tax front, the government followed other provinces by completely abolishing succession duties and gift taxes (a gradual elimination over several years), as well as easing and simplifying the capital tax for small businesses. At the same time, a number of small tax increases were introduced in the area of corporate taxation and the retail sales tax. Consequently, the net cash requirements were in the amount of $1,153 million, which constituted about 8 per cent of the revenues and were within the financing capacity provided by the province's non-public borrowing sources.

The first budget of the 1980s started with good news: the previous year's deficit was $500 million smaller than planned. The three traditional objectives of maintaining a favourable climate for job growth and economic expansion, ensuring a high standard of social services, and combating inflation by controlling government spending and minimizing deficit levels were reiterated. The minister noted the dramatically increased oil prices which contributed to inflation, in turn triggering 'soaring interest rates' – which were key words in the budget speech. Miller's assessment of the economy was pessimistic: announcing 'a more difficult year,' slower job creation, and possibly worse inflation. The minister insisted that he was presenting a budget that would provide a firm foundation for 'economic prosperity and social progress,' and small businesses, pensioners, and rural and remote communities were among the targeted public. New tax incentives would also promote energy conservation. There were no tax increases, and the resulting governmental net cash requirements would border on $1 billion. The 'year of economic uncertainty' was used as a reason to pause the deficit reduction strategy.

After two minority governments, the Progressive Conservatives (PCs) finally. succeeded in being elected with a majority in 1981, and Frank Miller could present his third budget. Again, the refrain was the fight against inflation in an environment of slow economic growth. Health care remained a key concern, and the budget recognized the priorities 'while taking into account the need for an appropriate level of revenues,' which could mean only one thing – new tax increases, including personal income tax, as well as tax increases on gasoline, fuel, cigarettes, tobacco, and domestic beer – all above $600 million, which allowed the government to keep the deficit below $1 billion.

The minister of finance promised to make the tax system more progressive: Ontario already had an income tax reduction program that eliminated the tax for more than 400,000 lower-income Ontarians. It was now expanded and more Ontarians were made eligible for assistance in paying OHIP premiums. Federal–provincial relations constituted an important concern for the government, and the need to renegotiate the fiscal arrangements was underscored, in particular concerning the equalization program. The regional fiscal disparities 'were so large that normally healthy interprovincial competition could deteriorate and lead to destructive protectionism and loss of national economic strength.'

A year later, Miller talked about 'some of the most difficult economic times facing Ontario,' concluding that the 'government cannot conjure up a way of paying for a decent standard of public services that does not involve some increases in tax levels or the deficit.' The major theme of the 1982 budget was 'getting people back to work.' The speech proposed to stimulate the economy with a major job creation program involving the employment of laid-off forest workers to work on forest management projects, a special mining employment program, and accelerating public investment projects in all parts of the province, with emphasis on those areas where unemployment was highest. A new initiative for stimulating housing construction was launched, and direct assistance to farmers was increased, as were new tax-reduction measures for small businesses. The financial consequence of new measures was a $672-million increase in net cash requirements over the previous year. The province raised additional tax revenue by broadening the retail sales tax base, and increasing, among others, revenues from alcohol and tobacco. To get inflation under control, the government was going to exercise restraint in wage increases, which would be cut to 6 per cent that year. The deficit was temporarily increased to $2.2 billion, and would be financed through non-public borrowing and liquid reserves.

The fifth and last budget prepared by Miller was supposed to 'encourage and sustain the economic momentum as the economy gains strength.' The government introduced measures which would help investment, such as expanding the tax exemption for production machinery and equipment, exempting from retail sales tax all purchases of certain transportation vehicles and equipment, and extending for two years the flat-tax provision for small corporations. To encourage consumer spending, the budget implemented a temporary program of retail sales tax exemptions for selected items, targeting narrowly products with high Canadian content. On the other hand, the retail sales tax on alcohol and tobacco was increased, as was the general rate of corporations' income tax. During the eighteen following months, a 5 per cent surcharge on Ontario personal income tax, called the social services maintenance tax, was going to be collected, an idea apparently borrowed from the New Democratic Party. Concerning the need to constrain government expenditures, the government created a formal program review process to examine all provincial programs to see where savings could be achieved. The target for 1983 was to identify $300 million of in-year expenditure savings, and as Miller stated himself, 'cabinet is sadly lacking in its applause for that one.' The deficit was going to be about $2.7 billion, financed primarily from non-public sources, but also from public capital markets.

In introducing the 1984 budget, Larry Grossman pointed to an economy that had recovered from recession. His budget speech underscored the commitment to economic transformation needed in times of a changing world economy, focusing on the ability to invent, create, and be entrepreneurial. The government wanted to 'invest vigorously in supporting and shaping change in Ontario. But in doing so, we must live within our means. Deficits must come down.' Already $350 million were cut from the planned deficit of the previous year. Also in 1984, provincial net cash requirements would be reduced, and the growth of revenues would be 2 points higher than the growth of expenditures. Consequently, the deficit was expected to represent 7.6 per cent of total government spending, with no public borrowing considered. Grossman decided to hold direct operating expenditures for most activities to the previous year's levels, instead of permitting them to rise with inflation.

172   Patrice Dutil, Peter Ryan, and André Gossignac

There was also a new approach to public policy: The government rejected temporary make-work schemes, choosing rather to make strategic long-term investments with a $500-million economic transformation fund 'to equip citizens and industries to meet the demands of a changing economy.' The budget significantly expanded and reformed support for youth employment and job access for women, introduced measures assisting older workers in acquiring new skills, strengthening the role and resources of learning institutions, quickening the modernization of Ontario's industries, stimulating innovation and small business, helping break the cycle of welfare dependency, and offering more independence to the elderly and the disabled. In spite of the high costs of these initiatives, there were no tax increases and the personal income tax surcharge of 5 per cent was going to expire as scheduled. Actually, this budget speech clearly differentiated from the majority of other speeches, where the subject of taxes was decidedly dominating the text. Here, such words as 'new,' 'provide,' 'program,' 'people,' 'training,' 'young,' 'youth,' 'help,' 'initiative,' and 'opportunities' came well before 'taxes.'[5]

The Nixon Speeches (1985–1990)

Before Bette Stephenson, the first woman to command the post of minister of finance, could present her first budget in 1985, the newly elected PC minority government was defeated in the legislature. The Liberals, strengthened by an accord with the NDP, would lead the government and Robert Nixon, the new minister of finance, presented the budget belatedly in October. In this first Liberal budget since 1943, the government aimed at 'carefully balancing social responsibility with fiscal responsibility.' Cashing out the fourth successive year of economic expansion, and a relatively low rate of inflation, the government was going to assure greater certainty in funding to local governments and the agencies providing health and education programs. The government's priorities focused on strengthening and revitalizing the post-secondary education system, meeting the needs in the health-care system associated with an aging population and new technologies, and fostering regional community-based economic development initiatives.

On fiscal measures, the Ontario government distanced itself from the PC federal government, whose tax measures were viewed as moving 'our overall income tax system in the wrong direction' and provided 'another large tax break for higher-income Canadians.' On this front, provincial Liberals were camped on the opposite shore, raising Ontario's general rate of personal income tax, imposing a surtax of 3 per cent on high-income earners, while at the same time enriching Ontario's tax reduction program by exempting another 50,000 low-income individuals from Ontario tax. And since 'fairness requires an appropriate balance between the taxation of individuals and that of the corporate sector,' additional charges were imposed on the latter. The budget speech included reviews of the proposed spending plans of each ministry, and limited their spending by $260 million. Three policy secretariats would be shut down, and certain Ontario delegations in the United States and in Europe would be closed. The budget also promised across-the-board reductions in government salary and wage spending. As a result, the net cash requirements totalled $2.2 billion (5.8 per cent of total government spending).

Nixon started his second budget speech in 1986 by presenting the beliefs underlying the government's economic approach and the

> conviction that the surest route to continuing prosperity is a combination of good business and businesslike government. The private sector's job is to create a competitive economy. The role of government is to help Ontario business get on with that job and to manage the province's own affairs in an efficient and cost-effective manner. This will be reflected in a move towards pay-as-you-go fiscal management, aimed at balancing operating expenditures with current revenues.

A new management system was also going to be implemented, the central feature of which was a capital account from which each ministry's capital requirements would be met. Allocating the money according to multi-year spending plans would give each ministry a certainty concerning its resources. Nixon warned, however, that it would be

> false economy to try to balance budgets by ignoring society's real needs ... We will face these problems directly while retaining our framework of fiscal responsibility. Our social programs are an integral part of the wealth creation process ... We need a healthy economy to pay for social programs; but social programs, in turn, help to build a healthy economy, by helping people adapt to the dislocations that economic progress sometimes creates. This is a budget that combines social concern with common sense.

This approach would include strengthening the links between the private sector and Ontario's universities, supporting new and growing companies, encouraging better training, and promoting excellence in education, which would be supported by a $1-billion technology fund for the next ten years. The role of the service sector was appreciated, and the government included service initiatives for small companies. There was another important increase in the budget for the Ministry of Agriculture (almost 40 per cent since 1984) and new social programs for shelter subsidies were introduced. The Ontario income tax reduction program for low-income people was broadened, and OHIP premiums were eliminated for some 35,000 other low-income Ontarians. The anticipation was that the government would close its books for that year with a $1.5 billion deficit. The public debt was expected to continue to grow, but at a slower rate.

The budget of 1987 emphasized education, technology development, and entrepreneurship, which were recognized as 'the surest foundations of Ontario's continued prosperity.' Among five priority areas were the promotion of economic expansion and job creation, the enhancement of opportunities in sectors and regions that were not fully participating in the benefits of economic growth, the rebuilding of aging infrastructure and accommodation of growth pressures, the improvement of important social programs and the fairer distribution of wealth in society, as well as maintaining vigilance over tax levels and the deficit. The importance of taking part in international exchanges, already present in several previous budgets, was again emphasized, as Ontario aspired to maintain and increase its share of world trade and investment. The speech also announced that the government would continue to ease the tax burden of low-income Ontarians: an additional 100,000 people could avoid paying Ontario income tax and 60,000 people paid less. Ontario reduced again the number of people paying health insurance plan premiums. The speech, finally, indicated that Ontario was studying major changes to the social welfare system which would abolish obvious disincentives to work. The provincial deficit was reduced to $980 million and the province's operating account essentially balanced.[6]

Nixon remained in his position after the Peterson government won a majority in September 1987. The budget speech for 1988 pointed to a well-performing economy, but raised concerns regarding the lack of productivity growth and the need to build a more competitive Ontario. The budget brought forward a new program in support of research and development, more resources for skills development and training, as well as a new program to assist industry and encourage the development of new technologies in Ontario. Anticipating attacks for his level of spending, Nixon maintained that it was still one of the lowest in Canada. He underscored as well the decreasing deficit and net cash requirements.

In 1989 Nixon announced the largest operating surplus in Ontario's history, with the deficit having been cut to $577 million, its lowest level in fifteen years. More than three-quarters of increased expenditures was dedicated to health care, education, housing, and social services, and major transportation investments were announced. To further support the growth of small and medium businesses, Ontario established a growth ventures programs. Not least, the health premiums were eliminated and replaced by a new payroll tax. Revenues were bolstered as the rate of personal income tax was increased by one percentage point. There was a new tax imposed on commercial property owners in the Greater Toronto Area (GTA), the rates of tax on gasoline and diesel fuel were increased, a new environmental technologies program tax was levied on fuel-inefficient cars, and a tax was established on the purchase of tires. Nixon announced that sustainable and environmentally compatible economic growth was going to be a priority.

Having finished 1989–90 with a budgetary surplus, and after eight years of economic expansion, Nixon would present a balanced budget addressing the realities of the 1990s in his sixth and last budget. He emphasized the government's response to an aging population, working families, a commuting labour force, the need for clean water, and the demands of competition in a global marketplace. At the centre of the government's strategy continued to be a healthy, well-educated, and adaptable workforce, continued development of the province's infrastructure, as well as high-quality social services and a fair distribution of the benefits of the provincial wealth. The health sector got several important budgetary increases, social programs would be modernized and enriched, and the decentralization of certain governmental offices and job continued. Not only was the budget supposed to be balanced, but the government would have enough surplus to pay back $430 million in debt, which would be the first reduction in Ontario's debt in forty-three years.

The Laughren Speeches (1991–1995)

The arrival of a recession radically changed the situation, and the NDP won the provincial elections in September 1990. Floyd Laughren would present the next four budgets. The 1991 budget speech presented the fiscal policy position of the new government and the belief that 'government can and would be active in supporting positive economic change and in ensuring that the costs of adjustment are shared fairly.' The budget aimed to put in place the foundation of 'a new economic strategy, a strategy which has sustainable prosperity as its central goal and fairness as its guiding principle. A prosperous and sustainable economy provides secure, well-paid jobs at high levels of employment. It is an economy where the quality, not just the quantity, of economic growth is important. Economic growth must be both environmentally and socially sustainable and all Ontarians must share fairly in prosperity.' 'Social partnerships' would be the basis for the economic strategy, including, among others, developing new working labour–business relationships, with the government 'creating the conditions which allow labour, business and communities to work out co-operative responses to economic change.' This cooperation would include increases to the minimum wage, pension reform, amendments to the Ontario Labour Relations Act, more regulated layoffs, and severance pay provisions.

According to Laughren, allowing the deficit to rise 323 per cent (from $3 billion to $9.7 billion, 23 per cent of governmental revenues – in fact, it rose to $10.9 billion) was 'not only justifiable, it is the most responsible choice we could make … to fight the deficit or fight the recession.' Instead of the budgetary deficit, there was talk about 'starting to reduce social deficits.' Education and health care in all its dimensions would be at the centre of these efforts, as well as social assistance, whose costs rose by 40 per cent, and provincially supported housing increased to an unprecedented level. The government offered direct employment to thousands of people through the $700-million anti-recession program, introduced the employee wage protection program, and reduced or eliminated taxes for people at the low end of the income scale. At the same time, there was an increase in the personal income surtax rate ('ensuring that those at the upper end of the income scale pay a greater share'), increases of the rates of tax on gasoline and diesel fuel, cigarettes and alcohol, reduced tax exemptions for small businesses, and increased capital taxes on banks and loan and trust companies.

Greater social equity, economic renewal, and fair and effective fiscal management were interdependent priorities of the 1992 budget that endeavoured to strike a balance of creating jobs, maintaining services, and controlling the deficit. Policies increasing productivity and encouraging innovation would secure investment in Ontario's future. But behind the slogans, some have called the real NDP approach a lot of 'tax and spend,' and although, after the spending explosion of the previous year, the government could claim to have the lowest rate of growth in total spending in thirty-nine years, again there was announced a $10 billion deficit. Among new initiatives, the Jobs Ontario training fund that would provide jobs and training for the long-term unemployed and 20,000 subsidized childcare spaces were made available to meet the needs of program participants.

New programs emerged. A transition fund was provided to help hospitals, schools, colleges, and universities restructure and reform their public services. Other programs included the Jobs Ontario homes fund, telecommunications projects, environmental projects, new investments to support state-of-the-art upgrades, and expansion of public transit. Ontario's corporate tax rate on manufacturing and processing profits, as well as farming, mining, logging, and fishing profits was rather slightly reduced, as was the corporate income tax rate for small business. New tax credits were designed to provide higher benefits to low-income seniors. On the other hand, the government was 'raising taxes in a way that shares the tax burden fairly,' increasing the Ontario personal income tax rate, raising the surtax rates on personal income, and drastically increasing the number of taxpayers who would pay it (an additional burden of $660 million). Since the profit level of the banking industry had improved, it caught a temporary income tax of 10 per cent and the capital tax rate on banks was increased. The employment health tax was also imposed on self-employed individuals. Looking for economies, the government froze salaries of cabinet ministers, MPPs, and most senior managers. Other government employees would have only a 1 per cent wage increase, while non-salary overhead costs for all ministries were being cut by 10 per cent.

The 1993 budget speech followed the previous year's address, with 'jobs' and 'services' as key words. For Floyd Laughren, this budget marked a turning point for Ontario at a time when winds battering the economy were gathering strength. After two weighty deficits, the government wanted to 'invest in Ontario's future rather than borrow from it … We cannot build our future on a foundation of debt. We must invest in jobs, make government more efficient and put public services on a sound financial footing.' Although, for the first time since 1942, operating spending would actually decline, the deficit was planned again to be around $10 billion, and what some have called a 'spending spree' continued. In the meantime, Ontario had become the largest borrower in the world at the sub-national level, borrowing on average more than

$1 billion a month, and spending more on interest costs than on schools. On the tax front, the government increased personal income tax for all taxpayers by three points, increased again the Ontario surtax rates,[7] extended the retail sales tax, ended some sales tax rebates, introduced a corporate minimum tax, and introduced or raised various other taxes, fees, and levies.

Simultaneously, the government imposed savings on internal government operations by reducing the cost of running government by 10 per cent: programs were streamlined, field offices rationalized, and the bureaucratic layers cut down. The number of ministries was reduced from twenty-eight to twenty, and their budgets for non-salary costs were chopped by almost one quarter over the previous two years. Looking desperately for revenues, the government assigned 147 staff to tax collection and audit positions to recuperate non-paid taxes.

In his fourth and last budget Laughren reduced again overall program spending, while at the same time preserving funding commitment to health, education, and municipalities. The budget cut taxes to encourage companies to hire new workers: businesses expanding their payroll were not to pay any additional employer health tax on their increased payroll for the first twelve months. There was also an innovation tax credit for small and medium enterprises (SMEs). Concerned with an excess of government red tape for new businesses, the government was moving to reduce the paperwork burden and to introduce one-stop registration for new businesses. Businesses would also be able to use a single form to remit retail sales tax and employer health tax. The government was committed to 'ending welfare as we know it and replacing it with a program that helps people get jobs.' The key element of the reform strategy was called Job Link, designed to increase the number of job placements and training opportunities available to social-assistance recipients and providing them with job-search skills. Enabling more people to buy their own homes should be done using a housing loan guarantee fund to help lower-income families buy homes through community-based initiatives. The year's deficit would approximate $8.5 billion (which still represented 20 per cent of the revenues).

The Ernie Eves Speeches (1996–2002)

Ernie Eves became the minister of finance under the Mike Harris Progressive Conservative government. There was no budget speech in the Legislative Assembly in 1995, but the Ministry of Finance published a detailed financial statement with an introduction that in its form and content resembled a budget speech. Five years after the social-democratic renewal of governmental policies, there was another renewal – this time a conservative one that would 'restor[e] confidence in this province.' In times when 'Ontarians want an economy that is freed from the burdens of red tape and overtaxation – where individuals have the opportunity and the means to set goals for themselves and for their communities,' the government's goal was to create 'an Ontario of opportunity rather than dependence, where genuine need is met with compassion and support, and where government is a partner in change rather than an obstacle.' This would be done by stopping government overspending, and getting Ontario out from under the burden of rising interest costs. The statement reiterated the ideological vision presented already in the *Common Sense Revolution*:

> The root of our debt problem is government overspending. As a result of the fiscal situation we inherited, currently the government spends $1 million an hour more than it receives in revenues. We are determined to stop that. In the last 10 years government spending has almost doubled, while the accumulated debt has almost tripled. What do the people of Ontario have to show for it? Fewer jobs today than in 1989, higher unemployment and nearly three times as many people on social assistance as 10 years ago. The experience of the past decade shows that overspending, high taxes and deficit financing do not create lasting jobs. In fact, they are barriers to job creation.

The document noted that after sixty-five tax increases in last ten years (of which eleven were income tax hikes), Ontario was still facing a potential deficit of over $11 billion.

The government presented deficit targets for the next five years, announced the creation of a contingency fund to cushion against unforeseen economic changes, and immediately cut spending by $2 billion, eliminating over thirty programs ('to serve people properly, governments must focus on priorities'). Reductions in many other programs and transfers were announced, touching also the always top-priority sectors of education and local government. Only the total spending on health would be protected. In addition, people receiving drug benefits were going to be asked to share the costs, following the scheme used in other provinces.[8] The cost of internal government administration would be cut by one third by the end of 1997–8. There was a new vision as well of how government would operate that vowed to 'stop focusing on process, and instead set its sights on constant improvement in performance.' New steps were taken towards open and accountable government, with full public disclosure of salaries and benefits paid to senior employees in the public sector. Rallies and demonstrations would occur in the months and years to come as the public reacted to the changes and cuts. There was also new accounting presenting a more complete image of the province's financial situation, including the cost of different liabilities and losses, and the full cost of public-debt interest incurred each year. Hundreds of government spending programs would be reviewed: 'For every program we are asking: is it in the public interest? Does it help or hinder job creation? Is it fair and equitable? And is it well managed?' All regulation affecting business would be reviewed.

In 1996 the budget speech justified the need to downsize services and programs by invoking 'actions to make a real and direct improvement in the lives of our children.' The government was going to leave more money in the hands of hard-working Ontarians, invest in programs in such priority areas as health care, education, and community safety, and reduce the size and cost of government. The objective was 'a society that not only believes in compassion and justice but has the financial capacity to make it a reality.' The deficit would fall to $8.2 billion. The government had already passed legislation to reform MPPs' compensation, get rid of hidden tax-free allowances, abolish their 'gold-plated' pension plan, and cut their pay by a further 5 per cent ('No consideration will be given to changing that level of compensation until the budget is balanced'). Trying to find the best way to deliver government services, the government was going to transfer different activities to the private sector or private-public partnerships, avoiding a large government bureaucracy. The business subsidy programs were eliminated as not creating lasting jobs. Instead, the first $400,000 in annual payroll was permanently exempted from the employer health payroll tax. Ontario's income tax rate would be cut by 30 per cent over three years, two-thirds of the benefits going to middle-income Ontarians. There was also a new rebate of land transfer tax for first-time buyers of new homes. Attached to the idea of progressivity, the PC government imposed the 'Fair Share' health-care levy on higher incomes.

In his third budget, Eves could announce a decrease of the deficit level to $6.6 billion and the projected elimination of the deficit in 2000–1. The budget speech recognized a need to cut taxes, to limit the size of the government, to continue to reduce the regulation and red tape that were discouraging business, and to create an environment that encourages communities and small businesses to grow and create jobs. Ontarians would be able to keep more of their money, and the government to invest the available resources in priority programs, while at the same lifting 'the burden of debt from our children's shoulders.' The budget aimed to invest and reinvest in health care, with the government willing to create the most comprehensive and effective health care services in the country. Among new initiatives, there were a rural job strategy, enhanced support for small-business lending, the acceleration of highway construction, an R&D challenge fund, and a new child-care tax credit.

Eves started his 1998 budget speech by noting that since the beginning of that year, Ontario had experienced a rate of job growth unprecedented in the past fifteen years, with more jobs created in a one-year period than in the entire history of the province. The finance minister was ecstatic: 'Today, Ontarians have a renewed confidence, a renewed optimism in the future. Today, Ontarians believe, as do we, that our province is once again the best place in the world in which to live, work and invest ... Tax cuts were a major part of this creating jobs and economic growth; tax cuts don't just create opportunities, they ensure a quality of life that allows all Ontarians to take advantage of these opportunities today and in the future.' The new budget was building on the foundations of the previous four years through further tax cuts, including to personal and property taxes ('Every Ontario taxpayer gets a tax cut'), additional improvements in health care, support for children, a new student assistance program, initiatives for safer communities, and investments in learning. The tax rate for small business corporations was going to be cut in half (from 9.5 per cent, the highest rate in Canada, to 4.75 per cent, the lowest), over the next eight years. There was a renewed pledge to balance the budget in 2000–1, while the 1998 deficit was planned to be $4.2 billion, including a $650-million contingency reserve fund.

The 1999 budget speech reiterated policy positions of the PCs, with tax cuts as the basis for a strong economy: 'This government believes we must continue to cut taxes, create jobs and further strengthen our economy ... High taxes kill jobs, they stifle prosperity and they threaten the government's ability to support the programs that Ontario families value most.' New tax cuts brought 'to 99 the number of tax cuts we are delivering to the people of the province of Ontario – 99 cuts, so you know who my hero is, Mr Speaker: Wayne Gretzky. Wayne Gretzky may be the greatest hockey player ever, but Mike Harris is the superstar of tax cuts.' Innovation was one of the key themes of the budget, the challenge being for all Ontarians to do their part in maintaining economic growth: But 'innovation does not mean just creating and using new technologies and it does not apply only to high-tech businesses. It means developing new ideas and seizing opportunities to ensure that Ontario remains competitive. The challenge is for all Ontarians – individuals, businesses, communities, institutions, organizations and governments – to do their part.' What the province needed was vision and the leadership necessary to build a strong economy: 'With a clear vision that tax cuts strengthen the economy and create jobs, we have been able to provide the means to invest in the priority programs that Ontarians value most.' Health was another of the priorities of this budget, with a second year in a row of important funding increases. For the fourth consecutive year the government had overachieved its deficit target, reducing it to around $2 billion, and the deficit would be eliminated completely the following year, as promised.

In his sixth and last budget, Eves, who stayed as minister of finance in the second Harris government, could finally start his address with 'The budget of Ontario is balanced.' Already the previous year the government had reduced the debt by several hundred millions, and the new goal was to more than double the promised $2 billion debt reduction during this mandate. Health care was a top priority for the government, with important spending increases for, among other things, restructuring and reforming the health care system to keep up with new technology and to meet the challenges of a growing and aging population. With the goal of giving Ontario's children a healthy start and a good education, the government expanded children's health programs and illness prevention, added additional funding to reduce class sizes, increased investments to expand and renew colleges and universities, and continued to 'provide parents and families with a greater voice in decisions about special education.' Meticulously counting his tax cuts, Eves proposed another sixty-seven tax cuts this year, including a comprehensive strategy to cut both the general corporate income tax rate and the manufacturing and processing rate by almost half by the year 2005. There were also additional tax cuts for Ontarians with lower incomes and for middle-income taxpayers.

When Eves decided to leave his political career in the beginning of 2001, Jim Flaherty was named as minister of finance, and introduced the third balanced budget in a row – the first such achievement in

nearly one hundred years. The budget plan was based on fiscal responsibility, growth, and accountability to the people of Ontario:

> That plan is … both responsive and responsible. It speaks to the issues that
> people talk about … The initiatives that I'm announcing … stem from
> weeks of extensive consultations with my colleagues, business people,
> community organizations and other people from across the province of
> Ontario. People know that we have come a long way in Ontario since
> 1995. They know that they're better off. People have told us that they want
> to preserve and build on those successes … The people of Ontario are ask-
> ing us to think ahead and exercise discipline through strong leadership
> and prudent management of their money. They are asking us to focus on
> those things that matter to them the most.

The budget pledged to continue to cut taxes, to pay down debt, and to
introduce sweeping reforms to hold the public sector more accountable
to taxpayers. Apart from the traditional priorities of health, education,
efficient transportation, and low taxes, there was also a new priority for
clean air and water with increased investments in the environment. The
budget continued increasing health-care spending, but underscored
the necessity of a fundamental reform to control its spiralling costs.
Another priority was to care for the most vulnerable. After having paid
down another $3 billion of the debt, the government promised to elim-
inate the personal income surtax for middle-class families.

After the retirement of Mike Harris in April 2002, Eves took over as
premier, while Janet Ecker became finance minister. In an open and
trade-oriented Ontario economy, the global economy of 2001 started to
slow down after the events of 9/11. Prudent management, and the use
of a $1-billion reserve, allowed the government to balance the budget
the previous year and to again take $127 million off Ontario's accumu-
lated debt. The budget was sticking to the fundamentals of the Common
Sense Revolution, trying to find a balance 'between meeting today's
needs and investing for tomorrow's.' 'Prudence and frugality' were announced as contributions that government could make to prosperity,
continuing to pursue tight fiscal discipline, a balanced budget, and debt
reduction to efficiently and effectively provide more resources to priority areas, including major investments in health care, in education, and
in a clean and safe environment.

Except for these sectors, overall program spending was going to decline by 2 per cent. In a difficult economic situation, some planned tax

cuts were delayed for a year. The government continued, however, to cut taxes for small businesses, which were creating nearly half of new jobs, and to remove modest-income people from the income tax rolls. Additional revenues would be won from an increased tobacco tax. The government continued to reform its way of working, incorporating zero-based budgeting principles into a business planning process. Every ministry was required to review its entire program spending over a four-year cycle to determine program effectiveness and efficiency. The following year the government would also move towards a multi-year approach to budgeting and funding.

In 2003, for the first time in Ontario's history, the budget was not delivered in the legislature, but the pre-election spending plan, in which everything was 'important' or 'very, very important,' was presented by Ecker in a TV broadcast from the Brampton headquarters of auto-parts manufacturer Magna International.[9] Responding to the priorities of health care and education, the budget continued with 'the building blocks that are key to a strong and resilient economy: competitive tax rates, lower taxes, balanced budgets, prudent fiscal management, cutting waste and the strategic investment of public dollars in key priorities.' Affected by the SARS crisis, and facing the first job losses in eighteen months, the province was trying to avoid further economic losses by introducing a sales tax holiday on tourist accommodations and attractions, allowing money for marketing and promotion, and compensating those whose lives had been affected by the SARS outbreak. The budget was still supposed to be balanced, although the fiscal year 2003–4 finished finally with a $5.5 billion deficit.

Using Digital Humanities Techniques and Methods to Reveal Differences

Even as they cope with new economic forces, ministers of finance (with their political staffs) and the key budget drafters in the bureaucracy choose a range of words to describe the context in which they operate and what they wish for in terms of their budget. The selection of words used is, in and of itself, indicative of what is preponderant in a minister's thinking. They create the narrative as a guide for the future of Ontario's economic well-being. The choice of words will also reflect, to varying degrees, the political and ideological sensitivities of the minister, and of his staff. The choice of words similarly can help attest to the kinship between various communication approaches and the degree to which they are original.

In order to control the biases of the software available to analyse word use, five distinctive applications were applied to deconstruct the Ontario Budget Speeches (OBS) and to establish the variations in their style and content.[10] Digital tools allow for a visualizing and comparison of key words as data. They can count all the words in a document and their frequency of use, which can be used to establish a document's main themes. They can compare key words across a number of documents to demonstrate stylistic variations. They can create visualizations of the different patterns of stylistic variations among different documents using statistical means like Principal Components Analysis (PCA). These three methods were used to dissect the OBSs.

Word Frequency and the 'Top Report' Themes

Word frequency lists were created for each of the thirty-five speeches using the TaporWare Word List software, and were colour-coded to track the top thirty-five unique words in all of the parties. Table 6.1 shows the language used most frequently during each partisan period, which offers a broad entry point into understanding the words in the OBSs as data. In terms of frequency, the top thirty-five words made up roughly 30–45 per cent of the unique words in these documents; their intended frequency therefore made for a reliable indicator of the major themes in each of these periods. Key concepts in these clusters were revealed as follows:

1 PCs, 1968–84: an emphasis on 'tax,' 'reform,' and 'growth'
2 Liberals, 1985–90: an emphasis on 'programs,' 'health care,' and 'social assistance'
3 NDP, 1991–5: an emphasis on the particular 'Ontarian' context at the time and the increasing 'deficit'
4 PCs, 1996–2003: an emphasis on 'cut,' 'health care,' and 'education'

The speeches clearly had different priorities in mind, and point to various social agendas and economic concerns. A run-down of the list shows how the word 'new,' for instance, appears often between 1968 and 1984 (an average of 31 appearances per year over 16 years), but drops dramatically under the Liberal (19 mentions per budget speech) and the NDP (18 mentions) governments, only to be revived (36 mentions per budget) by the PC government under Ernie Eves. The word 'program/s/ mmes' shows an interesting pattern. The Tories mentioned the word

Table 6.1 Top 35 unique words by party and period

AGGREGATE_PC1968_1984		AGGREGATE_LIB1985_1990		AGGREGATE_NDP1991_1995		AGGREGATE_PC1996_2003	
Unique Words 6733	Total 63151	Unique Words 3609	Total 18367	Unique Words 3288	Total 17426	Unique Words 4554	Total 29695
Words	Counts	Words	Counts	Words	Counts	Words	Counts
tax $	1315	million	292	ontario	302	ontario	569
ontario	781	ontario	269	government	262	tax $	400
government	721	tax $	213	year	203	government	353
million	677	year	190	tax $	192	year	277
new	498	government	182	jobs *	191	million	266
year	486	million	163	million	160	new	253
cent	475	budget	152	new	156	care *	248
federal	407	program	132	services	143	people *	234
budget	399	new	124	billion	116	health *	220
economic	351	federal	114	public *	111	jobs	175
increase	341	capital	101	budget	111	province	174
provincial	326	health *	93	people *	107	budget	169
province	290	programs	92	economic	102	years	168
fiscal	267	economic	91	social *	93	ontario's	155
economy	263	support	90	years	90	provide	154
income	255	funding	87	program	89	education *	150
reform *	246	increase	86	health *	87	today	141
growth +	246	services *	86	province	79	federal	129
capital	238	provide	84	ontarians *	78	support *	128
spending	238	years	80	care *	75	help *	126
total	235	assistance *	79	support	74	billion	126
local	222	fiscal	78	training *	74	economy	124
provide	212	province	77	provide	74	plan	121
programme	207	development *	70	spending	73	ontarians	121
development *	202	care *	70	capital	72	growth +	117
revenue *	201	social *	69	economy	71	children	114
public *	201	income	66	work	66	program	111
investment	194	additional	65	plan	66	funding	110
years	194	ontario's	64	deficit ^	65	taxes $	108
taxation $	191	billion	62	assistance	65	sector	107
program	190	total	61	pay	65	make	103
financial	189	growth +	59	help	60	families	102
policy	189	plan	59	ontario's	60	business	102
taxes $	188	increased	59	programs	59	research	100

Note: * indicates new term; ^ indicates expenditures; + indicates growth; $ indicates tax

an average of 24 times, while the Liberals practically doubled the rate to 44 mentions. Floyd Laughren spoke much less about programs (29 times average) and Ernie Evens sliced that rate in half with an average of 15 mentions. The career of the word 'health' is instructive also, with hardly a mention in the early Tory speeches, but frequent mentions by their successors.

The speeches were also tested for key concepts that may not appear in the top thirty-five issue units above, but which can be revealing of partisan and periodic markers. To do this, the HyperPo keyword in context (KWIC) function was used to present how these terms were used in different periods for each of the OBSs. Table 6.2 reveals the significance of

Table 6.2 Use of key economic concepts

Key word	PC 1968–1984	Lib. 1985–1990	NDP 1991–1995	PC 1996–2003
City/cities	0.0002	0.0001	0.0002	**0.0003**
Debt(s)	0.0007	0.0008	**0.0019**	0.0014
Deficit(s)	0.0018	0.0014	**0.0037**	0.0018
Efficiency	**0.0006**	0.0005	0.0004	0.0002
Equity	**0.0006**	0.0003	0.0017	0.0003
Employment (and variations)	0.0039	0.0010	**0.0044**	0.0020
Excellence	0.0000	0.0007	0.0000	**0.0007**
Expenditure(s)	**0.0052**	0.0020	0.0022	0.0001
Free trade	0.0000	0.0002	0.0002	0.0000
Global / globalization (0)	0.0000	0.0004	0.0002	**0.0005**
Growth	**0.0052**	0.0036	0.0028	**0.0056**
'Health' care	0.0022	0.0051	0.0050	**0.0074**
Imagination	0.0000	0.0000	0.0000	0.0000
Inefficiency/inefficient	0.0000	0.0000	**0.0001**	0.0000
Inflation	**0.0032**	0.0007	0.0005	0.0001
Infrastructure	0.0001	0.0007	0.0010	**0.0011**
Job(s)	0.0038	0.0025	0.0129	**0.0083**
Labour	0.0007	0.0007	**0.0019**	0.0002
Municipal/municipalities	**0.0059**	0.0027	0.0018	0.0017
Northern Ontario	**0.0007**	0.0009	0.0009	0.0004
NAFTA / 'Free Trade Agreement'	0.0000	0.0001	**0.0002**	0.0000
OHIP	0.0003	0.0003	0.0002	0.0000
Revenue(s)	**0.0064**	0.0030	0.0025	0.0009
Rural	0.0002	0.0001	0.0003	**0.0014**
Stimulation	**0.0013**	0.0005	0.0002	0.0003
Surplus	**0.0005**	0.0003	0.0002	0.0002
Unemployed	**0.0015**	0.0000	0.0011	0.0002
Urban	0.0004	0.0004	0.0000	0.0003

Note: Bold = highest amount in the row

certain economic concepts by time period and partisanship. The numbers have been reduced to ratios based on the size of the speech in terms
of word frequency (i.e., a ratio is produced by dividing the number of
times a word such as 'city' is used in a budget speech by the number of
words in that particular speech; the ratio helps to establish the proportional use of the word in each budget speech). It is interesting to note,
for instance, that the word 'inflation' is a key concern through the 1980s
and 1990s, but diminished during the later PC's Common Sense

Table 6.3 Budget speech comparison

'Austerity' budgets		'Neutral' budgets		'Spending' budgets	
Laughren NDP 1995	0.001434	McKeough PC 1975	0.016758	Laughren NDP 1992	0.022155
Eves PC 1998	0.007088	McKeough PC 1971	0.017097	McKeough PC 1972	0.022329
Nixon Lib 1988	0.007235	McKeough PC 1978	0.017491	McNaughton PC 1970	0.022404
Eves PC 1996	0.009129	Nixon Lib 1985	0.018081	McKeough PC 1976	0.022586
Eves PC 1999	0.010146	Laughren NDP 1991	0.018443	Laughren NDP 1993	0.022943
Eves PC 1997	0.010862	McNaughton PC 1969	0.018759	Grossman PC 1984	0.023154
Miller PC 1983	0.013478	White PC 1973	0.020619	Miller PC 1979	0.024796
Laughren NDP 1994	0.014046	Eves PC 2000	0.020845	Nixon Lib 1990	0.025345
Miller PC 1982	0.014978	Nixon Lib 1986	0.020946	Miller PC 1980	0.025954
McKeough PC 1977	0.015259	Miller PC 1981	0.02206	White PC 1974	0.026794
Flaherty PC 2001	0.016713			Ecker PC 2002	0.028336
				Nixon Lib 1989	0.03023
				McNaughton PC 1968	0.032399
				Ecker PC 2003	0.041592
				Nixon Lib 1987	0.04418

Revolution as it ceased to be perceived to be a threat. Ministers of finance were evidently comfortable in talking about 'efficiency' and 'excellence' in budget decisions, but avoided terms like 'inefficient' or
'imagination.' The term 'deficit' was used more frequently in economically challenging years, but it is interesting to note that the words 'expenditures' and 'revenues' were abandoned as concepts after 1995.

This software also depicted how austerity budgets used words differently than those aiming to increase government spending. Multiple
variations of the terms 'assets,' 'development,' 'increase,' 'investment,'
'outlay,' and 'spending' were tracked as indicators of 'Christmas tree
budgets.' 'Scrooge budgets' were tracked using words such as 'cuts,'
'decrease,' 'reduce,' and 'savings.' Based on their frequency of use, the
budgets were classified into three categories using the ratios of word
use in each speech (see table 6.3). The formula revealed that most of the
speeches fell within an expected place on the spectrum, based on the
descriptive analysis in the first half of the chapter. Rhetorically, however, there was an interesting surprise: specifically, Grossman's 1984
speech, which announced itself as an austerity budget, but evidently
sent a different message, judging from the basket of selected terms
tracked by the software. This budget actually discussed spending more
than cutting.

Style Analysis[11]

What key themes differentiate the OBSs over the years, and how can
those differences be explained? Statistical breakdown of word usage
revealed a number of tendencies in the OBSs beyond the simple frequency of words demonstrated above. First, there was a clearly consistent style in the way the budget speeches were drafted over this
thirty-five-year period, even though many of the documents present a
distinct style by party and minister. The component plots in figure 6.1
illustrate the level of originality in each document by comparing the
top 250 key words used in each document (Component Factor One, the
X-Axis), alongside simultaneously the manner in which the words used
compare to the other OBS documents (Component Factor Two, the
Y-Axis). Documents that, in previous studies, have appeared in the upper left quadrant are highly original, displaying a rich vocabulary and
a creative use of language. The works of William Shakespeare or the
early work of Henry James, for instance, appear in this quadrant.[12]
Documents plotting on the lower-left quadrant use a rich vocabulary

and a great deal of variation among documents (e.g., comparing two dictionaries in completely different languages). Speeches delivered by business and political leaders have appeared in the bottom-right quadrant, indicating a less rich vocabulary and less consistency. Documents plotting on the upper-right quadrant use a less rich vocabulary and show a greater degree of consistency. In other words, they are less creative. There is evidence of a consistent, institutional style of language employed in the budget speeches over these years, undoubtedly showing the strong contribution of the public service.

As such, this statistical treatment a reveals a clear split between the first PC dynasty (1968–84) and the later OBSs (1985–2003), with a distinct break between the Miller and Nixon speeches in particular (see figure 6.1). The figure shows a real fracture in the style of language used in the budget speeches starting in 1985. The SPSS statistical plot of the OBSs in figure 6.1 identifies the speeches by using the first three letters of the minister's name and the year of the speech (e.g., Floyd Laughren's 1994 speech would be represented as 'lau1994,' which appears in the very top right-hand corner of figure 6.1). The position of Laughren's work demonstrates a richer vocabulary and a more imaginative use of words, while the speeches delivered by MacNaughton, in contrast, show much less craft (White's 1973 speech being the nadir of creativity). A close-up view of figure 6.1 demonstrates that the OBSs clustered in terms of time period and often by individual finance minister. The top bolded sphere broadly identifies the OBSs from 1991–2003, the middle broken-line sphere identifies Nixon's OBSs that overlap slightly with two of Miller's later speeches, and lastly, the bottom dashed-line sphere identifies the speeches of the Progressive Conservative ministers of finance between 1968 and 1985.

It is evident from the factor analysis of the OBSs in figure 6.2 that the keywords that made the patterns above would also be distributed in a manner consistent with the three periods highlighted using Principal Components Analysis (PCA). Transposing the data used to craft figure 6.2 demonstrates how words, as issue units, plot out to create the pattern. Not surprisingly, the findings demonstrate that the 1960s and 1970s speeches used a broader variety of language, and that the range of words and their usage shifted in the 1980s and 1990s. Because of this transposition of data, the differences in language identified in figure 6.2 can be directly mapped on to figure 6.1 to understand how the particular words are associated with each OBS using the same groupings within each sphere (e.g., the solid-line, long dashed-line, or dotted-line

Figure 6.1 Finance minister and OBSs, 1968–2003

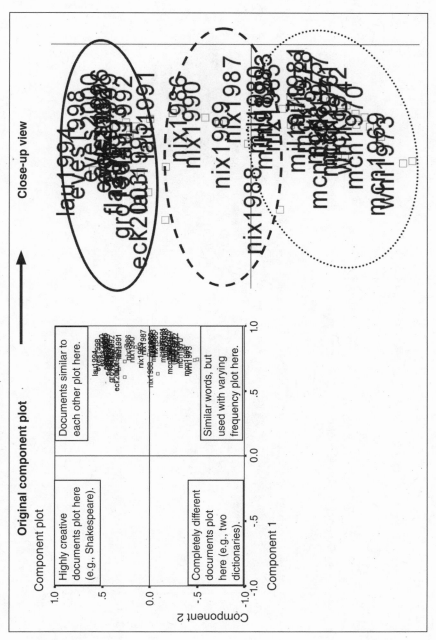

Figure 6.2 OBS key words, 1968–2003

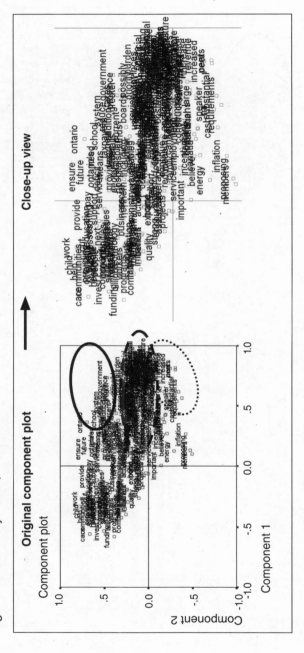

Words that appeared in the top left-hand corner were not as directly linked with the individual periods because they were also situated in other OBSs, but their position confirms the more evident focus on 'child,' 'communities,' 'education,' and 'help' in the 1991–2003 period. The close-up view of figure 6.2 offers a focused perspective of these word clusters. The anatomy of key-word patterns identified using this technique confirms an alignment with the three periods identified using simple key-word frequencies as follows:

1 MacNaughton, McKeough, Miller OBSs (1968–84): Canada, Incentives, Increase, Inflation, and Revenue (the bottom dotted-line circle)
2 Nixon OBSs (1985–90): Costs, Employment, Family, Infrastructure, and Municipalities (the middle dashed-line circle)
3 Laughren/Eves OBSs (1991–2003): Burden, Deficit, Hospital, Ontario, Reduce, and School (the top solid-lined circle)

The two-dimensional visualizations in figure 6.2 can also be presented in linear or three-dimensional formats to better understand the patterns of data. For example, figure 6.3 presents the same information as figure 6.2, simply in a linear format. The dendrogram (from Greek *dendron* 'tree,' *-gramma* 'drawing') is usefully described in the Merriam-Webster dictionary as a 'branching diagram representing a hierarchy of categories based on degree of similarity or number of shared characteristics.' It is typically used in describing biological taxonomy or to illustrate the clustering of genes. In understanding Ontario budget speeches, the cluster lines on the right side of figure 6.3 demonstrate the hierarchy of links among the documents in increasing convergence and similarity of word use. The 'number' column simply lists the document number in chronological order of year.

The clustering tendency by party and minister was reinforced by the fact that the speeches clustered together based on the period in which they were written, thereby indicating a commonality of style. This was eloquently attested to in the case of Darcy McKeough. His speeches from two different periods (1971–2 and 1975–8) show significant similarities. A few anomalies appear, but most of these can be explained rather easily. For instance, McNaughton's 1968 speech stands on its own because the frequency of words in it is significantly less compared to the longer speeches produced by the PCs in the 1969–73 period. This also helps to explain why White's 1974 OBS is proximal to McNaughton's

Figure 6.3 Dendrogram of the OBS, 1968–2003

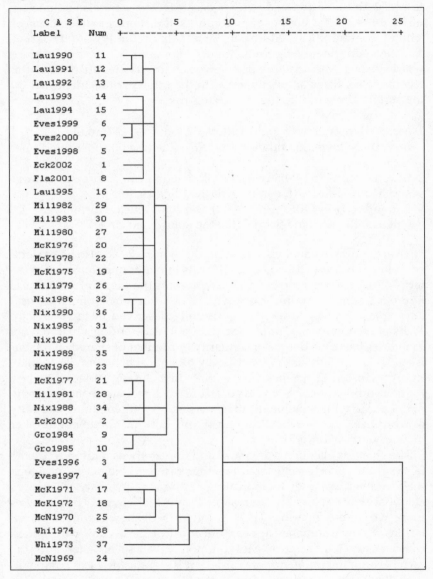

1968, and why two of Ernie Eves's longer speeches are located near the longer 1969–73 PC OBSs.

While length and similarity in the use of a party's vocabulary only explains some of the patterns here, other anomalies are not so easily ·identified. Nixon's 1988 speech (with a length of 6020 words) bears more striking similarities in terms of word usage to Ecker's 2003 speech (4291 words) than to the rest of his speeches. Grossman's single 1984 speech similarly locates itself among McNaughton's 1968 and White's 1974 speeches. The documents were analysed chronologically to address these anomalies.

1968–1984

The patterns of word usage indicate the kinship between the various styles of budget speeches. Once charted, they illustrate how budget speeches compare with each other in their choice of words and in the frequency of word usage; they also reveal a distinct level of personalization. The speeches made by MacNaughton, while similar to White's, are distinct in their style from that delivered by Miller. Grossman's only speech stands out, indicating a wholly different approach to words and style as well as a departure from the institutional style. It would seem to indicate that this speech was the product of Grossman (and his personal staff) far more than the product of the Department of Treasury and Economics (indeed, it could be said that Grossman pulled more towards Shakespeare than his predecessors and successors).

1985–2003

The years 1985–2003 featured a radically changed political landscape in Ontario, as all three parties in the legislature took turns in governing. Collectively, the OBSs show a dramatic shift in the PCAs, as evidenced in figure 6.5. Table 6.4 shows how Nixon's liberal speeches during relatively stable economic times were drastically different from the block of PC speeches during the Common Sense Revolution, as well as the Laughren speeches leading into the economic downturn. The differentiation in the use of language is similarly presented in the transposed component plots, where 'cuts' and 'private' interests figure more in the PC years and 'growth' and providing a fair 'share' were more evident in Nixon's speeches.

Figure 6.4 PC finance minister OBSs, 1968–84

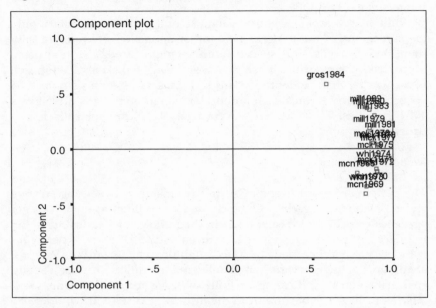

Figure 6.5 Finance minister OBSs, 1985–2003

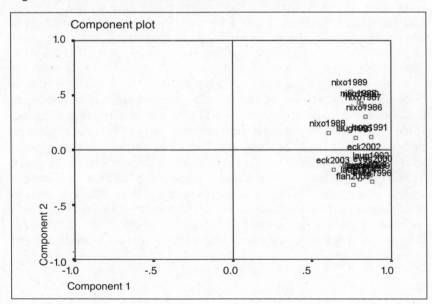

Table 6.4 Speech personalization

Key word	PC 1968–1984	Lib. 1985–1990	NDP 1991–1995	PC 1996–2003
I	**0.0208**	**0.0169**	0.0075	0.0111
You	0.0008	0.0008	0.0002	0.0008
We	0.0165	0.0149	**0.0296**	**0.0310**

Note: Bold = highest amount in column

Table 6.5 and figure 6.6 present some interesting stylistic conventions in the OBSs using similar key-words analysis methods. Conventional wisdom has it that budget speeches are not used to attack other parties, and this was borne out by the software when it tested for attributions. The use of the personal 'I' in budget speeches was popular with Tory finance ministers before 1985. With the Peterson Liberals, the voice shifted in favour of the more inclusive 'we,' perhaps indicating the more collaborative approach brought to budget making as cabinets became heavily institutionalized and as the premier's office began to play a more important role in setting priorities. Nevertheless, the term 'premier' and the premier's name were rarely ever used in the speech. The Tories of the mid-1990s–2002 were exceptional in this respect, invoking the name of Mike Harris twelve times in their speeches and also using the term 'premier' the most (forty times in the Harris years). 'Premier' was evidently used to demonstrate his agency in making dramatic changes.

Digital humanities software can also assist in easily identifying words that do not appear in the top twenty-five to establish the level of attention given to particular issues. Figure 6.6 presents words associated with key socio-economic phenomena in Ontario during this period. Some social-group indicators have yet to make it into the OBSs (e.g., 'diversity,' 'ethnic/ethnicity,' 'immigrants/immigration,' 'sexuality,' 'religion'), while other terms have shifted in their use over time. For example, the shifting language on health care has changed from focusing on 'home care' to 'long term care' and 'primary care.' The historical shift to the importance of 'computers' and 'information technology' is readily apparent using frequency alone, as is the consistent dominance of 'child care,' 'education,' and 'health care' as the main budget issues, which not surprisingly follows along the federal/provincial split of constitutional powers. It is interesting to note that 'housing,' by contrast, has been abandoned in recent years as an issue unit.

Table 6.5 Key issues and omitted words

Key word	PC, 1968–84	Lib., 1985–90	NDP, 1991–5	PC 1996–2003
Aboriginal(s)	0.0000	0.0000	**0.0006**	0.0000
Computer(s)	0.0001	0.0002	0.0000	**0.0005**
Day/child care	0.0002	**0.0012**	0.0006	**0.0012**
Disabled/disability	0.0003	0.0010	0.0003	**0.0012**
Diversity	0.0000	0.0000	0.0000	0.0000
Education	0.0014	0.0032	0.0024	**0.0052**
Ethnic	0.0000	0.0000	0.0000	0.0000
Family/families	0.0013	0.0019	0.0011	**0.0046**
First Nation(s)	0.0000	0.0000	**0.0001**	0.0000
Grandchildren	0.0000	0.0000	**0.0001**	**0.0001**
Handicapped	**0.0001**	0.0003	0.0000	0.0000
Health care	0.0005	0.0016	0.0025	**0.0055**
Home care	**0.0001**	0.0000	0.0000	0.0000
Homosexual/sexuality	0.0000	0.0000	0.0000	0.0000
Housing	0.0015	**0.0026**	0.0014	0.0003
Human	0.0001	0.0000	**0.0004**	0.0000
Immigrants/immigration	0.0000	0.0000	0.0000	0.0000
Indian(s)	**0.0001**	0.0000	0.0000	0.0000
Long term care	0.0000	0.0002	**0.0003**	0.0002
Man/men	0.0002	0.0002	0.0001	0.0002
Primary care	0.0000	0.0000	0.0000	**0.0002**
Religion	0.0000	0.0000	0.0000	0.0000
Sexual assault	0.0000	0.0000	**0.0001**	0.0000
Information technology/ highway	0.0000	0.0000	0.0001	**0.0003**
Youth/young	**0.0021**	0.0013	0.0008	0.0025
Woman/women	0.0003	0.0002	0.0015	**0.0008**

Note: Bold = highest amount in column

RéseauLu Issue Networks

The RéseauLu software tool[13] allows for another type of cluster analysis visualization, and it also confirms the linkages between the various budget speeches.[14] Figure 6.6 presents the top twenty-five key words from each speech compared to all the other speeches. Three distinct clusters take shape based on word usage: the late-Robarts/Davis period 1968–84, the Liberals and the NDP 1985–95, and the later PCs 1996–2003. Grossman's 1984 speech is again completely anomalous, but is now in the same issue cluster as other years in the same decade. Laughren's 1995 speech and Nixon's 1988 speech are also remarkable in their proximity with the budget speeches of the later PC OBSs. These two speeches link through the use of words such as 'education' and 'jobs' at roughly the same frequency as those speeches, which brings them into that cluster.

The graph also demonstrated the consistency in thought and word usage, for instance, of the speeches delivered by Ernie Eves and Janet Ecker. The speeches delivered by the pre-1985 Tories are vastly different, less inter-linked, and show more individual personality. The speeches delivered by Robert Nixon and Floyd Laughren group together, but there are interesting exceptions. The Nixon speech of 1988 distinguishes itself by its links with the Eves speeches. Once again, the Grossman speech stands out in its originality, on the side of the Laughren/Nixon family of speeches, and far removed from those of either the pre-1986 or the post-1995 Tories.

RéseauLu also shows where words were emphasized more often. The word 'fiscal' (at about 4 o'clock on the chart), for instance, was a more frequent concern to those writing the MacNaughton and Nixon speeches. 'Health' appears in the upper-left shaded area, clearly as a priority for the Tories, but one that was close to the Liberals also. The word 'tax' appears right in the middle of the chart, evidently the concern of all ministers of finance, but the word 'taxes' was more often mentioned by Eves, Miller, and McKeough. White seemed to prefer the word 'taxation.' The words 'families,' 'children,' 'businesses,' 'care,' and 'education' are emphasized by the Eves/Ecker budget speeches, but only Grossman seemed concerned about 'youth' and the 'young.' Laughren, with Nixon and Grossman, talked less about 'business' but more about the 'economy' (and 'economies'), and more about 'support,' 'training,' 'assistance,' 'funding,' 'investment' (in the singular), and 'social.'

Conclusion

Budget speeches in and of themselves do not shed light on where governments actually choose to spend money or effect cutbacks (only financial statements can provide a true picture), but in this case they do

Figure 6.6 Top 25 key words, 1968–2003

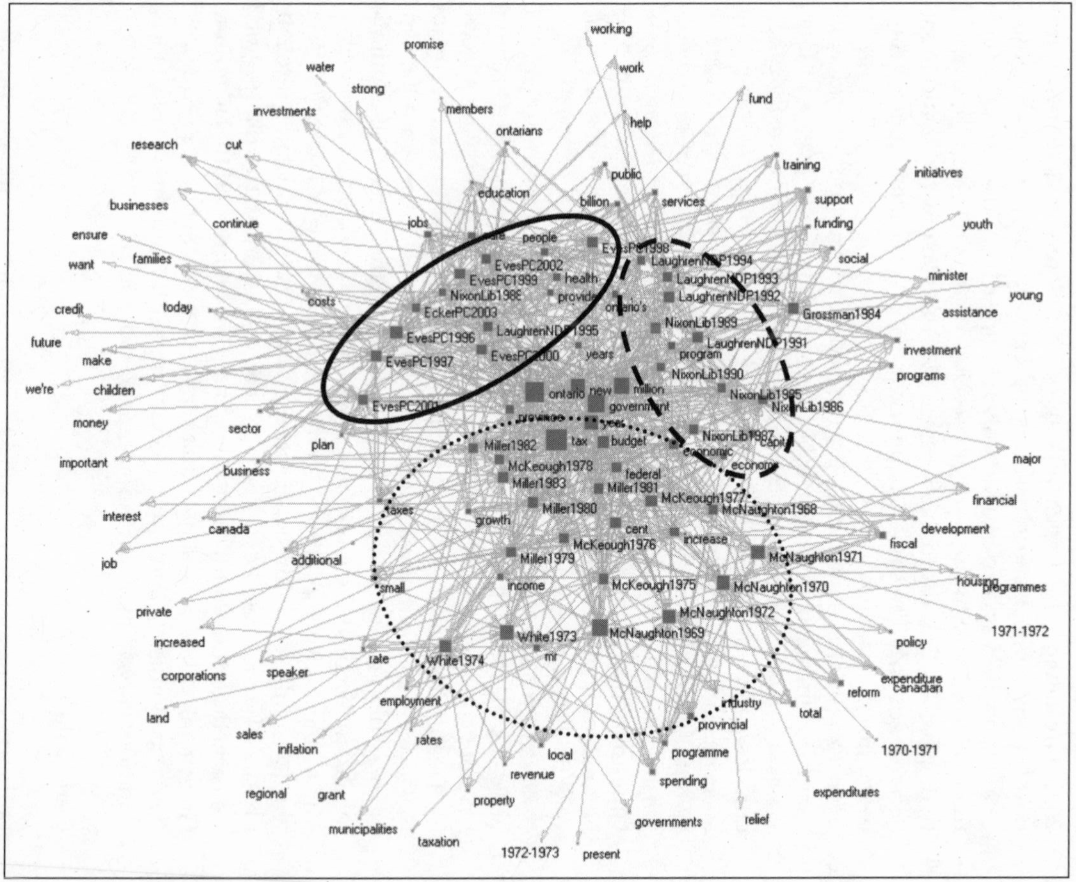

offer a clue to how the needs of Ontarians and the economy were articulated by each finance minister and as such are vitally important instruments of democracy. Budget speeches are simultaneously symbolic documents for politicians, working papers for public servants, and a ritualized document for the public and media which will only pay scant attention to it. That being said, they sit at the core of responsible government, and the budget, after the speech from the throne, is the most significant document tabled by the government. They are also fascinating literary documents that convey a variety of messages. Key among those are the themes that are accentuated by the presenting minister, but below the surface are a whole range of messages that are articulated by the emphasis on particular words, concerns, and ideas.

This *essai* (in the literal use of the word) showed that several subjects overshadowed almost every speech in this period: education, health care, and local government. On the economic side, prominent issues were productivity, competiveness, jobs, inflation, interest rates, small business, farming, mining, and recession (obviously, in recession years). Finally, given that more than three-quarters of the budgets showed a deficit, discussion of deficit and debt were very often at the centre of these critical speeches.

The issue differentiation of the OBSs also presents the case that different parties did provide different economic agendas for the province, which either built on, or reacted to, past efforts. In other words, based on word (or issue) usage, different economic plans emerged from the different parties; the issue is what creates budgetary decisions as responses in terms of the allocations of funds towards or away from an agenda or issue. There are even clear differences in the agendas developed among party ministers, enough for certain budget speeches to cluster into a unique style. The close clustering of Ontario budget speeches showed that teams like the Tory Big Blue Machine used a limited vocabulary and tended to use it consistently; evidently the words did not change too drastically over their term, suggesting that the economic and fiscal situation of the province did not require – or did not allow – the use of words and concepts that would alienate any of its audiences. The political need for consistency and reassurance certainly was respected, but there were other factors that evidently guaranteed a similarity of style. Certainly, the speeches shared common elements that could be explained by the strong, consistent contribution of the staff of the finance department. Len Roozen noted that until the 1970s, the deputy minister or an assistant deputy minister would hold the lead pen in writing the budget, but that even junior staff could see their own words show up in the text. In later years, early drafting responsibility shifted to ministers' staff, later supplemented (or replaced) by 'professional speechwriters.'[15]

This analysis has demonstrated that investigation into the stylistic and textual differences among the budget speeches can yield interesting insights, but modesty is in order and more work needs be undertaken in using the methods that have been used to uncover themes and links in the Bible, French literature, or gender, race, and nationality in black drama over the past 150 years. For the student of government budgets, those words can provide clues to the cohesion of the messages across the years, and a measure of the stylistic particularity of each budget speech. The use of digital humanities software opens a new window and offers a potentially rich tool to understand the orientation of budgets, not only in Ontario, but in other provinces and in the Government of Canada. It also opens the door to international comparisons.

NOTES

1 The author happily acknowledges the assistance of Ashley Walker in helping to document this chapter.
2 Our sample begins in 1968 for the simple reason that the budget speeches were only available in digital format beginning with that year.
3 See, for example, Noortje Marres, 'Net-work Is Format Work: Issue Networks and the Sites of Civil Society Politics' in *Reformatting Politics: Information Technology and Global Civil Society*, ed. Jodi Dean, Jon W. Anderson, and Geert Lovink (Routledge: New York, 2006), 3–17; or, Noortje Marres and Richard Rogers, 'Recipe for Tracing the Fate of Issues and Their Publics on the Web,' in *Making Things Public: Atmospheres of Democracy*, ed. B. Latour and P. Weibel (Cambridge, MA: MIT Press, 2005), 922–35.
4 It should be noted that before 1993 the term 'Minister of Finance' was not used, and under different governments the titles of 'Treasurer,' 'Minister of Economics,' or 'Minister of Economics and Intergovernmental Affairs' were used. For the purpose of this analysis, we will use 'Minister of Finance' to be inclusive of these other positions.
5 How much this can be explained by the Red Tory policy position of Grossman is another research topic. The 1986 speech by Nixon, the 1993 and 1994 by Laughren, the 1995 Budget Statement, and the 1999 speech by Eves also

went in this direction (for instance, in 1995, the word 'taxes' appeared far less often than: spending, jobs, plan, services, costs, new, interest, provide, public).

6 Nixon claimed to have reduced the deficit in his first three budgets using different possibilities of defining it; in reality, however, the total deficit stayed the same during the minority government of Peterson. The fiscal year 1988–9 was the first when the deficit was significantly reduced (cf. Canada, Department of Finance, *Fiscal Reference Tables* [Ottawa, 1996]).

7 'The wealthiest in our society will pay the most' – as a result, a typical family saw their income tax going up by above $350.

8 However, social assistance recipients and seniors receiving the Guaranteed Income Supplement were going to pay a small flat co-payment per prescription.

9 The word 'important' had been used 40 times, four times more than 'Ontario.'

10 For more on Digital Humanities methods see *A Companion to Digital Humanities Computing* (2004), or the journals *Digital Humanities Quarterly* and *Literary and Linguistic Computing*. Briefly, the methods used here aim to control the biases of the software available. To analyse word use, five distinctive applications were applied to deconstruct the Ontario Budget Speeches (OBS) and to establish the variations in their style and content. Three different software tools were used to identify key words that represented the dominant issues in each year of the reports. First, the TAPoRware List Words software (www.tapor.com) was used to create a basic concordance of all the words in each of the texts. TAPoRware simply strips out all of the words from the texts and measures their absolute frequency using raw counts. Second, to ensure valid results, TAPoRware's identification of key words was compared to the counts generated using the HyperPo program, a more dynamic software also provided in the TAPoR suite. The complete HyperPo keyword lists were then again refined into a list of the top 25 *issues* using HyperPo's keyword in context (KWIC) function. This function allows for an immediate check on the word sense and use of concordant words throughout a document in each sentence where a particular word is located. The check also ensures a disambiguation of synonyms that can limit the usefulness of the basic TAPoRware List Words software, because raw counts do not necessarily mean the word is used in the same way.

11 The third application was Intelligent Archive, a program developed by the Australian Shakespearean authorship-attribution scholar Hugh Craig.

Intelligent Archive performs a 'Principal Component Analysis' which provides a statistical treatment that first identifies the highest frequency variables in a set (or in textual analysis it finds the highest frequency of words in a given set of texts). It then provides a mathematical treatment of all the words in a text as data, with the exception of some 300 pre-selected stop words (such as articles, prepositions, adverbs, and modifiers). These word lists can then be compared with HyperPo's subset lists of word counts in order to triangulate meaningful word associations and omissions in the OBSs with the actors who created those documents.

After the set of texts and the set of highest-frequency words are identified, a factor analysis was performed on these 'principal components' of the text. Factor analysis in this case measures the two factors of the particular high-frequency words in each text (factor 1) and the differences in these variables among the set of texts (factor 2) by creating a coefficient based on the variance among the word frequencies reduced to data, thereby reducing the information to a manageable data unit for the program. These two factors were plotted on a two-dimensional matrix by using a fourth application, the standard statistical application SPSS software suite, to identify which texts had similar styles. Cluster analysis of the variables was also conducted using SPSS to identify the similarities of styles among texts. The purpose of using Intelligent Archive is simply to confirm the consistency of the TAPoRware results.

12 See Hugh Craig, 'Shakespeare and Print,' *HEAT*, 4, 2002, 49–63. Or Hugh Craig, 'Common-Words Frequencies, Shakespeare's Style, and the Elegy by W.S.' *Early Modern Literary Studies*, 8, Number 1, 2002. See also David Hoover, 'Corpus Stylistics, Stylometry, and the Styles of Henry James,' *Style*, 41, Number 2, 2007, 174–203.

13 The RéseauLu statistical analysis software package plots cluster analysis results using 'a visual node and hub model,' thereby establishing the links between different variables. This program yields imagery very different from that of TAPoRware, but in its way tries to measure how various texts relate to each other.

14 These statistical methods are based on a significant body of work in textual analysis, and afford the possibility of replicating these results for other researchers who are interested in these methods. Other work in this area includes Greg Elmer's research at the Infoscape Research Lab (see www.infoscapelab.ca), which uses experimental on-line methods to track informational politics in a similar line of word-count research. See Greg Elmer, David Skinner, and Zach Devereaux's 'Disaggregating Online News: The Canadian Federal Election, 2005–2006,' *Scan: Journal of Media Arts Culture*,

April 2006. Their research follows issues-based visualization work such as that of Christine Hine in *Virtual Methods: Issues in Social Research on the Internet* (New York: Berg, 2005), and Richard Rogers in *Information Politics on the Web* (Cambridge: MIT Press, 2004).

15 Len Roozen to Patrice Dutil, 31 December 2008.

7 The Ontario Ministry of Finance as an Exception in Canadian Public Administration

LUC BERNIER AND JOSEPH FACAL

> Macdonald and his remarkable group have developed the same sort of
> authority – the men with the best figures – that Quebec used to have in the
> mid-1960s.
>
> Jacques Parizeau, *Toronto Star*, 19 May 1973

Examined from a broad historical perspective, the state's responsibilities in Western societies were for a long time limited almost exclusively to maintaining order.[1] The great liberal philosopher Benjamin Constant (1767–1830) put it bluntly: 'Legislation, like the government, has only two purposes: first, to prevent internal disorder, and second, to repel foreign invaders.'[2] Police forces guaranteed social peace; courts settled legal disputes, the army protected the nation from outside threats. In addition, diplomatic responsibilities for the state in representing the 'people' to others were assumed, while economic functions were limited to issuing currency and collecting taxes.

Starting in the nineteenth century, but particularly in the second half of the twentieth, new responsibilities were added to the state's original functions. Three key interrelated factors were behind this development: the growing influence of doctrines preaching state intervention to offset market dysfunctions, the need for governments to react to the disorganization brought about by the economic crisis of the 1930s and the destruction caused by the two world wars, and the now constant pressures from different social categories with ever-growing demands: workers, farmers, employers, the middle class, the liberal professions, women, seniors, and youth. In the great majority of Western societies, the state has gradually taken charge of organizing most aspects of education, providing health care, promoting the arts, culture, and sports, and protecting heritage and the environment, as well as establishing numerous social programs to shield individuals from the costs and risks related to aging, accidents, unemployment, or extreme poverty. To differing degrees depending on the country, the economic situation, and the ideology of the government, the state has also gradually assumed responsibility for stimulating and regulating economic growth, encouraging job creation, building transportation and communication infrastructures, promoting such strategic niches as innovation and high tech, bailing out industries in difficulty, and even taking control of whole areas of the economy through public corporations.

Today, in most Western societies, it is the ministry/department of finance (or the 'treasury') that defines economic and fiscal policy. It typically plays the role of a 'guardian,' to borrow Wildavsky's term, but at moments it also plays a role as a central agency. In a federal and parliamentary system such as Canada's, a wrinkle is added: the economic and fiscal role is shared between the federal and the provincial ministries of finance. How different are they? Can they both play similar roles as central agencies or as 'guardians'? The purpose of this chapter is to put in perspective the Ontario Ministry of Finance's experience as it stretched beyond 'guardianship' and assumed a central agency role by offering a comparative perspective with its counterparts in Quebec and in Ottawa.

Comparisons between Quebec and Ontario are of course nothing new. In particular, attempts to explain their different standards of living over the last decades are too numerous to mention, though the traditional gap favouring Ontario has steadily diminished in recent years. Geographic reasons were obviously one part of the answer: Ontario is a hub in Canada and in North America, and therefore at the crossroads of many more continental economic activities. Toronto has emerged over the past forty years as the financial centre of Canada, gradually replacing Montreal. Ontario is also the most populous and industrialized province in Canada. In addition, the auto industry, and a good proportion of Canada's manufacturing, has been concentrated in Ontario to take full advantage of the hub effect.

What role did the Ontario Ministry of Finance play in assisting this rising level of prosperity? Certainly, the contributors to this book make a compelling case that it has played a vital role in defining policy since the days of George Drew. Elsewhere, commentators have noted, for example, the singular influence of different departments. The extraordinary prosperity that Ireland has experienced over the past decades has been explained, for instance, by pointing to the dynamism of some of its development agencies, such as Forfas, IDA-Ireland, and Enterprise Ireland.[3] The policy capacity of the Ministry of International Trade and Industry (MITI) of Japan has also been celebrated. How can it be compared with other similar organizations in Canada and elsewhere in highly developed capitalist societies?

The thesis developed here is that in the 1960s and 1970s, when Keynesianism was in vogue and budgets and bureaucracies were growing rapidly across North America, the Ontario Treasury morphed into an exceptional – and unmatched – role. Many public servants situate the 'golden age' of Finance between 1966 and 1974 before institutionalized cabinets.[4] Jacques Parizeau, a former public servant and eventual premier of Quebec, was a leading light of the Parti Québécois when he cast his sparkling judgment on the MOF in 1973. This chapter will put his remark in perspective, showing that Ontario experimented boldly in positioning its Ministry of Finance at the centre of the decision-making apparatus.

The Department of Finance of Canada

In Ontario, as in Quebec, the 1960s–1970s were critical for province-building and modernizing the state apparatus at a time when policy coordination was still in its infancy.[5] In Ottawa, the Department of Finance is considered one of the four central coordinating agencies (along with the Privy Council Office, the Treasury Board Secretariat, and, to an increasingly important degree notwithstanding its political purpose, the Prime Minister's Office), even though it is a regular government department.[6] But such categorizations miss the nuanced evolution of this critical department of the government of Canada. The ascendency of Finance in Ontario in the late 1960s and 1970s actually coincided with the end of an important phase in the history of the influence of the Department of Finance as a central agency in Ottawa.

The role that the state can play in the economy varies according to the dominant ideology, the political forces, and the policy instruments and institutions that it has developed. The formulation of fiscal policy has been the domain of the Ministry of Finance in Ottawa, even though there has been a Department of Revenue since 1927 and a minister in charge of the Treasury Board since 1967. Financial matters and government incomes were also managed by Finance, often creating disequilibrium among ministries.[7] In sum, the essential institution of economic policy in Ottawa has long been the Department of Finance. It is also an institution of policy coordination, the eldest in the federal system. David Wolfe has explained it this way:

> Within the Canadian state, the Department of Finance occupied a central role from the outset. It evolved as a centre for co-ordinating government policy as a result of its minister's critical position in the financial committee of Cabinet concerned with the allocation of resources among government departments. Its role in the supervision and control of all financial affairs, revenues and expenditures was modelled directly on that of the British Treasury. Given the importance of public finance for the creation of a transportation infrastructure during the formative stages of Canadian economic development, it is not surprising to find the Department of Finance at the centre of the state bureaucracy.
>
> The predominance of Finance was confirmed during most of the postwar period by the absence of any other department that could act as a significant locus for economic decision-making. However, disenchantment with the effectiveness of Keynesian policy during the 1960s resulted in a period of institutional innovation in the federal bureaucracy. The creation of new supply-oriented departments during the 1960s fragmented economic policy-making, as they began to compete with Finance for the Cabinet's attention. The introduction of the Cabinet planning system by the Trudeau government challenged the pre-eminence of Finance in economic policy and restricted its role to a reactive one based on the exercise of its still considerable veto power.[8]

Other scholars have confirmed this view of Finance in Ottawa. For Ted Hodgetts, it had become 'the centre for co-ordinating total governmental programmes.'[9] He observed that this role began to change in 1962 when the Royal Commission on Government Organization recommended that a new cabinet post, President of the Treasury Board, be instituted.[10] For Richard Phidd and Bruce Doern, that department's role was different: it encompassed policy advice, initial policy implementation, and policy evaluation.[11] Bob Bryce, an eminent mandarin, noted that the Treasury Board was different in that its role was to scrutinize how effectively policy was managed after the government had made a decision.[12]

Thirty years ago, Colin Campbell and George Szablowski examined five central agencies in Ottawa: the Prime Minister's Office, the Privy Council Office (PCO), the Federal-Provincial Relations Office (FPRO), the

Treasury Board Secretariat, and the Department of Finance.[13] The presence of the Federal-Provincial office in this list was surprising at the time. Officially created in 1974–5 from a branch in PCO, it had developed a particular importance with the accession to power in Quebec City of the Parti Québécois in 1976, and it is interesting to note that in a later book, Campbell did not mention Finance as a coordinating department.[14] Certainly, there was a parallel between FPRO and the Department of the Treasury, Economics and Intergovernmental Affairs. But where FPRO's role was focused on constitutional affairs, Ontario's office was tied to issues of fiscal federalism in addition to constitutional issues. Clearly, central agency powers were more dispersed in Ottawa than in Ontario.

With the dismantling of the complex Trudeau cabinet planning system in 1984, Finance was restored to its former prominence and for a time all memoranda sent to Cabinet was filtered by Finance. Again in Wolfe's words:

A small core of technocratic expertise was concentrated in the Department of Finance with increased influence over the entire scope of public policy. The prerequisites of Keynesian policy entailed that Finance pass judgment on the degree to which individual policy initiatives launched by departments or agencies corresponded to the macroeconomic policy objectives of the government as a whole. This authority effectively gave Finance veto power over any policy deemed inconsistent with its macroeconomic objectives. Similarly, important policy initiatives that could be rationalized in terms of Keynesian objectives were assured easier passage through the policy process.[15]

It was clear that Pierre Trudeau was more interested in increasing the ability and capacity of the PMO and PCO, not of Finance, to coordinate policy.[16] He expected the Privy Council Office to have the capacity to challenge the 'excesses of a monopoly of ideas' which emerged from the Department of Finance.[17] With the development of an office of the macroeconomic policy adviser in the PCO, and the separation of fiscal policy and expenditure control, the Trudeau era spelled the end of the dominant role of the Department of Finance in Ottawa for a time.

In *Governing from the Centre*, Donald Savoie confirmed the resurgent power of the Department of Finance. He noted that Prime Minister Jean Chrétien once observed that he could not afford any light to show between his minister of finance and himself.[18] For Savoie, Finance covered the entire range of government activity. 'They are concerned with fiscal and tax policy, federal–provincial relations, government expenditures, international trade and finance, and social and economic policies,' he writes. 'In short, they are guardians of the public purse.'[19] Savoie also quoted Bob Bryce, noting that 'much of the work of the Department of Finance is of the nature of a critical appraisal of the proposals of others.'[20] Savoie added that the department was very jealous of its position and prerogatives: 'not only should there be no light between the prime minister and the minister of Finance, the department's economic theology should not be exposed to a light other than its own.'[21] Although Savoie reports that Finance officials see themselves as the best department of economics in the country, that position was truer before Trudeau challenged it.[22] David Good, in his *Politics of Public Money*, also noted that while important functions around budget-making and tax policies were shared between Finance and the 'priority setters,' there was no doubt that the former was the most critically important ministry in determining expenditures and revenue policies.[23]

Ontario's TEIGA

The evolution of the structures of the Ministry of Finance in Ontario is explained in the preceding chapters, but a few of these elements are important to the arguments presented here. To recap: In 1956, the Department of Economics was created. In 1961, it and Federal-Provincial Relations were merged with the Department of Commerce and Development to become the Department of Economics and Development. In 1967, Economics was 'married' to the Treasury, thus creating Treasury and Economics. As explained in Penny Bryden's chapter, in Ontario Finance was also the central agency for intergovernmental affairs with the integration of the federal-provincial secretariat in 1967. In 1968, an independent Department of Revenue was created from a few ribs of the Department of Treasury and Economics. The role of Treasury as a central agency in government of Ontario came from its control of the budgetary process. Finally, in 1972–3, the Department of Municipal Affairs was absorbed and the department became the Treasury of Ontario and Ministry of Economics and Intergovernmental Affairs (or TEIGA). Several policy domains such as Northern Affairs were included. Under the administrative leadership of Ian Macdonald, the ministry had the responsibility for economic research, regional development, intergovernmental affairs, and statistics.[24] This name lasted until 1978, when the ministry lost responsibility over intergovernmental affairs, housing, and municipal

affairs. Such a concentration of intergovernmental affairs, urban planning, and financial matters was a unique feature of provincial administration in Canada in the 1970s.

It is notable that this growth in Finance occurred under a stable
Progressive Conservative Party in power since 1943. Leslie Frost, John
Robarts, and Bill Davis provided unmistakably conservative governments, but remarkably activist and expansionist ones.[25] Frost and
Robarts engineered a party capable of rejuvenating itself by changing its
leader roughly every decade. This was a period when much of the policy making was done in the line departments, with little need for policy
capacity at the centre.[26] Moreover, expenditures were not tightly controlled in an era when revenues were growing rapidly. Budgetary estimates even in the early 1960s were more an addition of documents
received from ministries than an exercise to limit expenses. As Schindeler
explained, analysts looked at new programs separate of the existing
ones.[27] The new ones were considered policy matters and 'are supposed
to be approved by the Treasury Board and the executive council.' In the
early 1950s, Premier Frost served as his own finance minister, as had
George Ross at the turn of the century and George Henry and Mitch
Hepburn in the 1930s and 1940s.

Frost contributed another particularity to the Ontario decision-making
structure by giving so much importance to the Department of Economics.
Its capacity to influence policy came from the ability to give sound policy
advice to the top of the government. In Don Stevenson's words, 'the
Department acted as a research and policy advisory body to the Premier.'[28]
It was this department that acted as a central agency, and it followed that,
when Economics was absorbed fully by Treasury in 1968, Treasury would
play what amounted to a 'central agency' role. And yet, among the former
deputy ministers and past assistant deputy ministers we interviewed,
none gave an impression of a sense of superiority or 'centrality' one
typically gathers from reading about the Department of Finance in the
government of Canada. According to the former deputy ministers we
interviewed, this central role had to do with the fact that the Ontario premier and his secretary to Cabinet did not want a large administrative apparatus around them and preferred to rely on Finance for policy advice. If
many authors would explain that in Ottawa the role of the Department of
Finance was to say no, Stevenson saw the role in Toronto differently:

> Our ministry is almost unique combining most of the above broad policy
> responsibilities with the central budgetary function of government.

Finance departments traditionally have been tagged with the label of being 'the No men,' fighting increases in expenditures and new programs.
Many of the program areas the ministry is involved in are those where
increasing expenditures will be required in the coming years.[29]

In order to play its role of adviser to the premier in the late 1960s, a
Policy Planning Division was created to provide a core of advice on
policy planning to the premier, the treasurer, and the Cabinet Committee
on Policy Development. In Macdonald's words, the division was designed to

– recommend alternative provincial and regional economic targets
  and goals;
– assess revenue prospects and recommend overall limits of expenditures for the budget and capital outlays;
– recommend economic and fiscal policies which ensure that targets
  are achieved in a consistent and economic manner;
– suggest priorities for expenditures, programs, and policies in order
  to obtain desired economic and financial returns;
– design regional development plans for the government's regional
  development program;
– advise on the overall consistency of government policy in federal-
  provincial matters, support the work of the Advisory Committee on
  Confederation, and fill a staff function for the Prime Minister;
– assess the merit of alternative taxes and propose tax policy and
  reforms.[30]

There was an economic planning function, but also the desire of Premier
John Robarts to have a leading-edge capacity in intergovernmental affairs. According to Stevenson, there has been a much greater role played
by finance departments and departments of intergovernmental affairs
in the development of federal-provincial policy in the social area than
by the program departments.[31] It is true also that Finance played an
important role in energy policy.[32] It was in the Department of Economics
under Frost, and again in Finance under Robarts and Davis, that the
idea of changing fundamentally the financial relations with the regional governments was initiated.[33] In short, building on the Department of
Economics and the Department of Treasury under Frost, Ontario's
Ministry of Finance has been a unique central agency from the second
half of the 1960s and the middle of the 1970s.

The Ministère des Finances du Québec

Provincial states obviously have had more limited powers and capacities than the Canadian government to affect the economic growth of their territory. From the 1960s to this day, the federal government has controlled the main economic instruments (not the least of which is critical taxation and monetary policy). The provinces, by comparison, have overseen only a share of taxation, regulation, subsidies, or fiscal policy. Many created their own public enterprises as flexible autonomous instruments of economic management.[34] There was simultaneously an opportunity for action at the provincial level because the provinces could act on a more homogeneous regional economy than the federal government. To a certain extent, strategic planning and policy coordination was more manageable than in Ottawa, at least from a size perspective. Ontario and Quebec seized those opportunities differently.

Much has been written about the 1960s in Quebec, a period known as the Quiet Revolution era.[35] Under the leadership of Premier Jean Lesage, the Quebec state experienced a rapid development. The Union Nationale party, returned to power under Daniel Johnson in 1966, continued the reforms in education, health, and economic management. It was a period of expansion of the state in an effort to modernize society and have government practices 'catch up' with developments elsewhere in North America.[36] It was also undeniably a period of neo-nationalism. The provincial government was viewed in those years as the only collective tool which francophones could control politically and use to enhance their social status. At the same time, the notions of a *Québécois* people and of a Quebec nation, both used indistinctly, emerged and took clearer shape, and the Quebec state was confirmed in its responsibility of protecting and developing the particular identity of this Quebec society.

The rapid development of the Quebec state apparatus during the 1960s and 1970s was made possible by the first large cohorts of truly well-educated francophones who, having often studied abroad, arrived on the labour market to discover that the private sector, in which almost all key positions were held by anglophones, did not promise upward-mobility possibilities. Thus, the new generation of public servants had a personal as well as a collective interest in the expansion of the Quebec government's size and role.

The key public institutions of the Quiet Revolution (Hydro-Québec, the Caisses de dépôt and placement) have been under heavy media and academic scrutiny since their beginnings. Other economic bodies such as the Office de planification et de développement économique (OPDQ) have also been studied. In contrast, Quebec's Ministère des finances has not attracted much attention.[37] In his reflections on the evolution of the Quebec state, Louis Bernard, who had been chief of staff for René Lévesque and secretary to Cabinet, highlighted the Conseil exécutif (cabinet office) as a coordinating body, but not Finance.[38] Ambroise and Jacques, in their significant review of the transformation of the economic role of the state in Quebec during the 1960s, discussed the public corporations, but did not even mention the Ministère des Finances.[39] Gélinas defined it as a horizontal ministry with an external mission.[40] Bourgault, Dion, and Gow stand out in their consideration of Finance as a central agency.[41]

In part, this was a reflection of priorities. An important portion of the economic development portfolios in Quebec was put in the hands of public corporations such as Hydro-Québec to the point where some said it had become 'a state within the state.' The Department of Natural Resources was responsible for Hydro-Québec, but because of the revenues it generated, Hydro-Québec was also given a reporting relationship to Finance. This was also true for other public corporations. Only the Lottery Corporation and the Liquor Board (Loto-Québec and the Société des alcools) report exclusively to Finance.

The evolution of fiscal and taxation ministries in Quebec was also different than in Ontario. The Ministry of Finance managed both revenue and expenditures in the 1960s. In 1961, a distinct Ministry of Revenue was spun out, a model that would be adopted in Ontario much later. Over the 1970s also, cabinet committees were established that would play a great role in coordinating policies. Over the period 1970–82 the federal model was adopted to control expenditures.[42] A Treasury Board was established in 1970, later than in Ottawa and Toronto. As in Ottawa, however, Finance continued to play the principal role in the development of economic, fiscal, and budgetary policy. Finance also continued to do its own analyses on various programs that could have an impact on economic policy.[43]

The centrality of Finance in Quebec was never as evident as it has been in Ontario at the same period. As André Bernard has observed, when Jean Lesage took power in 1960 and became premier, financial management was still framed by laws adopted at the end of the nineteenth century.[44] 'Finance' was still about the budgetary management of a very small organization, something Lesage was determined to change.

As Leslie Frost had done in Ontario, the Quebec premier decided to be minister of finance. According to Georges-Émile Lapalme, one of his ministers who also had been the previous Liberal leader, Lesage was fascinated by public finances.[45]

As in Ontario under Frost, the office of intergovernmental affairs was installed close to that of the premier. To reach his modernization objectives, the premier also aimed to get 'access to the international system.'[46] As international affairs became an important issue in the 1960s, the mandate of intergovernmental affairs was expanded. The Department of Intergovernmental Affairs was formally established in 1967, and then reorganized in 1974 with a mandate to oversee both federal–provincial and international relations – a unique entity in Canada.[47] Under the stewardship of Claude Morin as deputy minister it still remained a relatively small shop. Morin did not want to manage a large staff and it is quite possible that his influence in this regard was detrimental to the development of the state apparatus.[48]

Unlike in Ontario, the policy work on urban planning stayed with Municipal Affairs. Later, there would be a temporary Ministère de la métropole (mostly concerned with Montreal), as there have been various incarnations of the Ministry of Regions. It was never clear among deciders (and much less among observers) whether this department was dedicated to planning or economic development. It was moved back and forth between Economic Development (formerly Industry and Trade) and Municipal Affairs over the years. Another critically important planning effort was done far away from Finance, in Agriculture. The protection of land for agriculture was always a closely followed policy in the province.

Beyond urban development issues, various agencies were created over the years to work on economic development and planning that were certainly not organized in the coherent manner of the Ontario government. Policy planning, for instance, was awarded to the Conseil d'orientation économique.[49] Its effectiveness was limited, however, as its mandate was to provide *non-binding* advice to the government that included both economic and regional planning.[50] The advice was usually ignored, and the Conseil was replaced in 1968 by the Office de planification et de développement économique (OPDQ), which owed much to the French model of a Secrétariat général au plan and was also interested by regional planning.

In terms of fiscal and economic policy, Finance officials in Quebec never controlled the process like their colleagues in Toronto or Ottawa.

In Quebec, policy advice came from the cabinet secretary and the premier's office. Lesage, content with conducting the orchestra, formed a strong cabinet with ministers who initiated important reforms. In choosing to assume himself the position of minister of finance, Lesage might have hoped that his ministry would play a central agency role, especially as the need for coordination increased with the growth of state activities. Yet Finance was never allowed to rise to the occasion.

This may have been a matter of executive style on the part of Lesage. He would ask separate advisers to work on one file, as much as possible not indicating that different people were working on similar issues. Once he had their reports, he would compare them and form his own opinion. This would allow him to have various options to choose from, and of course to test the integrity of the counsel.[51] Staffs in Finance were mostly accountants – it would have been impossible for economists in Finance to have the influence they had in Ontario, so they went elsewhere. Under Lesage, a few ministers (René Lévesque, Paul Gérin-Lajoie, and later Eric Kierans and Pierre Laporte) formed an inner cabinet. Each of these ministers had their own policy staff. Policy was thus developed by ministers and Lesage would lead them, but not initiate the reforms.[52]

Under Premier Daniel Johnson, policy on key issues was developed by the premier with the higher civil servants that Lesage had hired.[53] Johnson had a far weaker cabinet than Lesage, and so invested in building up the Ministère du Conseil exécutif (MCE) – a strong cabinet office that would become, and remain, an important force. Although there is usually a minister responsible for the portfolio, the influential Secrétariat aux Affaires intergouvernementales canadiennes was located within the MCE.

Remarkably, Johnson kept most of the advisers he had inherited from Lesage: Claude Morin and Jacques Parizeau remained close to the premier, even though Johnson had promised in the 1966 campaign to get rid of them. Johnson, sometimes presented as indecisive, used a competing system of advice, pitting technocrats and political advisers on critical issues so that none of the central agencies could have a pre-eminent role.[54] The institutionalization of the premier's office and of the MCE continued in the 1970s with Bourassa, and especially in René Lévesque's government, where the influence of Louis Bernard was capital. The MCE would become more important with the creation of various secretariats such as Aboriginal Affairs. In economic matters, the OPDQ was also directly related to the premier's office.[55]

Where Ontario built up its Ministry of Finance in the 1960s and 1970s to provide more coherence to its policy apparatus, particularly in the areas of economic development, Quebec chose a different route. To paraphrase Daniel Latouche, the Quebec experience was guided by a dramatic decision that something radical had to change, but the vision that guided the Quiet Revolution was at best 'haphazard,' with 'chance' and a 'small group of civil servants' not particularly tied to the ministry of finance playing critical roles. Latouche argued that, in the end, a 'limited degree of differentiation [was] achieved by the Quebec process vis-à-vis similar experiences of province building elsewhere in Canada.'[56]

This is not to say that the Quebec Ministry of Finance was insignificant. Its role depended in part on how the machinery of government was organized but it also was affected by the personality of the minister of finance. For example, in their account of the budgetary process under the Lévesque government in Québec, Dion and Gow underline the important presence of Jacques Parizeau. Because of his proven commitment to his political party, his reputation as a mandarin, his economic expertise (the first French-Canadian to receive a PhD from the London School of Economics), and his roots in Montreal's bourgeoisie, he was an essential cabinet member in addition to practically owning the finance portfolio.[57] But Parizeau proved to be an exception – no other minister having so much influence on the premier.[58]

The Search for Effective Models

In their frustrations with trying to conjure logic out of organizational charts, scholars often describe public administrations as organized anarchies. In the model initially developed by Cohen, March, and Olsen, and simplified by Padgett, it is assumed that the complexity of the objectives pursued by governments often include contradictory themes. Because outcomes are necessarily uncertain and because unintended consequences inevitably blemish accomplishments, incremental approaches are usually favoured.[59] Decision making has to be iterative because consequences are too numerous and difficult to predict. To complicate matters all the more, a course of action can also change from one government or from one minister to the next. Nevertheless, such systems work.

The Tommy Douglas government in Saskatchewan worked hard to build expertise in its department of finance and was recognized as such by the mid-1940s. Saskatchewan, a much smaller province than

Ontario in terms of population and economy, had a relatively malleable bureaucracy and its system was not as stable as in Ontario. By 1947, the 1946 solution was already evolving,[60] and with the defeat of the Saskatchewan CCF-NDP government in 1964, many of the leading lights in Saskatchewan Finance had left to work in Ottawa or in other provinces.

During the 1960s and 1970s, the two largest provinces and the federal government each adopted distinct approaches to their departments of finance. Ottawa's experience was one of steadiness of purpose and mandate. Finance attracted some of the best minds in the government of Canada, and its importance was not doubted. In Quebec, because the dominant ideology in Quebec before 1960 militated against state intervention, the government of Quebec had only played a marginal role in the province's economic development until the Quiet Revolution. (It should be remembered that education and health policies were mostly designed and implemented by religious and civil organizations over which the state had little control and that the first nationalization of electricity in Quebec took place in 1962, forty years after Ontario.) In such a context, Finance could play nothing more than a cautious, book-keeping role, and would continue on this path through the Quiet Revolution.[61] Real power in terms of economic and budgetary policy was in the hands of a small group of advisers located in the Ministère du Conseil exécutif and in the premier's cabinet until the early 1970s.

The Ontario experience with Finance stands out as an exception among Canadian provinces. In the 1960s and early 1970s, the Department of Treasury, Economics and Intergovernmental Affairs became a de facto central agency without the counterweight of an Ottawa PMO or PCO or of an MCE in Quebec City. The policy advice structure in Ontario may not have had the formal elegance and equilibrium of the Trudeau cabinet committees and secretariats or the structures and disciplines Louis Bernard built in Quebec City for the first Lévesque government, but highly efficient and influential it certainly was.

The strength of the Finance staff in Ontario certainly affected federal–provincial relations, but in a manner that was very different than with Quebec. Quebec demanded more from Ottawa in terms of constitutional powers and the funding that went with them, often framing these demands in terms of the need that the original spirit of confederation be respected. Both Ontario and Quebec wanted Ottawa to assume a smaller place in the fiscal area, but whereas Quebec wanted to increase its influence, Ontario often said it simply wished to keep things transparent and cleanly accounted for. Ontario sought solutions that were practical and efficient for Ontario. Such an option was not possible in Quebec, where federal–provincial relations have taken a quasi-bilateral nation-to-nation dimension since the 1960s.

This peculiarity of Quebec within Canada derives from the fact that it is the only society with a French-speaking majority and a well-defined territorial base on the North American continent, giving it a distinct culture and collective identity. This society was aware of its specificity even before the birth of modern Canada and has always claimed a status and powers enabling it to preserve and strengthen its identity. Furthermore, Quebec signed the 1867 constitution on the basis of what it saw as a pact between two founding French- and English-speaking peoples, two nations, thereby establishing a federal system in which the two orders of government would be, so it was thought, sovereign in their respective spheres of jurisdiction.

Finance in Ontario survived well the many transformations that were brought to its structures in the 1970s and later. It could be said that from that point onwards, however, the structure of Ontario's department of finance lost much of its exotic features and that it became very similar to its counterparts in Quebec and Ottawa.

This exceptionalism of the evolution of the Ontario Ministry of Finance deserves to be explained. The influence of the premier is of course part of the explanation. After five years in office, John Robarts came to the conclusion that Finance's central functions of budget making and devising tax policy would be buttressed by a solid grounding in economics. Since Frost's last days, the province had undertaken important works in infrastructure, and now education and health demanded more attention. That core domestic need was amplified by the federal government's growing intervention in the economy. To respond effectively, a stronger team that combined economists and financial experts was needed, in addition to intergovernmental officers dedicated to the task of positioning Ontario in a rapidly redefining confederation.

A second factor was the quality of the team assembled under Ian Macdonald. Jacques Parizeau had reason to admire the staff at Finance: it was agile, smart, capable of countering Ottawa's intelligence, and alert to Ontario's short- and long-term interests.

There were limits to the success, however. For all the *dirigiste* potential of the Ministry of Finance, Ontario remained a laissez-faire economy and government's role in actively developing regions remained limited. As two noted scholars of the Ontario economy have noted: 'As

Canada's industrial centre benefitting from national policies, the
Ontario state never forwarded an industrial strategy beyond resource
exploitation and the "extensive accumulation" of laying infrastructure
supportive of urban growth, and indeed sprawl, that eventually created the 200-kilometre city around Toronto.'[62]

Where Ontario took advantage of federal policies to focus its power
demands on the nuclear option, Quebec chose a more autonomous and
interventionist economic policy in harnessing hydro-generated power.
But there were other features to Quebec's chosen path. It left economic
responsibilities dispersed between various agencies. Many of its best
trained economists were not working in Finance in the 1960s. They
were deployed in other institutions deemed essential to the Quiet
Revolution. There would not be in Quebec a golden age for Finance.

Conclusion

Ontario's exceptionalism lies in the folding of economics, regional development, and intergovernmental affairs into the portfolio of Finance,
and in the fact that Frost, Robarts, and later Bill Davis both relied on
this ministry implicitly for a wide range of policy advice. In a very
pragmatic fashion, they decided to work with the available resources at
Finance and not duplicate staff by adding policy capacity closer to the
premier. The role of any ministry necessarily varies over time. But in
the critical years of the 1960s and 1970s, which were crucial for both
Quebec and Ontario, it is striking to note the diverging paths of the respective ministries of finance.

The Ontario 'moment,' of course, did not last. The Davis government
opted to strengthen its own premier's office and its cabinet office in the
early 1970s. Its Treasury Board Secretariat sought more involvement in
policy making and implementation, and a number of ministries assumed a more important place in 'development' portfolios. Northern
Development, Environment, Municipal Affairs, Industry, to name but a
few, soon had a hand in policy areas where Finance staff had hitherto
been uncontested. TEIGA seemed to work exceptionally well and is
fondly remembered as a 'golden age' by many of its employees. Asked
why he left Finance in order to become president of York University in
1974, Ian Macdonald answered, jokingly, that 'it was not fun anymore!'[63]
What the joke meant was that with TEIGA, the necessary procedures
and institutions had been put in place and that, personally, Macdonald
had by then developed what he wanted to build. He did not leave

because he was not satisfied by the evolution of the department, but because he had a very interesting opportunity elsewhere.[64] One can only speculate that he had a hunch that the scope of government activities the department was expected to cover could not be sustained for a long period and effectively would not be maintained.

In both Ontario and Quebec, the committees of the 1970s, the program reviews of the 1990s, the business plans of the early years of this decade were all attempts to filter information and get an overall view of the business of the state. Modern states can certainly do more than their predecessors, but they all still search for the tools that will give them coherence. Though the Ontario TEIGA was only temporary, it remains a fascinating example of public administration innovation and policy entrepreneurship.

NOTES

1 The concept is discussed at length in Joseph Facal, 'L'État: Définition, formes et tendances,' in *Sociologie de l'entreprise*, ed. J.-P. Dupuis (Boucherville: Gaétan Morin, 2007), 99–131.
2 Quoted by C. Debbasch and J.-M. Pontier, *Introduction à la politique* (Paris: Dalloz, 1995), 54.
3 See Frank Barry, 'Institutional Capacity and the Celtic Tiger Economy,' paper prepared for the 8th INFER Annual Conference, Cork, 22 September 2006.
4 See Luc Bernier, Keith Brownsey, and Michael Howlett, eds, *Executive Styles in Canada: Cabinet Structures and Leadership Practices in Canadian Government* (Toronto: University of Toronto Press, 2005).
5 See Bryan Evans, 'Capacity, Complexity, and Leadership: Secretaries to Cabinet and Ontario's Project of Modernization at the Centre,' in Patrice Dutil, ed., *Searching for Leadership* (Toronto: University of Toronto Press, 2008), 126.
6 Robert J. Jackson and Doreen Jackson, *Politics in Canada*, 6th ed. (Toronto: Prentice Hall, 2006), 288.
7 André Bernard, *Politique et gestion des finances publiques, Québec et Canada* (Sainte-Foy: Presses de l'Université du Québec, 1992), 127.
8 David Wolfe, 'The Canadian State in Comparative Perspective,' *Canadian Review of Sociology and Anthropology* 26 (1989), 108–9.
9 J.E. Hodgetts, *The Canadian Public Service: A Physiology of Government 1867–1970* (Toronto: University of Toronto Press, 1973), 95.

10 Ibid.
11 Richard Phidd and Bruce Doern, *The Politics and Management of Canadian Economic Policy* (Toronto: Macmillan, 1978), 196.
12 Ibid., 212.
13 Colin Campbell and George J. Szablowski, *The Superbureaucrats: Structure and Behaviour in Central Agencies* (Toronto: Macmillan, 1979).
14 Colin Campbell, *Governments Under Stress* (Toronto: University of Toronto Press, 1983), 77.
15 Wolfe, 'The Canadian State in Comparative Perspective,' 109.
16 Campbell and Szablowski, *The Superbureaucrats*.
17 Savoie, *Governing from the Centre* (Toronto: University of Toronto Press, 1999), 164.
18 Ibid., 156. See also David A. Good, *The Politics of Public Money* (Toronto: University of Toronto Press, 2007).
19 Savoie, *Governing from the Centre*, 156.
20 Ibid., 162; quoted from Phidd and Doern, *The Politics and Management of Canadian Economic Policy*, 210.
21 Savoie, *Governing from the Centre*, 157.
22 Ibid., 160–1.
23 David Good, *The Politics of Public Money: Spenders, Guardians, Priority Setters, and Financial Watchdogs inside the Canadian Government* (Toronto: University of Toronto Press, 2007), see chapter 2 especially.
24 Donald W. Stevenson Papers, 'Notes for Paper to Be Given to the Regional Group, Institute of Public Administration of Canada. February 11, 1972,' pp. 2–3.
25 Evans, 'Capacity, Complexity, and Leadership,' 129–30.
26 Ibid., 123.
27 See F. Schindeler, *Responsible Government in Ontario* (Toronto: University of Toronto Press, 1969).
28 Donald Stevenson Papers, 'Notes for Possible Use at Niagara Institute Seminar,' 17 November 1977, p. 3.
29 Ibid., 'Major Intergovernmental Policy Issues to Be Faced by the New Ministry of Treasury, Economics and Intergovernmental Affairs, Notes for Possible Use at the National Defence College Briefing, September 18, 1972.'
30 H. Ian Macdonald, 'The Solemnization of an Institutional Marriage (or the Joining of the Treasury with Economics), 1969.' Minor editorial adjustments have been made to this text.
31 Donald Stevenson Papers, 'Distribution of Responsibility for Services (Education, Public Health, etc) and Fiscal Policy Relating to Them,' draft of paper to be given at Columbia University, 17 April 1978.

32 Donald Stevenson Papers, 'Energy Issues Facing Canada: Three Perspectives, Prepared for a Seminar on Energy Policy and Federalism in North America, Banff, Alberta, May 14–16, 1980.'

33 Donald Stevenson Papers, 'Federal-Provincial-Municipal Relations – The Management of Canadian Federalism in the 1970s – The Provincial Point of View,' Notes for address to the Institute of General Management, Ottawa, March 7, 1973.

34 See Luc Bernier, 'The Foreign Economic Policy of a Subnational State: The Case of Quebec,' in *Perforated Sovereignties and International Relations*, ed. Ivo Duchacek et al. (New York: Greenwood, 1988), 132.

35 See Kenneth McRoberts, *Quebec: Social Change and Political Crisis*, 3rd ed., with postscript (Toronto: McClelland and Stewart, 1993); and Luc Bernier, 'The Beleaguered State: Québec at the End of the 1990s,' in *The Provincial State in Canada*, ed. Michael Howlett and Keith Brownsey (Peterborough, ON: Broadview Press, 2001).

36 See Gérard Bergeron and Réjean Pelletier, *L'État du Québec en devenir* (Montreal: Boréal Express, 1980).

37 See Bernard, *Politique et gestion des finances publiques*.

38 Louis Bernard, *Réflexions sur l'art de se gouverner: Essai d'un praticien* (Montreal: Québec/Amérique, 1987).

39 Antoine Ambroise and Jocelyn Jacques, 'L'appareil administratif,' in Bergeron and Pelletier, *L'État du Québec en devenir*, 110–12.

40 André Gélinas, *L'administration centrale et le cadre de gestion* (Quebec: Les Presses de l'Université Laval, 2003), 19.

41 Jacques Bourgault, Stéphane Dion, and James Iain Gow, 'Evolution of the Role of Central Agencies in the Quebec Government, 1960–90,' in Alain G. Gagnon, ed., *Québec, State and Society*, 2nd ed. (Scarborough, ON: Nelson Canada, 1993), 224.

42 Bernard, *Politique et gestion des finances publiques*, 128.

43 Ibid., 141.

44 André Bernard, 'Vingt-cinq ans de changements dans le domaine de la gestion financière du gouvernement du Québec,' in *L'administration publique québécoise: Évolutions sectorielles 1960–1985*, ed. Yves Bélanger and Laurent Lepage (Sainte-Foy: Presses de l'Université du Québec, 1989).

45 Pierre O'Neill and Jacques Benjamin, *Les mandarins du pouvoir* (Montreal: Québec/Amérique, 1978), 29. See also Claude Morin, *Mes premiers ministres* (Montreal: Boréal, 1991).

46 Daniel Latouche, 'State Building and Foreign Policy at the Subnational Level' in *Perforated Sovereignties and International Relations*, ed. Ivo Duchacek et al. (New York: Greenwood, 1988), 33.

47 Ibid., 37.
48 Luc Bernier, *De Paris à Washington: La politique internationale du Québec* (Sainte-Foy: Presses de l'Université du Québec, 1996).
49 Dale C. Thomson, *Jean Lesage and the Quiet Revolution* (Toronto: Macmillan, 1984).
50 See chap. 3 in James Gow, *Administration publique québécoise* (Montreal: Beauchemin, 1970), 40 and 46.
51 O'Neill and Benjamin, *Les mandarins du pouvoir*, 36.
52 Ibid., 28–37.
53 Ibid., 51.
54 Morin, *Mes premiers ministres*; O'Neill and Benjamin, *Les mandarins du pouvoir*.
55 Lionel Ouellet, 'L'appareil gouvernemental et législatif,' in Bergeron and Pelletier, *L'État du Québec en devenir*, 83.
56 Latouche, 'State Building and Foreign Policy,' 35. See also Bernier, *De Paris à Washington*.
57 Stéphane Dion and James Iain Gow, 'The Budget Process under the Parti Québécois, 1975–1985,' in *Budgeting in the Provinces*, ed. Allan M. Maslove (Toronto: Institute of Public Administration of Canada, 1989).
58 See Pierre Duchesne, *Jacques Parizeau, Le Baron*, vol. 2 (Montreal: Québec/Amérique, 2002) and Graham Fraser, *René Lévesque and the Parti Québécois in Power* (Montreal: McGill-Queen's University Press, 2001).
59 Bernier, *De Paris à Washington*, chap. 1.
60 See A.W. Johnson, *Dream No Little Dreams* (Toronto: University of Toronto Press, 2004), 122 and 169.
61 Luc Bernier and Guy Lachapelle, 'Budgets et changements sociaux: La Révolution tranquille a vraiment eu lieu,' in *Le processus budgétaire au Québec*, ed. G. Lachapelle et al. (Sainte-Foy: Presses de l'Université du Québec, 1999), chap. 1.
62 Robert Macdermid and Greg Albo, 'Divided Province, Growing Protests: Ontario Moves Right,' in *The Provincial State in Canada*, ed. Michael Howlett and Keith Brownsey (Peterborough: Broadview Press, 2002), 167–8.
63 Interview with Luc Bernier, Toronto, 7 February 2007.
64 Interview with Luc Bernier, Fredericton, 25 August 2009.

SECTION 3

The Guardian and Budget Making

8 Coping with Complexity: Innovation and Resistance in Crafting the Expenditure Budget, 1961–1985

CAROLINE DUFOUR[1]

As the Robarts government assumed a broader range of responsibilities and deepened its impact on the provincial economy through its spending and its programs, the task of creating a budget became more demanding. The response came in three parts. First, budget responsibilities (especially around drafting the actual budget) were transferred from the Department of Economics and Intergovernmental Affairs. The second step was increasing and improving the bureaucracy's capacity to understand economic trends and, just as important, to explain them to both politicians and to itself. It was not just a question of hiring the right individuals, however. With new people came a thirst to create a system that would allow the government to anticipate expenditures more effectively from year to year and to foresee liabilities and commitments deep into the future. Ontario was not alone in this regard, as the Canadian and United States governments undertook similar experiments with their own budget process to improve the decision-making system.

The Treasury Board Secretariat (TBS), some remnants of the old Department of Economics, and, from 1971, the Management Board (MB) and its Secretariat (MBS) were all involved at one point or another in the modification of the budgetary function. One of the tasks the TBS and the new MBS performed in relation to this consisted of crafting the process by which the expenditure budget would be defined and executed. It was a search for a new 'style' that would have three purposes: to control, to manage, and to plan the use of funds as voted by the legislative powers.[2] Depending on the style chosen, one of these dimensions was inevitably accented.

The objective of this chapter is to bring to light the evolution of the style of the expenditure budget in Ontario between 1961 and 1985, a period during which political and administrative authorities demanded change. The debates on the style of the expenditure budget were revealing because they demonstrated how the Treasury and, later, the Ministry of Finance, had to work with other ministries to finally define its annual budget. The evolution of the style of the expenditure budget in Ontario between 1961 and 1985 was particularly important as the government undertook a number of experiments aimed at improving the process of budgeting and, in a way, simultaneously challenged some of the Treasury's authority. These experiments in increasing control, efficiency, and management were significant steps in the evolution of the budgetary process because they impacted the thinking and preparation of the budget.

1961–1974: The Rise and Fall of PPBS

John Robarts became premier of Ontario in November 1961, knowing well that the role played by the government in the provincial economy would face an important change in orientation. Similarly to its counterparts in other industrialized societies, the Ontario government wished to combat recession and unemployment. It also aimed to modernize the provincial economy and spent massively on the social and economic infrastructure. Between 1960 and 1965, the net general expenditures of the Ontario government went from $900.9 to $1263 million, an increase of 40 per cent.[3] In parallel with this change of economic orientation, the Government of Ontario's relations with the Government of Canada cooled, leading Queen's Park to announce its intention of being financially autonomous. The financial gap to be filled due to the adoption of this measure was considerable. At the time, the combined expenditures of the provinces were about half of the federal government's.[4]

These two shifts in the economic context of the province were reflected in the rapid growth of the provincial budget, which in turn was used by the mandarins of the Ministry of Finance as a tool to control the short-term performance of the economy. The logic behind this choice was that 'since the budget assumed a proportionally greater share of the provincial total product and was growing faster than federal expenditures ... it could be used as a stabilizing force in the economic system.'[5] In the budget speech of 1966, the Treasurer offered four principles that guided the use of the budget as a tool of economic intervention: (1) the establishment of expenditure priorities on the basis of their contribution to growth and productivity; (2) the introduction of long-range planning; (3) the coordination of all policies and programs within the long-range plan; and (4) coordination with the federal and municipal governments.[6] This approach to social and economic development was not unique to Ontario. Governments throughout Canada, the United States, parts of Europe, and Japan in the same decade started using their budget as a policy tool to address similar social and economic issues.

With the implementation of new interdependent budgetary and economic principles, governments had to overcome a variety of administrative barriers. One was the absence of planning, coordination, and development structures in the administration, which led to the creation of organizations dedicated to one or another of these tasks. Another problem lay in the inadequacy of the style of the expenditure budget. In Ontario, it was the Committee on Public Accounts of the Legislative Assembly that first alluded to this reality. In its annual report of 1966, the committee argued that the government needed to have better control over its programs and their costs and should try to adopt a new form of budgeting.[7]

It was evident that in regard to the principles enumerated by the treasurer (particularly the preoccupation with expenditures and long-range planning), the style of the expenditure budget of the time did not meet the government's needs. The line-item style of budgeting, also known as traditional or object-budget, was the standard in Ontario at this time, as it was in all public bureaucracies. Public administrations had adopted this approach during the nineteenth century and continued to use it with minor tinkering. The main purpose of this approach was to empower the legislature to control governmental expenditures by focusing on the money required by ministries rather than on what was accomplished with the money. Because the control was exerted a priori, the budget was based on pre-established objects of expenditures or items (salary, office supplies, transportation, etc.). The annual expenditure budgetary process started with each ministry preparing a budget, all using the same items and indications. All of the ministries' budgets were added up and thus constituted the government's expenditure budget, which in turn reflected the organizational structures of the administration. With each succeeding budget, the same items were presented, but the amounts of money grew somewhat with each fiscal year to accommodate various increased costs. This is why some analysts qualified the practice of line-item budgeting as an incremental model.

Three aspects of this budgeting style were particularly problematic for the Ontario government in regard to the new uses being made of the budget. First, it made the funding of new programs difficult. New initiatives are given low priority because of the absence of means to evaluate the programs already in place and the incremental logic. Second, because of the budget's input orientation and its annual cycle, the main emphasis was put on immediate expenditure levels. There was no space for the concepts of planning and long-range costs. Third, the only form of control exercised by this style of budget on administrators was to evaluate their ability to spend within the limits of the pre-established budget. The efficiency or the reach of organizational objectives could not be evaluated because the line-item budget did not produce information that could allow such appraisal.

The solution to the problem of the style of the expenditure budget came in the form of the Planning-Programming-Budgeting system (PPBS), suggested by the Committee on Public Accounts in its 1966 report. The adoption of PPBS by public administrations was an international trend and the history of its beginnings is well known. In 1961, the American Department of Defence implemented a budgeting system that promised to manage public money not by controlling, as the line-item approach did, but by planning.[8] It created great hope in public administrations, and within ten years several governments in both developed and developing countries aimed to adopt it. PPBS represented the first attempt to move government budgeting away from the incremental decisional process and into a rational mode. The PPBS approach borrowed from the concept of 'systems,' a notion widely used in both natural and social sciences. It was said to be simple and rational in its approach: planning objectives, developing programs based on objectives, translating the programs into budgetary requirements, and evaluating the programs' performance.[9] Applied to public administration, the new system offered seductive promises. During the initial 'planning' phase, the government would identify from among a set of objectives the ones it wished to follow. A second step involved an analysis of the possible options available to reach the objectives in light of the available resources. This led to the preparation of 'program packages' that could solve the same issue while presenting different costs and benefits. Once a program was finally chosen, efforts would be made to evaluate its costs over many years. At the end of the cycle, through program evaluation, the government could choose to keep a program, terminate it entirely, or modify some aspect of it.

PPBS emphasized programs and tied their objectives to the budgeting process without considering the organizational structure. The program structure presented the hierarchical listing of programs, activities, and sub-activities that contributed to the achievement of government objectives.[10] This approach emphasized what the government intended to do with the money allocated by the legislative power, and not what it needed, as the line-item model did. Another difference from the line-item model was the emphasis put on long-term planning, rather than annual spending. It meant the expenditure budget had to present the expected cost of each program for a certain number of years, including in some cases the context of past years. The program structure also served as a framework for the evaluation of the effectiveness of programs. By knowing how much a program was supposed to cost, it would be possible to control the amount of public funds spent and to measure the efficiency of the program managers. In addition, there was the possibility of conducting accurate cost-benefit analyses. This model, if applied completely, could serve as the format for the estimates, thus offering the opportunity to the legislature to be involved in control of program administration. More than a simple device presenting numbers annually about the government's needs, PPBS could become an extraordinary management tool.

To the Government of Ontario, PPBS looked like an attractive solution. Following the suggestion of the Committee on Public Accounts, James Allan, treasurer of the province, announced to the House on 31 May 1966 that the government had adopted program budgeting in principle – the first Canadian government to do so, although the first studies on the topic had been carried out by Ottawa, following a recommendation of the Glassco Royal Commission on Government Organization in favour of program budgeting.[11] The overall objective in introducing PPBS in the Ontario administration was to increase the effectiveness and efficiency of services delivery through better planning and management of government programs.[12] The system was designed to assist the Cabinet and its committees in improving decision-making about policies and resources allocation. This system would also allow the legislature to get a better grip on the estimates as the amounts of money submitted showed the meaningfulness of each program.[13] In contrast to the general enthusiasm for PPBS, however, few resources were devoted to its implementation at the outset. The treasurer expected it could be achieved through training programs or by gradually recruiting people with the applicable skills during the normal turnover process.[14] More important, it was the Program Review Branch of the Treasury Board Secretariat that would be charged with the responsibility of coordinating its development and implementation.

PPBS had a rocky beginning in the Ontario administration. Following Treasurer Allan's announcement in the House, a pilot project conducted with the Department of Health was unsuccessful.[15] Attempts to define an overall program structure for the government and to develop performance indicators also failed. The hiring by the TBS in October 1968 of a coordinator responsible for the development of the system eased the situation. He quickly developed a flow chart showing a management cycle based on the four activities central to the system and a definition of the roles of each political and administrative actor within this cycle. The following year, TBS distributed a critically important policy piece, *Effective Management through P.P.B.S.*[16] and organized courses and seminars designed for middle managers. Soon, a plan was ready calling for a fully operating PPBS in the whole administration by April 1971.

The administrative emphasis was first put upon the development of a limited number of aspects of PPBS, including the standard Multi-Year Plan (MYP), or Multi-Year Forecast (MYF) as the government called it. A central element of the planning dimension of Ontario's PPBS, the MYF was designed to assist the Cabinet in establishing funding priorities for existing programs and for implementing new ones. In concrete terms, it linked the process of developing policy and planning new programs within the actual operations of the government.[17] Public servants were encouraged to establish priorities for program implementation and ensure that the financial, human, and material resources could be made available to continue existing programs, introduce new ones, and phase out others.

The initial MYF was launched in 1968 and provided a straight projection of program costs for five years. An important characteristic of this plan lay in the absence of government objectives, despite the theoretical obligation that they be included. It led to the development by each department of its own program structure: another twist to the classic PPBS approach.[18] The consequence was that the programs as defined by the departments became the keystones of the budgeting system. Government objectives, if any were formulated, would not have their own program structure, as prescribed by PPBS. Moreover, activities which contributed to a specific objective, but were located in different departments, would be grouped in different programs.[19] In other words, the structure still followed that of the departments, as it had with the line-item style. Because this approach centred on ministerial programs and structures, PPBS could not be implemented in Ontario following a top-down approach, but instead was accomplished 'bottom-up.' Thus, each department submitted its own plan to be included in the government's MYF.

The net effect of the practice was that the Cabinet's attention was centred not on program priorities as established in the departments' plans, but on their financial implications for the first few years. In other words, plans were used to identify the potential financial issues which would have resulted if more stringent priorities and control of costs were not introduced.

The implementation of PPBS also gave birth to a plan to alter the format of the estimates, which indeed had to be modified to allow better oversight by the members of the legislature. For the fiscal year 1969–70, the intention was to abandon the practice of having members of the Legislative Assembly vote funds by organizational unit and objects of expenditure. Instead, MPPs would vote on programs and objects of expenditure. This said, an analysis of the TBS at the time noted that there was still 'a strong emphasis on the goods and services being purchased to operate individual programs,' even if the goal was to give more insight into the results expected to be achieved with the money spent.[20] TBS was scarcely more encouraged by the development of appropriate measures of output, benefits, and effectiveness of individual programs. It found it almost impossible to establish meaningful measures because departments were still reluctant to specify their program and activity objectives. The implementation of this element of the system was thus postponed until the start of the MYF in 1973–4.[21]

Working documents of the Committee on Government Productivity (COGP) published in 1970 and 1971, which presented rich insights into the working of the Ontario budgetary system, bear witness to the struggles associated with the implementation of the PPBS.[22] Composed of five senior public servants and as many private-sector executives, the COGP was appointed in 1969 by Premier Robarts with the mandate of reappraising all aspects of the provincial administration in order to gear it towards the 1970s. It was expected to introduce more rationality in the policy-making process and its terms of reference allowed it 'to inquire into all matters pertaining to the management of the Government of Ontario and to make such recommendations as in its opinion will improve the efficiency and effectiveness of the Government of Ontario.'[23]

The growth of the provincial expenditures ($3 billion in 1969–70 compared to $1 billion in 1962–3) and the increasing role the provincial government expected to play in the coming decade, motivated the creation of this committee. PPBS had made some progress since its beginnings when the COGP investigated it. By December 1970, program analysis coordinators were appointed in most departments to direct the introduction of the system. The format and use of the MYF, which by then had to present not only natural growth but also a constraint forecast, had been improved, and departments admitted it provided them with substantial benefits, even though most of their MYF did not contain the elements they were supposed to in the framework of PPBS.[24] Departments were also developing their programs and objectives and the estimates were to be prepared on the basis of programs and activities for the fiscal year 1971–2.

A report prepared to provide the COGP with background material on PPBS underlined a list of problems and obstacles to its implementation that inevitably diminished its progress.[25] The first of these problems was the concept of 'program.' The COGP discovered that departments were at vastly different stages in the development of their goals and program structure, making the global functioning of PPBS difficult. Moreover, the programs did not include all the costs related to them. The report also indicated that there were program overlaps between departments. Finally, several issues linked to the development of a program structure were identified. These difficulties had a common origin: the Cabinet did not define the overall government objectives that should be guiding departments. By not focusing on a program system, a bottom-up approach developed and the purpose of having a planning, programing, and budgeting system lost a significant part of its meaning. This situation led the COGP to conclude in a November 1971 project report that the planning function was deficient in the Ontario administration and that what did take place did so outside of the PPB system.[26]

The MYF was the second PPBS component that caused trouble for the departments. The tool itself, as mentioned above, was considered generally useful. It was the conditions associated with it, including little feedback from central agencies, the short time given to departments to complete the exercise, the impression of producing useless analysis and data, and the lack of top-down participation, that contributed to the questioning of the validity of the MYF, and indirectly made the implementation of PPBS difficult. It was clear that the two main central agencies involved in the MYF, the TBS and Taxation and Fiscal Policy Branch of the Department of Treasury and Economics, were in conflict.

On one hand, the TBS had an expenditure-oriented approach and envisaged the MYF as 'the programming device which expresses anticipated accomplishments ... together with the costs, physical and human resources required for a number of years into the future.'[27] The first year of such a plan had to provide guidelines for the preparation of the estimates, taxation proposals, and fiscal policies, in addition to performance targets. On the other hand, the Taxation and Fiscal Policy Branch was more concerned about the implications for planning. It considered a medium-term forecast such as the MYF had three limited purposes: to provide continued balanced-budget capacity based on refined information about on-going and new programs, to be a vehicle to display and receive global priorities, and to respond flexibly to federal fiscal policy initiatives. The differing perspectives paralysed a good part of the process. As of 1971 no evaluation had been made by central agencies on MYF's value as an operational budgetary instrument.

Despite these difficulties, the COGP did not recommend abandoning PPBS. Instead, COGP integrated it in the ambitious administrative reorganization it proposed to the government to improve the efficiency and the effectiveness of government operations. In the plan, PPBS effectively became the vehicle of greater flexibility in resource utilization for managers and improved accountability.

The implementation of the COGP's recommendations regarding the reorganization of government gave PPBS its second wind, and the MBS appeared optimistic about its implementation.[28] This re-launch was supported by the creation of a Management Policy Branch in the MB whose responsibility included the development of PPBS.[29] Many ministries would have to adjust to new responsibilities assigned through the implementation of the recommendations. First among them was the requirement for major revisions of their goals and objectives. In some cases, this meant that some ministries had to explicitly establish goals and objectives. The concept of current level of service (the identification of sufficient policy and programing options to give a degree of choice in applying any necessary budgetary constraint) was added to the MYF in 1972, and would prove one of the more successful components of PPBS. The MYF process was also modified to involve political input at an early stage, putting increased emphasis on projections into future years, and to accelerate the transition from forecasting to planning.

Importantly, the requirements for Cabinet submissions were to be more formalized. Despite past efforts to give the estimates a format coherent with PPBS requirements, their presentation using the categories of 'programs' and 'activities' had more form than substance. In 1972 a multi-stage process was introduced for changing the form of the estimates to encourage consideration of program outputs along with traditional input information. That year, twenty-four ministries and agencies established at least one commitment to undertake work involved in starting PPBS, and many had organized staff committees dedicated to the task.[30] In the end, in addition to all the investments put into the technical aspects of PPBS, success depended on the development of a results-oriented attitude among government managers and administrators, an element that was only taking root a full six years after the ministerial announcement of May 1966.

A few months after the COGP's report, the secretary of the MB reiterated the government's interest in PPBS when he wrote to the deputy ministers that 'the philosophical underpinnings of the system of management described in the guide *Effective Management Through P.P.B.S.* continue to be favoured in Ontario.'[31] However, numerous problems remained to be solved. Among them, according to the chairman of the board, was the presence in PPBS of elements too complex, or made too complex by the public service, to be understood by the politicians, an opinion shared by some consultants hired to examine the issue.[32] In addition, ministries identified issues link to PPBS, namely, the conflict between the MYF and the estimates, for which no solution could be developed.[33]

As part of a process aimed to provide a last chance for the implementation of PPBS, many initiatives were undertaken. They included the distribution of a questionnaire to all ministries to enquire about deputy ministers' perceptions on PPBS, the formation of an inter-agency task force to monitor the technique and processes of the MYR and the annual estimates, the revision of the *Effective Management through PPBS* guide, and the visit by the administration to an American state where PPBS had been installed with some success. A significant initiative remained though the revision of the role and responsibilities of the MB and hence its Secretariat. In its third interim report, the COGP suggested an expanded role for the MB which included ensuring programs were managed effectively and efficiently by ministries. The committee's report also recommended that the annual estimates proposed to the MB include a statement of measurable outputs and that ministries could be controlled in their performance as well as for their expenditures.[34] The analysis conducted by the officials of the MBS on the subject painted the picture of an organization searching for its purpose. For

PPBS, the officials asked questions about all its dimensions, including the relation the MBS had (and should have) with it.[35] The exercise had the merit of inciting the actors involved to implement a clear definition of their responsibilities in this budgetary system.

Parallel to these initiatives to buttress the implementation of PPBS were signals coming from different parts of government that its demise was near. At the beginning of 1973, PPBS seminars were cancelled by the Civil Service Commission. Within the ministries, some deputies were distributing the well-known article 'A Death in the Bureaucracy: The Demise of Federal PPB' to their staff.[36] More significant was a speech given by an official of the MBS at a personnel management conference held the same year, which expressed the view that the implementation of PPBS was beyond the capacities of the public service. He argued that the ministries still did not have the analytical resources to carry out a comprehensive planning function. Finally, it seemed that the time available to cabinet ministers was already overcommitted to make room in their schedule for a meaningful participation in PPBS.[37] Seven years after the first works on PPBS, the Government of Ontario recognized the enterprise had not been successful. In 1973 the only component of the system that remained was the MYF, which had gone through significant changes to be a useful tool, and it was abandoned in 1976.

Beyond identifiable elements such as personalities, time constraints, and resources allocated to the project, conceptual and practical factors played a role in the failure of the implementation of PPBS in Ontario's public administration. In the first case, whether the government was aware of it or not, PPBS presented flaws that affected all administrations that tried to adopt it.[38] First was the difficulty of applying a budgeting system developed in the world of defence to social policy fields: Defining concrete objectives, developing tools to measure desired end results, and establishing clear relationships between means and ends was logical for a government department with a predictable policy field. For a government trying to make sense of social interventions, PPBS's tools proved to be clumsy. Second, the terminology of PPBS did not have the same meanings for the persons involved. One official in the Ministry of Revenue declared it an exercise in jargon whereby people worried more about the definition of terms than about the specific results. The obvious conceptual differences of the TB and the Taxation and Fiscal Policy Branch of the Department of Treasury and Economics illustrated the point.[39] Third, and more fundamentally,

PPBS implied a long-term planning that did not match the political instincts of the cabinet or economic circumstances.[40]

That political dimension also had a determining influence at the practical level. One aspect of it resided in the Cabinet's non-involvement with the implementation of PPBS that undermined the implementation of the new budgetary style. Ministries were not subjected to general government objectives. Instead, they tended to continue fulfilling administrative and technical functions as well as organizational units: a program could therefore frequently contribute to several objectives of the government. Second, when it happened that a general end was identified, it was not unusual to find many programs sprawled among ministries contributing to it. Third, programs could be interrelated, contributing to each other, rather than being aimed at one broad objective. The complexity of the program structure simply took the administration away from an ideal PPBS structure based on decision-making alternatives.

Instead of an approach based on programs, ministries decided to use one reflecting their own organizational structure. This had the virtue of making their programs workable for the preparation of the estimates voted on by the legislature. In essence, there were two parallel program structures in the administration. One was made from the point of view of the central agencies and reflected their vision of the programs in place, not that of the line ministries. The other structure was developed by each ministry for the purposes of the estimates. The authority of program managers was threatened by the PPBS. It was easier to supervise budgets following organizational lines than try to account for them if they covered more than one ministry. This double structure led some actors to describe the situation of PPBS in Ontario as at best an uneasy mixture of program and organization, unevenly distributed in the administration.[41]

A method of 'crosswalking,' created to accommodate organization and program arrangements, was considered to resolve the dispute between operational departments and central agencies. It basically consisted of linking program and organizational structures by superimposing them. In theory, the model might have worked; in practice, the technique met resistance. Managers wanted clear accountability of all expenditures charges under distinct 'Vote and Item' in the House, and did not want to see their numbers subsumed into those of other ministries.[42] Ministries did not try to develop inter-ministry committees that would have worked on inter-ministry programs. Because ministries used a program structure for budget purposes, an inter-ministry structure would had created important problems for the development of a budget as well as for reporting and controlling.[43]

In sum, PPBS had few friends. On one hand, the executive power, by not setting government objectives, tacitly allowed a parallel program structure to be created that could not meet the ends aimed for by PPBS. The ministries were also resistant. Any attempt to match the two program structures was prevented by their dogged determination to follow the estimates presentation guidelines. Despite its interest in policy evaluation, the legislature offered little help. PPBS was thus allowed to die on the vine. It would be remembered as a good theory whose time simply had not come.

1974–1985: The Implementation of the MBR and ZBB

Until 1974 the Government of Ontario had been managing the budgetary growth of a prosperous province. By 1975, the economy had started to stall and the government's fiscal position had deteriorated. Emerging world-wide inflationary pressures triggered by rising oil prices and a provincial deficit of almost $2 billion led to a policy of fiscal restraint. The Davis minority government responded by reducing the number of public servants, working to improve the productivity of the administration, and streamlining rules and regulations. In sum, it wanted to 'trim the fat of the system.'[44]

It was under these circumstances that it imitated other governments dealing with similar issues and decided to introduce in the administration a system named Management by Results (MBR). Also known as Management by Objectives (MBO), its purpose was to manage programs and develop the expenditure budget. Popularized by management guru Peter Drucker, MBR focused on three key concepts.[45] The first one was goals setting, which consisted of determining long-term and operating objectives. Priorities were usually set in terms of anticipated results to be achieved over a certain period of time. 'Participation,' the second key concept, introduced the urgency for superiors and subordinates to work collaboratively in the identification of organizational goals and objectives, planning, and resources allocation. This was considered to be an important strength of MBR because it could heighten commitment and morale, lead to team building, greater coordination, and the development of better management information systems.[46] Finally, with MBR the organization could receive feedback, as progress towards stated objectives could be tracked.

MBR focused on government actions and their consequences, not their costs.[47] The approach could be linked to the budgeting process when the objectives outlined in the budget were implemented by means of the MBR system.[48] In a well-designed system, there was a clear relationship between the level of performance and the resources required to achieve it. MBR was said to enable the government to determine more rationally the level of funding it was willing to provide for a particular program as well as the level of performance expected of a program manager.

The adoption of MBR by the Government of Ontario was gradual. The restraint policy of 1975 triggered its implementation, although the approach had been mentioned earlier in some government documents.[49] The formal introduction of MBR followed the COGP's final report, when PPBS was still a going concern in the administration and the government had decided to restructure and expand the role of the Management Board. As the board had to ensure that programs were managed efficiently and that its recommendations included statements of measurable output in the estimates, MBR was envisaged as a possible alternative to PPBS.

In fact, MBR was seen as springing out of the PPBS management framework (along with other systems such as the goal-setting and review system) because of the common concern with the effective and efficient utilization of resources and the emphasis on output rather than input.[50] While PPBS made policy making and policy review central tasks, MBR saw the results of the policy-making process as a way of ensuring that what Cabinet decided to do got done. This took the form of a two-stage process in the provincial administration.[51] First, a ministry would commit itself to the attainment of quantifiable and measurable objectives, win the endorsement of Management Board, and receive the resources needed to achieve them. Second, the ministry would report on actual achievements and had to account for any deviations from the stated objectives. It was expected that a program manager would be concerned with avoiding over-expenditures and underachievement.

The extension of the principles of MBR into the Ontario budgeting process was ambitious and was made to provide a common basis for the establishment of policy priorities, the estimates review process, and the monitoring of performance.[52] Decision packages were the basis of the system, as they were used to establish funding priorities and developed to reflect varying levels of output with corresponding levels of input. After program priorities were established and output levels determined, they could be expressed in terms of MBR. The MBS would review the estimates using the numbers presented in the exercise and selectively monitor results as a means of exercising central control. The first experience with MBR was judged satisfactory (during the 1974–5 estimates process, thirty-three MBR projects were presented by four-teen ministries).[53] As a result, the government decided to proceed with a four-year plan to implement MBR where feasible; this at the time was estimated to be about 70 per cent of government programs. In 1976 MBR projects covered about 40 per cent of the provincial budget.

Concurrent to the implementation of MBR, the Ontario government put an end to its anti-inflation program, one year after its introduction. The financial situation of the province was hardly a bed of roses. The Cabinet continued its search for better management of the economy and asked the Cabinet Committee on Wage and Price Guidelines to as-sess Zero-Base Budgeting (ZBB), a technique to improve the manage-ment of the budget.[54] This style of expenditure budget was seen as an innovative concept when it was introduced in the public sector in the 1970s, although it was first conceived in the literature in 1924.[55] Texas Instruments had first adopted this approach to expenditure budgeting in 1969. It gained notoriety few years later through Georgia governor Jimmy Carter, who imported the system into his state administration in 1971. The concept rapidly spread to other countries during the 1970s and the 1980s, although its diffusion and its popularity never compared to that of PPBS. In Canada, a few provincial governments introduced ZBB, on an experimental basis. The federal government never paid real attention to it.[56]

ZBB was presented as a budgeting tool that did not take existing pro-grams or their funding level for granted, as traditional budgeting typ-ically did. Instead, it required a review of each program before any resources were assigned. Rather than an incremental change from the preceding year, every dollar had to be justified. The first step in such a budgetary system consisted of dividing the organization into decision units (budgetary program, operation or activity), which made it pos-sible to adapt ZBB to an existing organizational structure. Once the units were chosen, managers had to survey all plausible ways to achieve objectives and select the best one. This led to the preparation of decision packages, that is, simple budgets.[57] The supervisor then ranked the de-cision packages in the order of their utility.

In submissions presented in October 1976 and January 1977, the MB recommended that Cabinet adopt ZBB.[58] Considering its successful use by both private and public organizations, this approach to the allocation of annual expenditures seemed appropriate and applicable to the Ontario government. Management Board's proposal was for the implementation of a modified version of ZBB that would be piloted in a limited number of ministries. The application of a pure ZBB in Ontario public administration was judged impractical and unnecessary because of the onerous amount of analysis required. Management Board also considered that there was no need for Cabinet to review all components of each program every year. Instead, it proposed to differentiate between those expenditures which could be varied in a particular year and those which, for practical purposes, could not. ZBB, in this application, would only apply to the variable expenditures. These were in fact the expenditures the government wanted to keep an eye on in a period of restraint. In a clear reference to the PPBS experience, the Management Board's submissions stated that for ZBB to work, the government had to be committed to making it work by having the ministries carry out the necessary analyses.

Some officials of the Management Board Secretariat remained doubtful, if not sceptical, of the enterprise.[59] It was not that they questioned the logic or the technical aspects of ZBB. In light of the PPBS experience, they were concerned about the time commitment of the ministers and ministries, and the bureaucracy's commitment to adopting a new system. Others were aware that ZBB presented limits: its difficulty with defining the decision packages and alternative levels of output and input, the amount of paperwork that it could generate, and the possibility of departments 'gaming' the system to the point where it would lose its integrity. Nonetheless, they supported its introduction for a number of convincing reasons:[60] First, it undermined the weakest features of incremental budgeting, which the government described as 'taking existing programs for granted and increasing their funding levels each year to allow for inflation and workload increases.'[61] As the government recognized, incremental budgeting 'worked' when funds were plentiful. When funds were in short supply and reductions had to be applied, however, this budget practice simply led to the application of arbitrary or across-the-board cuts in programs. There was no way to distinguish essential programs that should not suffer money cuts from those that could, and managers had to face the same consequences, whatever their effectiveness. It was hoped that ZBB would offer a rational method of establishing funding priorities. Second, ZBB made the identification of areas and programs of duplication easier. Third, it provided a rational approach to establishing priorities and making trade-off decisions. Finally, it could be tracked by ministers, deputy ministers, and program managers.

The adoption of ZBB did not mean that MBR had to be put aside. Many authors have noted that MBR was 'first a management technique and only secondarily ... a budgeting system.'[62] In fact, ZBB's advocates believed it was a constituent of MBR, or at least consistent with it.[63] This was why establishing a clear relationship between ZBB and MBR was a key element in the implementation strategy of the new budgetary system. The administration trusted that ZBB offered the best mechanism for tying MBR to the planning, budgeting, and estimates processes. Therefore, it was considered imperative that MBR and ZBB be put in place in tandem.

The Management Board Secretariat did not try to implement ZBB across-the-board, as it had tried with previous initiatives, a decision shared by other provincial governments, namely, those of British Columbia and Newfoundland.[64] Rather, ZBB was first adopted on a voluntary basis, through pilot projects, for the purpose of establishing priorities within ministries for budgetary decision making. One ministry from each policy field was involved to ensure that methods and procedures were workable in the ministries. Such an approach would allow developing both expertise and advocates for the new system. Five ministries participated in the experiment, and ZBB became a publicly known budgeting tool when Darcy McKeough mentioned it in his 1977 budget address.

The results of the ZBB pilot projects were rather positive. A summary written in November 1977 indicated that the ministries that had participated found it advantageous in analysing components of their divisions. Many reported success in developing divisional priorities for service levels and contingency analysis, and for reviewing the operation and utilization of resources at the branch and section level.[65] ZBB also integrated well with the existing budgeting process, despite the need to refine it to reduce the amount of paperwork. Ministries identified another pressing need: to train personnel in budgeting and planning and in performing supportive backup analyses. There was one final advantage: implementation within ministries could be phased in by division. In the end, the approach was judged good enough to be spread through the administration. The decision to adopt ZBB, however, was not left to volunteering ministries. Interestingly, the more efforts ministries put into planning, the more likely they were to adopt ZBB.[66]

While ZBB was being implemented, MBR's situation was also progressing. The Cabinet had reaffirmed its commitment to Management by Results, and most ministries had plans for its full implementation by April 1978. For the Management Board, the main impact that MBR had had was on the relationship established between the board itself and the ministries favouring better management and control.[67] The most tangible result was that in fiscal year 1977–8, more than half of the internal estimates prepared by the ministries followed that model and 95 per cent of the government's budget was described in terms of 'Results Abstracts' – a document outlining program objectives and results closely linked to MBR.

MBR had thus become a central practice of the administrative and political actors when the provincial auditor's mandate was amended to allow cost-benefit evaluations of government programs. The legislature asked him to examine and report on whether satisfactory systems were in place to measure the economy, efficiency, and effectiveness of programs. The change in mandate was hardly unique to Ontario, as similar transformations were taking place in other provinces as well as at the federal level and in several developed countries.[68] The development of the state and the concurrent growth of the power of public administration led to a concern, namely, among officers of legislative assemblies. A 1971 international auditing conference discussing the broadening of auditors' powers and discussion about this issue among the auditing community during the same time frame are illustrations of the movement. The origin of the change in the role of auditors in Canada can be placed in 1975, with the Independent Review Committee on the Office of the Auditor General of Canada. The committee recommended the introduction of comprehensive auditing in the mandate of the auditor general that would giving him the right and the obligation to scrutinize the capacity of public administration to reach its goals as well as the economic efficiency with which it does so. The auditor's mandate was amended to include the evaluation of the 'value for money' of programs, and the same year the auditor general made the now famous declaration that the government and Parliament were 'close to losing effective control of public purse' in addition to criticizing the format and the content of the estimates.[69] The creation of the Royal Commission on Financial Management and Accountability (Lambert Commission) closely followed. The provinces quickly reacted to Ottawa's situation: in 1977, eight of them had passed or modified auditor-general acts for the purpose of examining their systems of accountability and management.

The Ontario auditor's new mandate seemed timely, as in 1979 the government objectives were to reduce the spending growth rate for established programs to 6 per cent. His first and unflattering report on the topic noted the absence of guidelines for setting MBR objectives, the lack of measurable goals and objectives, as well as an inadequate measure of performance.[70] This remark was only the tip of the iceberg. The Management Board Secretariat soon grew impatient with the quality of the MBR abstracts and came to the conclusion that the estimates were still prepared on the basis of an incremental model, a situation not appropriate in a period of budgetary restrictions.[71] Two explanations were offered for the weak commitment of the ministries to MBR. First, they had come to the conclusion that MBR results were not being seriously considered in budget allocations. Second, there was still a paralysing lack of expertise in MBR throughout the bureaucracy.[72] As for the latest initiatives conducted by the MBS to improve Management by Results, they were too recent to be evaluated at this time.

A mandate to assess the status of MBR in the Ontario government was given to a group of six senior executive directors from line ministries. The group, known as the MBR Task Force, was created in November 1980. In its report submitted in January 1981, the task force stated that the difficulties encountered by MBR in Ontario resided more in its implementation than with the concept.[73] Remarkably, the task force judged that too much investment had been put into MBR for it to be abandoned, and that other alternatives could not guarantee a better performance. On this basis, it recommended strengthening MBR rather than replacing it. This led to the approval by the Management Board and Cabinet of a 'Managing by results improvement plan' calling for significant improvement within a two-year time frame. In this plan, the Management Board Secretariat, as the custodian of the planning and control process, had to ensure the resource allocation and the estimates process were oriented towards results.

The submission of the MBR task force's report coincided with the suggestion by an inter-ministry committee for a new format and content for the estimates, which had not significantly changed since 1971–2.[74] Even though there was no formal request or proposal from the legislature or the provincial auditor, the Management Board Secretariat felt the government had to be ready to answer the questions the other provinces and the federal government were being asked in respect to the estimates.[75] The Management Board, however, judged the recommendations made by the committee as too bold and instead adopted a three-year action plan that would eventually lead to the implementation of new printed estimates and briefing books in 1983–4.

In January 1983 the MBS introduced a crucial element in favour of the implementation of MBR in the internal guidelines for the analysis of the estimates submissions. If a ministry failed to cooperate in the negotiation process with the MBS, which included in the quality of the material submitted and respect for the deadline of presentation, major consequences could occur. The ministry case could become an issue at the MB during the estimates approval, and the funds could be held back until the abstract submitted was considered to be of adequate quality. Despite these incentives, in April 1984 the MBR coordinator of the Management Board Secretariat reported that considerable improvement was required in the MBR abstracts submitted by the ministries. He concluded: 'MBR Improvement appears to have survived its infancy, but there is still considerable growth to be achieved. MBR has been implemented, but it is not yet institutionalized.'[76] The same year it was decided that the form and terminology of the abstracts were no longer mandatory. In the end it seemed the enterprise was worth it, as four years later the system was still in place and considered well established.[77] As a comparison, by that time Newfoundland and Saskatchewan had abandoned ZBB on the basis that it did not help in meeting the needs created by the fiscal crisis of the 1980s.[78]

As was the case with PPBS, both MBR and ZBB presented conceptual weaknesses that may have harmed their implementation. In the case of MBR, it is well known to be a measure of program performance based on the results over a single year and does not include benefits that could spread over many years or unexpectedly reveal themselves in the future. As for ZBB, it is interesting to note that the Management Board Secretariat decided to shy away from the use of its name, since it was believed 'the introduction of new jargon does more to hinder than help the acceptance of a new idea,'[79] and thus could have led to another ill-fated implementation. Moreover, the 'zero' factor never made sense for many managers, even if in Ontario the application of ZBB was limited to specific programs. Oddly enough, some weaker conceptual elements of this style of expenditure budget may have helped its introduction in the government of Ontario. As in the American experience, its superficiality and production of results so resembled those of the incremental approach that it actually helped the penetration of ZBB.[80]

At the practical level, the implementation of MBR and ZBB was strongly linked to often interdependent political and institutional factors. MBR could be performed with a certain independence from the executive power as it did not require the development of broad government objectives or program structure, and thus did not need decisions or actions of the Cabinet to proceed. A second source of political influence came unquestionably from the legislature, namely, the provincial auditor's enhanced powers giving him the mandate to evaluate the administration's productivity through cost-efficiency analysis. The auditor's interest in the concept of MBR and the recommendation of the task force (exploiting the argument of the efforts invested in it so far) to retain this management system cemented its position in Ontario. The main incentive to make MBR a real style of budgeting came from the renewed role the estimates came to play in the light of the auditor's concern. As they were used to communicate to parliamentarians what ministries do, how they do it, and with how much money, the ministries did not have the choice but to present analysis using MBR, which was seen as the best instrument to prepare the estimates at the time if one was to offer more control to the members of the legislature. The threats over funding formulated by the Management Board reinforced this movement: the prospect of having difficulties getting funds if they did not use MBR to prepare their estimates was an incentive to adopt this style of budgeting, even if it was imperfect. The adoption of ZBB, even though it came after MBR, played an important role in its implementation. It acted as the missing piece between MBR and the hard reality of the budgetary process. ZBB could be used without the intervention of the executive power and its occasional adoption allowed for some budgetary controls in some ministries. Without bringing a perfect solution to the style of expenditure budget, the implementation of MBR and ZBB led to more satisfactory outcomes in the Ontario government.

Conclusion

In 1968, Treasurer Charles MacNaughton discussed the reform of the expenditure budget in Ontario and argued that 'the changes which have been introduced have been piecemeal and of necessity superimposed on an existing system which cannot utilize the new tools to their full potential.'[81] Unknown to the treasurer, his declaration summarized the path budgeting reform was to take in Ontario for the next twenty years. The attempts to improve the style of expenditure budget in Ontario between 1960 and 1985 proved to be frustrating, particularly when it came to PPBS. But it was the experience with this style of budgeting that led the provincial administration to think in terms of programs. The legacy of PPBS stopped there, as the effort to penetrate the administration stumbled against the robust resistance of the line-item budgeting style. This inertia was particularly ill fated because it prevented an effective response to the changing needs of the government in financial management and in producing a new format for the estimates to support the legislative control of public spending.

Even though they could not be fully implemented and did not lead to complete reform of the budgeting system, the cases of MBR and ZBB showed that some change was possible. MBR was intended to provide a simpler means of measuring public benefit and program performance. Its implementation, along with ZBB's, allowed the style of expenditure budget in Ontario to depart from its long-lived emphasis on control and shift to a more managerial approach.

The comparison of the implementation attempts of PPBS, MBR, and ZBB demonstrates the weight some variables had in the process. The involvement of the Cabinet in the expenditure budget process was critical. The implementation of PPBS, which necessitates this involvement, failed, while MBR and ZBB could function without any political commitment made to them. Second, central agencies had a clear role. PPBS failed during a period of reform, where the Management Board and its Secretariat were questioning their roles, including in relation to PPBS. The Secretariat would be far better involved with the implementation of MBR and ZBB. Finally, the format of the estimates proved to be the most important element of inertia in the system. The format (i.e., how and what information is presented) shapes the use the legislature can make of it. In the present case, this format resisted changes even if central agencies wanted to adopt new ones. Ministries did not have an incentive to adopt a new style because they could get their funding from the legislative assembly, which had made no request for radical reform. From this angle, PPBS would not be implemented because the costs for managers in changing the rules of the game were not worth it. The format of the estimates only changed when the provincial auditor intervened, and in turn, the new styles of expenditure budget, namely MBR and ZBB, became possible when the new format for the estimates was adopted. As such, the legislature and the provincial auditor especially, had a considerable influence on the evolving style of the expenditure budget. Without downplaying the roles of the other factors discussed in this chapter, the interest of the legislative assembly in the format of the estimates proved to be a crucial starting point.

The Ontario experience showed that a clear distribution of responsibilities between the political and administrative actors and a coincident agreement on the format of the estimates to adopt can lead to the conditions that will transform the style of the expenditure budget, an important managing tool. The hierarchical power under which the executive power controls public administration is not always sufficient to modify the managing rules of public monies. The parliament also bears responsibilities and powers. This conclusion seems to go against the commonly held idea that in parliamentary systems, the legislature exercises little real power over budget matters because the executive controls the assembly. This is certainly worth further reflection. In the same vein, the reasons underlying the level of interest of the executive and legislative powers in the issue of the style of the expenditure budget would merit investigation considering the effects it can have on the public finances.

On this last point, it is difficult to evaluate the exact impact in terms of money that the problems with the implementation of a new style of expenditure budget had on the MFO. The MFO may have been a microcosm of the administration from this point of view, as it did not pay real attention to an issue that seemed technical even though it was highly political.

NOTES

1 The author wishes to thank the staff at the Archives of Ontario for its help, especially Sarah Fontaine, and Ryan Ayukawa for his research assistance.
2 Kenneth Kernaghan and David Siegel, *Public Administration in Canada*, 4th ed. (Scarborough, ON: Nelson, 1999), 620.
3 Amounts are given in constant dollars of 1967. D.R. Richmond, *The Economic Transformation of Ontario: 1945–1973* (Toronto: Ontario Economic Council, 1974).
4 Kenneth Bryden, 'The Politics of the Budget,' in *The Government and Politics of Ontario*, ed. Donald C. MacDonald, 3rd ed. (Scarborough: Nelson, 1985), 386.
5 K.J. Rea, *The Prosperous Years: The Economic History of Ontario, 1939–75* (Toronto: University of Toronto Press, 1985), 227.

6 Richmond, *The Economic Transformation of Ontario*, 18–19.
7 Legislative Assembly of Ontario, *Standing Committee on Public Accounts, Report*, 1966.
8 There is no shortage of literature on the travails of the PPBS in the Western world. The government of Canada's experience is well covered by Donald Savoie in his *Politics of Public Spending in Canada* (Toronto: University of Toronto Press, 1990) and David Good, *The Politics of Public Money* (Toronto: University of Toronto Press, 2007). The experience of PPBS at the provincial level has not been the object of much study, with the exception of Raymond Garneau, 'La budgétisation par programmes: Rationalité budgetaire contre rationalité politique,' in *Le processus budgétaire au Québec*, ed. Guy Lachapelle, Luc Bernier, and Pierre P. Tremblay (Quebec: Presses de l'Université du Québec, 1999).
9 Joon Chien Doh, *The Planning Program Budgeting System in Three Federal Agencies* (New York: Praeger, 1971), 39.
10 Archives of Ontario (AO), RG 27-29, Management Board Secretariat, Planning and Development Branch files, R.D. Carman, Effective Management Systems – A Review of PPBS and Possible Approaches or the Future, 30 May 1973, file 'PPBS Review – Questionnaire, Status Report – PPB-2,' p. 17.
11 James Iain Gow, *Learning from Others: Administrative Innovations among Canadian Governments* (Toronto: Institute of Public Administration of Canada, 1994), 145. Gow also makes the interesting remark that the interest for PPBS in Canada occurred around the moment when the United States government was officially letting go of it.
12 AO, RG 27-29, Management Board Secretariat, Planning and Development Branch files, Planning and Development Branch, P.P.B. Status Report, 12 May 1972, file 'PPBS Review – Questionnaire, Status Report – PPB-2.'
13 AO, RG 6-14, Correspondence of the Deputy Provincial Treasurer, file 'Budgetary planning file,' Hon. C.S. MacNaughton, Statement re Format of the Estimates for 1967-68, 15 February 1967.
14 Ibid., Hon. C.S. MacNaughton, Opening Statement at the Seminar on Program Budgeting, 7 June 1968.
15 AO, RG 6-14, Correspondence of the Deputy Provincial Treasurer, Background material for consideration at Steering Committee Meeting, 22 July 1970, file 'Committee on Government Productivity,' p. 2.
16 Treasury Board of Ontario, *Effective Management through P.P.B.S.* (Toronto: The Board, 1969).
17 AO, Planning and Development Branch, P.P.B. Status Report.
18 AO, Carman, Effective Management Systems.
19 Ibid.

20 AO, Planning and Development Branch, P.P.B. Status Report, 14.
21 Ibid., 17. Another element, the program memorandum, was supposed to be used for the creation of new programs and the modification of existing ones by the Cabinet in the PPBS framework, but was never actually used.
22 AO, RG 27-29, COGP, Discussion paper on roles & responsibilities in the priority setting system, working copy. Project 51, November 1971; ibid., Management Board Secretariat Planning and Development Branch files, file 'Committee on Central Roles & Relationships – Reports.'
23 Kenneth Bryden, 'Executive and Legislature in Ontario: A Case Study on Governmental Reform,' *Canadian Public Administration* 18, 2 (1975), 239.
24 AO, Planning and Development Branch, P.P.B. Status Report, 14; RG 6-14, COGP, Financial Management Systems, 17 December 1970, Correspondence of the Deputy Provincial Treasurer, file 'Committee on government productivity.'
25 AO, COGP, Financial Management Systems.
26 AO, COGP, Discussion paper on roles & responsibilities in the priority setting system.
27 Ibid., 18–21.
28 AO, Planning and Development Branch, P.P.B. Status Report. All the information presented in this paragraph about the state of PPBS in 1972 comes from this report. In 1972, the Management Board and the MBS succeeded the Treasury Board and its Secretariat in the framework of the government reorganization, while departments were renamed ministries.
29 AO, RG 27-29, Management Board Secretariat, Planning and Development Branch files, file 'M.B. 1.4 M. B. Analysis', Secretary of the Treasury Board, Report to the Treasury Board, 27 September 1971.
30 AO, Planning and Development Branch, P.P.B. Status Report.
31 AO, RG 27-29, Management Board Secretariat, Planning and Development Branch files, file 'PPBS Review – Questionnaire, Status Report – PPB-2,' G.H.U. Bayly, Memo to all Deputy Ministers (draft), 14 July 1972.
32 AO, RG 27-29, Management Board Secretariat, Planning and Development Branch files, file 'CO-5 Committee on Central Roles and Relationships – Minutes, correspondence,' R.D. Carman, Meeting on central roles and responsibilities, 30 June 1972 and Minutes of meeting between C.S. MacNaughton, G.H.U. Bayly, and R.D. Carman, 18 July 1972.
33 Meeting between C.S. MacNaughton, G.H.U. Bayly and R.D. Carman, 2.
34 AO, RG 27-31, Management Board submission, analysis and decision files, 1971–1996, file 'ED-16 82-85 Managing by results,' Staff of MBS and CSC, The managing by results, and goal setting and review systems, 19 February 1975, p. 3.

35 AO, RG 27-29, Management Board Secretariat, Planning and Development Branch files, file 'M.B. 1.4 M. B. Analysis,' R.D. Carman, Memo to D.E. Bogart, 20 June 1973.
36 Allen Schick. 'A Death in the Bureaucracy: The Demise of Federal PPB,' *Public Administration Review* 33.2 (1973), 146–56; AO, RG 27-29, Management Board Secretariat, Planning and Development Branch files, file 'P.P.B. Miscellaneous – PPB7,' Memorandum from R.D. Carman to G.H.U. Bayly and al., 20 June 1973.
37 AO, RG 27-29, Management Board Secretariat, Planning and Development Branch files, file 'Evaluation (Performance Follow-Up) Reports & Charts – M.B. 1.13,' R.D. Carman, presentation for the International Personal Management Association, Miami Beach, 1973.
38 C. Lloyd Brown-John, André LeBlond, and D. Brian Marson, *Public Financial Management: A Canadian Text* (Scarborough: Nelson Canada, 1988), 161.
39 AO, COGP, Discussion paper on roles & responsibilities in the priority setting system; RG 27-29, Management Board Secretariat, Planning and Development Branch files, file 'Ministry of revenue – IM–5,' R.D. Carman, minutes of a meeting with Messrs. Callaghan & Crosbie on PPBS, 6 September 1972.
40 David Novick, *Program Budgeting* (Cambridge, MA: Harvard University Press, 1965), 25.
41 AO, RG 27-21, Management Board Secretariat, Expenditure Policy and Divisional Services operational files, file 'PED systems reviewed 1981–82 – ADM 1-3-1,' G. McAllister, Programs and estimates division systems review, 13 May 1981.
42 Ibid.
43 R.D. Carman, Progress Report on Management Board and the Management Board Secretariat, 25 September 1972, RG 27-29 Management Board Secretariat Planning and Development Branch files, file 'MB 1.1'.
44 Michael J. Prince. 'The Bland Stops Here: Ontario Budgeting in the Davis Era, 1971–1985,' in *Budgeting in the Provinces: Leadership and the Premiers*, ed. Allan M. Maslove (Toronto: Institute of Public Administration of Canada, 1989), 98.
45 Brown-John, LeBlond, and Marson, *Public Financial Management*, 153.
46 Ibid., 155.
47 Carl Grafton and Anne Permaloff, 'Budgeting Reforms in Perspective,' in *Handbook on Public Budgeting and Financial Management*, ed. Jack Rabin and Thomas D. Lynch (New York: Marcel Dekker, 1983), 101.
48 Wallace K. Swan, 'Theoretical Debates Applicable to Budgeting,' in *Handbook on Public Budgeting and Financial Management*, ed. Rabin and Lynch, 53.

49 AO, Bayly, Memo to Deputy Ministers (draft), 14 July 1972; RG 27-29,
    Management Board Secretariat, Planning and Development Branch files,
    File 'Estimates submissions & Review 1973–74,' R.D. Carman, Revised
    draft, 25 September 1973.
50 Staff of MBS and CSC, The managing by results, and goal setting and re-
    view systems.
51 Ibid., 4.
52 AO, RG 27-31, Management Board submission, analysis and decision files,
    1971–1996, file 'MB 1-9 Zero base budgeting 78/9 & 77/8,' MBS, Adminis-
    trative policy branch, Results based management system, 30 June 1977,
    p. 10.
53 Staff of MBS and CSC, The managing by results, and goal setting and re-
    view systems, 5.
54 AO, RG 27-5, Management Board Secretariat, Projects and Special Studies,
    1970–1998, file 'Zero base budgeting, Oct. 76,' O.M. Berg, memo to R.M.
    Dillon et al., 3 November 1976.
55 Swan, 'Theoretical Debates Applicable to Budgeting,' 6.
56 Ian Gow, Learning from Others, 149.
57 Grafton and Permaloff, 'Budgeting Reforms in Perspective,' 103.
58 AO, RG 27-5, Management Board Secretariat, Projects and Special Studies,
    1970–1998, file 'Zero base budgeting – Oct. 76,' Cabinet Submissions,
    27 October 1976 and 4 January 1977.
59 Ibid., file 'ZBB – General,' R.D. Carman, Memo to W.A.B. Anderson, 8 June
    1977.
60 AO, RG 27-31, Management Board submission, analysis and decision files,
    1971–1996, file 'MB 1-9 Zero base budgeting 78/9 & 77/8),' 'A system for
    the rational establishment of priorities,' no date.
61 AO, Management Board, Submission of 27 October 1976.
62 Barry Bozeman, Public Management and Policy Analysis (New York: St Mar-
    tin's Press, 1979), 235.
63 Grafton and Permaloff, 'Budgeting Reforms in Perspective,' 102.
64 Gow, Learning from Others, 149.
65 AO, RG 27-5 Management Board Secretariat, Projects and Special Studies,
    1970–1998, file 'ZBB-CCR,' Dave Hipgrave, ZBB pilot project, 23 Novem-
    ber 1977.
66 AO, RG 27-5, Management Board Secretariat, Projects and Special Studies,
    1970–1998, file 'Zero base budgeting – Oct. 76,' D.R. Peebles, Memo to
    George R. McCague, 25 August 1978.
67 AO, MBS, Administrative policy branch, Results based management sys-
    tem, 3.

68 *Learning from Others*, 152–3. The rest of the section on the auditor general also relies on Gow's work.
69 Quoted in AO, RG 27-5, Management Board Secretariat, Projects and Special Studies, 1970–1998, b323594, *Two-day analysts' workshop – Book I*, June 1982.
70 Provincial Auditor of Ontario, *Annual Report for Year Ending March 30, 1981*, sections 1.6 and 4.
71 W.A.B. Anderson, Memo to all deputy ministers, re: zero base budgeting, 16 November 1977, p. 3; RG 27-5, box 8, 30 June 1977, Administrative Policy Branch.
72 AO, RG 27-31, Management Board submission, analysis and decision files, 1971–1996, file 'MB 3-7 1981–82, Managing by results guidelines,' no author, no title, no date; RG 27-21, Management Board Secretariat Expenditure Policy and Divisional Services operational files, 1971–1992, file 'Division meetings 1981–82, ADM 1-4,' R.C. Norberg, Memo to J.W. Keenan, 21 April 1981.
73 AO, RG 27-21 Management Board Secretariat, Expenditure Policy and Divisional Services operational files, 1971–1992, file 'Interprovincial meeting – budgeting practices 1981–82, ADM-1-12 (81–82),' Draft – Manager's guidelines to managing by results, MBR Improvement project, April 1982.
74 AO, RG 6-125, Management Board Secretariat, Programs and Estimates Division, Fiscal Planning Policy Branch program files, file 'Mgt Board Misc.,' Status Report, Format and Content of the Estimates, 6 January 1981.
75 AO, RG 27-21, Management Board Secretariat, Expenditure Policy and Divisional Services operational files, 1971–1992, file 'ADM-1-12 (81–82),' Paul Gélinas, Estimates Format and Content, 10 March 1982
76 AO, RG 27-31, Management Board submission, analysis and decision files, 1971–1996, file 'ED 16 82–85 Managing by Results,' John R. Allen, Report on the Quality of MBR abstracts submitted with ministries' 1984/85 estimates, 26 April 1984.
77 Brown-John, LeBlond, and Marson, *Public Financial Management*, 466.
78 Gow, *Learning from Others*, 150.
79 AO, RG 27-5, Management Board Secretariat, Projects and Special Studies, 1970–1998, file 'ZBB – general,' D.R. Peebles, Memo to members of the administrative policy branch, 3 June 1977.
80 Allen Schick, 'The Road from ZBB,' *Public Administration Review* 38.2 (1978): 177–80, quoted in Gow, *Learning from Others*, 150.
81 AO, RG 6-14, Hon. C.S. MacNaughton, Opening Statement at the Seminar on Program Budgeting, 7 June 1968.

9 Budget Making in the Ontario Ministry of Finance, 1985–2000

KEN OGATA AND GARY SPRAAKMAN

Provincial government fiscal planning has evolved over time, influenced by a variety of factors including economic conditions, budgeting philosophy, political expediency and ideological direction, coercive pressure from financial markets, public and ministerial requests for new programs and policy initiatives, and changes in accounting policy. Prior to 1960, Ontario generally followed the principle of balanced annual budgets and pay-as-you-go capital financing. As such, the government's annual budget was described as a form of 'accounting exercise,' providing details about the allocation of government resources to particular programs, balanced by the associated tax revenues necessary to fund these programs. This budgeting philosophy downplayed political expediency while constraining governments from unduly increasing spending. However, the growing ideological influence of Keynes for economic policy and Beveridge for social welfare led to a dramatic increase in the scale and scope of Canadian government programs after 1960, fuelled in part through the growth of government debt. By the 1990s, though, financial markets and debt rating agencies rendered this strategy increasingly unsustainable, leading to a series of government reforms both federally and provincially.

This chapter will examine the Ontario budget-making process leading up to and including this transition period, and corresponding changes to the government and its budget. In particular, we focus upon the role and influence of the Ontario Ministry of Finance (MOF) through the annual budget process, and the extent to which the MOF has both changed and helped promote change within government. In building upon the premise of this book, we examine how the MOF may serve as a microcosm of change within the Canadian public sector as a whole, and the extent to which the MOF was both constrained and influenced by its environment. In other words, although governments and their central agencies often seek to shape their environment and society in general through their policies, we describe how the Government of Ontario's fiscal policy was conversely shaped by these forces.

The mixed-methods approach of this study used both quantitative and qualitative data, drawing upon a variety of data sources. Government documents and media sources were used to establish the societal context for budget making and the prevailing budgeting philosophy in effect at that time (e.g., increased spending, debt financing, reduced taxes). Financial data such as the Government of Canada's Fiscal Reference Tables were used for comparability reasons to establish the broader budget-making pressures and trends by other Canadian governments over this period. Media sources were used to gauge 'public' reaction to the Ontario budget, noting the themes reflected with respect to budget-making positives and negatives. Media sources were also used to identify and gauge the public reactions of the credit rating agencies to the province's budgeting practices, and the pressure upon government to respond accordingly. Interviews with ministry participants provided additional insight into the province's budget process, as well as their assessment of the nature of shifts in the province's budget-making practices over time. Finally, government documents related to the budget process, including the annual budget, budget estimates, annual reports, provincial auditor reports, and associated documents (e.g., Ontario Financial Review Commission), were also reviewed.

The years 1985 to 2000 represented a period of dramatic shifts within Ontario that spanned the political spectrum. Although David Peterson's Liberals (1985–90) represented a partial extension of the prior Progressive Conservative government dynasty (1943–85) with their middle-of-the-road approach, Bob Rae's NDP (1990–5) represented an uncharacteristic and unexpected turn to the left, followed by a harsh swing to the right with Mike Harris's neo-Conservatives (1995–2000). At first blush, one might expect that these divergent positions in political ideology would have translated into major changes in the budget-making process. While this was true to an extent, particularly with respect to the state of the province's overall finances, and each party did attempt to redefine Ontario in accordance with their political perspective (e.g., NDP Social Contract, Conservative Common Sense Revolution), we contend that larger macro pressures seemed to exert a greater influence in shaping the government's ultimate budget strategy. As one former official put it:

Well, I thought the uncertainty covering from the 70s to the 2000 kind of time frame, some of the things that come to mind is that it's certainly bigger than it was, far more open to outside, more transparent in terms of the business that it does, considerably more cooperation inside the ministry, and between the ministry and other ministries. I'd say it's a more disciplined organization, there are also more strictures – it's not as loose an organization as it once was ... There's a lot more accountability and responsibility around reporting and that sort of thing than previously was the case. (MOF Official 1)

For example, the general approach of David Peterson's Liberals to budgeting reflected a 'tax and spend' approach, raising additional revenue to finance increased program spending, which may be regarded as consistent with the stereotypical Liberal approach. Ontario's actions, though, were also largely typical of Canadian government budgeting practices across the political spectrum at that time (i.e., deficit financing and the expansion of social programs), notwithstanding Treasurer Robert Nixon's pride in presenting a balanced budget in 1990. As a former official remembered,

The prior government, I don't know that there's anyone who hasn't had to put some water where they want, who hasn't had to do things that they probably wouldn't imagine themselves doing. I don't know that the Conservative governments from 1995 onwards thought that they would put as much into health care as they did, but they put a lot of money into health care. They made a number of spending decisions which were probably well in excess of what they thought they would do ... So how do they reconcile their ideological positions? ... I'm sure each one of them has had to really struggle to – I think that Floyd Laughren, of all ministers of finance, ... I'm sure that he wrestled with that very hard as part of his discussions, ... I think there is a certain pragmatism [required] and they cannot live in the world of one stakeholder. (MOF Official 3)

Table 9.1 provides a summary of Ontario's annual revenue, expenditures, deficits, and accumulated debt between 1985 and 2000, while figures 9.1 and 9.2 graphically present this information. As shown by the

Table 9.1 Ontario's annual revenue, expenditures, deficits, and accumulated debt, 1985–2000

Year	Revenue			Expenditures			Deficit (-) or surplus	Net debt
	Own source revenue	Federal cash transfer	Total revenues	Total program expenditure	Debt charges	Total expenditures		
1984–5	18,810	4,578	23,388	23,530	2,417	25,947	-2,559	22,634
1985–6	21,103	4,682	25,785	25,604	2,795	28,399	-2,614	28,919
1986–7	24,345	4,870	29,215	28,638	3,211	31,849	-2,634	31,531
1987–8	27,174	4,984	32,158	31,171	3,476	34,647	-2,489	34,020
1988–9	31,878	5,113	36,991	34,703	3,767	38,470	-1,479	35,499
1989–90	35,861	5,364	41,225	37,318	3,817	41,135	+90	35,409
1990–1	37,130	5,762	42,892	42,145	3,776	45,921	-3,029	38,438
1991–2	34,429	6,324	40,753	47,487	4,196	51,683	-10,930	49,368
1992–3	34,253	7,554	41,807	48,942	5,293	54,235	-12,428	61,796
1993–4	36,603	7,071	43,674	47,747	7,129	54,876	-11,202	80,599
1994–5	38,432	7,607	46,039	48,336	7,832	56,168	-10,129	90,728
1995–6	41,857	7,880	49,737	50,062	8,475	58,537	-8,800	101,864
1996–7	43,936	5,778	49,714	48,012	8,607	56,619	-6,905	108,769
1997–8	47,684	5,098	52,782	48,019	8,729	56,784	-3,966	112,735
1998–9	51,535	4,515	56,050	49,036	9,016	58,052	-2,002	114,737
1999–2000	59,157	5,885	65,042	53,347	11,027	64,374	+668	134,398

Source: Government of Canada Fiscal Reference Tables, September 2001.

Figure 9.1

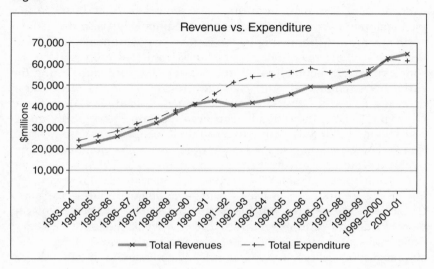

Figure 9.2

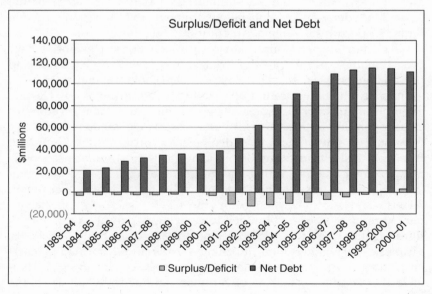

table and figures, Ontario's financial situation fluctuated significantly over this period, moving from surplus to huge deficits, and back to surplus again, in part reflecting economic conditions, but also the general approach towards budgeting by the respective governments of the day. Bob Rae's NDP government sought to introduce a more socially responsive government, although the depth of the recession during the early 1990s, combined with coercive pressure from the debt rating agencies to reduce the size of the deficit, forced Treasurer Floyd Laughren to table more fiscally conservative (and ideologically divergent) budgets. Although Laughren sought to adopt a more progressive, 'fair tax' system, going so far as to appoint a Fair Tax Commission, the overall softness of government revenues ultimately required raising personal income tax rates. The need to demonstrate fiscal restraint also led to the infamous 'Rae Days,' which involved public-sector wage freezes and unpaid days off to address the stubbornly persistent gap between revenue and expenditure due to a weak economy. Debt and deficit pressures among the other Canadian governments prompted similar responses to restore fiscal order (e.g., Federal Liberals, Alberta Conservatives, and Saskatchewan NDP). In brief, fiscal realities combined with credit tightening overrode political ideology during the first half of the 1990s.[1] Table 9.2 summarizes the fiscal position of the Canadian federal and provincial governments over this period, while figure 9.3 portrays the rate of expenditure.

Mike Harris's neo-Conservative 'Common Sense Revolution' approach managed to reduce the size of government while introducing personal income tax cuts; however, efforts to contain spending in areas such as health and education ultimately proved unsuccessful. Despite attempts at austerity measures, the government was later forced to increase spending in these areas. While a case can be made that Harris's Conservative government was ideologically consistent on the budget front, particularly in terms of reducing taxes to stimulate economic growth, their budget-cutting program mirrored similar downsizing and restraint programs initiated earlier by the federal government, Alberta, and Saskatchewan (see figure 9.4). Of these, only Alberta embarked upon its course of budget downsizing as part of an explicit political agenda (i.e., Klein Revolution). In fact, during the late 1990s, virtually every government in Canada experienced normative, coercive, and mimetic (follow-the-leader) pressure to cut spending and balance their budgets.[2] Just as governments mimetically followed the example of others in expanding social programs through the 1960s to

Table 9.2 Federal and provincial fiscal positions ($ millions)

Fiscal year	NF	PEI	NS	NB	QC	ON	MB	SK	AB	BC	Federal
1980–1	($87)	($14)	($142)	($114)	($3,481)	($1,297)	($90)	$233	$1,404	($212)	($14,556)
1981–2	($148)	$1	($382)	($160)	($2,621)	($1,780)	($251)	$140	$2,133	($141)	($15,674)
1982–3	($191)	($25)	($371)	($392)	($2,463)	($3,189)	($435)	($227)	($796)	($1,241)	($29,049)
1983–4	($326)	$4	($316)	($276)	($2,164)	($3,153)	($429)	($332)	$129	($963)	($32,877)
1984–5	($252)	($4)	($368)	($279)	($3,873)	($2,559)	($483)	($380)	$1,245	($822)	($38,437)
1985–6	($253)	($20)	($353)	($213)	($3,473)	($2,614)	($528)	($579)	($761)	($857)	($34,595)
1986–7	($231)	($13)	($277)	($368)	($2,972)	($2,633)	($559)	($1,232)	($4,033)	($635)	($30,742)
1987–8	($197)	($17)	($227)	($336)	($2,396)	($2,489)	($300)	($542)	($1,365)	$71	($27,794)
1988–9	($226)	($11)	($242)	($79)	($1,704)	($1,479)	($141)	($324)	($2,007)	$930	($28,773)
1989–90	($175)	($8)	($267)	($25)	($1,764)	$90	($142)	($378)	($2,116)	$496	($28,930)
1990–1	($347)	($20)	($257)	($181)	($2,975)	($3,029)	($292)	($360)	($1,832)	($667)	($32,000)
1991–2	($276)	($50)	($406)	($355)	($4,301)	($10,930)	($334)	($842)	($2,629)	($2,340)	($34,357)
1992–3	($261)	($82)	($617)	($265)	($5,030)	($12,428)	($566)	($592)	($3,415)	($1,476)	($41,021)
1993–4	($205)	($71)	($547)	($256)	($4,923)	($11,202)	($431)	($272)	($1,384)	($899)	($42,012)
1994–5	($127)	($1)	($235)	($68)	($5,821)	($10,129)	($196)	$128	$958	($228)	($37,462)
1995–6	$9	$4	($201)	$51	($3,947)	($8,800)	$157	$18	$1,132	($317)	($28,617)
1996–7	($19)	($4)	($116)	$115	($3,212)	($6,905)	$91	$407	$2,527	($753)	($8,897)
1997–8	($7)	($7)	($442)	$35	($2,157)	($3,966)	$76	$35	$2,639	($167)	$3,478
1998–9	$4	$6	($385)	($164)	$126	($2,002)	$31	$28	$1,026	($1,003)	$2,884
1999–00	($23)	($5)	($773)	$8	$30	$668	$11	$83	$2,717	$40	$12,298
2000–1	($33)	($7)	($199)	$33	$500	$3,192	$26	$58	$6,388	$1,498	$17,148

Source: Government of Canada Fiscal Reference Tables, September 2001.

Figure 9.3

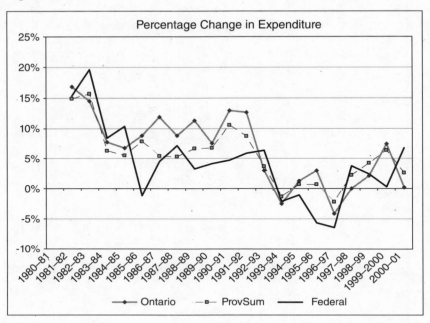

1980s, so too they began to exercise fiscal restraint beginning in the mid-
1990s. Government reform and fiscally responsible budgeting were in
vogue, supported by the New Public Management[3] and Reinventing
Government[4] movements. Although few governments adopted the
Harris approach of cutting taxes and government spending simultaneously, Ontario's course did not veer substantively from this broader pattern within the public sector. As an official remembered:

> Political expectations have changed over the years. What a politician ex-
> pects the Ministry of Finance or [the department of] Treasury and
> Economics to do for them has evolved a lot, and partly it's the maturation
> of politicians and political leadership and what premiers do and what
> prime ministers do and what's expected of them, which has changed a lot.
> That obviously affects the organization and I might think about a couple
> of other things, but one of the basic ways in which you see that is that in
> the 70s period we weren't afraid to make a mistake, but ministries today
> are horrified to make a mistake, and that reflects the fact that the polit-
> icians have become intolerant of being seen to be wrong. (MOF Official 1)

Figure 9.4

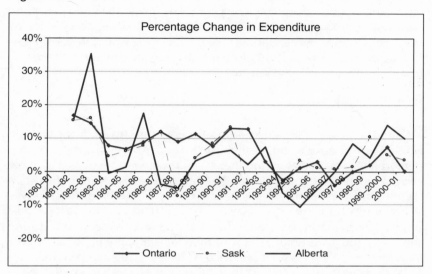

Overview of Budget Process

McElwain identifies three main phases to the budget process that apply well to the period in question: preparation, approval, and accountability.[5] Preparation involves development of the budget, including the province's fiscal plan, revenue and expenditure forecasts and decisions, new policy directions, and the allocation of resources among ministries. This process culminates with the tabling of the budget and associated estimate details in the legislature in the spring. Approval involves legislative review of the detailed estimates by the all-party Standing Committee on Estimates, and approval by the House, typically late in the calendar year. Accountability involves the year-end review of government activities and tabling of the Public Accounts, as well as the provincial auditor's report. Governments have also increased efforts to measure and report on the results of their programs. While these phases are defined as distinct, increasingly the process has begun to blend together, with annual cycles overlapping and leading into each other. The budget is now a year-round process, and one that is subject to increasing public scrutiny.

Two central government agencies are involved in this process. First, and the focus of this book, is the Ontario Ministry of Finance, which provides economic forecasts, options on the overall fiscal strategy, revenue adjustments and policies, and analysis of significant expenditure issues and policy decisions. The other key central agency is the Management Board Secretariat (MBS), which is responsible for preparing the detailed expenditure estimates that accompany the budget, and ensuring that actual expenditures are appropriate.

Budgetary Reforms

During the period 1985–2000, several changes occurred in the Ontario Ministry of Finance's budget-making process. Among the more prominent changes were the following: First, the government has actively sought greater public input into the budget process through the establishment of an all-party legislative standing committee that receives submissions from citizens, industry associations, and interest groups. Second, particularly in light of the fiscal pressures experienced during the 1990s, the government has sought to 'educate' the public about the state of the province's finances, such as by releasing an economic outlook statement in the fall. Third, the public sector has moved away from cash-based accounting to accrual accounting like the private sector, which has significantly changed the valuation of and investment in capital assets. Finally, the scope of government has changed, with third-party public organizations (e.g., hospitals, schools, universities) now included within the provincial government reporting entity.

However, we suggest that several of these changes were more the result of a gradual evolution in broader public-sector management practice, punctuated by some major events and decisions, rather than in response to dramatic shifts in governing political ideology within Ontario. The broader societal push for better standards of accounting, combined with demands for increased accountability, greater government transparency, and improved coordination and communication among ministries has prompted many of these changes. Changes to the process were less the result of ideological influences, and more a necessary response in terms of 'technical' enhancements that the government would have instituted regardless of the province's fiscal situation. In many ways, the experience of the Province of Ontario with respect to management of the budget process and public finances is reflective of changes that occurred on a larger scale within the public sector in Canada and internationally. 'Yes I see it now, obviously. I watched the process,' one official remembered:

I'm a student of it now as opposed to part of it directly and yes it's quite different as I described before. It's the inclusiveness – the secrecy hasn't changed – and the competencies of the people involved haven't changed. The issues have changed, the depth of analysis has changed, there are far greater expectations like transparency and accountability on what government can do today than they were in 70s and 80s. You didn't worry very much about whether it was technically correct back then. You do now, and you have to have a lot more rigour to the whole process and make sure everything is airtight, and that we're meeting all standards that anyone would reasonably expect on a fiscal level for instance, that these government documents and numbers are in accord with the public sector accountability act and the PSAAB and other things that now drive good financial reporting. That's a huge change from years ago when financial reporting was whatever we said it was. Now financial reporting accords with the generally accepted accounting principles, the PSAAB rules, the CICA [Canadian Institute of Chartered Accountants], and you can look at that stuff now with confidence in terms of those numbers being correct. (MOF Official 4)

Notwithstanding these broader trends, we acknowledge the significant role played by province's negative fiscal situation over this period, combined with the ideological stance of the governing parties, and the coercive pressure for fiscal restraint exerted by the credit rating agencies. The recession of the early 1990s, rapid growth of government debt, and Mexican currency crisis in 1994[6] translated into nervousness in the capital markets, as evidenced by increased credit rating agency scrutiny and subsequent downgrades. Although we will describe this in greater detail later, we characterize the rating agencies as 'silent' during the Nixon era (active but not vocal), 'cautionary' during the Laughren era (active and publicly vocal), and 'placated' during the Eves era (inactive and nonvocal). 'The second thing, which is probably a good thing, in the public interest,' observed one official, '[are] the rating agencies [...] You remember what happened in Ontario when Rae wound up [with] that 13 billion dollar deficit and the bottom dropped out of the rating agencies? You have to really say for that reason we had to rethink our whole policy thinking and direction. That's a pretty important one' (MOF Official 2).

Liberal Reforms (1985–1990)

Between 1985 and 2000, the budget process in Ontario slowly shifted from an environment of centralized, secretive budget making in the

1970s, where the treasurer (i.e., minister of finance) prepared the budget with limited input from the public or other ministries, to an increasingly open and cross-government coordinated process by 2000. This is not to suggest that the budget process, similarly to that of municipal governments, has become 'public,' as the tenet of budget secrecy has been preserved as a guiding principle (though some have questioned the need for this), but merely that increased opportunities now exist for broader input from the public and the rest of government. Liberal reforms beginning in 1985 started this process of pushing the MOF towards the current framework.

Near the beginning of the Peterson minority government, the first influential budget event involved the tabling of Treasurer Nixon's 'Reforming the Budgeting Process: A Discussion Paper.'[7] As shown in table 9.1, the new Liberal government had inherited a sizable deficit of $2.6 billion (1984–5) from the departing Progressive Conservative government. Ongoing annual deficits and growing accumulated debt caused the bond rating agencies to be concerned about the stability of government finances.[8] In November 1985, early in the Liberal mandate, the Ontario government's bond rating was reduced from AAA to AA+ by Standard and Poor's.[9] This downgrade increased debt servicing costs, making financing of the province's accumulated deficit ($23 billion) more expensive, as well as signalling reduced confidence in how the province's finances were being managed. The AAA rating was restored in 1988,[10] though the province's annual and accumulated deficit situation would soon take a turn for the worse.

Nixon declared the purpose of the 'Reforming the Budgeting Process' document to be 'to improve the pre-budget consultation process' by encouraging greater involvement of the public and the members of the Ontario legislature. His initiative for reforming the Ontario budget-making process was part of larger concerns being raised in Canada about the need for changes in the federal government's budget-making process.[11] Key among those budget-making concerns were the need for a regular annualized process, greater involvement of the elected officials, and alternatives for promoting public discussion of budget issues before commitments were made in the budget.

Previously the budget-making process had been conducted by the MOF, largely in isolation. Groups were invited by the treasurer to share their insights at various times of the year, but no formal public process existed. Consultations with the treasurer were in camera.[12] Other groups requested meetings to discuss their special concerns with the treasurer, although the overall number of such consultations was limited (practically and by choice). Greater involvement by the public and other departments was further inhibited by the inflexible principle of budget secrecy. This principle contributed to the insularity of the MOF, combined with their perceived lack of need to consult others on fiscal matters due to their level of technical expertise. 'We believed we knew what the answers were, and we didn't need to have a lot of people tell us how to deal with the issues that were there,' observed a former official. 'And that partly reflects the fact that it was budget making, and budget making was secret ... Budgets have gradually evolved from those secret documents where nobody knew what was going on to more open documents. The openness varies – in Ontario they're still pretty tightly held ... It was so important not to have anyone be aware of it that drove you to do things on your own' (MOF Official 1).

With due respect to the MOF, while the principle of budget secrecy constrained broader public consultation, more limited opportunities to seek 'informed' input into significant economic and public policy issues necessitated their past reliance upon internal expertise. In order to open up the process, Nixon recommended the establishment of a new legislative committee, the Standing Committee on Finance and Economic Affairs (SCFEA), with the following responsibilities:

– receive the Ontario Economic and Fiscal Outlook;
– hold pre-budget hearings;
– review all tax legislation arising from the budget; and
– prepare recommendations for the budgeting of revenues, expenditures, and additional cash requirements.

As noted in Robert Nixon's statement to the legislature on 11 July 1985, the proposed annual budget process would start with the Ontario Economic and Fiscal Outlook, which would be released by the MOF in the fall of each year to provide the economic context and background for developing rational budgets. The Outlook was intended to provide 'a comprehensive and formalized statement on Ontario's economic and financial outlook at the beginning of the budget consultation cycle [that] would assist in focusing debate on appropriate fiscal policy for the province.'

The public consultation process was to be expanded and made more transparent:

Briefs prepared by the groups would be tabled and transcripts of the consultations made available. Members of the Committee would have the opportunity to bring varying perspectives to discussions on a wide range of issues. The Committee could encourage participation from groups that have not previously taken part and from private individuals. It could hold hearings outside of Toronto and be open for media coverage. The Committee could synthesize the views expressed and provide recommendations to the Government.

The Committee's assessments and recommendations on revenues, expenditures, and the requirements for additional cash were to provide a means for passing public opinions on to the government and treasurer. While it was expected that SCFEA members could have differing opinions, this would also provide richer insights for the budget-making process. These recommendations, though, did not 'remove the responsibility of the Treasurer to make the final decisions respecting spending and revenues.' The SCFEA was expected to start sitting no later than one week after the beginning of the fall sitting of the legislature. However, this seldom happened; and most hearings took place in January and February, thereby resulting in limited input into the upcoming provincial budget. See table 9.3 for the annual activity of the SCFEA. The SCFEA consultations have become an integral part of the budget process. At their close, the committee reports on its observations, and provides recommendations. The reports have evolved into a standardized format with various themes based upon participant comments. For example, the 1998 report included the following information and associated themes:

– commentary by the Minister of Finance and ministry staff,
– macroeconomic issues and fiscal matters,
– taxes (e.g., sales tax harmonization),
– transfer partners, including municipalities, colleges, universities, schools, and hospitals,
– spending programs (e.g., infrastructure, social health, justice, and agriculture),
– sectoral activities (e.g., construction, transportation, energy, tourism, hospitality, and finance), and
– job creation

Treasurer Nixon also suggested an annual or predictable cycle for the budget-making process (tabled near the beginning of the government's

Table 9.3 Data from pre-budget hearing

Budget year	Number of written submissions	Number of oral submissions
1987	92	145
1988	130	109
1989	64	44
1990	70	43
1991	95	69
1992	72	47
1993	50	69
1994	55	54
1995	78	62
1996	111	80
1997	45	36
1998	94	90
1999	No session – the House prorogued	
2000	159	118

Source: Ontario, Standing Committee on Finance and Economic Affairs, Pre-Budget Consultations, minute books.

fiscal year – 1 April), but admitted that given that a major source of the province's revenue was the federal government, and the timing of the federal budget was uncertain, this was difficult to achieve. The provincial auditor in his 1987 annual report also expressed concerns with the estimates review process:

– Estimates were always considered during the fiscal year in which they apply, often late in the year. This meant that much of the debate on spending took place after the fact.
– The backlog that developed in the review process at the end of the session might result in some estimates receiving a cursory review or in not being considered at all.
– The time allocated to the estimates review process was insufficient for a meaningful review.
– During the hearings Members tended to concentrate on constituency matters and broad policy matters rather than on the scrutiny of government spending. This could be attributed in part to the difficulty in interpreting the information provided in the estimates books.[13]

The provincial auditor recommended the establishment of a separate committee to review the estimates. This all-party Standing Committee on Estimates (SCE) was established in 1989 with responsibility to conduct a detailed review of the estimates, approve the estimates, and submit a report. The SCE is to consider in any calendar year the estimates of not fewer than six and not more than twelve ministries or offices. All other estimates are deemed to be accepted and thereby passed by the committee (subject to final approval by the legislature). The SCE's report to the House could include recommended changes. A subsequent amendment addressed the section of the estimates or ministries/agencies to be reviewed by the committee: members of the Official Opposition party choose first, members of other parties choose next, and members of the government choose last.[14]

NDP Reforms (1990–1995)

The NDP unexpectedly formed the government in late 1990. However, their timing for finally achieving power was unfortunate, as Canada would go through a significant recession in the early 1990s[15] which significantly restricted their fiscal-policy room to manoeuvre, and thereby their ability to act in accordance with their ideological leanings. As indicated in table 9.1, although Peterson's Liberal government managed to produce a small surplus for 1989–90 after several years of annual deficits, the early 1990s recession wreaked havoc upon the province's finances, with provincial revenues dropping in 1991. The recession both reduced revenues and increased expenditures, in part owing to the NDP's expansion of the social safety net. Consequently, this led to relatively larger deficits and accelerated growth of the net provincial debt, which in turn drove up debt-servicing costs, exacerbating this already negative situation. Figures 9.1 and 9.2 illustrate the province's declining fiscal position.

To service this burgeoning provincial debt, the Ontario government had to borrow at ever-increasing market rates. Although the government was initially able to borrow at favourable rates due to the province's AAA credit rating, growing concerns about government debt in the financial markets drove up borrowing costs. Ontario's credit rating was reduced from AAA to AA- during the NDP reign in three steps (see figure 9.5), one notch at a time in May 1991, May 1992, and November 1993.[16] Treasurer Floyd Laughren remarked about the pressure exerted

Figure 9.5 Province of Ontario credit rating

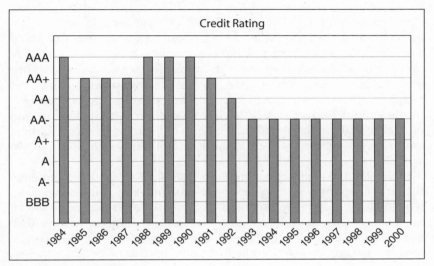

Source: Standard & Poor's.

by these downgrades upon the province's finances, and the subsequent need to enact publicly unpalatable restraint measures. Confidence in the province's fiscal plan declined during their tenure as the government as they continued to exceed market expectations regarding the size of the deficit. They made frequent revisions to these forecasts, but were still unable to meet stated revenue, expenditure, and deficit targets. 'He inherited probably the most significant downturn in a long time,' observed a former executive in the Ministry of Finance, 'and yet he had to wrestle with declining revenues and expectations from the public. He was very pragmatic – both the Premier Rae and Floyd Laughren' (MOF Official 5). Another remembered:

> What occurred at that period was ... there was growing international pressure around the idea of a debt wall. And when the NDP came in, right or wrong, they found themselves with a lot less dollars than they committed to spend ... It meant then that there was almost a move away from being able to just do your base line and as well to toss up a wish list to a really drastic change in terms of thinking towards almost a zero-based budgeting mentality. (MOF Official 6)

Notwithstanding these fiscal pressures, the NDP also sought to introduce additional changes to the government's budget-making process. Floyd Laughren used his first budget speech to introduce several proposals.[17] He announced the establishment of a Cabinet Treasury Board to examine the structure of government programs to ensure clear responsibility for the management of expenditures. Second, he announced further initiatives to open up the budget-making process. Treasurer Laughren also increased pre-budget consultation for the 1991 budget. In his second budget (1992), he introduced further changes in pre-budget consultation, expanding the types of forums and meetings held with interest groups, as well as additional internal evaluation of the process.[18]

Moreover, 1990 marked the first time the SCFEA received representation from groups active in economic and financial forecasting. Consequently, the committee proposed that pre-budget hearings should be more concerned with the economic outlook and fiscal framework than with detailed expenditure review.[19] Starting in 1991, the SCFEA began holding hearings outside Toronto to expand representation; nevertheless, Toronto has remained the dominant location for pre-budget hearings.

Laughren's pre-budget information consisted of three parts. First, an economic outlook paper was issued in December 1991 just before the pre-budget consultation program. As its title implied, it dealt with what was expected for the Ontario economy over the next few years. Second, a few months later, Laughren issued a fiscal outlook paper to provide information on the government's revenue and expenditure forecasts. That document also presented scenarios about 'what would happen to the province's fiscal situation if no measures were taken to control spending and bolster the economy.' Third, a Budget Guidebook was issued. Its intent was to make the process more transparent to the public by outlining the actual process as well as summarizing information on the current and expected fiscal situations. It also included a copy of Premier Rae's televised address describing the seriousness of Ontario's economic situation.

Consultations also changed. The treasurer began meeting with seven to twelve interest groups at a time on a sector or thematic basis, such as agriculture and food, social and employment equity, and tourism. As many of the sessions dealt with both revenue and spending, the appropriate line ministers chaired the sessions, with Laughren attending all sessions. He also held roundtable discussions with selected members of Premier Rae's Councils on Economic Renewal and Health, Well-Being, and Social Justice. Finally, Laughren met with other groups, and encouraged participation by all Ontarians, receiving a record 4300 letters and submissions from individual residents.[20]

Both the Liberal and the NDP governments sought to increase the involvement of the public and of members of the Legislative Assembly in the budget process. These changes allowed many more public groups to make representation on a much more diverse range of interests. In addition, members of the legislature had the opportunity to hear and read the concerns of ordinary citizens. Finally, the revised budget-making process encouraged the involvement of independent analysts and forecasters, prompting critique and subsequent refinement of the data used in the process. 'Floyd didn't change the nature of the process that much,' noted a former official, 'but one of the things Floyd would say, I believe, was that most of his party ... came in with a very sceptical and readiness not to trust the bureaucracy, and Floyd I think played a significant role, because he very quickly adapted and got close to the ministry ... So I don't think he changed the process much, but he did enable the process to do what it did' (MOF Official 1).

Progressive Conservative Reforms (1995–2000)

In July 1995, shortly after being sworn in, the new minister of finance, Ernie Eves, established the Ontario Financial Review Commission (OFRC), with the mandate to 'review the Province's accounting, reporting, and financial management practices.'[21] This review process matched that previously employed by Saskatchewan and Alberta. In November 1995, the commission produced its report, 'Beyond the Numbers: A New Financial Management and Accountability Framework for Ontario.' The partisan starting point of 'restoring credibility and confidence' was made very clear in the report's introduction:

> To find ways of 'restoring credibility and confidence' in the financial reporting of a $50-billion-a-year enterprise is no small task. When the enterprise in question is a provincial government that shares responsibility for educating our children, taking care of our sick, policing our communities and preserving our quality of life in many other ways every day, it becomes truly daunting.

Finance Minister Eves asked the OFRC to address three high-level goals:

1 come up with a framework for forecasting revenues and planning spending that was prudent and realistic;
2 look at ways of improving financial management of government; and
3 explore how government could report on its financial position more quickly and meaningfully.

The commission was dominated by financial auditors. The OFRC had eight commissioners, six men and two women. The men were all from external or financial audit firms. The two women included the president of the Canadian Bankers Association, and a member of various boards (including her family's firm). The OFRC also relied upon the provincial auditor and two members from his staff as special advisers. Although the government's responsibilities include education, health, policing, and 'preserving quality of life,' they approached their review in a fashion befitting financial auditors, rather than employing program evaluation techniques.

The OFRC found that the 'competent and hard-working public servants ... are held back by an existing system that may frustrate efforts to detect waste, and can discourage efficiency.' This is not unlike the findings of the Alberta Financial Review Commission when reporting on its province's finances. Consistent with the New Public Management perspective,[22] the OFRC advocated the following changes:

- produce business plans for government as a whole, its ministries and agencies;
- build a contingency fund into the budget in case of worse than forecasted economic conditions;
- set rigorous goals for performance, report on results, and use that information to enhance the next year's performance;
- set debt and deficit reduction targets and be measured against them;
- provide incentives for improvement, and remove the current disincentives;
- allow for a meaningful and informed legislative review of ministries' business plans before debating spending authority, because the commission believed the legislature was the proper forum for public accountability;
- have an integrated financial management and reporting system for all government activities;
- set consistent planning and reporting standards; and

- speed up the planning, reporting, and evaluating cycle so that plans
  were reviewed in time to make useful changes, and results produced earlier.

The OFRC was critical of the government's existing process for planning, reporting, and evaluating its activities. Although the budget was the primary planning process for the Government of Ontario, the OFRC deemed it to be deficient. The commission's findings with respect to the budget-making process noted two specific shortcomings: it did not provide a plan, and it did not include performance goals. Consequently, the reporting and evaluation of those plans was also deemed inadequate.

The budget-making process at the MOF changed in some significant ways after the OFRC's report. It became more business-like in a financial accounting sense. Financial accountability and reporting became more dominant. The government shifted from a modified cash-basis accounting system to a modified accrual-based system that was more consistent with the private-sector GAAP approach. Reporting and accounting were standardized within ministries and across ministries. A new enterprise resource planning system, the Integrated Financial Information System (IFIS), was implemented to enable and to speed up standardized reporting and accounting across the Ontario government.

Associated with the adoption of IFIS was an increasingly comprehensive approach to managing government. Horizontality and the cross-coordination of government planning and activities became increasingly important, particularly when they involved the formerly 'independent' MUSH sector (municipalities, universities, schools, and hospitals). The planning perspective became a multi-year horizon, and budgeting became linked to business planning.

Although the Harris government instituted many changes to the machinery and process of managing government finances (e.g., forecasting, accrual accounting, consolidation, accountability), it was their actions with respect to allocating and acquiring resources that garnered the most attention. The Common Sense Revolution built upon principles advocated under New Public Management and Reinventing Government, along with expenditure restraint measures previously adopted by Alberta, Saskatchewan, and the federal government. Notwithstanding their desire to restrain and reduce government spending, cuts to federal transfer programs as part of meeting the federal government's own deficit reduction targets would likely have necessitated corresponding actions at the provincial level regardless of which party was in power.

Rather than comment upon the specific fiscal actions undertaken by the Harris and Rae governments, we have attempted to focus upon the role of the MOF in facilitating and implementing the policy directions espoused by the government. Ministry officials commented upon the 'similarity' between governments in terms of their role in the process, and the type of advice provided to the government of the day. The MOF has maintained its posture as a part of the public service, responding to these shifts in political ideology and providing rational, quality, non-partisan assistance. While it is not possible to provide objective measures of professional relations among the minister, government, and MOF officials, the collegial relations and freely offered notes of respect provided by the former finance ministers at a conference in 2006 speak to the professionalism of service provided. 'If you ask Floyd and Ernie, it reflects the similarity between them,' noted an official.

> They have a role to do; they often face very similar circumstances. Everyone would go to them saying I need this I need that, but they were the voice of no, we can't do everything – that's what the Premier needed them for. Their jobs played out very similarly. Floyd came in and raised taxes all over the place. Ernie cut them. There were obviously different circumstances that enabled that and political philosophies were definitely different. Treasurers will always be different because they have the control of raising money, and they do say no, sometimes they're listened to and sometimes they're not, but no one else is minister of money raising. No one else is a minister of the Premier's tax system. (MOF Official 1)

As noted by Savoie in his *Governing from the Centre*, the relationship between the finance minister and prime minister/premier is one where there can be no perception of 'light' between them, no opportunity to attempt an end run or divide-and-conquer strategy to exempt programs or enact new spending, particularly during a period of restraint, lest it invite an unravelling of the whole.

Evolution of the Process

Pre-Budget Consultation

Perhaps the most significant change to Ontario's budget process is its formal legislative pre-budget consultations, which have only been adopted by one other province (British Columbia). McLellan, in a review of the pre-budgeting consultation process for 1985–2000, found that Ontario had been

the provincial pioneer in formal pre-budget consultations.[23] Other provinces have experimented with variations on this consultation process, but only the federal model parallels Ontario's all-party legislative committee. These hearings can be seen as part of the broader process of ensuring that governments are held accountable for the decisions they make and public funds they spend.

Although the pre-budget consultations were originally intended to take place in the fall to enable meaningful input into the upcoming budget, the meetings have tended to start in January or February, thus limiting their influence on that year's budget (though they may affect future years budgets). The SCFEA reports have generally not provided a unanimous position. As would be expected, divisions in opinions have been along party lines. The Opposition parties have submitted dissenting reports which are included as appendices. Nevertheless, McLellan identifies six positive features of the Ontario pre-budget consultation process:[24]

– Committee members establish budget consultation with the public.
– With financial information prepared and distributed by the MOF, the committee contributes to informed discussions.
– Witnesses contribute important information – statistical data, sector profiles, industry surveys, etc. – for further informing the discussions.
– The committee considers competing, independent economic information to that provided by the MOF, which ensures quality information for the discussions.
– The committee extends the budget time horizon to consider long-range topics such as taxation, wealth generation, international trade agreements, etc.
– The committee makes transcripts of all proceedings available to the public.

Overall, the budget-making process has become much more expansive and open to the public. Before 1985, budget making was largely an internal exercise conducted by the Ministry of Treasury and Economics (and its predecessors), in part due to a high level of internal expertise

280 Ken Ogata and Gary Spraakman

and a lack of public consultation by the government in general. Changes to this insularity began in the 1970s, and continued throughout the period covered by this chapter. Three explanations are offered. First, stakeholders typically did not challenge the MOF's assumptions or policy position in the 1970s, and usually deferred to their analysis. Since then, stakeholder challenges have increased together with additional demands by stakeholders for information and input into the process. Although specific instances of government 'failure' with respect to improper budget analysis may not have prompted stakeholder questioning, the persistence of government deficits and inability to meet forecasts have left the public sector open to challenge and increased scrutiny. Improvements in the MOF's capacity to process information together with this broader stakeholder input have elevated the resultant quality of the budget. 'In the early years the Ministry would do its policy development and we would figure it out and we knew we were right without bothering to ask anyone else – we just took it as a given and those budgets would reflect it. But the world is different – stakeholders did not challenge in those days,' noted one former official. 'Governments received deference that people did not choose to criticize governments openly, or challenge them is a better word, as they do today ... So I think that's been the single change – the cultural shift and the shift in relations with the public. The third dimension is the growth of outside stakeholders and stakeholder involvement in policy themselves ... I think the government just reacted to it. I don't think the government every consciously encouraged it. I think they suddenly realized it was happening and followed the trend' (MOF Official 4).

Second, with the increased complexity of the government, the MOF could no longer practically prepare budgets without the involvement of the public and other ministries. A cultural shift occurred in the MOF's openness to the involvement of others, combined with increasing need for cross-governmental coordination of programs, initiatives, and communication strategies. As more public-policy issues began to impact multiple policy areas, the need for more coordinated action by government, both unilaterally and between levels, has resulted in expanded consultation. Third, enhanced capabilities by outside stakeholders such as banks and consulting groups to undertake public-policy analyses and related research have provided a check on what the MOF (and government in general) have proposed. Consequently, the MOF has had to take these external stakeholder positions into consideration. 'There has been an enormous growth in the number and sophistication of NGOs,' observed one long-time executive in the Ministry of Finance. 'These have developed into a major source of spending pressure as well as a rich source of budgetary ideas. Coupled with the Internet-fuelled growth of grass-roots democracy, budget making today is a pluralistic endeavour.'[25]

Increased Government Coordination

Another key change over this period (1985–2000) can be described as greater collaboration between the MOF and other ministries. The complexity of public-policy issues requires increased collaboration and consistency in approach. Greater involvement by the public and other stakeholders has also led to the premier becoming much more involved the budget-making process. According to ministry officials, in the past, the premier would not be briefed about the upcoming budget until it had largely been completed, usually just before its release. While the budget still belongs primarily to the minister of finance, the premier can no longer afford to remain a passive observer of the process due to the potential political ramifications. By 2000, the premier, his office, and the Cabinet office had become active participants in the process. Consistent with Savoie's observation of the centralization of power in the Prime Minister's Office, the need to control the government's message demands earlier and more active participation in the budget process. Along with this predisposition towards greater control has been the trend towards 'error-free' government, to minimize the potential for challenges from stakeholders and/or the Opposition. The premier's involvement, though, has also facilitated greater policy alignment, as well as improved communications on the budget. One former official put it this way: 'There is much greater alignment of policy overall in the government than there would have been 20 or 30 years ago. The communications are very carefully managed and coordinated, and the policy is as well. Coordination is tied together through the premier's office and the Cabinet office. So as a central agency it's quite different than it would have been 20 or 30 years ago ... So by the time they get to Cabinet, those issues have been completely explored at the staff level – ministers have been briefed, deputies have been briefed, everyone knows the content so there shouldn't be any surprises, because if there are then we haven't done our homework and neither has the ministry' (MOF Official 4). Another noted: 'The budgets have increasingly become the Premier's documents, the Government's documents, and the

Ministry of Finance, Treasurer's documents. The Premier's office, because they are essentially how the Premier gets most of his information, again an evolution – an observation from my standpoint is the power of the Premier's office has grown significantly' (MOF Official 1).

Changes in Financial Management

With the greater influence of outside advisers, the province's financial reporting practices have correspondingly changed over time. Ontario, like many other provinces, has adopted financial reporting guidelines that are consistent with generally accepted accounting principles (GAAP). The Public Sector Accounting and Auditing Board (PSAAB) guidelines follow a modified accrual accounting approach similar to those stipulated by the CICA for private firms (i.e., GAAP). For example, moving from a modified cash basis to accrual accounting means that the cost of capital assets is now expensed over its useful life (i.e., depreciation), rather than according to when built or acquired (i.e., pay-as-you-go financing). This has smoothed the expenditure profile for new capital construction and acquisitions, facilitating the use of alternative financing options, including revenue bonds and public-private partnership arrangements. Governments now recognize the value of capital assets such as buildings and roads held on their books, rather than carrying them at nominal value (i.e., $1). This has increased attention to the importance of maintaining an accurate inventory of these assets, including monitoring and maintaining their condition to provide service. Also, the net income of government enterprises such as the Liquor Control Board of Ontario is treated differently. The 'need' to adopt these changes was heightened by the OFRC's recommendations in their final report. Two former officials reflected on the new accounting rules:

> They also probably quite frankly didn't have to deal with all the accounting rules that we have now. We're not complaining because it's all good stuff and evolution but it's considerably more overhead to do something now than it would have been then ... You have to do it properly and of course with public sector accounting board requirements now and consolidations and all kinds of stuff that people probably wouldn't have worried about before. It's a complexity. (MOF Official 3)

> Just to repeat, greater standards and openness and transparency. We have legislated dates to introduce our first quarter, both economic and financial

statement reports. And those are progress reports. So our first report has to be by such a date, second quarter, and third quarter. There are legislated timeframes; we never had that before. In the document, movement towards budget before the end of March, there are higher standards and expectations around accountability. (MOF Official 5)

The OFRC report also recommended integrating the different accounting systems within the various ministries and agencies under an enterprise resource planning (ERP) system, in order to consolidate financial statements across the government and thereby provide better financial information to aid management. The result was the Ontario government's Integrated Financial Information System (IFIS), which as of the end of 2000 was still being implemented, but which ministry officials indicated has greatly facilitated their ability to track and manage the government's finances. IFIS contributes to better standards of accounting, greater accountability, greater transparency, and more disclosure by consolidating this information.

This enhanced financial reporting was accompanied by budgets being used for planning purposes rather than merely short-term expenditure control. The outcome was business plans that looked beyond the current budget year, using a multi-year planning horizon. The numbers behind the budget/business plan cover a four-year period in terms of considering fixed expenditures and number of employees. Ministries have benefited from this approach, as it provides a preliminary indicator of their future budgetary allocations, as well as an indication of future cost pressures.

By 2000, budget-making has become a year-round process. While there are still peak periods, with the summer reporting of the public accounts, quarterly reporting, the fall economic statement, followed by the pre-budget consultations before the actual budget making, the process now occupies the entire year. However, despite the collaboration with the ministries and the involvement of the premier and the public, budgetary secrecy remains a guiding principle.

Conclusion

According to ministry officials, in the past the provincial budget represented more of an accounting exercise, providing a detailed breakdown of the allocation of resources to particular programs, along with the revenue measures necessary to pay for these programs. As indicated by ministry officials, along with the researchers' accounts of shifts in the nature of public administration and public finances, the Ontario government and Ministry of Finance have responded to increased demands by the public for greater budget details, government accountability, and participation and input into the process. Over the period from 1985 to 2000, the Ontario government has adopted several measures to open up the process and facilitate public participation, although the tradition of budget secrecy has been preserved.

Along with greater public input has come greater inter-ministry consultation and collaboration. A long-term executive in the MOF noted that 'there is far more interaction among ministries and central agencies … [and] … the MOF and the Premier's office.'[26] He went on to say that by the time a policy arrives at Cabinet, all members and their relevant ministry people are briefed.

Although the MOF required the cooperation of ministries to prepare the annual budget, the shift towards greater coordination and consistency of government actions has dramatically escalated the need for integration and communication. Along with greater government integration has been the increasingly prominent role of the premier's office in the development and communication of government direction.

The adoption of government-wide financial information systems such as IFIS is indicative of this evolution, though one necessitated by expansion of the scope of the provincial government (MUSH sector included within the consolidated reporting entity). The shift to GAAP-like public-sector accounting practices (PSAAB), along with strictly defined legislated time frames for the production and release of government financial information, has served to promote a more 'business-like' approach to the public sector as a whole. However, this does not mean that the outputs and outcomes are better understood and managed, only that the inputs are subject to greater scrutiny and accountability.

Although the Peterson (Liberal), Rae (NDP), and Harris (PC) governments each attempted to redefine Ontario in accordance with their political perspective, employing the annual budget as a key mechanism in their efforts to promote change, broader trends within public administration have had equal if not greater influence upon the MOF and its activities. Increased demands for public accountability, greater scrutiny and challenge by various stakeholders, the deterioration of Canadian public finances combined with tightening credit, and the influence of New Public Management principles have all contributed to changes in the Ontario government's budget process beyond those advocated and pursued by the government itself. The budget-making process has become more open to the public, but also more open to Cabinet, owing to the need for collaboration. The trend towards greater government accountability combined with increased public challenge and scrutiny of the government and its policies has escalated the need for proper 'due diligence' and careful consideration of the implications of new policies and programs. Whether this shift towards more 'business-like' practices represents a more professional and effective process is subject to interpretation.

NOTES

1 Christopher G. Reddick, 'Long-Run and Short-Run Budgeting: Theories and Empirical Evidence for Canadian Provinces,' *International Journal of Public Administration* 4 (2003), 427–53.

2 John W. Meyer and Brian Rowan, 'Institutionalized Organizations: Formal Structure as Myth and Ceremony,' *American Journal of Sociology* 83 (1977), 340–63. Normative pressure refers to what governments philosophically 'should do,' coercive pressure to what they are 'forced to do,' and mimetic to 'copying' what others have done to attain/maintain legitimacy.

3 Patrick Dunleavy and Christopher Hood, 'From Old Public Administration to New Public Management,' *Public Money & Management*, July–September 1994, 9–16; Peter Aucoin, 'The New Public Management: Canada in Comparative Perspective' (Montreal: Institute for Research on Public Policy, 1995); Donald J. Savoie, 'Fifteen Years of Reform: What Have We Learned?' in *Reforming the Public Sector: Taking Stock*, ed. G.B. Peters and D.J. Savoie (Montreal: McGill-Queen's University Press, 1998); Jan-Erik Lane, 'New Public Management and Public Administration in Canada' (Toronto: Institute of Public Administration of Canada, 2000); Christopher Pollitt and Geert Bouckaert, *Public Management Reform: A Comparative Analysis* (Oxford: Oxford University Press, 2000).

4 David Osborne and Ted Gaebler, *Reinventing Government: How the Entrepreneurial Spirit Is Transforming the Public Sector* (New York: Plume Books, 1992).

5 Mark McElwain, 'Ontario's Budgetary Process,' in *The Government and Politics of Ontario*, 4th ed., ed. G. White (Scarborough, ON: Nelson Canada, 1990).

6 Donald J. Savoie, *Governing from the Centre: The Concentration of Power in Canadian Politics* (Toronto: University of Toronto Press, 1999); 'Moody's

Downgrades Canada's Rating, Pressuring Government to Reduce Debt,' *Wall Street Journal* 225, no. 72 (1995), A2.

7 Robert F. Nixon, 'Reforming the Budget: A Discussion Paper,' Ministry of Treasury and Economics, 1985.

8 For example, see John Cruickshank and Robert Stephens, 'Tories Accused of Deal for Rating,' *Globe and Mail* (Toronto), 30 October 1984, A4.

9 See, for example, George Brett, 'Lower Rating for Ontario Viewed Calmly,' *Toronto Star*, 13 November 1985, G1.

10 See, for example, Brian Fox, 'Credit Rating Rebounds,' *Windsor Star* (Windsor), 6 July 1988, A1.

11 Evert A. Lindquist, 'Consultation and Budget Secrecy: Reforming the Process of Creating Revenue Budgets in the Canadian Federal Government,' Conference Board of Canada study no. 86 (February 1985).

12 Ibid.

13 See Ontario, Office of the Provincial Auditor, *Annual Report*, 1987.

14 Ray McLellan, 'Restructuring the Estimates Review Process in Ontario,' *Ontario Legislative Library*, Current Issue paper 173 (May 1996).

15 An examination of Statistics Canada data for real quarterly gross domestic product growth shows that during 1990 and 1991 there was a recession – more than two quarters of back-to-back negative real growth.

16 See, for example, Gene Allen and Harvey Enchin, 'Ontario Credit Rating Lowered – Rae Says Deficit Not Sole Factor,' *Globe and Mail*, 17 May 1991, A1; Kevin Ward, 'Bond Rating – 2nd Service Drops Rate for Province,' *Ottawa Citizen*, 13 May 1992, E1; and Derek Ferguson, 'Province's Credit Rating Chopped 3rd Cut in 3 Years Will Add Millions to Borrowing Costs,' *Toronto Star*, 25 November 1993, A1.

17 G. Bruce Doern, 'Fairness, Budgetary Secrecy, and Pre-Budget Consultation in Ontario, 1985–1992,' in *Taxing and Spending: Issues of Process*, ed. A.M. Maslove (Toronto: University of Toronto Press, 1994).

18 Ibid.

19 Ibid.

20 Ontario, Standing Committee on Finance and Economic Affairs, 1992, app. B.

21 'Ontario, Beyond the Numbers: A New Financial Management and Accountability Framework for Ontario' (Ontario Financial Review Commission, November 1995).

22 Pollitt and Bouckaert, *Public Management Reform*.

23 Ray McLellan, 'The Ontario Pre-Budget Consultation Process,' *Ontario Legislative Library*, Current Issue paper 202 (January 2000).

24 Ibid.

25 Interview with Len Roozen, 31 December 2008.

26 Ibid.

10 'Guardian' as 'Spender': Infrastructure Investment, 1960–2005

GERVAN FEARON[1]

This chapter explores the trends and drivers of infrastructure expenditures conducted by the Ontario Ministry of Finance in the latter half of the twentieth century. According to the Canadian Institute of Chartered Accountants the term 'infrastructure' can be defined as any non-financial asset having physical substance that is acquired, constructed, or developed, and (1) is held for use in the production or supply of goods and services; (2) has a useful life extending beyond an accounting period and is intended to be used on a continuing basis; and (3) is not intended for sale in the ordinary course of operations (Ontario budget, 2001).[2] On a simply cumulative basis, the Ontario government spent $87 billion on infrastructure between 1960 and 2005. The Ontario Ministry of Finance estimated the value of the province's infrastructure in 2001 at $210 billion. Of this, 52 per cent was considered to be owned by the provincial and municipal governments, 26.8 per cent owned by utilities, and the remainder held by the federal government and institutions such as hospitals and educational institutions. Four years later, the Ministry of Public Infrastructure Renewal estimated the value of the province's infrastructure complex at $266 billion.

As this chapter will show, successive treasurers/ministers of finance wholeheartedly endorsed the need to spend tax dollars on infrastructure in their budget speeches. But for the most part, those displays of enthusiasm camouflaged a reality: as a percentage of total expenditures, the government's commitment to infrastructure declined from over 40 per cent of the budget in 1960 to under 4 per cent in 2005, representing a shift from capital to operating expenditures.

The attraction of ministers of finance to infrastructure can be explained in a number of ways. First, many finance ministers liked to be seen as 'builders' for good reason: they are tangible examples of 'government at work.' Second, the timing and level of these expenditures were also 'responsive' to economic and demographic forces. Infrastructures were thus seen as vote-getters because they correspond to a real need in the community. The third is related to 'patronage': builders, developers, and real estate holders have tended to be friends of government, and infrastructure spending was long seen as a legitimate way to win influence that, in turn, might help fuel an election campaign. But funding infrastructure depends on the fiscal capacity of government (i.e., its ability to raise the funds necessary through taxes and borrowing), and here the staff in Treasury have played an all-important role. The economic framework defined by the bureaucracy helped to predict outcomes and socio-economic impacts of infrastructure expenditures and policies. This in large part was the product of a binding collaboration – an ability to link visions and actions – with line ministries and agencies that were tasked with determining infrastructure needs and expenditure recommendations. This ability to collaborate on spending as well as to maintain a productive dialogue with the Ontario government bureaucracy added to the mutual trust that was shared between the public service and the treasurer/minister of finance and the premiers.

As previous chapters have shown, the Treasury under Leslie Frost worked closely with the Department of Economics to determine planning and fiscal initiatives. This present chapter shows that the ministry also used commissions and task forces to study policy options and make recommendations to successive ministers of finance. These studies often formed the basis for policy formation and shaped expenditure programs. Institutions were also used as public-policy instruments to channel infrastructure spending.[3] For instance, the Ontario Hydro-Electric Power Commission of the early 1960s continued to provide a basis for future infrastructure expenditures and arrangements. More recently, the Ministry of Public Infrastructure Renewal, established in 2004, represented a further evolution in the continuum of institutional changes as a step to better meeting the infrastructure needs of the province.

Institutional changes also included innovative use of public-policy instruments to deliver infrastructure initiatives such as the Ontario University Capital Aid Corporation, Urban Transportation Development Corporation, and the Ontario Development Agency in the 1960s and 1970s. In the 1980s, the Board of Industrial Leadership and Development (BILD) spearheaded planning, policy, and programs aimed at infrastructure investment. The 1990s saw the evolution of the Jobs Ontario Capital Fund and Loan-based Financing instruments and, later, the

SuperBuild Growth Fund (Ontario SuperBuild Corporation) as instruments for pushing infrastructure investment in the province.

The institutional changes were accompanied by changes in the tools of analysis and the procedures for economic planning. For instance, in the mid-1970s, the development of various financial and economic models sharpened decision making: the Financial Information System (FIS), Quantitative Tax Analysis or General Income Tax Analyzer (GITAN), the Corporation Income Tax Analyzer (CORTAN), and experiments with Planning Programming Budget Systems (PPBS) as well as econometric and input-output economic models of the Ontario economy. These tools provided the Ministry of Finance with new frameworks for analysis and planning. Clearly, the tools developed were based on the economic framework and principles of the time. Econometrics was dominated by Keynesian economics and input-output models, which tended to see technological relationships as fixed. These models implied that infrastructure spending involved a constant return to scale underlying production technology. The tax analysers tended to define tax revenue independent of government expenditures, and financial information systems tended to assume that the aggregation of the parts was equal to the impact of the whole budget. The Keynesian framework also tended to suggest that government spending constituted a component of aggregate demand and that infrastructure expenditures could be a mechanism to stimulate the economy. That idea was challenged by neoclassical economic growth frameworks (supply-side) of the 1990s, which viewed public infrastructure as intermediate inputs in private and/or household production technology, possessing increasing returns to scale underlying production technology, and characteristic of a mixed-public good. In recent years, both demand and supply-side economics have been used to plan the province's infrastructure needs. While the primary tools available still rely on the demand-side analytical frameworks which were created in the 1960s and 1970s, the underlying conceptual framework of treasurers/ministers of finance evolved in response to the contemporary economic theories of their time.

Those analytical frameworks evolved over time in response to attempts to balance changes in the conceptual framework with two primary forces – demographic trends and economic imperatives. Demographic trends defined the underlying demand (why) for roads and highways, water and sewage, electricity and telecommunications, education and hospitals over the last fifty years. The economic imperative of developing a competitive and 'full' employment-driven economy defined the 'when, what, and where' of Ontario's infrastructure expenditures. External forces such as inflation, stagflation, and recession also defined the fiscal capacity of governments to meet their planned infrastructure investment targets. If governments had the 'why, when, what, and where,' it was these exogenous forces that defined the 'how.' Unanticipated economic shocks repeatedly altered the course of the province's infrastructure development, leaving a gap between existing capacity and desired infrastructure levels dictated by the demands of demographic trends and the desire to attain economic competitiveness. The need for the development of financing mechanisms that better addressed the long-term planning horizon of infrastructure investments further insulated these long-term infrastructure decisions from short-term economic shocks, and also facilitated risk-sharing factors that shape institutional change and infrastructure expenditure trends.

Trends, Economic Setting, and Ministers of the 1960s and 1970s

Trends in Infrastructure Expenditures

The 1960s and 1970s saw significant growth in the level of Ontario's infrastructure expenditures. Figure 10.1 shows the trends in net capital disbursements during the 1960s and early 1970s.[4] The infrastructure spending of the 1960s established the foundation for Ontario's contemporary infrastructure. It was aimed at facilitating exports, employment, and production. It was also a period of substantial investment in educational facilities, health care, roads and highways, rural electrification, public buildings for the growing numbers of civil servants, water and sewage, and regional-rural development. Net capital disbursements as a percentage of total expenditure averaged over roughly 20 per cent during this period. The infrastructure investment also focused on the construction of highways and secondary roads, hydro-electric works, water treatment plants, and municipal projects. There was also a growing recognition of the importance of public transportation to the vitality of Toronto and southern Ontario, which was reflected in the establishment of GO Transit in 1965–6 and the rapid expansion of the Toronto subway system. It is interesting to note that the rapid population growth of the 1960s and 1970s resulted in a decline in net capital disbursements per capita even though aggregate levels were increasing. In addition, infrastructure investment as a percentage of overall expenditures had actually declined to 15 per cent by 1970 (see figure 10.2).

Figure 10.1 Net capital disbursements, 1960–1975

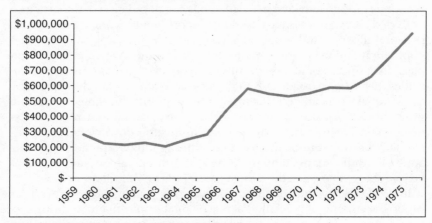

Source: Ontario government budgets, 1959–75.

Figure 10.2 Net capital disbursements as percentage of net ordinary expenditures, 1959–75

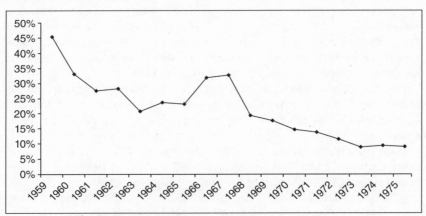

Source: Ontario government budgets, 1959–75.

The economic environment in the 1960s was characterized by strong economic growth at over 6 per cent, while the population of the province exceeded six million for the first time. Exports, employment, production, personal income, and retail sales were all growing rapidly. This rapid population and economic growth as well as a quest for modernization placed significant demands for numerous items, such as educational facilities, health care, roads and highways, access roads to harvest resources, rural electrification, transmission lines, public buildings to house a growing civil service, water and sewage expansion, and regional development. For instance, Ontario Hydro-Electric Power of Ontario increased the distribution of electricity through 1600 kilometres of line added to rural Ontario, with up to 491,070 rural customers, and the number of motor vehicles in the province reaching 1.974 million in 1959.[5]

In 1964, the growth of the manufacturing sector and, in particular (upon the signing of the Auto Pact in 1965), the auto-manufacturing sector accelerated the demand for a skilled and trained workforce. This resulted in a need for infrastructure to foster both physical as well as human capital.[6] In May 1967, the Kennedy Round of the General Agreement of Tariff and Trade (GATT) talks resulted in an across-the-board tariff cut averaging 35 per cent. The International Monetary Fund had created the new international monetary reserves in the form of Special Drawing Rights and, additionally, the Canada-US Agreement on Automotive Products had been signed. The competitiveness of the province was viewed as being dependent on its infrastructure providing an impetus for the government's focus on capital expenditures.

The ministerial decisions pertaining to infrastructure expenditures were shaped by the economic setting of the period. James Allan and Charles MacNaughton each kept net capital disbursements at an average of over 20 per cent of total expenditures. For Allan, the emphasis was on the Hydro-Electric Power Commission of Ontario (later to become Ontario Hydro), which received $75 million in 1959 and another investment of $48.8 million at the end of his term in 1966.

Allan articulated the view that government should be engaged in the development of social security and infrastructure systems for the betterment of the population of Ontario, and in supporting the modernization of the province. He was also concerned about interrelationship between governments at all levels, including the coordination and harmonization of federal, provincial, and municipal government policies. Allan's administration suggested that the demand for public services was positively related to per capita income and prosperity. Increased prosperity would, for example, lead to an increase in the number of automobiles per capita and a resultant increase in the demand for roads and bridges. Allan translated his social and economic views from vision into action through the establishment of commissions, followed by the establishment of corporations or programs to implement identified initiatives. In just two years, 1960 and 1961, several commissions were established that would have a direct impact on infrastructure building: the Ontario Hospital Services Commission, Ontario Water Resources Commission (originally established in 1957), Ontario Hydro-Electric Power Commission, Ontario St Lawrence Development Commission, Ontario Mental Health Foundation, and the Civil Service Commission (for its impact on government facilities).

A set of corporations and programs emerged from the Allan-mandated commissions and guided much of the government's infrastructure expenditures during his tenure. These corporations included the following: the Ontario Municipal Improvement Corporation (1960), Ontario Universities Capital Aid Corporation (1964), Ontario Housing Corporation, Metropolitan Toronto Housing Authority, Retarded Children Education Authority (1965), a re-fitted Ontario Research Foundation (1965), and GO Transit (1965). Other institutions such as the Ontario Water Resources Commission and Ontario Hydro-Electric Power Commission were also strengthened.

Allan's early view was that the role of government was to foster a stable environment for economic growth. However, this view evolved by 1962 to consider the role of government as oriented towards the betterment and well-being of the Ontario population; orderly and efficient development of communities and industry; and efficient government operations and value-for-money budgeting. By the latter part of Allan's tenure as the treasurer of Ontario, this focus further shifted towards government as an instrument of leadership, transformation, and meeting needs, including full employment.

Allan was also particularly concerned about the inability of the private sector to meet the demand for housing driven substantially by booming immigration. Consequently, the Metropolitan Toronto Housing Authority was established to speed up the development of public housing in the Toronto area through non-profit and low-income housing as well as rent subsidies. It is worth noting that by the late 1960s, Ontario accounted for over 70 per cent of all the public housing starts in Canada. Allan's commitment to the development of human capital can be observed in his focus on education. Maintenance and capital grants to colleges stood at $29.9 million in 1960–1, and $36.6 million in 1961–2. In 1962–3 provincial grants to universities for maintenance, capital goods, and special grants averaged $45.5 million. The Ontario University Capital Aid Corporation facilitated some $53.6 million of investments in universities in the province.[7] It is also worth noting that the Department of University Affairs was established in 1965, in part to monitor what the universities were doing with the infrastructure dollars.

The expenditures on infrastructure declined as a percentage of the budget as the 1960s wore on, moving from 45 per cent of total amounts to less than 15 per cent at the end of the decade. MacNaughton invested in municipal infrastructure even more than in the Hydro-Electric Power Commission. The growing recognition of the importance of public transportation to the vitality of Toronto and southern Ontario was reflected in the establishment of GO Transit in 1965–6 and the rapid expansion of the Toronto subway system by the government. This new emphasis on public transportation corresponded to modest investment of $31,000 in 1965–6 that jumped to $9.2 million in 1966–7, totalling over $20 million between 1966 and 1969.

Did Ontario's massive investment in infrastructure – in combination with building across the country – contribute to inflation? Possibly – and over the decade it would become more transparent. By 1970, the Prices and Income Commission became an instrument for fighting inflation by seeking voluntary restraints on prices and income in all sectors of the economy. At the same time, federal–provincial relations were being tested by disputes surrounding the federal-provincial fiscal imbalance. The Tax Structure Committee failed to resolve these issues and the Ontario government could not look towards increased revenue-sharing with the federal government as a solution to the province's budgetary constraints. Nonetheless, the 1970 budget review concluded that the federal government's funding of national medicare had gone far in fiscal redistribution – possibly further than any other Western country.[8] By 1970, the slowing of the economy, credit constraints, and rising interest rates along with concerns about inflation were defining the bounds of provincial government fiscal policy.[9] The economic growth and exuberance of the 1960s were further fading and being eclipsed by inflation, unemployment, and, ultimately, stagflation.[10]

Darcy McKeough, who briefly served as treasurer in 1971–2, considered that government's role was to foster the greatest level of private-sector activity and investment.[11] The economic principles guiding

McKeough involved policies aimed at full employment, controlling government expenditures to limit their impact on taxation and inflation, provincial-municipal reforms, and economic growth with responsible preservation and conservation policies for the environment. Tax cuts, cost controls, and program reviews were conducted in the spirit of this role of government. Policies were put in place to limit the size of government, which stood at 69,118 public-service employees in 1971 (e.g., procyclical contractionary policy driven by a balanced-budget constraint linked to government's immediate revenue prospects). Limiting the size of the public sector, however, implied a slowing in the need for public works and construction of government buildings to house an increasing number of civil servants who had come into the workforce in the 1960s under Allan and MacNaughton. A new Ontario Land Acquisition Corporation was established to acquire land for future provincial usage, including parks, transportation, recreation, and housing. This corporation was responsible for coordinating land-use planning and urban development.

McKeough established a full employment budgetary framework that involved estimating the full employment level of GDP, determining the full employment level of tax revenues, and matching government expenditures to this level of revenues.[12] In many respects, McKeough moved to modernize the budgetary process by unifying the provincial budgetary system in 1972, including administrative budgeting, cash budgeting, national account budgeting, and financial transactions. The Quantitative Tax Analysis or General Income Tax Analyzer (GITAN) was introduced to compute tax incidence and revenue effects of personal income taxation, while the Corporation Income Tax Analyzer (CORTAN) conducted a similar analysis on the business side. Provincial and regional econometric models, along with input-output tables and the economic intelligence system (i.e., data and opinions on economic indicators used to analyse the financial markets), were developed to support the budgetary process. Finally, an attempt to introduce a planning-programming-budget system (PPBS) was made (see the chapter by Caroline Dufour). These systems formed the integrated financial and economic planning framework that provided the computational and analytical mechanisms for fiscal planning and infrastructure investment.

John White continued in the same vein. His concerns were to support a guaranteed annual income plan, full employment, restraints on government spending, and redistributive tax policies to promote fairness.

Large capital expenditures of $164 million were made on education facilities, as well as some $269.9 million on housing and urban development. Expenditures to improve transportation were also made, with $35 million allocated towards GO Transit and another $2.5 million to establish a new computer traffic and communication system to improve traffic flows. Municipal water and sewerage grants were also increased to enhance the supply of serviced lots aimed at boosting construction and better meeting the demand for housing in the province.

By the time of McKeough's return to office in 1975, the economic environment was characterized by stagflation and the rising cost of public debt. A Special Program Review Committee established in 1976 recommended that all capital expenditure commitments receive pre-approval by the Ministry of Treasury, Economics and Intergovernmental Affairs. In addition, restrictions on government borrowing were established, including capital loan and debt guarantees used to finance Ontario Hydro. In 1976, Ontario Hydro construction at the Bruce Heavy Water Plant C was cut by $1.2 billion. The program review process, now mandatory, required that all capital expenditure commitments receive pre-approval. The contraction-oriented government economic policy was driven by the view that, given an inflationary gap, the appropriate government policy was to reduce government expenditures. The stagflation of this period demanded a refined balance between fiscal expenditure controls to dampen inflationary pressures and the accommodation of infrastructure investment to foster employment opportunities.

By 1978, consumer expenditures started to recover and, along with tax cuts, economic activity was revived. Government infrastructure spending also increased by 43 per cent to $688 million, with significant disbursements allocated to roads, highways, subways, and water and sewage. The second McKeough budgetary period represented a focus on consultative government aimed at reducing government's drag on the economy by devising policy through consultation with a wide cross-section of the economy. Premier Davis's priorities during this period also included encouraging price stability, improving the business climate and private investment, promoting exports and replacing imports, and reducing regional disparities. McKeough would continue to aim for full employment, but subject to government budget constraints within a balanced budget framework.

The Ontario government established new programs to support what could be called private infrastructure: the provision of housing for the growing population of the province. These programs included the

Ontario Housing Action Program, Home Ownership Made Easy, and the Grant for First Home Buyers. In terms of public infrastructure, the province established Wintario Lottery as an innovative mechanism for raising revenue for physical fitness, sports and recreation, and cultural activities and facilities. However, the Ontario Lottery Corporation Act would be modified in the late 1980s to facilitate the use of funds for selected health capital facilities.

The Ontario government moved to clarify its role as a lender and its approach in budgeting of capital expenditures. The Ontario Mortgage Corporation was wound down and the activities of the Ontario Land Corporation (OLC) were integrated into the activities of other Ontario crown corporations.[13] In addition, the government also changed its methodology for capital funding, moving to front-end capital grants that represented a pay-as-you-go mechanism. The pay-as-you-go approach was tantamount to cash accounting of capital expenditures, since expenditures are reported as the infrastructure announcement is made as opposed to being matched to the productive life of the asset.[14] It would be another twenty years before this decision would be fully reversed and accrual accounting for capital investment implemented for the province.

Trends, Economic Setting, and Ministers of the 1980s

The 1980s began with capital investment representing 10 per cent of total government expenditures and declined to 8 per cent by the end of the decade. This decline in expenditure is misleading, as the government's per capita expenditure on capital would increase from around $200 to nearly $335 per capita over the decade (see figure 10.3).[15] Indeed, capital investment increased from $1.7 billion in 1980 to $3.4 billion by 1989–90. The composition of capital investment would remain relatively stable over the decade. However, in the 1986–7 budget there was a sharp re-allocation of expenditures away from capital investment in health care, school and post-secondary education, and social services towards environment and resource and economic development. This adjustment in the proportional allocation of these categories of total capital investment reflected the rebalancing between economic competitiveness and demographic forces as drivers of infrastructure expenditures.

The demographic pressures of the 1980s resulted in infrastructure investment focusing on housing, water and sewer facilities, and transportation.[16] It was suggested that the aging of the population would require

Figure 10.3 Capital investment per capita, 1980–90

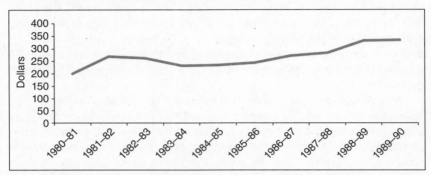

Source: Ontario budget papers, Ontario budget (1982), Budget paper C, p. 7, and, for population, Statistics Canada, CANSIM, table 051-0001.

an increased investment in facilities for the elderly over time. The demographic profile changes (i.e., a large portion of the population between five and nineteen years of age) also resulted in a focus on capital spending to build and improve educational facilities.

The early 1980s was a period of combating inflation (e.g., Inflation Restraint Act), rising unemployment, program review for all ministries, review of crown corporations, efforts to privatize or cost-recover, and the Canadian dollar hitting a (then) historical low against the US dollar at 72 cents. For instance, the rental charge for water to Ontario Hydro had been established in 1958, but came under review in 1984. In 1985, program review resulted in the elimination of the Ontario Universities Capital Aid Corporation (TOUCAC), which operated between 1964 and 1978 to advance funds for capital construction for universities, colleges, the Ontario Art Gallery, the Royal Ontario Museum, and the Ontario College of Art, as well as between 1966 and 1980 to fund capital expenditures for school boards. The government went further by writing off capital advances, including $184 million for Ontario Housing Corporation, $352 million for water treatment and waste control facilities, and equity positions in three crown corporations (Ontario Development Corporation – $7 million, Urban Transportation Development Corporation – $37 million, and Ontario Energy Corporation – $80 million). These were written off for $1. The entire debt forgiveness, relief of excess debt burden of municipalities, write-down, and write-offs totalled $3,699 million. This would form the foundation for greater municipal (local) engagement in infrastructure investment in years to follow. In addition, the government audit had shown that the province was paying out funds to repay loans owed to the province, so it only made sense to assume the loans and eliminate the liabilities owed to it by a host of provincial crown corporations.

Government budgeting was increasingly evolving to a pay-as-you-go fiscal management system aimed at balancing operating expenditures with current and projected revenues.[17] A new capital accounting method was established, with capital being allocated to each ministry on a multi-year basis. Management Board of Cabinet coordinated multi-year capital and other investment plans submitted by each ministry concerning future capital needs and the impact of new capital spending on operating expenditures. For instance, a multi-year hospital capital expansion was established for $850 million.

Budget Paper C, 'Public Investment and Responsible Financial Management,' raised concerns about government debt with interest on public debt reaching 9.6 per cent of provincial expenditures in 1981. Capital expenditures financed through debt were viewed as increasingly competing with private sector needs to finance operating and capital expenditures. Now, the debt financing of public capital expenditures would potentially crowd out private investment.[18] For instance, Ontario Hydro's debt of $14 billion accounted for more than 40 per cent of the provincial direct and guaranteed funded debt at $31.6 billion as of 31 March 1982. In comparison, provincial agencies, the local government sector, and the university and hospital sectors only accounted for 14.9 per cent, or $5.5 billion, of the $37.1 billion of the consolidated funded debt of the Ontario public sector. In this economic environment, the government would explore the development of new institutional mechanisms to finance the growing needs for provincial infrastructure expansion.

The policy direction of each minister of finance was instrumental in shaping the trends of this decade. The Frank Miller budgets were founded on the premise that the private sector performed best with minimal government regulation and that the economy would benefit from a reduction in red tape and a speeding up of government decision making. In this respect, Miller supported privatization and shared McKeough's views regarding the need to avoid government acting as an impediment to the private sector. It should be noted that Miller's views on reduced red tape extended beyond the boundaries of Ontario, with suggestions in the 1981 budget that there was a need for national policies that fostered productivity improvements, exports, import replacement, and energy substitution.

This emphasis on policy coordination was exhibited in Ontario with the establishment of the Board of Industrial Leadership and Development (BILD), which emerged out of the Building Ontario report, and the formation of the Employment Development Investment Fund. The BILD focused on coordinating and implementing economic development strategies in the province, including capital projects such as the Ontario Hydro Darlington project (accelerated by a $60 million additional investment); a $25 million investment in a transportation corridor from Toronto to Niagara; and the continued funding of the Urban Transportation Development Corporation.[19] In addition, Ontario Hydro capital requirements were funded by $500 million from the Canada Pension Plan to purportedly avoid pressure on capital markets. The Ontario government also invested in information technology, including computerized axial tomography (CAT) scanners to permit improved tele-medicine services for Northern Ontario. Government capital priorities were also changing as the government cut its expenditures on Toronto subway construction by $10 million while increasing its contributions towards highway construction by $19 million.

In 1982, the acceleration of provincial capital projects by $133 million was utilized to stimulate employment and economic growth. These projects included accelerating the repair and maintenance of public buildings, highways, roads, and municipal bridges, water and sewage treatment projects, renovation and repair of schools, colleges, and universities, and forest and fishery infrastructure. A number of youth employment initiatives were also established around the same period. It was viewed that government needed to alter its capital investment to reflect the demands of a maturing industrial economy and aging population.

In the 1982 budget, capital expenditure was defined as 'the creation or acquisition of assets that have a life span of more than one year and provide public benefits beyond the initial year.'[20] It was noted that, in the private sector, the matching principle involved capital expenditures being spread over the productive life of the asset (accrual accounting). A guiding principle for public sector capital investment was matching expenditures to the social benefits flowing from the expenditures.[21] These expenditures had previously been viewed typically as claims by third parties in the form of debt, such that the current expenditures to finance these debts are treated as current expenditures (cash-based accounting).[22]

In terms of decision structures, BILD remained an important instrument in financing infrastructure investment in the province. It focused on human resources, natural resources, electricity transportation, communication, and technology, with a five-year commitment of $775 million. These expenditures provided an overview of government priorities for infrastructure investment. The BILD initiative became a key mechanism for Ontario infrastructure expenditures, with expenditures through this program often being matched to job creation. For instance, in 1983, accelerated federal-provincial capital work projects of $247 million coordinated under the BILD were viewed as generating 12,000 jobs (the provincial share was $167.5 million).[23]

The computer age redefined infrastructure expenditures within the 1983 budget as provisions were made for the Ministry of Education to provide 7000 desk-top computers and software packages for use in elementary and secondary schools. The government also noted the need to invest in knowledge-intensive industries, allocating $50 million to establish centres for the promotion of new technology and advanced applied research.[24] In addition, $21 million was allocated towards high-technology equipment and training support for universities and colleges, along with $41 million to promote technological advancement in the agriculture, forestry, and minerals sectors. This increasing interest in information technology also spilled over into 1984, during Larry Grossman's tenure as treasurer, with $4 million being invested in 4000 computers placed in communities across Ontario by the Ministry of Citizenship and Culture to enhance citizenship and civic engagement.

Robert Nixon served as the Liberal government's finance minister between 1985 and 1990. Clearly, at this point his staff as well as staff inside the Treasury and Economics ministry were concerned about the province's deteriorating roads, bridges, and highways. By 1988, $7 billion in capital projects had been committed to ameliorate what was called the 'backlog' in needed public capital facilities. Capital expenditure of $290 million was allocated towards roads, highways, and transit in support of further construction of the 407, 403, and 416 highways. A Municipal Industrial Strategy was established to support the cleaning up of beaches as well as the improvement of municipal water and sewage infrastructure. A Green Paper on 'Financing Growth-Related Capital Needs' was conducted in 1989 by the Ministry of Municipal Affairs to support municipal front-end financing initiatives.[25]

The Liberals focused on the expansion and modernization of Ontario's infrastructure. There were several forces now affecting Ontario, including global integration, immigration, an aging population, and increasing demands for an expanded social infrastructure. Ontario's competitiveness was viewed as dependent on the level of its infrastructure. In the 1989–90 budget, $3.236 billion in capital expenditures were announced out of a total of $41.29 billion in total operating and capital expenditures. In 1990, a five-year strategy was established involving $2.0 billion being spent on transportation, including $1.2 billion on provincial highway projects, $0.4 billion on GO Transit, and $0.4 billion on municipal roads and transit. In addition, educational capital expenditures were increased, water and sewerage capital programs were expanded, and a new crown corporation was established in support of the government's clean environment focus.

Nixon's early view – that government was responsible for establishing a supportive environment for business to improve its competitiveness through productivity gains – evolved to the belief that government must be committed to a durable prosperity that is shared by all.[26] Nixon now considered efficiency and equity to be forces to be held in balance. His action to support efficiency was already clear.

To promote equity, the government now established the $220 million Assured Housing Strategy, which resulted in an additional capital construction for more affordable rental housing. The minister of housing, Alvin Curling, signed a multi-year agreement with the federal government to provide 6700 non-profit and co-op housing units in the province. Furthermore, the Ontario Lottery Corporation Act was modified to permit the funding of cancer treatment facilities and the increase in capital-funding investment to hospitals. To support the efforts towards modernity and equity, a number of studies and task forces were initiated, including a Green Paper on Financing Growth-Related Capital Needs, the Premier's Council on Technology, the Premier's Council on Health Strategy, a Strategic Procurement Program, Ontario Round Table on the Environment, Social Assistance Review Committee, and a Task Force on Illegal Drug Use in Ontario. Hence, the 1980s ended with a view that capital expenditures where needed to support efficiency and equity throughout the economy.

Trends, Economic Setting, and Ministers of the 1990s

The 1990s began with total capital expenditures at $3.2 billion and ended with expenditure levels at $4.5 billion. These expenditures were relatively stable at just over $3 billion for the first half of the decade, when they began to diminish as escalating government deficits began to constrain investment in the future (i.e., infrastructure) in favour of addressing immediate demands. Specifically, the potential of public expenditures

Figure 10.4 Capital investment per capita, 1990–2000

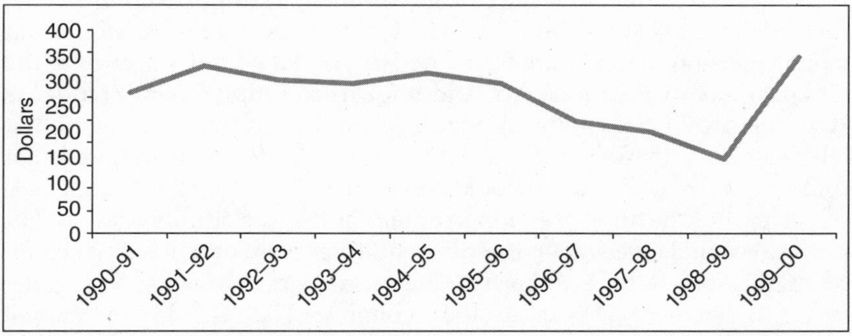

Source: Budget papers and, for population, Statistics Canada, CANSIM, table 051-0001.

crowding out private investment, noted by McKeough and Nixon in prior years, became a real policy concern in the 1990s. Hence, infrastructure expenditures reached as low as $1.9 billion, based on the 1998–9 budget figures. The decline in infrastructure expenditures was finally reversed in the 1999–2000 budget, as these expenditures reached $4.5 billion. The above trend in government expenditures are reflected in the per capita data presented in figure 10.4. The composition of capital investment in Ontario remained relatively stable during the decade until 1999–2000, when there was a substantial re-allocation away from environment, resource, and economic development and towards health care and school and post-secondary education. The first budget by Floyd Laughren, presented on 29 April 1991, came at a time when the real economic growth was negative 3.3 per cent, unemployment stood at 10 per cent, and inflation was 5.6 per cent. The recession suggested that economic restructuring was needed to support positive economic growth, sustainable prosperity, and fairness through social partnerships and counter-cyclical economic measures.

Demographic forces and economic imperative acted as twin drivers behind the decisions of the ministers of finance. The first budget tabled by Floyd Laughren involved expenditures of $52.8 billion and revenues of $43.0 billion and translated into a deficit of $9.726 billion. Laughren's budget differentiated between human capital (e.g., education and training) and physical capital (e.g., infrastructure). Human capital was viewed as complementary to the utilization of physical capital as a mechanism for improvement in economic growth. For human capital, the Laughren budget reflected the government's supportive sentiments towards labour. This labour agenda included an increased minimum wage, pension reform, amendments to the Pay Equity Act and the Ontario Labour Relations Act, and reforms to Employment Standards Act. The provincial capital expenditures of $4.3 billion were aimed at job creation and supporting economic growth. It was anticipated that these capital expenditures would result in 70,000 new jobs being creating as part of the anti-recession program of the Rae administration. For physical capital investment, these expenditures were part of a set of counter-cyclical policy tools to balance the business cycles owing to private-sector investment shocks to the economy. The $4.3 billion capital expenditures of the government were focused on hospitals, education (i.e., school boards, universities, and colleges), municipalities, government buildings, roads, public transit, bridges, and water and sewer systems. These expenditures represented only one of two major capital expenditure thrusts of the government. The primary infrastructure thrust was the 'Let's Move' program, involving $50 billion in public and private sector funding over ten years towards capital infrastructure.

Laughren's secondary infrastructure thrust stood on two platforms, namely, jobs and partnership. The Jobs Ontario Capital Fund was established as part of the 1992 budget, with $2.3 billion allocated to a strategic capital program for transportation, communications, and environmental systems. It was anticipated that in the first year the fund would spend $500 million and generate 10,000 jobs. In terms of partnerships, the Telecommunications Advisory Committee and the Sectoral Partnership Fund are two specific examples. It is interesting to note that telecommunication had become a strategic component of the government's infrastructure program and was now viewed as a vital component of the information and knowledge economies. By 1992, the Ontario government capital strategy had evolved into a three-pronged approach, including base capital, the Jobs Ontario Capital Fund, and loan-based financing. Total capital expenditures between 1992 and 1994 hovered between $3.5 and $3.1 billion. The base capital expenditures focused on the traditional capital infrastructure investments. The Jobs Ontario Capital initiative remained a key component of the government's infrastructure strategy, and each year the associated employment numbers were reported as symbols of success (e.g., 8400 full-year jobs were viewed as created through the program in 1992–3 and $700 million was to be spent in 1993–4). The Jobs Ontario Capital Fund was modified to include a new loan-based financing system for colleges, universities, schools, and hospitals.

By 1993, the anticipated short-lived recession had now stressed the Ontario economy for over two years and government revenues were suffering. This was reflected in mounting government deficits. The province's capital expenditures would begin to diminish, reaching $3.594 billion for the 1992–3 budget and $3.096 billion for the 1993–4 budget. On the operating expenditure side, the government planned to achieve $6 billion in savings through an Expenditure Control Plan ($4 billion) and the Social Contract ($2.0 billion). Asset sales was also an integral part of these savings, totalling $915 million, including the sales of SkyDome ($140 million), GO Transit rolling stock ($325 million), land and buildings through the Ontario Realty Corporation ($250 million), and Suncor shares ($190 million). The government also attempted to increase revenues through aggressive service levies and permits.

Laughren moved in 1993 to establish new mechanisms to support the government's capital investment strategy. These were manifested through new legislation, namely, the Capital Investment Plan Act, which resulted in the formation of four new institutions – the Ontario Transportation Capital Corporation, Ontario Clean Water Agency, Ontario Realty Corporation, and Ontario Financing Authority. The latter was aimed at facilitating the implementation of the government's capital investment approach in centralizing financing arrangements and minimizing borrowing costs by avoiding duplication, improving coordination, and leveraging its bargaining power. Similar approaches to the Ontario Financing Authority had been taken in other provinces, most notably British Columbia and Saskatchewan, each having NDP governments around this period. The Ontario Transportation Capital Corporation would become responsible for the arrangements to build Highway 407. The efficiency gains from these arrangements (e.g., public–private sector initiatives) were highlighted by the assertion that the 407 would be completed in 1999 – sixteen years ahead of the original schedule. The Canada-Ontario Infrastructure Works Agreement established in 1994 represented a partnership between the federal government, province, municipalities, school boards, colleges, and universities. Under the agreement, there was a commitment to build four new subway lines, the Mississauga Transit-way, and the Guelph Food Technologies Centre.

Laughren considered that the cash accounting method for capital dating back to 1968 exaggerated the fact that operating expenditures (i.e., programs) were vastly greater than capital expenditures. He thus proposed a new definition for capital expenditures for the acquisition or construction of infrastructure. Infrastructure was defined as including tangible assets such as land, buildings, major engineering structures, public facilities, and significant additions and improvements to existing structures. Equipment was excluded because of its short-term life span. Capital fund expenditures were now reported separately from operating expenditures. Treasury Board was given the responsibilities of implementing a multi-year budgeting strategy as well as improved capital-budgeting decision making.[27] The Financial Administration Act was amended to support the policy agenda of the government.

The economic environment affecting the Eves budgets had been expected to feature low inflation, steady economic growth, and moderate job growth (i.e., all near the 2 per cent level per annum). However, by 1997, it was clear that unemployment was higher than anticipated (e.g., 7 to 8 per cent) and economic growth had picked up (e.g., around 4 per cent) in a relatively low-inflation environment. Job creation was a priority; however, the government's philosophy suggested that this was the responsibility of the private sector and outside the fundamental responsibilities of government.

Ernie Eves's vision was initially articulated in his 1996 budget and was fully manifested in the 1999 document. Eves was focused on implementing the 'Common Sense Revolution,' which spoke to a sense of rebuilding the grandeur and competitiveness of Ontario (e.g., investing in transportation for economic development), establishing an inheritance for future generations, and striving towards a balanced budget agenda. Government, it was suggested, should focus on establishing an environment for growth as opposed to being a purveyor of social welfare outcomes. It was in this environment that Eves's vision begins to be manifested. In 1996, the Ontario Financing Authority responsibilities were extended to cover the managing of all the borrowing that relied on the province's credit strength to facilitate the risk management of interest rates and currency fluctuations. A review was initiated under the Ontario Financial Review Commission that resulted in the standardization of all budgetary reporting and an updating of the Public Sector Accounting and Auditing Board (PSAAB) in accordance with the recommendations of the Canadian Institute of Chartered Accountants. In 1997–8, organizational performance and benchmarks were established across the government.

Between 1996 and 1997, the clarification of who-does-what was manifested by devolution and elimination. In the 1996 budget, the Ontario

Development Corporation was closed at a cost of $63 million to government. In 1997, the Ontario Housing Corporation responsibilities were transferred to the municipalities for the management of the public housing stock. This transfer involved the devolution of $429 million in provincial monies and $100 million in federal assistance to Ontario Housing Corporation for capital repairs and renovation to the municipalities. The Jobs Ontario Capital initiative was eliminated.

By 1997, the government began to acquire a landscape that it felt no longer needed ploughing, so it was time to cultivate. Total capital expenditures reached $2.75 billion, with a key policy initiative being the government's participation in the extension of the Canada-Ontario Infrastructure Works (COIW). This initiative resulted in some $325 million in joint federal-provincial dollars and $134 in local government funding flowing to infrastructure as part of the overall expenditure of $459 million under the initiative. In addition, the government made available $800 million in municipal capital and operating restructuring funding for water and sewerage systems, non-profit and cooperative housing, transportation, and unallocated funds.[28] The government also contributed $500 million to a Research and Development Challenge Fund that aimed, along with other measures, to trigger total investments of $3 billion over ten years.

In 1998, the government continued its efforts towards improving Ontario's competitiveness by investing $30 million into the Telecommunications Access Partnership program. Regional development would also play a part in the government's infrastructure thinking, as reflected by a $820 million investment in Ontario highways with specific reference to Northern Ontario.

It would be in the 1999 budget, more than any other, that Ernie Eves's efforts on infrastructure would be seen in their full force. The SuperBuild Growth Fund was introduced as a five-year initiative aimed at investing $20 billion in Ontario infrastructure. An amount of $2.9 billion was included in the 1999/2001 budget, aimed at funding partnership arrangements, universities, colleges, health care, roads and bridges, the information highway, environmental initiatives, and community support across the province. Educational infrastructure improvements benefited substantially from the SuperBuild Growth Fund. As early as the 1998 budget, it was noted that Ontario needed greater investment in post-secondary education to ensure that the demand for labour and, particularly, occupational needs were met. Correspondingly, $1.9 billion was allocated towards new school construction to create spaces for up to 170,000 students. Next, transportation benefited from $936 million in additional funding, while health services received $504 million. In 1999–2000 the SuperBuild Growth Fund included an additional $742 million for universities and colleges to facilitate the construction of new classrooms and labs to support the growing student population.

The Ontario Innovation Trust was established, with $250 million for Ontario universities, hospitals, and colleges for labs, high-technology equipment, and other research infrastructure. Investment in smart libraries entailed assisting Ontario libraries and improving community health access to the Internet. Volunteerism was viewed as important to the society, so investments were made to establish Internet connections in libraries through what was to be referred to as 'volunteers@action.' Centres of Excellence were funded, with an emphasis on a Centre for Information Technology at the University of Toronto, Centre for Environmental and Information Technology at the University of Waterloo, and the McMaster Engineering and Science Rehabilitation Program.

The need for further government investment in infrastructure to support the knowledge economy was exhibited in the $150 million Access to Opportunities Program (ATOP). ATOP was aimed at doubling the number of graduates in computer science and engineering. The program allocated $500 million for strategic skills training at community colleges and $600 million to the Ontario Student Opportunity Trust Fund to help 185,000 community college and university students. In addition, the law and order agenda of the government was reflected in a $189 million capital expenditure for correctional and court facilities in the 1999/2000 budget.

In the 2000 budget, Ernie Eves outlined some of the accomplishments of his government, namely, balanced budgets and debt pay-down. For infrastructure, the budget would set the stage for the years to come as it outlined a further integration of infrastructure capital expenditures under the SuperBuild program. The program would focus on the following: health services ($1 billion to accelerate capital restructuring), research investment ($250 million), private–public sector partnership ($1 billion over five years) and sports, culture, and tourism ($300 million), and highway system ($1 billion). These infrastructure expenditures were often driven by studies commissioned by government bodies such as the Health Service Restructuring Commission (HSRC) and the Learning Opportunity Task Force.

Infrastructure investment was seen as a mechanism for regional and urban development, while tax policy was viewed as an instrument favouring competitiveness and job creation. Tax policy was viewed as setting the foundation for economic opportunity as well as creating the incentives for economic growth in much the same way that previous governments had defined infrastructure investment. On the other hand, the 'who does what' review process was starting to be translated into action. For instance, the Local Service Realignment (LSR) initiative resulted in a transfer of social housing and social assistance from the provincial governments to local municipal governments. The provincial government's direct role in social housing established under the Allan budgets of the 1960s was now ending. Correspondingly, the Ontario Housing Corporation, Central Mortgage Housing Corporation, and Metropolitan Toronto Housing Authority role had faded over the years.

Trends, Economic Setting, and Ministers of the New Millennium

In the 2000–3 period, the drivers affecting infrastructure expenditures would remain demographics and economic imperatives. However, the prior decade-long effort to redefine capital expenditures along the lines of an accrual basis as opposed to a cash-accounting basis would finally gain currency, and its implementation culminated in not only changes in accounting principles, but also the disentanglement of the Ministry of Finance from the fundamental management of the province's infrastructure investments. The Ministry of Public Infrastructure Renewal was established.

Capital infrastructure investment increased from $2.1 billion in 2000–1 to over $3.1 billion after 2002–3 (see figure 10.5). Capital infrastructure investments in 2004 and 2005 were actually larger than the numbers for the previous years of the 2000 decade. When adjustments for project delays, re-allocation of capital expenditures, and depreciation are taken into account, per capita infrastructure investment diminished by an average of $70 per capita (i.e., without adjustment $269 and $288.75 per capita; with adjustments, these amounts were $207 and $210, for 2004–5 and 2005–6, respectively). Figure 10.5 shows provincial capital investment per capita with and without the adjustment for investment in capital assets. The substantial changes in the responsibilities of the Ministry of Finance and the emergence of the Ministry of Public Infrastructure Renewal in determining the province's infrastructure investment initially did not result in a substantial change in the proportional allocation fund towards the key areas of health care, school and post-secondary education, social services, environmental initiatives,

Figure 10.5 Capital investment per capita, 2000–2006

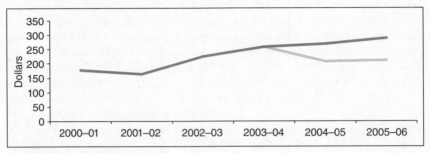

Source: Ontario budget papers.

resource, and economic development, and general government and justice. There were material changes made to the composition of expenditures within specific broad categories, such as transit infrastructure. Expenditures increased from $193 million in 2002–3 to $359 million in 2003–4, reaching $513 million by 2005–6. Similarly, there was a substantial increase in municipal and local infrastructure expenditures.

For the 2002–3 budget, the economic environment was supportive of the government's agenda, given overall economic growth, at 3 per cent, and relatively low unemployment, at just over 6 per cent. The Flaherty budget, entitled 'Responsible Choices,' utilized the construct that there were unlimited wants and limited resources. It was a statement of scarcity, choice, and trade-offs. For instance, Flaherty suggested that 'the people of Ontario know that government can only give them what the government has taken away from them through taxes in the first place.' He was most proud of the government's achievement of a balanced budget over three consecutive years, noting this had not been achieved in Ontario for the last one hundred years.

Flaherty's views on infrastructure investment depicted a minister concerned about the public good, economies of scale, externalities, and efficiency. It was under Flaherty that there would be a major consolidation of the trends in the thinking and best practices underlying government infrastructure management. The role of government in infrastructure was defined as that of a regulator and facilitator of infrastructure investment aimed at fostering private-sector involvement (i.e., consistent with the World Bank's views). The government looked externally for principles and best practices to guide its infrastructure decisions. For instance, the World Bank and the United States (e.g., the

US Transportation Equity Act) were quoted in illustrative examples supporting the government's infrastructure decisions. In addition, the government looked at best practices as well as the Canadian Institute of Chartered Accountants' views on the reporting of tangible capital assets to develop a framework for treating infrastructure expenditures. The CICA defined tangible capital assets as non-financial assets having physical substance that are acquired, constructed, or developed, and (1) are held for use in the production or supply of goods and services; (2) have useful lives extending beyond an accounting period and are intended to be used on a continuing basis; and (3) are not intended for sale in the ordinary course of operations.[29]

It was noted that the acceptable international accounting community principle for treating tangible capital assets was the historical cost/net book value method (book value being equal to the historical cost less depreciation). In contrast, the government's practice in 2000 involved expensing the full cost of tangible capital assets in the year of acquisition or construction. Once the construction was complete, the asset no longer appeared on the government's books; as a result, government tangible-capital-asset financing was complicated by budgetary shocks from unplanned future operating, maintenance, and replacement costs.

Ontario's infrastructure challenges included new technology and an aging population, depreciation, replacement, and repair costs, congestion and gridlock, technological intensity (e.g., Service Ontario kiosks, traffic monitoring cameras, computers in classrooms), and the composition of Ontario's infrastructure (e.g., bricks and mortar as opposed to technology).[30] The immediate drivers of Ontario's infrastructure needs, promoting its role in economic growth, were identified as population growth and urban centres. On the other hand, infrastructure was no longer viewed as an instrument or component of the government's social policy.

The Harris Government suggested that government action was appropriate when a natural monopoly (e.g., water and sewage), economies of scale, large capital outlay, and enforcement/control of billing were involved. Principles for infrastructure investment would include the beneficiary pays principle (e.g., toll roads such as Highway 407 in Toronto), unbundling to allow competition (e.g., in hydro-electric production), or a transfer of either operating or financial risk to the private sector.

For financial reporting, the Ontario Financial Review Commission would serve to define many of the reporting requirements and guidelines for Ontario's infrastructure and the Ontario SuperBuild Corporation.

The guidelines included the following: the corporation developing options for infrastructure investment to be considered by government; showing costs and the depreciation of existing assets; and adopting the Public Sector Accounting Board's standards in the reporting of tangible capital assets.

The Ontario SuperBuild Corporation, established in 1999, had its role clarified by 2001: it was now to act as a catalyst for the fostering of first-class infrastructure in Ontario for the twenty-first century. This theme would resonate in many of the subsequent Ontario budgets, even after 2005. The Ontario SuperBuild Corporation would become the key instrument for achieving the province's infrastructure objectives. The corporation's policy priorities reflected the thinking and best practices of the times regarding public infrastructure investment and administration. Based on the 2001 budget, these priorities were as follows: to increase the amount invested in infrastructure to accommodate growth; to bring and keep existing assets in good condition; to develop strategic policy for key infrastructure sectors; to undertake long-term capital planning, including 'wise' asset management and open financial reporting; to develop new and better ways of financing infrastructure, including public-private partnership and user-pay arrangements; and to advise the government on potential privatization.

The Ecker 2002 budget speech, putatively about 'values and choices,' was entitled 'Growth and Prosperity – Keeping the Promise.' The 'values' focused on were education and the environment, along with those values articulated in the Common Sense Revolution. The economic climate was supportive of the government's agenda given overall economic growth at 3 per cent and relatively low unemployment at just over 6 per cent. In this environment, total gross capital expenditure was set at $3.17 billion, representing a 17 per cent increase over the previous year's level.

Conclusion

There was an evolution in the way Treasury officials explained infrastructure expenditures. Allan viewed public infrastructure investment as key to the standard of living and betterment of the citizens of Ontario as well as a mechanism to provide the necessary facilities to promote employment and economic opportunities. By the late 1960s, MacNaughton would consider public infrastructure investment as a component of fiscal policy that could be used within a Keynesian economic framework to stabilize fluctuations in the province's economic activity. Infrastructure expenditures were part of the industrial and social policy of the provincial government. In the 1970s, fiscal policy and budgetary mechanisms became the dominant context for infrastructure expenditures. In the 1970s, the Treasury also moved to increase its fiscal policy coordination and leverage the government's financial capacity to undertake infrastructure expenditures.

The job of determining how infrastructure dollars would be spent was tossed around repeatedly over the last forty years, but the Treasury / Ministry of Finance played an important role, ensuring that the expenditures were made within a framework of fiscal and project management capacity. In the early 1960s, under James Allan, Treasury (assisted by the Department of Economics) was able to finance the province's infrastructure needs directly out of the government's purses. For instance, the government's expenditure of $48.8 million to support Ontario Hydro was paid for with general government revenues.

In the mid-1960s, to cope with the wide range of infrastructure needs of the province from transportation, to electricity, housing, and education, the government established specialized 'single purpose' corporations to oversee construction and maintenance. The government fuelled the capacity of these corporations, authorities, and commissions by making monetary infusions. In this respect, these agencies held monies outside of the consolidated revenue funds of government, yet represented multi-year commitment to initiatives. The government also permitted these agencies to borrow from government to the point where it leveraged its own borrowing capacity to provide them with cash.

In the mid-1970s, the rising cost of public debt convinced the Treasury that the government could not use its borrowing capacity to leverage capital on behalf of its agencies without limits. By 1978, it was recognized that the gap between the government pay-as-you-go approach (cash accounting) and the spread of capital costs over the productive life of the asset (accrual accounting) was growing far too wide. For instance, Ontario Hydro's debt of $14 billion in 1982 represented 40 per cent of the Ontario government's entire provincial direct and guaranteed funded debt.

In the early 1980s, Treasury developed a multi-purpose-agency approach to infrastructure expenditure, as opposed to having several single-purpose agencies. The establishment of the Board of Industrial Leadership and Development (BILD) represented such a multi-purpose agency. In 1985, the government wrote off the debt of numerous single-purpose agencies, such as the Ontario Universities Capital Aid Corporation, Ontario Housing Corporation, Ontario Development Corporation, Urban Transportation Development Corporation, and Ontario Energy Corporation. In total, $3.7 billion was written off and these single-purpose agencies closed.

As the 1980s wore on, Finance's role was diminished. It was the Management Board of Cabinet that emerged as the important coordinating body of multi-year capital investment for the province. This was particularly true for the hospital sector. Similarly, the Ministry of Municipal Affairs became an increasingly important player in Ontario infrastructure expenditure decisions by front-ending the financing of municipal capital expenditures. Later, the Treasury Board of Cabinet would replace the Management Board on the infrastructure portfolio.

In 1992, the government's desire to manage the consolidated revenue fund better as well as to improve the efficiency of its access to capital markets resulted in the formation of two 'super-agencies.' The establishment of Jobs Ontario Capital Fund and Loan-based Financing was responsible for financing a wide range of infrastructure projects, such as those associated with colleges, universities, schools, and hospitals. The establishment of the Ontario Transportation Capital Corporation, Ontario Realty Corporation, and Ontario Financing Authority furthered this trend. The Ontario Financing Authority, for instance, was responsible for a centralized approach to establishing financial arrangements and minimizing borrowing costs by avoiding duplication, improving coordination, and leveraging its bargaining power. On the other hand, the Ontario Transportation Capital Corporation became responsible for arranging the building of Highway 407 (super-fund and financing authority instruments).

The establishment of the Ontario SuperBuild Corporation, along with the SuperBuild Growth Fund, placed in one agency a broad range of infrastructure responsibilities, which included: to increase the amount invested in infrastructure to accommodate growth; to bring and keep existing assets in good condition; to develop strategic policy for key infrastructure sectors; to conduct long-term capital planning, including 'wise' asset management and open financial reporting; to develop new and better ways of financing infrastructure, including public-private partnership and user-pay arrangements; and to advise the government on potential privatization. Correspondingly, the Cabinet Committee on Privatization and SuperBuild, comprising six ministers, examined privatization and capital partnership. Its key decision was to sell Highway 407 for $3.1 billion in 1999 (in a 99-year lease arrangement), signalling an opening for the role of the private sector in provincial infrastructure arrangements.

On the policy side, the formation of the Ontario Ministry of Infrastructure was significant in that it was staffed to a significant degree by former Ministry of Finance officials. On the operational side, the formation of the Ontario Financing Authority and the Ontario Infrastructure Corporation would ensure follow-through. The Ontario Infrastructure Corporation aimed at fostering public-private partnerships, first in the hospital sector, but with the intent to examine the feasibility of extending the practice to a wide range of infrastructure investments aimed at meeting the public good. There might be a pendulum swing at work: the policy framework has been assumed increasingly by the Ministry of Energy and Infrastructure.

Treasury and Finance maintained the view that the role of infrastructure expenditures was to further the prosperity of the province. In addition, innovations in public-policy instruments were aimed at leveraging government's bargaining power in capital markets, promoting the efficient coordination of financial needs, enhancing capital-project risks management, and providing appropriate incentives to facilitate private-sector involvement in large-scale public sector–driven capital projects.

Many of the economic tools used in evaluating and developing fiscal and budgetary policy were established in the 1970s, including the Quantitative Tax Analysis or General Income Tax Analyzer (GITAN), the Planning Programming Budget System (PPBS), its Zero-Based Budget variant (ZBB), and econometric models. In the 1970s, the Ministry of Finance also moved to increase its fiscal policy coordination and leverage the government's financial capacity in conducting infrastructure expenditures. In the 1980s, the Ministry of Finance made attempts to improve financial management and the accountability of expenditures as well as to enhance the use of its capital-market access powers to leverage funds for provincial capital expenditures. It was in this period that the Board of Industrial Leadership and Development (BILD) would evolve and become a key instrument guiding capital expenditures over the decade. For the 1990s, the economic challenges faced by the province resulted in a strong linkage being made between job creation and capital expenditure decisions, as exhibited by the Jobs Ontario Capital Fund. The review of the ministry's role, within the context of the residual claim of the provincial government relative to municipal government and the private sector, resulted in devolution of some government activities (e.g., public housing). Nonetheless, the broad trend of the Ministry of Finance involved a further concentration of capital expenditure decisions within the framework of the ministry, as can be seen in the establishment of the SuperBuild Growth Fund in 1999, consisting of a $20 billion mandate for capital investment over a five-year period.

The vision of the ministers of finance has been a significant driver affecting the composition and level of capital expenditures in the province. This vision was bounded by the institutional framework of the Ministry of Finance, which aimed at balancing and aligning effective governance, efficient capital market assess, and prudent expenditure management in an environment that demands responsiveness to periodic economic shock, risk management compliance, and demographic pressures. In this complex environment, economic theory has played a significant role in defining the underlying premise of provincial infrastructure expenditures. The view of fiscal policy as an instrument for stabilizing economic fluctuations emerged from the Keynesian economic framework, and the definition of public capital stock as an intermediate input in production emerged from endogenous growth theory.[31]

In the 2000s, the concentration of policy and expenditure responsibilities for capital expenditures, within the governance framework of the Ministry of Finance that had developed over the previous four decades, became the catalyst for the establishment of an independent Ministry of Public Infrastructure Renewal. The new ministry's mandate was oriented towards meeting the infrastructure requirements of the province in the twenty-first century. The previous four decades also saw the tools promoting public infrastructure investment evolve (e.g., cash versus accrual accounting) and the policy instruments for implementing initiatives develop (e.g., public–private sector partnership, centralization or decentralization). From Allan in 1960 until the end of the Eves era of the 2000s, vision has competed with pragmatism in driving infrastructure expenditures aimed at achieving modernity and social betterment for the people of Ontario as well as Canada. The institutional changes at the Ministry of Finance, and its interaction with the Ministry of Public Infrastructure Renewal, will determine the course of future infrastructure policy in the province. Past and future innovation in the public policy instruments used to finance infrastructure development will continue to help determine how vision, policy, and economic imperatives are translated into action for the benefit of the people of Ontario in the years to come.

NOTES

1 I would like to thank Steven Wald for the use of his Ontario budget collection. In addition, I would like to thank Patrice Dutil, Carlyle Farrell, and Jean De Sousa for their review of the manuscript.
2 Infrastructure includes educational facilities, health care, roads and highways, rural electrification, public buildings, water and sewage, and regional rural development (see 1960 budget statement). Harry Kitchen in *A State of Disrepair: How to Fix the Financing of Municipal Infrastructure in Canada*, C.D. Howe Commentary no. 241 (2006) provides a useful definition of municipal infrastructure. It is worth noting that evaluations of infrastructure spending are complicated by a change in the accounting practices of the government of Ontario as it moved from cash accounting to accrual accounting over the period. The use of cash accounting between 1960 and 2000 suggests that capital disbursements may overstate the contribution to new capital formation, as a portion of these funds were used to maintain the productive life of existing assets. In contrast, accrual accounting addresses depreciations as well as contributions towards the productive life of the asset. The movement from the GAAP to PSA precipitated by the introduction of the Public Sector Accounting Board (PSAB) standards on tangible-capital-asset accounting (in 2002) has had a tremendous impact on the government capital expenditures, the institutional structures used to implement infrastructure projects (e.g., private- and public-sector partnerships) and the comparability of the public-sector capital expenditures between 1960 and 2005. This paper aims to provide an understanding of the demographic, economic, and socio-political factors affecting infrastructure expenditures on Ontario. Accounting principles and policies have also had a significant impact on these expenditures, but remain beyond the scope of this paper and represent an opportunity for future research.
3 The government's use of studies, commissions, and task forces as precursors to institutional change and public-policy instrument innovation is a theme that is repeated by nearly all ministers throughout the study period.
4 Between 1959 and 1975, there are two periods of significant growth in infrastructure expenditures (1965–7 and 1973–5) following periods of relatively stable expenditures levels. The underlying accounting system during this period was cash accounting. Hence, the periods of significant growth in expenditures represent a combination of new capital formation as well as repairs to maintain the productive life of existing capital stock. It should also be noted that no attempt is made in this chapter to establish a rigorous quantitative relationship between the key budget announcements of successive provincial governments and the trend observed in the actual level and

composition of infrastructure spending. Data limitation affected the analysis conducted in this study. For instance, the amount announced in any budget as infrastructure expenditures may not all be spent in the year announced and reported expenditures may be revised in later years. Furthermore, since 2001, there has been an attempt to record infrastructure expenditures (investments) on an accrual basis as opposed to on a cash basis.

5 1960 Budget Statement, 25.
6 1964 Budget Statement, 8.
7 1964 Budget Statement, 14.
8 1970 Budget Statement, 80.
9 See 1969 Budget Statement, 40, and 1970 Budget Statement, 31.
10 Ibid.
11 1972 Budget Statement, 5.
12 McKeough's focus on full employment was also seen in the introduction of the Municipal Employment Incentive Program and continued utilization of the Ontario Seasonal Employment program.
13 Budget Paper C, 1978, 10.
14 See Budget Paper C, 1978, 10–12.
15 The growth in program expenditures (e.g., health and social services) accounted for much of the significant drop in infrastructure expenditure's share of total spending.
16 See Budget Paper A, Budget Statement, 1981, 12.
17 1986 Budget Statement, 1.
18 The crowding-out effect implies that the incremental increase in capital financing costs (e.g., interest rates and constrained capital availability) to the private sector must be deducted from the rate of return to public capital investment.
19 The increase in funding for Ontario Hydro represented a reversal from McKeough's policies of the mid-1970s. In the Miller years, the key drivers of infrastructure expenditures included the provincial population and demographic changes, economic patterns and growth, urbanization and regional growth, the capital financing capacity of the province, and fiscal policy (e.g., anti-inflationary policy or counter-cyclical Keynesian policy). Miller's budgets tended to be counter-cyclical, while McKeough budgets were often pro-cyclical within a Keynesian context.
20 See Budget Paper C, 1982, 4.
21 Budget Paper B, 1982, 5.
22 Budget Paper C, 1982.
23 It is also worthwhile noting that the federal government initiative, the Community Services Contribution Program (CSCP), was established in

1978. By 1979, CSCP involved $400 million in expenditures for Ontario for water and sewerage projects and neighbourhood improvement.

24 Interestingly, the establishment of the information-technology infrastructure (e.g., fibre optics) was done primarily through the private sector (e.g., Bell and Rogers) as opposed to the public sector. This points to the capacity of the private sector to access capital markets through the use of its current and future stream income (i.e., capitalization/securitization).

25 Budget Paper E (1989) was particularly focused on municipal financing.

26 1987 Budget Statement, 1.

27 Kitchen and Slack, in a working paper entitled 'Trends in Public Finance in Canada' (2006), and Harry Kitchen, in 'Physical Infrastructure and Financing' (research paper prepared for the Panel on the Role of Government in Ontario, 2003) stress the need for the application of multi-year capital budgeting for infrastructure expenditures planning. In his *A State of Disrepair: How to Fix the Financing of Municipal Infrastructure in Canada* (C.D. Howe Commentary no. 241, December 2006) Kitchen suggests that bond financing, as opposed to pay-as-you-go financing, is likely more appropriate given the multi-year nature of these assets.

28 In 1998 the restructuring of the municipalities also resulted in the Toronto Transit Commission receiving $828 million.

29 Another definition suggested at the time by government for decision-making was 'economic capital,' meaning tangible capital assets that constitute public infrastructure regardless of their accounting classification or the source of funds.

30 Budget papers for the period suggest that several forces affected infrastructure decisions, including: (1) vision and role of government; (2) economic trends and policy, i.e., a movement from the betterment of Ontario to Ontario in the global economy; (3) demographics and social policy; (4) institutional and organizational change; (5) accounting and budgetary principles; (6) urbanization and regional growth; (7) expenditure drivers, e.g., (a) social welfare (including demographic drivers, etc.), (b) economic efficiency (includes productivity and employment drivers), (c) competitiveness (includes access to markets and shipment drivers), (d) threat management (e.g., flexible transportation systems), (e) environmental balance (public transit), and (f) maintenance and component failure (upkeep and public safety).

31 Private investment (I) shocks are often considered to be a significant source of economic fluctuation in the Keynesian framework. Public infrastructure (capital) investment can therefore be viewed as stabilizing total capital stock (Keynesian) and/or total capital per capita (neo-classical economics or endogenous growth theory) within the economy.

11 Guardians in Check: The Impact of Health Care on the Ontario Budget, 1960–2004

PATRICE DUTIL[1]

Whenever you touch the health-care system, people get very upset.

Floyd Laughren[2]

Wisely, guardians do not buy the assertions of priority setters that because health is dominant all new money should and will go there and nowhere else.

Janice MacKinnon, Saskatchewan Minister of Finance (1993–7)[3]

At the height of his career, Aaron Wildavsky, the undisputed American dean of public-sector financial management studies, published an article in *Canadian Public Administration* on the topic of 'spending limits' in American and Canadian budgeting.[4] Voicing his frustration with the inability of governments to curb spending, Wildavsky probed both systems for clues as to why public sectors in both countries proved unable to withstand the demands on the public purse. In his vain search for an explanation, he examined a number of factors, ranging from efforts to install program-based budgeting systems to political inertia. Twenty-five years later, and fifteen years after his death and the coincident drive in Canada and in the United States to successfully cut spending, the weaknesses in Wildavsky's model are starting to show.

It is incontestable that Wildavsky changed the way scholars looked at the budget-making process. First, he cast a new light on the drama and importance of budget making, bringing to life what appeared to be drab, insignificant processes. Second, he dwelled on a point that all practitioners took for granted: that the budget only changes incrementally in ordinary time. Indeed, he practically taught students of public administration to measure 'ordinary time' by examining budgets. Finally, he gave his actors almost cinematic names: on one side were the 'spenders' – most of the people in government, as a matter of fact. Facing them were the 'guardians' – typically the public servants who animated the Ministry of Finance. Wildavsky created a model that demanded tinkering and testing and in the process attracted the interest of many fine Canadian scholars. In his *The Politics of Public Spending in Canada* Donald Savoie documented in fine detail the intuitions Wildavsky had revealed in his 1983 article in *CPA*. Writing fifteen years later, David Good's *Politics of Public Money* added more players on the Wildavskian stage: priority setters and financial watchdogs.

Wildavsky and his followers produced insightful portraits of the budget-making process. Based on private interviews with key players, they probed behaviours and spotted strategies. But by focusing on comportment in narrow time frames scholars run the danger that some fiscal realities will escape their notice. The framework that depends on 'spenders,' 'guardians,' 'priority setters,' and 'financial watchdogs' too often diverts its attention from where the money is actually going. They all pointed out that while 'spenders' vastly outnumbered 'guardians,' the guardians could withstand a great deal of enemy fire. They also all implied that there was evenness among the spenders, that with some exceptions, spenders roughly competed with each other on a same footing for additional dollars.

The evolution of the budget in Ontario – particularly if seen through a wider lens of time – forces a different perspective on the model and reveals an even more dynamic system. Over the forty years examined in this paper, the budget of Ontario has changed dramatically. Spenders have assumed different proportions, and the guardians have had to pick their fights. In Ontario, the budget was transformed by the revolution of health care. This phenomenon – where the state assumes the responsibility of not only providing universal insurance but of managing the health care infrastructure – transformed budget making by implicitly creating a new rule: all spenders can come to the table, but only after Health Care will be sated. The consequence of this first 'iron rule' points to a significant reality in Ontario's budget making, namely, that health care is the first priority and that in the face of this truth premiers of all stripes and the decision makers in the ministry of treasury/finance over two generations have been powerless.

The guardians, in this case, have been helpless. Disarmed by 'priority setters' who responded to the public will, health care has grown from a marginal concern of the government of Ontario to its prime occupation. In 1959, health care expenditures in Ontario constituted 5 per cent of the province's budget. By 2003 (a date chosen for a few reasons described below), health care had grown to assume 41.25 per cent of the budget.

This reality reveals other iron rules of budget making in the province over the past forty-odd years: that regardless of economic conditions, the general budget will grow faster than inflation, that a big part of that reality can be explained by the fact that health care expenditures (which run at a higher rate of inflation consistently) keep growing, and that, finally, health care expenditures continually assume a larger share of the government's budget.[5] These certainties helped to shape the behaviour of the ministry of finance.

The evolution of this reality has been assumed, but has not been documented or explained. It has instead become part of the fabric of the province's politics and culture. This critical budget issue has touched every Ontarian's life, from the richest to the poorest. It has driven the political fortunes of premiers, given a heart attack to a minister of health, directly caused the downfall of one flamboyant minister of finance, and frustrated all of them. Remarkably, the issue has not been the subject of great commissions or of collective declarations. Instead, it has simply kept its inexorable motion as it consumed more of the province's treasury. The evolving importance of health care expenditures also allows for a reinterpretation of the Ministry of Finance's role in managing its greatest expenditure and puts into a different light its putative role as 'guardian.' In the face of this voracious consumer of public funds, one is led to conclude that the guardian was forced by one spender to change its behaviour. One scholar has concluded that in this regard, the Ministry of Finance actually became a spender itself.[6] This is true, but the rising cost of health care also forced another behaviour: Finance would have to assume an even greater role as guardian in the face of *all the other spenders* in order to supply enough money for health care expenditures. All the attempts to control budget expenditures – from planning programming budget systems to expenditure managing systems – simply failed in terms of health care. Successive ministers of finance have lamented this reality, and many have pointed to a variety of factors from the obvious ones, such as the aging of the population, to declining federal contributions. All of them have been very creative in selecting time frames to bolster their claims and to blame their predecessors. To document the evolution, two sources were primarily used: budget documents (which are forward-looking), to illustrate the views of the succeeding governments, and the government's public accounts (which provide audited numbers). Invariably, there is a discrepancy that shows that health care expenditures are very difficult to predict and that budget execution in terms of health care has been less than disciplined. This being said, this chapter is not about budget efficiency. It aims instead to document how ministers and officials have experienced the incremental growth of health care in Ontario over the longer duration and to explore how they have reacted to it.

Following the Saskatchewan example, the idea of a health insurance scheme for Ontarians was first articulated by the CCF (the official opposition in Ontario from 1948 to 1951) as a hospital insurance program. In the 1951 election, the idea was also passionately promoted by Liberal leader Walter Thomson.[7] In 1954, the Leslie Frost government commissioned Malcolm Taylor, the young University of Toronto political scientist who had focused his PhD dissertation at Berkeley (1948) on the Saskatchewan Hospital Services Plan, to examine the insurance system in the province and how hospital insurance could be improved. Taylor actually had an office in the Frost Building, next to George Gathercole, the deputy minister of Economics.[8] Taylor, who had been an adviser to the Saskatchewan government and would later act as director of research for the Hall Commission that called for a universal medical insurance plan, confirmed many hunches: the system was not adequate. Although 66 per cent of Ontarians had some sort of insurance coverage, according to Taylor, there were not enough beds in the hospitals, the cost of hospital stays was growing dramatically, and the few provincial and municipal grants were not making up for the costs.[9]

Ontario was spending money in health care before those years on hospitals, public health programs, and asylums for the mentally disabled, but it was telling that in the period 1943–62, the province spent a total of $2,186,762,710 on education. Highways and roads had consumed $1,596,200,411 and health 1,085,553,037.[10] Ontario was spending on children and universities, and building its infrastructure. Health care was lower priority.

Ontario introduced its Hospital Insurance Plan in January 1959, and created a Hospital Services Commission to carry out extensive studies of hospital usage in the province and articulate standards of care. Under this insurance scheme, a single person would pay just over $25 a year, while a family could be covered with contributions of just over $50. Ontarians responded, and within a year the province spent $77 million on its new hospital insurance scheme.

The program proved popular: by the end of 1960, 95 per cent of the population was enrolled and covered. In 1960–1, Ontario citizens were paying $82.5 million in premiums for a system that was costing $246 million. Ottawa was contributing $87.1 million, and various revenues ranging from 'miscellaneous income' to laboratory fees contributed $76.9 million. The remaining $500,000 was absorbed by the general treasury. In other words, the system was balanced, with contributions from Ontarians, the federal government, government services, and the Treasury itself.

The equilibrium was soon upset. Expenditures in the Department of Health increased again by $40.3 million in 1961–2 due to an increase in capital spending. The Province's contribution to the Ontario Hospital Care Insurance Plan (OHCIP), moreover, was significantly affected. It went from $18 million in 1960–1 to $50 million in 1961–2, a $32 million (or 178 per cent) increase. This amount, according to the budget statement, did not include the cost of administration of the OHCIP. 'In order that everyone may understand the astronomical rise in the cost of Ontario's hospital and health services,' the Treasurer candidly said.

> I am including here a statement comparing the expenditures being made on Ontario's hospital and health services. We in Ontario … have been faced with rising hospital costs. Last year these costs increased by 20 per cent, an experience common to virtually all Canadian provinces. Such increases arise from a variety of causes as discussed in the Committee on Health. It should be pointed out that salaries and wages represent 70 per cent of the new operations costs of all public general hospitals and these have risen by 52.5 per cent in the last three years alone. Neither present Federal-provincial contributions nor the revenue from hospital insurance premiums at present rates are sufficient to finance these rising costs.[11]

The health insurance scheme had barely taken its first steps and already expenses defied expectations. In its budget statement for the new fiscal year 1962–3, the Ministry of Finance pointed to new challenges and breakthroughs. It described the treatment of the baby victims of thalidomide (a drug taken by expectant mothers that sometimes deformed the limbs of their fetus) and pointed to impressive successes in combating tuberculosis. Mental-health expenditures alone were expected to total $58.9 million, an increase of $4.9 million over the previous year. 'As one problem is overcome, another arises; it is our aim to keep abreast of these new challenges,' said the Budget Statement for 1962–3.[12]

In 1964–5, the Ontario government added a number of services to its menu of covered benefits: radiotherapy for the treatment of cancer for outpatients, physiotherapy, occupational therapy, and speech therapy. Not surprisingly, the treasurer reported that OHCIP costs had already doubled from the program's inception five years before, amounting to $320.6 million. At the end of 1963, 98.1 per cent of the growing population of Ontario was covered under the plan. The treasurer also noted a 'general increase in hospital utilization.' Costs were spiralling upwards, according to the Budget Statements: 'As new hospital beds and facilities become available, they are immediately put into service. In keeping with all other components of daily living, the per diem costs of hospital care have risen, mainly because hospital salaries have now reached a level that is more in keeping with rates of pay in other fields.'[13] In light of the growth of expenses, the province would inject another $50 million. Noting the growing demand and the extension of services, however, it passed down the cost of the increase to the citizen. Effective 1 July 1964, OHCIP premiums were raised to $3.25 per person per month and $6.50 for a family. The health budget in 1964–5 would consume 11.6 per cent of the Ontario budget, still much less than highways and roads, at 23 per cent, and far less than education, which would consume 31.6 per cent of the budget.

Health insurance grew very popular in John Robarts's Ontario as Emmett Hall's Royal Commission on Health Services toured the country to investigate the health needs of Canadians. In 1964 the commission recommended the Canada-wide adoption of the public insurance system for health care that had been pioneered in Saskatchewan. In Ontario, 99.2 per cent of the population was already covered under the hospital insurance program, but the Robarts cabinet could easily see that its reputation and popularity would grow by paying more attention (and money) to this file.

Inspired by the Hall report, the province launched its new Medical Services Insurance Plan (MSIP) on 1 April 1966. It was anticipated that health care expenditures would double in order for the province to provide for the new services. Under the new plan, the MSIP would be available to all residents of Ontario, and be automatically extended to those receiving welfare payments. Low-income individuals and families could apply for reduced premiums. In addition, dependents up to the age of twenty-one and attending school could be included in the family rates. In terms of sourcing the money, the government arranged for $50 million of the MSIP to be administered by the Department of

Health; another $8.9 million would be delivered by the Department of Public Welfare. Total expenditures (including hospital costs, capital expenditures, etc.) of the Department of Health would top $244.1 million, an increase of $75.8 million over the estimated net expenditures of 1965–6, a 45 per cent increase.[14] Health care costs were now expected to eat up 13.5 per cent of the annual Ontario budget.

The Hall report had a formidable impact on Charles MacNaughton, the treasurer. 'The Ontario Government is vitally interested in improving the well-being of every person and every family in this province,' the Budget Statement of 1967–8 declared.[15] This time, $311 million would be allocated for health expenditures, representing yet another increase of 32 per cent over the previous year. It is worth noting the degree to which the Robarts government was concerned with mental health. In that year, a new Mental Health Act was passed, and spending for mental health was given a boost of $16 million. Ontario was now spending almost one-third ($100 million) of its health budget on the treatment of psychiatric diseases. In addition, the Ontario Hospital Insurance Plan would get an injection of $40 million in 1967–8 (the first increase since 1964, since previous growth was paid for with increased premiums), bringing the overall *government* contribution to $90 million in that year.

By 1967–8, the cost of funding hospital insurance had exceeded $500 million, again up 20 per cent from the year before. Costs for the Ontario Medical Services Insurance Plan (OMSIP) were also reported to have risen substantially, mostly because of the inflating fee structure of Ontario physicians, but also because of the addition of more out-patient benefits (including eye examinations) and the steady expansion of the population. Within a year, costs for OMSIP alone would climb to $129 million, adding pressure to the provincial purse. In 1968–9, $78 million would be required to support the hospital plan and $27 million to subsidize OMSIP.[16] The government raised the premiums that year in order to 'more closely reflect the true cost of operating these plans.' They were increased to $5.50 per person per month, and $11.00 for families as the government announced that more increases were planned for the next two years. The new premiums were expected to contribute $157.5 million in 1969–70 and $309.6 million in 1970–1, but expenses on insured services grew dramatically to $571.96 million in 1969–70 from $394.87 million in 1968–9.[17]

Government was able to control spending to a certain degree. Total spending on health care actually declined in 1969–70 as a result of a reduction in construction grants for hospitals, and because of a reduction in the government's contribution to the Ontario Hospital Care Insurance Program. It was, in the words of the 1970 budget, 'a policy of severe and deliberate expenditure restraint.'[18] All the same, health care expenditures now constituted 16 per cent of the total budget.

Part of the help also came from Ottawa. Responding to the Hall report in 1966, the Government of Canada offered to pay half the cost of medical care if the provinces agreed to a number of conditions. The Medical Care Act required that the provinces offer 'public administration' of the medical plans as well as universal and comprehensive coverage. Ottawa was willing to pay for half of the cost of health insurance, so long as it was portable, comprehensive, run by the state, and universal. Ontario, however, refused to participate in the federal program. 'The decision by Ottawa to force the introduction of medicate at a time when all governments know what the financial future is going to be seems to us, therefore, ill-considered and irresponsible,' declared the Minister of Finance Charles MacNaughton. 'What guarantee have we that, in a few years from now, the federal government will not dump the full responsibility for this program on the provinces, and close off or limit its contributions after it has obliged the provinces to embark on this slippery slope?'[19] The premier himself, reading from a text prepared by senior officials in the Treasury, spared no words: 'We object very strenuously to the use of the federal spending power to really alter the Constitution ... Medicare is a glowing example, a Machiavellian scheme ... one of the greatest political frauds that has been perpetrated on the people of this country.'[20]

Another minister of finance would later complain that 'the federal government chose to lever Ontario into Medicare against its own better judgment.'[21] That position, however, was costly for the province: Ontario was losing out on an estimated $175 million per year, and simply could no longer afford to decline Ottawa's dollars. Provincial legislation to authorize new arrangements was passed in June 1969.[22] The impact on the budget was dramatic. With Ottawa willing to match, dollar for dollar, provincial expenditures in the area, expenditures rocketed upwards in terms of the overall budget, matching the moneys spent by the Ministry of Education, Colleges and Universities for the first time in 1970–1.[23]

Pressures were brought to bear on the Ministry of Health to try to control the relentless growth of expenditures. In an effort to streamline operations and improve accountability, the government consolidated the hospital and health services insurance plans in 1972. It also disbanded the Hospitals Services Commission and made hospitals directly accountable to the Ministry of Health 'to get a better handle on what seemed to be uncontrolled grown in hospital spending.' In the 1972–3 budget, the only increase was allowed in health and welfare, and most of that increase of $137 million (or 13.3 per cent) was to cover what the government called 'new programs for nursing and home care benefits and increased hospital operating costs.'[24] The ministry also initiated policy work on adopting a more local model of health governance that would eventually lead to the creation of the first District Health Councils. The idea was to give DHCs a mandate to do long-range planning for a given region's medical needs, including hospital beds and new programs, and to develop a list of spending priorities.

To complicate matters, the government was receiving significantly less money from premiums in 1971–2 (a decline of $53 million) as a number of Ontarians could not afford them. Indeed, by 1973–4, health premiums were contributing 7 per cent of the provincial revenue.[25] The 1975 budget document included a discussion of galloping health care costs and noted a cooling of Ottawa's commitments. In reaction to the federal government's budget that year, the Government of Ontario offered a new deal. It would assume complete responsibility for all health care programs in exchange for 17 points of personal income tax.[26]

The following year, the budget documents identified for the first time 'the problem of escalating costs' and a 'Health Financing Gap.' Noting that expenditure on insured health services had more than doubled from 1970 to 1975, the statement concluded that the 'health insurance plan has consumed a rapidly growing share of the Government tax revenues and created an ever increasing drain on the province's economic resources.'[27] It detailed the reasons for the increase, including wage hikes for nurses and hospital staff, rates of service utilization, and reduced revenue from the federal government. According to government documents, premiums covered 44 per cent of costs in 1970–1. By 1975–6, premiums covered only 23 per cent of costs, leaving a shortfall of $788 million to be made up from the general revenues of the province.[28] At this point, 20 per cent of the population was no longer contributing to OHIP covered because of age or income. Most of the revenue – $459 million of $564 million – came from employers. To compensate for the loss, the government increased OHIP premiums by $5 per month for single persons and $10 per month for families effective 1 May 1976. It was estimated this would generate $790 million in revenue, an increase of $228 million per year, but still only 28 per cent of the per capita cost of insured services for that year. In 1976, health care costs amounted to 28 per cent of expenditures, while education cost 26 per cent. Health Minister Frank Miller was mandated to close small community hospitals, and the ministry did identify ten likely candidates. Angry protests forced the minister to back down, however. The stress this caused him was directly blamed for a mild heart attack.

Darcy McKeough, the minister of finance, noted that 'the utilization rate is a serious problem – in Ontario medical visits per person are 20 per cent higher than they were four years ago, and the rate of hospital admission is now growing at double the rate of population increases.' McKeough blamed the principle of universal medicare and its 'built-in price incentive for people to seek frequent medical attention' and 'the high doctor-to-population ratio.'[29] Expenditures were expected to grow by 14.5 per cent in 1976–7 and 9.2 per cent in 1977–8.[30]

To complicate matters, Ottawa simultaneously reviewed its contribution to health. As provinces responded to the growing demand for health services, Ottawa soon found itself unable to anticipate its yearly bills, and moreover felt its important contribution was insufficiently visible. In 1977 it took a new approach: it replaced its shared-cost programs for health and post-secondary education and combined these into a single unconditional block fund called Established Programs Financing. Under this new plan, a province was no longer required to demonstrate that the federal funds were spent on health or post-secondary education. Simultaneously, it reduced its tax bite on personal income by 13.5 per cent, and allowed the provinces to increase their bite by an equivalent amount. Darcy McKeough was satisfied: 'The federal government won its basic objectives of greater control and certainly over its financial outlays; the provinces gained greater flexibility in the design and administration of their health and post-secondary education programs, something they have sought for a long time.'[31]

The Bill Davis government decided to take more steps to resolve the problem of financing. A few weeks into the fiscal year 1977–8, it appointed a small committee of senior public servants and Ontario Medical Association (OMA) executives chaired by Allyn Taylor to 'recommend cost control possibilities in the health care field where expectations and mounting expenditures are outstripping resources.'[32] Taylor – the chairman of Canada Trust – was the only outsider on this committee of experts. Representing the government were Rendall Dick, the deputy minister of Treasury, Economics and Intergovernmental Affairs,

J.G. Parr, the deputy minister of Colleges and Universities, and Boyd Suttie, the assistant deputy minister of Community Health Services in the Ministry of Health (in other words, the biggest spenders in the government). They were joined by three key directors of the OMA, the organization that represented physicians: A.K. Gillies, the executive director, R.S.H. Twidle, the honorary treasurer, and William Vail, a general surgeon and vice-president. The committee first met in July 1977 and submitted its report right after Christmas that year.

The committee heard from a variety of experts representing professional associations, institutional associations, educational institutions, volunteer organizations, consumer associations, and a few district health councils. The introduction of its final report made a revealing observation that gave a hint about where it sought inspiration:

> Ontario's health care system is firmly in place and no single massive move will redesign it. As Peter Drucker has said, the moment government undertakes anything it becomes entrenched and permanent. Therefore, the battle must consist of a series of unspectacular skirmishes on four front – users, providers, institutions and government – with the hope that the result will be containment of costs in balance with the resources available.[33]

The committee came to two key conclusions that would guide its recommendations: first, that the health care system was rife with 'misuse of facilities, duplication and waste'; and second, that solving this problem would be difficult, for 'the various components of the health care delivery system are highly interdependent and there is danger in attempting specific correction in one area for fear of creating new inequity or new imbalance in the other.'

The committee proposed twenty reforms to contain the costs triggered by the users, the providers, the institutions, and the government. Revenue had to increase, which meant that the users had to pay more. They should pay higher OHIP premiums, be charged a 'substantial amount' for the first day of each hospital admission (up to a maximum of two days per year), and that a daily fee be levied for chronic hospital care after a three-month stay. It also recommended that those categories of the population not paying OHIP premiums be asked to contribute. To satisfy doctors who complained that their revenues were being limited, the committee recommended that 'balance billing' be introduced: in other words, that physicians be allowed to extra-bill charge their patients for services above the fee schedule even if they operated under the OHIP system (only physicians who had opted out of the OHIP system could bill their patients directly). Finally, it proposed that the system reduce its expenditures: that the existing list of insured services be trimmed, that access to the Drug Benefit Plan be limited, and that constraints be placed on the introduction of new technologies.

To further control costs, the committee advised that medical school enrolment be reduced, and that outpatient surgeries be promoted. Furthermore, the government was tasked with undertaking a thorough review of its relationship with hospitals to reduce red tape. Finally, the committee recommended that the District Health Council program be moved out of its pilot stage so that local authorities across Ontario might be in a better position to gauge needs and manage expectations. The august composition of this committee of experts notwithstanding, the minority Davis government chose to wait until its next budget to act.

On 7 March 1978, in his budget speech, McKeough declared that 'the control of health costs continues to be a high priority' and proposed a dramatic 37.5 per cent increase in OHIP premiums. (This represented an increase of $6 per month per person, for a total payment of $22 or $264 per year, while families would pay an additional $12 per month for a total of $44 or $528 per year.) Intended to generate an additional $271 million, the premiums would cover one-third of the costs of services.[34] Health care was allocated an additional $276 million, an increase of 8.1 per cent.[35]

Ontario, Alberta, and British Columbia (and to a certain extent Quebec, in which employees and employers co-paid the premium) were the only provinces collecting premiums. McKeough argued that the increase was necessary because the 'financing of health costs continues to be unbalanced' and because health care premiums had to 'retain a visible link with the services.' 'Consequently,' he concluded, 'I am proposing to increase OHIP premiums to restore the balance in financing.'[36]

For the treasurer, the situation demanded immediate action. A week after his budget speech, Darcy McKeough told the Toronto Association of Business Economists that Ontario health costs were likely to rise again by 8.1 per cent in the new fiscal year.[37] The Opposition saw things differently, and resisted the idea that premiums be used to pay for the cost increases. With McKeough's plan, OHIP premiums would have doubled since 1976. The *Globe and Mail* observed that low-income earners would actually be paying more in OHIP premiums than in income tax to both the federal government and the province.[38]

The reaction was swift. The Social Development Committee of the Ontario legislature was the first to embarrass the government. Apparently, the Ministry of Health documents that had been given to the committee were visibly incomplete. Amidst accusations that his office was deliberately concealing evidence produced by his own ministry, Dennis Timbrell produced the missing pages of the briefing note. The revelations were embarrassing to the minister. According to the ministry briefing notes, 'The premium system is of limited effectiveness in raising consumer cost awareness ... Moreover, it is recognized that the premium system is expensive to administer, and is regressive in comparisons with income taxation.'[39] While Timbrell protested that he had no intention of misleading the committee, and that the government had the right to take its own counsel, the minister was subjected to repeated calls for his resignation.

The Opposition did not hesitate to threaten to defeat the minority government if it pursued this approach, and by the end of April a compromise was reached. OHIP premiums would be increased by 18.75 per cent – $3 per person or $19 a month and $6 per family or $38 a month – half of what the minister of finance had proposed. The resulting loss in revenues was calculated at $145 million. To make that up, the government committed to find $73 million in cuts elsewhere – the Ontario Development Corporation's loan program, the Ontario Housing Corporation, highway construction, university capital fund projects, and the Northern Regional Priority Program were declared major targets – and increased the corporate income tax rate by 1 per cent.[40]

The minister of finance sensed he had lost credibility. 'I'm satisfied today that my goals are intact and in place,' McKeough said. 'My principles are intact ... I don't feel limp or weakened,' he told the media. 'I neither feel strengthened by this experience nor weakened. Obviously it's been interesting. There are a number of things you learn, some of which I may have controlled better or explained better and some of which I didn't. I know a couple of areas where we could have done a better job, certainly ... of explaining what we were up to.'[41] McKeough quit his post a few months later, and left politics altogether. Health care had claimed its first political victim. Frank Miller, a former minister of health, assumed the mantle of finance.

As a compromise, the Davis government also agreed to create a Select Committee on Health Care Financing and Costs, chaired by Dr Robert Elgie, the MPP for York East. Elgie was soon after made minister of labour and was replaced by Bruce McCaffrey, the MPP for Armourdale.

Like the committee of experts the year before, the select committee was tasked with reviewing Ontario's health care costs, health care financing methods, and alternative methods of financing the health care system. The committee held twenty-one days of hearings and heard from ninety-four witnesses during the summer of 1978, and submitted its report that fall.

In trying to understand what accounted for the growth of expenses, the select committee's report cited a study by Professor Robert Evans that categorized the sources of rising medical costs. As one of the key factors from the 1950s to 1977, for instance, the growth in costs was directly attributed to increases in physician incomes and in the number of physicians in the province. The growth in hospital costs, for its part, was simply attributed to growth in utilization. In its forty-eight-page report, the committee recommended that the premium system be allowed to continue, but that the subsidy mechanism be revised so that citizens who were entitled to receive premium assistance received it. It also recommended that 'any increase in personal income taxes during the current economic period should be regarded as both ill-advised and inconsistent with the public welfare.'[42]

In his address to the select committee Frank Miller argued against removing the health insurance premiums (something both the NDP and the Liberal Party advocated), noting that premiums provided $1 billion, or about 8 per cent of budgetary revenue. They covered almost 30 per cent of the money spent on insured health services and about 25 per cent of the entire Ministry of Health budget.[43]

A few months later, Miller delivered his own first budget speech and insisted that the government would be better able to keep expenses in check. In the early 1970s, he observed, the cost of providing insured health services escalated at an average annual average of 15 per cent. In the three years after 1976, this rate of increase had been held to an average of 8 per cent.[44] In terms of broader spending, health care was growing a little more slowly, moving from 27 per cent of the budget in 1975 to 28.7 per cent in 1981.

The government had to continue to raise revenue through the health care premiums, Miller noted, but he used a new argument. 'Since 1959 the annual compound growth rate of our gross provincial product has been 10.3 per cent ... while the hospitals budget has increased 14 per cent annually on the same basis. Looking at it another way, since 1959, our gross provincial product has increased 539 per cent. In the same time period, our expenditures on hospitals alone increased by 1,108 per cent.'[45]

The government had to be creative in raising more money. It was hoped that the federal government would invest some of the funds it had gathered from its Lotto Canada operations in Ontario hospital construction projects, but those were dashed.[46] To make matters worse, OHIP fees paid to doctors went up 14.75 per cent in 1981, simply based on volume. To help control costs, the OMA and the province signed a five-year fee schedule agreement in 1982 that included ten-stage increases, starting with a first hike in 1982. To raise revenue, premiums were increased in 1980 by $1 per person and $2 per family and were again increased in 1981 by $3 per month for single persons (to $23 per month) and $6 (to $46 per month) for families. There was to be another increase of $4 per persons and $8 for families in October 1982. Despite the increases, OHIP premiums were now covering less than 20 per cent of health care costs, a drop of another 10 per cent in five years.[47]

Desperate to control costs, the government again turned its attention to the system's ability to live within its means. In 1983 Larry Grossman, the health minister, launched the BOND (Business-Oriented New Directions) program for hospitals in the hope that administrators would learn to see their enterprises as businesses. The Ministry of Health would allow hospitals to keep any surplus their activities could generate – encouraging them to go beyond recovery costs in the way they managed their public areas (parking lots, shops, cafeterias, etc.). Grossman would soon change jobs, replacing the retiring Frank Miller and moving, like his predecessor, from Health to Finance. He wasted no time in assigning blame. At a meeting of ministers of finance in December 1983 he pointed his finger at Ottawa, noting that 'the federal share of health care spending had dropped off sharply in recent years.' He observed that 'in 1979 the federal government still paid 49 per cent of health care costs in Ontario. In less than four years, it was paying 41 per cent. In terms of actual cash payments the federal share has fallen from 29 per cent sent in 1979–80 to 24 per cent in 1983–84.'[48]

The BOND initiative proved to be of limited impact. In the budget for 1983–4, the treasurer declared that 32 per cent of the Ontario expenditure budget was now allocated to health care. In 1983 alone, health care expenditures increased by $800 million, compelling the government to increase OHIP premiums by almost 5 per cent. The extra $1.40 per person per month and $2.80 for families would contribute an additional $69 million. 'I believe there should be a clear and continuing link between premiums and the cost of health care,' stated Minister of Finance Grossman, echoing his predecessors.[49] He pointed to the fact that the reductions in federal financial commitments to the provinces were creating 'increasing cost pressures on the system' even as the population was growing older. Grossman hoped that Ottawa would engage 'to reexamine the mechanisms we have in place to pay for health and social services for the elderly.' He articulated the idea of introducing a special weighting into the federal Established Programs Financing (EPF) formula to reflect the impact of an aging population on the health care system so as to give the provinces 'the financial means to adjust their systems in line with the realities of the changing needs of their people.'[50]

The defeat of the Progressive Conservative government led by Frank Miller in 1985 changed the situation in terms of funding trends. The first budget presented by Robert Nixon of the Liberals committed to an increase of 8.3 per cent in funding for the operations of hospitals. In October 1985 the province lost its Triple A rating, largely as a result of the decision to raise the deficit in order to provide more money for hospitals and schools. The following year, the Liberal government committed an additional $850 million for hospital expansion, the first time since the mid-1960s that hospitals had received such an increase in building funds. It also provided reductions in OHIP premiums ranging from 25 per cent to 75 per cent for low-income individuals and families and announced that extra-billing by doctors would no longer be allowed.

Ontario estimated that it would lose $16 million, but still expected to collect $1,653 million from OHIP premiums. At the same time, payments to physicians and practitioners grew by $65 million, payments to discharge hospital bridge financing by $126 million, and the Drug Benefit Plan by $41 million.[51] By 1987, the health care budget had passed the $11 billion mark, amounting to $1200 per person, while the government simultaneously reduced the number of Ontarians who paid OHIP premiums by an estimated 40,000 people. It was now becoming even more difficult to estimate health costs. OHIP premiums accounted for 5 per cent of the budget, while health care constituted 32 per cent of expenditures. In fact, the treasurer reported in mid-year that the Ministry of Health required an additional $370 million, the insurance plan and the drug benefit plan a further $181 million, and hospitals an additional $84 million. All the same, the government embarked on a campaign to start reducing hospital beds – something the Davis government, despite its best intentions – was unable to do. It also sought advice as Dr John Evans, a former leading Liberal Party member and former president of the University of Toronto. He was asked to head an 'Ontario Health Review Panel' in the fall of 1986 and submitted his report in June 1987. There was no salient breakthrough in its recommendations, except to propose that a 'Premier's Council' be established to thoroughly investigate the situation.

As the number of claims for services increased from 57 million in 1977–8 to an estimated 94 million in 1987–8, revenues were declining on a number of fronts. Ottawa was contributing less and less. In 1979–80, its EPF contributed 51.8 per cent of Ontario's funding. By 1987–8, it was contributing 39.3 per cent. OHIP premium rates, frozen since 1984, made funding for health services all the more dependent on the general treasury. Meanwhile, the Ministry of Health was estimating that it would spend $1.2 billion more on health care in the following year:

> Expenditures for OHIP payments to physicians and other practitioners have quadrupled, from $.9 B in 1977 to $3.6 B in 1987–88. Annual percentage increases in OHIP expenditures have fluctuated in a range from 9.7 per cent recorded in 1979–80 to a high of 19.7 per cent in 1982–83, averaging 15 per cent over the period as a whole. On a per capita basis, OHIP expenditures rose from $108 to $391, an average annual rate of 13.8 per cent over the period. More recently, for the period from 1981–82 to 1986–87, OHIP expenditures grew from $1.5 B to $3.2 B, representing an average annual rate of increase of 15.5 per cent.[52]

The treasurer noted that the health care tax bill would amount to $12.7 billion, over $2.1 billion more than the total yield from Ontario's personal income tax, and constituting 33.2 per cent of government expenditures. Robert Nixon's Ministry of Finance used bolder language than previous administrations. 'If health care costs continue to escalate at rates experienced in the recent past, other social and economic priorities will be placed at risk,' Nixon noted.[53] In 1987–8, an additional $198 million 'for increased utilization of insured services and for negotiated adjustments to the physicians' schedule of benefits' was budgeted. Desperate for money, the minister of finance announced in his budget speech of 1988 that the government would introduce legislation to let some lottery proceeds go to hospitals (lottery profits were projected at $465 million for that year).

In response to the increasing pressures brought about by the health sector, the Peterson government decided to study the issue more intensely. It established a Premier's Council on Health Strategy, as proposed by Evans, a Hospital Operational Review, and a Joint Task Force on the Use and Provision of Medical Services with the Ontario Medical Association. In addition, the MOH undertook its own review of the drug benefit program as well as the home care program.

Early in 1988, the Ministry of Health reviewed the operations of twenty-three hospitals and found a catalogue of management difficulties that, in one way or another, accounted for growing costs. Issues as broad as 'difficulties in coping with an aging population' and 'difficulties in coping with rising costs of medical services and technology' were added to important policy and incentive issues. Nine hospitals reported that they had created or added new programs to their services 'beyond' MOH approval.[54] Responding to a query in question period, the minister of health, Elinor Caplan, pointed out that 'over the past three years – in fact, since the 1984–5 budget – we have increased funding to hospitals in their base operating budget by some 39 percent.' She continued, prompted by the leader of the Opposition: 'Over the past 10 years, the hospital sector alone has received a 250 per cent increase. In the past four years, that increase has been 40 per cent.'[55]

All the hospitals in the study reported that they did not have long range plans, and twenty-one of the twenty-three had never performed impact analyses on their work. Nineteen of the hospitals reported 'a passive management that does not fully participate in major decisions, weak governance and direction by board, and conflict between groups.'[56] The report recommended that the MOH 'should issue a clear policy statement stating the need to re-align, reduce, cap or eliminate certain services and programs, to balance the global budget' and that 'each hospital should implement the bonafide [sic] efficiency improvement and revenue generation opportunities identified in the specific reviews.' For the longer-term time frame, the report was hardly original: the Ministry of Health 'must require all hospitals to function within an operating plan which covers both operating costs and capital requirements' and 'must approve annual budgets (bottom-line only) in a timely manner, and must not accept or fund a deficit budget.'[57]

The Peterson government chose to grapple with the growing health care funding issue by appealing to a broader range of individuals than the officials of the Ministry of Finance or Health. It commissioned three reports on health care that were received in 1987. *Health for All Ontario* (known as the Spasoff panel) developed a series of health goals. *Health Promotion Matters in Ontario* (the Podborski committee) focused on illness prevention, and the Evans panel produced *Toward a Shared Direction of Health in Ontario.* The three papers emphasized partnerships and community-based care networks and also noted that the health care system needed financial strategies in order to achieve its objectives.

The Premier's Council on Health Strategy delivered its report, *From Vision to Action*, in 1989. Chaired by Roy Aitken, executive vice-president of Inco, the committee focused on funding the health care system, and proposed a mix of ideas. On hospital funding, it recommended a 'modified global funding arrangement using a case mix approach.' It also recommended more specific targets to shift resources to outpatient and community services, giving hospitals greater flexibility to allocate services within their budgets, and involving physicians in the budgeting process. The committee also proposed a roll-back of the capital funds set aside in 1986 to build more hospital capacity unless 'other mechanisms such as community based services' were shown not to be able to respond.[58]

The committee also focused on physicians because it concluded that the oversupply of doctors and the multiplication of procedures on patients were adding heavily to the cost of health care. It pointed out that total OHIP payments had gone from $900 million in 1977–8 to $3.6 billion in 1987–8 – a growth rate of 15 per cent per year. It concluded that a 'mix' of payments ranging from fee-for-service, capitation, and salaries be pursued. (The response would be very slow in coming: in 1987–8 Ontario doctors were given a fee hike of 4.8 per cent, adding up to a 66.58 per cent increase since 1981.) More to the point, the committee noted that expenditure planning had to be improved. Finally, it looked at the relationship between the health care system and the community to see what savings could be realized by transferring expensive, professionally provided services to community organizations. Noting that many ideas of this sort had been advanced before, the committee acknowledged that 'the principal challenge to the committee was to understand why past recommendations have not been implemented and to identify strategies to overcome implementation barriers.'[59] Again, it was an issue of execution – budget discipline and difficult policy work: 'We clearly need to develop incentives for cost control.'[60]

Financing the health care system in Ontario took two important turns in 1989. First, the federal budget announced a reduction of $560 million in its transfer payment to the province for health care and education.[61] Almost simultaneously, Robert Nixon announced that OHIP premiums would be eliminated on 1 January 1990, thereby fulfilling a promise that had been made by the Peterson Liberals during the 1985 election campaign. A fixture in the funding of health care in the province would be replaced by a new Employer Health Levy of 1.95 per cent of payroll for companies with more than $400,000 in salaries. Special provisions were made for employers with smaller payrolls (less than $200,000). Officials in the Ministry of Finance hoped this shift in the revenue structure would bring in more cash. Health care, now consuming 33.3 per cent of the budget, needed more revenue. It was estimated that the loss of $1,843 million in OHIP premiums would be made up with revenues of $2,114 million from the Employer Health Levy.

The Liberals were defeated in 1990 and the province's first New Democratic Party government took power. Floyd Laughren's first budget, even with its commitments to dramatic funding increases, reflected concerns that were familiar: 'The costs of our health system are threatening to overwhelm all other Government expenditures.'[62] The government's response was to deal first with the payments to physicians. It capped payments to doctors and immediately reduced payments for medical services received outside the country. A year later, reflecting on average annual increases of 11.2 per cent over the previous ten years, Laughren announced that 'this high level of growth is simply not sustainable' and expected to hold the increase in health care expenditures to 2 per cent in 1991–2 and to 1 per cent in 1992–3. Key among the reforms was the introduction of differential fees for new physicians in areas of oversupply and a reduction in medical school enrolments, ideas that had been advanced by the various study groups spawned by previous governments.

The measures succeeded, and for the first time in thirty years, health expenditures actually declined. As part of the 'Social Contract' provisions, the government estimated that it would save $434 million in medical costs in 1994–5 and 1995–6 by seeking more efficiencies in, and limiting the entry of new doctors into, the system[63] In 1995, Laughren noted that 'even though our total spending on programs is falling, we will spend almost $300 million more on health care this year than two years ago.'[64] Perhaps the most important provision was the introduction of photo health cards that were aimed at preventing up to an estimated $60 million in fraud. The measures did not leave workers in the health care sector happy. Infrastructure repairs to Ontario hospitals went undone, growth in services to match the growing population was halted, and doctors and nurses chafed at the salary freezes.

Notwithstanding the success of the NDP in harnessing health care costs, the province faced a new challenge to its funding. In his budget speech of March 1995, the federal minister of finance, Paul Martin, announced a dramatic cut in transfers to the provinces in health care funding. As the NDP government was swept out of office in 1995, a new government – elected on a platform to slash spending – would have to face the double threat of diminished federal funding and pent-up frustrations from many parts of the health care community.

The response was rapidly articulated. 'Everyone knows that simply throwing more money at health care is not the answer,' the Progressive Conservative Speech from the Throne declared in September 1995.[65] Ernie Eves, the minister of finance in the Mike Harris government, said that the government 'remained committed' to protecting the $17.4 billion health care budget: 'Yet this is not a commitment to maintain the status quo. We need to find savings in some areas in order to meet new needs in other areas – for example, to provide new technologies, to reduce waiting lists, and to meet the needs of an aging population … We believe savings must be identified before new spending on health care can be undertaken.'[66] The Harris government's first step in financing health care was to cut the Employer Health Tax so that by 1999, the first $400,000 of payroll would be exempted. It was estimated that by 1999, 88 per cent of private-sector employers would no longer have to file a payroll tax return. Instead, the government adopted a surtax on the Ontario Income Tax that had been installed by the NDP government and dedicated it wholly to what was called a Fair Share Health Care Levy (FSHCL). The hope was that once fully phased in, the FSHCL would equal 20 per cent of Ontario income tax in excess of $3,845 plus 36 per cent of Ontario income tax in excess of $4,800. The Employer Health Tax was not eliminated, however, and would contribute close to $3 billion through the late 1990s to provincial coffers. In 2001–2, $529 million of provincial revenue from charity casinos and slot machines at race tracks would be dedicated to support health care.

The Harris government brought a new approach to budgeting, slashing 14.2 per cent of the 1994–5 Ontario budget. The health sector was not spared: the new budget bill proposed user fees for prescription drugs used by seniors and low-income earners. By 1996, 25 per cent of the 32,000 acute-care beds that had existed in 1991 had been closed.[67] In his November 1995 economic statement, Finance Minister Eves announced plans to reduce the grants to hospitals by $1.3 billion. A year later, the government's subsidy of malpractice insurance ($36 million) was eliminated, and then restored, and while the clawback on physician billings was continued, it was reduced, while at the same time the total income cap that had been imposed on physicians by the Rae government was lowered.[68] In 1997 the clawbacks were ended, and a 1.5 per cent increase was allowed. The government also established a Health Care Restructuring Commission to make recommendations as independently as possible on hospital closures and modernizations.

The Ontario PC government had a difficult job in justifying itself. In 1998, Elizabeth Witmer, the minister of health, responded to a query in question period by saying, 'Our government has not made any cuts to health in Ontario. As the member well knows, the only people who have made cuts are the federal government. In fact, they have made somewhere in the neighborhood of $2.5 billion that we have lost in social and health transfer payments from the federal government.'[69] In response to a query during question period on 30 April 2001, Tony Clement, the minister of health and long-term care articulated the Tory case: 'Health care spending has increased at a dramatic pace,' he told the assembly, '27 percent in five years, 19 percent in the past two years alone. However, double-digit increases in health spending are no longer sustainable. At the current rate of increase, within five years health spending would consume 60 percent of the Ontario government's operating budget, up from 44 cents on every dollar today, and 38 percent since our government was first elected.'[70] A few months later, he pointed to the dramatic drop in the federal contribution to health care. 'Ever since Jean Chrétien has been elected,' he responded during question period in 2001, 'the percentage of federal spending is lower than it was in 1993. Since 1994–95 we've increased our spending in the province to $23.7 billion, an increase of over 35 percent, and yet the federal Liberal government has increased their revenue by over $8 billion but the health and social service transfers have increased by a paltry $400 million. We spend in Ontario, as a provincial government, over $750 a second on health care. Ottawa contributes just $107 in the same time period. It's clear the federal government is not living up to its responsibilities.'[71]

Health care spending in the Harris government would indeed continue to grow. For 1997–8, it was predicted that $18.5 billion would be spent on all aspects of health care, ranging from services to restructuring and capital construction. A major change was the federal contribution. On 1 April 1996, the federal government replaced the Established Programs Financing and the Canada Assistance Plan with the Canada Health and Social Transfer (CHST). The net effect was that federal transfers to Ontario would decline by $601 million in 1997–8 from 1996–7 levels. Compared to what it had received in 1995–6, federal payments to Ontario would be cut by $2.12 billion in 1997–8. In 1998, the government budgeted $471 million for capital construction.

Health care costs, in terms of both operating and capital expenditures, were adding up to $22.3 billion, and featured increases of close to $2 billion each year. In the Harris years, health-based operating spending increased by $6.1 billion, bringing total health care costs to over $25 billion in 2002–3, and assumed a larger portion of the budget than ever. In 1995–6 base health care operating spending made up 38 per cent of government program expenditures (excluding capital costs and public debt interest). Health care's share grew to 45 per cent in 2001–2 and would increase to 47 per cent in 2002–3 as a succession of finance ministers (James Flaherty assuming the position in 2001, and Janet Ecker in 2002) tried in vain to control costs.

From 1994–5 to 2002–3, Ontario's health care spending (operating and capital) increased by $10.3 billion. Ottawa's CHST transfers to Ontario did not keep up. The federal minister of health, Allan Rock, proposed an initiative to 'save medicare,' but it drew such hostility from the provinces, which insisted that funding the CHST adequately had to be a priority, that it was almost immediately withdrawn.[72] In the federal budget of 2003, Ottawa confirmed new funding, including a $967 million contribution to Ontario to deal with immediate needs within the province's health care system.

Expenditures continued to be unpredictable. An additional $158 million was allocated in year 2001–2 due to a higher-than-anticipated utilization in drug programs in the Ministry of Health and Long-Term Care.[73] In 2001, Jim Flaherty, the minister of finance, noted that 45 per cent of the programing budget was spent on health, and predicted that by 2006, 60 per cent of programing dollars would be consumed by heath. 'This rate of increase simply isn't sustainable.'[74] Management was a problem: 'All of the health care system needs more effective and efficient government.'[75] Since 1998–9, operating grants to hospitals had increased by 50 per cent, the Tories argued. And in 2003–4, health care was expected to consume 46 per cent of program expenditures. The government that year proposed a Public Sector Accountability Act that required hospitals to balance their budgets and to adopt rigorous business plans.

The McGuinty Liberals came in with similar pledges to control health care costs when they were elected to office in the fall of 2003. Within ten years, from 1994 to 2004, expenditures on health care had consumed another 5 per cent of the budget. In 2004, the government was expecting to pay $2441 per person on health care. Since 2001, total operating spending had increased by $7.7 billion, growing at an average rate of 7.7 per cent. Finance Minister Greg Sorbara emphasized that the government wanted the health care system 'measured ... on results [with ...] funding ... targeted to ensure that the results Ontarians want are met, including reduced wait times and access to primary care.'

> Sustainable health care spending is not about cutting health care spending – that is neither desirable, nor realistic. It is about investing wisely in a system that delivers tangibles results in an accountable, efficient and cost-effective manner and that not only focuses on curing illness, but also on health promotion and prevention. Health care costs cannot continue to grow faster than the rate of economic growth over the long term. The province is devoting an increasing share of its program spending to fund health service ... There are many pressures on the health care system such as an aging and growing population, rising utilization for existing service, the costly demand for access to new medical technology, wage settlement and emerging public health threats from an increasingly connected world. This rate of increase is not sustainable, and can only lead to the continued 'crowding out' of available funding for other priorities in the future.[76]

The government created an Ontario Health Quality Council with a budget of $1 million. The key to the Liberal government's approach, however, was the return of the premium, this time called the Ontario Health Premium. Levied at 6 per cent of taxable income in excess of $20,000, the full premium would be payable at a taxable income of $25,000. In 2004–5, it was expected to inject $1.6 billion into the system, still short of the additional $2.1 billion the government was promising to spend on numerous initiatives designed to cut costs and improve accountability.

The Liberals argued that in 1994 Ontario dedicated the equivalent of 6 per cent of the Gross Provincial Product to health and long-term care. That figure fell to 5 per cent during the Harris years, before rising to reach 5.5 per cent in the Tories' last year in power, 2003 – about 2.3 billion, or 9 per cent more. Ottawa's cash contribution to health care in Canada peaked at $8.2 billion in 1993–4 and fell to a low of $5.4 billion in 1998–9. By the time the McGuinty Liberals assumed power in 2003, it still had not reached the numbers of 1993–4. A *Toronto Star* editorial put it plainly: 'Ottawa spent far less on health care for all Canadians than consumers spent on tobacco and alcohol.'[77] The campaign led by the provinces – with Ontario as a key player – proved convincing. The Martin government agreed to provide $41 billion in federal transfers to provinces for health care to fund special initiatives to cut wait times for particular surgeries.

Conclusion

The guardians of the Ministry of Finance were placed in a difficult situation when it came to health care financing. There were three sources of funds for health care in Ontario, and all three proved less then dependable. The first one, of course, was the general treasury. Funded by taxation and borrowing, it sustains the system and can be drawn upon to realize the project. A second source was the dedicated insurance premium levied on citizens. Governments succeeded each other in raising the premiums until they were abandoned altogether, proving to be insufficient, regressive, and inefficient. They would be reinstated in the form of a tax in 2004. A third source was federal government transfers. Ottawa, in this case, proved to be a frustration. In the 1970s, it helped fuel expenditures and expansions with its offer to match provincial spending, only to suddenly and then steadily diminish its contribution.

If there were limits on the revenue that could be depended upon to pay for health care in the province, there were none apparent on the capacity to spend. All through these years, ministry staff was clearly aware that there was no solution to the problem and stood helplessly by as health care consumed more tax dollars and apportioned to itself a steadily growing share of the government's operating budget. By the early 1970s, health care had eclipsed expenditures for roads and highways. By the early 1980s it had overtaken education as the greatest spender.

There were reasons for this. In part, certainly, it was a growing and steadily aging population that demanded health care. In part, it was also the absence, for a long time, of any checks and balances on the system. Stakeholders – doctors, nurses, technicians, hospital administrators, patients – drew on the health care account with scarcely a concern that their expenses would not be covered. Politicians were also helpless. Clearly, the priority setters felt as though they had no choice but to continue to spend without asking too many questions. Health care was a popular program in the province, surely one of the most in demand. It would not be an exaggeration to say that Ontarians have come to see the provision of health care as a birthright.[78]

Figure 11.1 Net health-care disbursements as a percentage of
net ordinary expenditures, 1960–2005

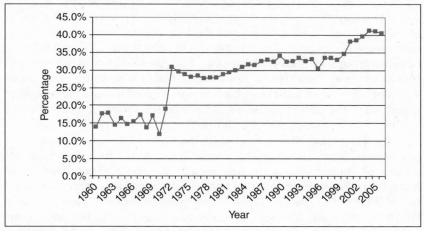

Source: Ontario Public Accounts, 1960–2005.

As an entitlement, health care has distorted the provincial government's priority-setting abilities. While the provincial budget dedicated
progressively more of its revenue to health care, other areas were inevitably neglected. Infrastructure – particularly energy generation –
was allowed to stagnate. Transfers to municipalities were cut as were
moneys invested in education. Ontario would lag other provinces in a
number of areas. As Janice MacKinnon, minister of finance in
Saskatchewan in the 1990s, observed:

> Health care is engaged in a David and Goliath battle for scarce provincial
> resources. The Goliath is a public so committed to medicare that it evokes
> terror in its politicians who would rather face angry students over high
> tuition fees or disgruntled mayors complaining about crumbling infra-
> structure than confront irate seniors or baby boomers concerned about
> health care … The Davids are the other funding priorities – education,
> training, research and development, poverty reduction, environment and
> infrastructure – which always play second fiddle or poor cousin to the
> mightily Goliath of Health care.[79]

A choice was made by Ontarians that health care insurance was the most prized of government services. It was telling that this was probably the area where the core of government had the least control. The vast majority of the service providers are not government employees and, save for a few years in the 1990s, could tap at will into the provincial treasury. A striking feature of the evolution of the health care files was that it was never seriously examined by a government commission. While a number of study groups were created over the years, their work was hardly comprehensive and their recommendations quickly forgotten. Clearly, this was a policy area where a consensus was perceived to exist. Government could make the critical decisions as long as the system was allowed to evolve in the manner prescribed in the 1960s.

In the face of this strategic vacuum, the staff in Treasury/Finance had to adjust in its role as 'guardian.' In many respects, although ministerial statements pointed to the unsustainable trends in expenditures, the Ministry of Finance was unable to resist the pressures exerted on it by the politics of the priority setters. The guardians in this case had little support: their calls for more revenue never seemed to be sated; their demands for more control of expenses could not withstand the impossible appetite for health care services. Were the guardians defeated? Darcy McKeough undoubtedly was undermined fatally in 1978 over the issue of funding health care. But he was hardly the only minister to be defeated by it. The issue of health care funding demonstrated the limits of the guardianship entrusted to the staff of the Ministry of Treasury/Finance. Health care takes no prisoners.

NOTES

1 My thanks to Ron Branker and Ashley Walker for their research assistance and to Alvin Ing for his help with the chart.
2 Cited in Matt Maychak, 'NDP Poised to Cut Health-Care Services,' *Toronto Star*, 2 May 1992, A16.
3 Janice MacKinnon, *Minding the Public Purse: The Fiscal Crisis, Political Trade-Offs, and Canada's Future* (Montreal: McGill-Queen's University Press, 2003), 176.
4 Aaron Wildavsky, 'From Chaos Comes Opportunity: The Movement toward Spending Limits in American and Canadian Budgeting,' *Canadian Public Administration* 26.2 (1983), 163–81.
5 A point also made on occasion in Harvey Lazar and France St-Hilaire, eds, *Money, Politics and Health Care* (Montreal: Institute for Research in Public Policy, 2004). Many have taken a different angle on the issue, arguing that health care spending has 'crowded out' other expenditures. A recent study

of provincial government expenditures from 1988 to 2004 argued that there was no evidence that increased health care expenditures resulted in lower levels of spending on other categories of government expenditures. See Stuart Landon, Melville McMillan, Vijay Muralidharan, and Mark Parsons, 'Does Health-care Spending Crowd Out Other Provincial Expenditures?' *Canadian Public Policy* 32.2 (June 2006). The argument rests on a study of 14 relatively consistent years of budgeting.

6 Michael Prince, 'The Bland Stops Here: Ontario Budgeting in the Davis Era, 1971–1985,' in Allan M. Maslove, ed., *Budgeting in the Provinces: Leadership and the Premiers* (Toronto: Institute of Public Administration of Canada, 1989), 100.

7 See Kenneth Bryden, 'How Medicare Came to Ontario,' in Donald C. Macdonald, *Government and Politics of Ontario* (Toronto: Macmillan Co., 1973), 36; Roger Graham, *Leslie Frost: Old Man Ontario* (Toronto: University of Toronto Press, 1990), 187–8.

8 I am in debt to Don Stevenson for this information.

9 This was not an accident. Taylor had been thinking about health care for a long time. He wrote his PhD dissertation on the topic and in 1954 published 'Government Planning: The Federal-Provincial Health Survey Reports,' in the *Canadian Medical Association Journal* 70 (February), 204–9, and 'The Social Assistance Medical Care Plans in Canada' in the *American Journal of Public Health* 44 (June), 750–9. For a general overview of Taylor's work, see Malcolm Taylor, *Health Insurance and Canadian Public Policy* (Montreal: McGill-Queen's University Press and Institute of Public Administration of Canada, 1978). See also Graham, *Leslie Frost*, 234–5.

10 Budget Statement, 1962–3, 52.

11 Budget Statement, 1960–1, 13.

12 Budget Statement, 1962–3, 14.

13 Budget Statement, 1964–5, 15.

14 Budget Statement, 1966–7, 16.

15 Budget Statement, 1967–8, 12.

16 Budget Statement, 1968–9, 14.

17 Budget Statement, 1971, table C3, 95.

18 Budget Statement, 1970, 20.

19 Hon. Charles S. MacNaughton, Statement to the Federal-Provincial Meeting of Finance Ministers, 4–5 November 1968, cited in 'Ontario's Experience under Cost-Sharing,' *Supplementary Actions to the 1975 Ontario Budget* (July 1975), 3–4.

20 Statement of the Hon. John Robarts, Constitutional Conference, 10–12 February 1969, cited in 'Ontario's Experience under Cost-Sharing,' 4.

21 'Ontario's Experience under Cost-Sharing,' 4.

22 See Kenneth Bryden, 'How Medicare Came to Ontario,' in Donald C. Macdonald, *Government and Politics of Ontario* (Toronto: Macmillan Co., 1973),
44.
23 Ontario Budget 1973, Financial Statements, chart 2.
24 Ontario Budget, 1972.
25 Ontario Budget, 1972. Revenues from premiums were $473,181 in 1969–70,
$613,770 in 1970–1, and $560,200 in 1971–2.
26 'Ontario's Experience under Cost-Sharing,' 11.
27 Ontario Budget Statement, 1976, 4.
28 Ibid., 8 (see chart, p. 9).
29 Ontario Ministry of Finance Library, 'Reforming Fiscal Arrangements and
Cost Sharing in Canada: Statement by the Hon. W. Darcy McKeough to the
Meeting of the Ministers of Finance, July 6–7, 1976,' 9.
30 Ontario Budget, 1978–9, 15.
31 Quoted in *Globe and Mail*, 22 March 1982, 6.
32 *Report of the Joint Advisory Committee of the Government of Ontario and the
Ontario Medical Association on Methods to Control Health Care Costs* (Queen's
Printer, 1977), 1.
33 Ibid., 3.
34 Ontario Budget, 1978–9, 15.
35 Ibid., 10.
36 Thomas Claridge, '100 Percent Increase in Two Years, Ontario's Health
Premiums Double Those Elsewhere,' *Globe and Mail*, 8 March 1978, 11.
37 Angela Barnes, 'Health Costs Called Major Problem Area.' *Globe and Mail*,
14 March 1978, 11.
38 'Cost of OHIP,' *Globe and Mail*, 8 March 1978. A short glimpse of the internal discussions around the 1978 budget can be seen in a National Film
Board production entitled 'The Art of the Possible' (directed by Peter Ray-
mont). Typically with NFB productions, the real drama was not captured.
The firestorm surrounding the decision to increase OHIP premiums is only
vaguely referred to.
39 Cited in Norman Webster, 'Can Darcy Act Like Bamboo?' *Globe and Mail*,
12 April 1979, 7.
40 Editorial, *Globe and Mail*, 26 April 1978, 6.
41 Cited in Arthur Johnson, '"I don't feel weakened" McKeough Says of Defeat on OHIP Premiums,' *Globe and Mail*, 26 April 1978, 5.
42 Legislative Assembly of Ontario, *Report of the Select Committee on Health
Care Financing and Costs* (17 October 1978), 20. It is worth noting that Liberal MPPs Sean Conway and Jack Riddell included a statement in the
report against the premium system. 'We remain adamantly opposed to the

premium system and a Liberal government would move in its first term of office to abolish that system and replace it by a more adequate and progressive one' (23). NDP MPPs Bob Mackenzie and David Warner argued the same points in a separate statement.

43 Ontario Ministry of Finance Library, 'Statement to the Select Committee on Health Costs and Financing by the Hon. Frank S. Miller,' 14 September 1978.
44 Ontario Budget, 1981, 19.
45 Ontario Ministry of Finance Library, 'Remarks by the Honourable Frank S. Miller, Treasurer of Ontario at the Opening Luncheon of the Ontario Hospital Association Annual Convention,' 29 October 1979, 5.
46 Ibid., 17.
47 Ontario Budget, 1982, 12.
48 Ontario Ministry of Finance Library, 'Remarks by the Honourable Larry Grossman, Treasurer of Ontario and Minster of Economics, to the Meeting of Ministers of Finance,' 8 December 1983.
49 Ontario Budget, 1984, 18.
50 Ontario Ministry of Finance Library, 'Remarks by the Honourable Larry Grossman at the Primrose Club Luncheon,' 25 September 1984, no page number.
51 Ontario Budget, 1986, 44.
52 Ontario Budget, 1988, 76.
53 Ibid., n.p.
54 Ontario Ministry of Health, 'Report of the Conjoint Review Committee on the 23 Hospital Operational Reviews,' July 1988, 5.
55 Ontario Hansard, Oral Questions, 11 May 1988.
56 Ibid., 6.
57 Ibid., 14.
58 Province of Ontario, Premier's Council on Health Strategy, *From Vision to Action: Report of the Health Care System Committee* (Queen's Park, Toronto, 1989), 3 (see also p. 9).
59 Ibid., 4.
60 Ibid., 40.
61 William Walker, 'Budget Will Drive Us Away, Firms Say,' *Toronto Star*, 18 May 1989, A1.
62 Ontario Budget, 1991, 16.
63 See Thomas Walkom, *Rae Days* (Toronto: Key Porter Books, 1994), 179–85. It is interesting to note that Bob Rae never mentions health care in his memoir of his years as premier. See Bob Rae, *From Protest to Power: Personal Reflections on a Life in Politics* (Toronto: Penguin Books, 1996).

64 Ontario Budget, 1995, p. 11. A critique of the Rae government's dealings with the pharmaceutical companies is Thomas Walkom, *Rae Days* (Toronto: Key Porter Books, 1994) chapter 9.
65 Cited in Daniel Girard, 'Health Care Faces Change,' *Toronto Star*, 28 September 1995, p. A14.
66 Ontario Ministry of Finance Library, 'Speech to the Canadian Club by the Hon. Ernie Eves, Ontario Minister of Finance,' 1 December 1995.
67 John Ibbitson, *Promised Land: Inside the Mike Harris Revolution* (Toronto: Prentice Hall, 1997), 194.
68 Ibid., 198.
69 Ontario Hansard, Oral Questions, 15 December 1998.
70 Ibid., 30 April 2001.
71 Ibid., 27 November 2001.
72 See Gerard Boychuk, 'The Federal Role in Health Care Reform: Legacy or Limbo?' in *How Ottawa Spends, 2003–04*, ed. Bruce Doern (Toronto: Oxford University Press, 2003), 96.
73 Ontario Budget, 2003, 38.
74 Ontario Ministry of Finance Library, 'Notes for Remarks by the Honourable Jim Flaherty, Minister of Finance to the Canadian Club and Empire Club of Canada (May 10, 2001),' 6.
75 Ibid, 7.
76 Ontario Budget, 2004, Paper A, 15.
77 'A Desperate Need for More Funding,' *Toronto Star* editorial, 30 June 2003, A18.
78 The argument is developed in Candace Johnson Redden, *Health Care, Entitlement and Citizenship* (Toronto: University of Toronto Press, 2002).
79 Janice MacKinnon, *Minding the Public Purse* (Montreal: McGill-Queen's University Press, 2003), 246. The entire chapter 11 is devoted to the dislocation of finances brought about by the costs of health care.

Conclusion

PATRICE DUTIL

The evolution of public administration can be grasped through a number of methods. One of them examines how public service organizations are shaped by politicians in order to better deliver on the services the government of the day has promised. Another strategy is to examine how structural change is brought about by slower-evolving external forces such as socio-economic transformations, cultural changes, and ideological shifts. In cases such as these, scholars typically like to examine business plans, internal memoranda, annual reports, and program evaluations. A third strategy is to consider public administration through the eyes of the public servants themselves. In this case, scholars are interested in the ideas of the employees in an effort to gauge the originality of their thinking and the degree of to which they can be independent agents of the politicians. Of course, no strategy can be useful entirely on its own. Scholars necessarily must consider the wishes of the elected politicians, take the measure of outside events, and try to understand the bureaucracy itself to understand how a government department evolves over time. In his *The Canadian Public Service: A Physiology of Government, 1867–1970* the late Ted Hodgetts called this sort of combined approach a 'historical-analytical survey, mapping the profile and physiology of the public service.'[1]

The fancy term for this combination of methods of enquiry is historical institutionalism; in this case, it is applied to the study of a government department as it evolves through time. The preceding chapters have demonstrated that historical institutionalism can take on many forms and research strategies. It also showed that the Department of the Treasury of Ontario, as it went through numerous name changes, organizational transformations, and ideological regimes struggled to carve out a place for itself and remain relevant to the process and think-ing of governance.

Typical of departments of finance, the first mission of the treasury has been to gather money, and to do its utmost to ensure that government keeps it. Not surprisingly, through the years since the Second World War (some would say since the dawn of government), the prime concern of the executives in this department has been to ensure that enough taxes are raised to meet expenses. For a good part of this period in Ontario, the department had a predominant concern with two goals, namely, con-tinued growth and investment in the structures (ranging from hard assets to better schooling). For policy makers, the (always elusive) ques-tion was (and remains): how to dose taxation so that it had minimal consequence to the growth economy and supply the money necessary to realize a good society? This is what made the experience of the Ontario department of finance so alluring. Never straying from its mission to amass the province's treasure, the department took on many missions after the Second World War and redefined its 'guardian' mission.

George Drew, the crusty Progressive Conservative premier elected during the war, set a new direction in policy making that required bet-ter data and better interpretation. As Keith Brownsey demonstrated in his chapter, Leslie Frost, the young small-town lawyer who had never shown a particular interest in finances, took his cues from Drew and laid down the foundation for a treasury that, being far more than a mere sentinel at the gates, would grow to be the brain trust of the gov-ernment of Ontario. He wanted sober fiscal management, but he was equally sensitive to popular demands for more government services and was very concerned that it should be Ontario that provided those goods, not the government of Canada. Not surprisingly, in October 1946, Treasury produced a twenty-four-page report on interprovincial and dominion-provincial conferences since confederation, highlighting the Ontario position. It was the first of the sort, and announced a more systematic approach to policy making.[2]

Drew and Frost encouraged a certain philosophy of planning for the province, and mobilized the bureaucratic staff to deliver the intelli-gence necessary to carry it out. Chester Walters, the deputy treasurer, played an early role in this mission, as did his protégé, Harold Chater. Before the war was over, Ontario had been carved up into eighteen dis-tinct regions and the Office of the Chief Statistician generated reams of data on the micro-economy of each of them.[3] George Gathercole, who within a dozen years of joining the Ontario public service was deputy minister of the Department of Economics, assigned his staff to produce population projections for the regions, counties, and urban areas of Ontario and used those statistics to make comprehensive submissions to all sorts of parliamentary and government-sponsored enquiries into various policy matters.[4] Gathercole would be one of the most influential figures in Ontario in the 1950s and early 1960s.

In a paper he gave to the Conference of the Municipal Finance Officers' Association of the United States and Canada in San Francisco in May 1954, Gathercole explained the government of Ontario's approach to planning. 'By "planning,"' he said,

> I do not mean, of course, the establishment of a collectivist or planned economy in which all economic activity is directed by a single authority. When I speak of planning, I mean that we should handle our common problems rationally and with foresight. In this sense we are all planners. Planning, as I have defined it, has to do with people and their physical environment. It is concerned with the choice of different alternatives and the establishment of priorities. It should suggest how, under democratic processes, the needs and desires of the people can be achieved to best advantage from an optimum use of resources and fiscal capacity. Planning presumes a conscious selection from alternatives, preceding a course of action. Its essence, therefore, lies the probabilities of the future, necessitating projections of economic and social trends, and its watchwords are foresight and forethought.[5]

Gathercole, speaking not as a deputy minister in charge of municipal affairs or indeed as an official in the department of planning – he was listed as Provincial Economist and Assistant Comptroller of Finances – articulated high ambitions for the Ontario approach, even as this approach extended into the deepest reaches of municipal planning.

> Why do I believe this plan holds out so much promise for the regional planner? It is because it meets the needs of today and tomorrow. It strikes off the shackles of local boundaries and provides the machinery for co-coordinating basic municipal services and for pooling the financial resources of the whole region. It unlocks the door for new developments in the housing field. It contributes to the solutions of the deep seated social and economic consequences of derelict neighborhoods and impoverished communities. It opens the way for the establishment of parks, recreational centres and green belts. As never before, it gives the planner an opportunity

to coordinate comprehensive municipal service in conformity with economic realities of the regions and challenges him to combine beauty and functionalism.[6]

Hardly the rhetoric one would expect of a traditional 'guardian'!

Indeed, the approach of the 1940s and 1950s transformed the Department of the Treasury into a 'guardian' organization that had fingers in almost every file of the government, including the 'spending' portfolios. Its role was not just in allocating funds, but in deciding how priorities would be identified and acted upon. If the department had been 'path dependent,' or tied to binding traditions and mentalities inherited from ages past, it was rapidly getting rid of those shackles.

Nevertheless, it is clear that the system created by the alliance of George Drew, Leslie Frost, and Ontario mandarins such as Chester Walters and George Gathercole engendered policy approaches and a culture of trust and mutual reliance that had a long and deeply felt impact years after they left. Ian Macdonald adapted the tone in the 1960s and 1970s by forging a deep and abiding meeting of the minds with his ministers, but even more so with his premiers, John Robarts and William Davis. They shared a conservative, but ambitious view of the prospects of the province that demanded a certain dirigisme. 'In view of what lies ahead, the Province should give the most serious thought and study to its future financial policy,' George Gathercole wrote in 1962. 'It should attempt to plan its expenditures and revenues over the next five years in such a way that increases in expenditure are, wherever possible, financed out of the growth in revenues generated by expanding economic activity. In other words, we should endeavour to equate the increase in our expenditures to that of our revenues and as far as possible to the improvement in revenues from normal economic growth.'[7] The Treasury and, later, the Ministry of Finance thus articulated a unique brand of progressive conservatism, even when the government was led by political teams of red and orange stripes.

That unique symbiosis between the finance and economics departments and the political elites was established for a number of reasons. The first key factor was that the Treasury building developed the intellectual and managerial capacity to respond to myriad causes and to fashion programs and create agencies, boards, and commissions of all sorts – much more than merely preparing budgets or collecting taxes. Ten years after becoming premier, Frost pointed to a range of accomplishments such as unconditional per capita grants to municipalities,

payments to municipalities in lieu of taxes on provincial business prop-
erties, the establishment of the municipal corporation to assist municipalities in their credit financing, the creation of the Metropolitan
Toronto Plan, the establishment of the water resources commission, the
incorporation of equalization and growth need factors in determining
the province's grants to school boards, the distribution of free textbooks
and milk in schools, the establishment of a disabled persons' allow-
ance, the creation of provincial parks, the free polio vaccination program, the creation of the Princess Margaret Hospital for the treatment
of cancer, the creation of an atomic-reactor power plant, and scientific
forest management. Almost all of these were the products of either the
Treasury or the Department of Economics. That tradition of identifying
talent and promoting expertise would have a lasting effect. Most deputies in this period were trained within the department, and many of its
employees went on to become senior executives in line ministries and
agencies. A number of them sought election to the legislative assembly
and the House of Commons and were elected.[8]

If talent was important, the structure of the department also evolved
frequently to match its new missions. The chapter by Patrice Dutil and
Devyn Leonard shed light on the reality that the 'guardian' – keeper of
the budget and careful calibrator of taxes and expenditures – assumed
new roles as the years wore on. Ian Macdonald was noting the obvious
when he announced that the unification of the Departments of Treasury
and Economics in 1967 was the solemnization of a long union. Both had
played a role in setting government policy in one way or another since
the war. In its new incarnation, the Department of Treasury and
Economics would be relied upon to take on more roles. The 'treasury'
was now a planner, both for provincial resources and programs and for
regional government. That role evolved again in the late 1970s and
since. Today, the Ministry of Finance's structure is leaner and more focused. Many agencies have been done away with, and many of the coordinating functions have been passed on to Cabinet Office.

A second factor was the department's impact on policy making outside the regular confines of 'treasury' portfolios. As Bryan Evans and
John Shields demonstrated in their chapter, it was a department that
reassessed constantly the prevailing wisdom of how provincial finances
should be managed. Treasury, like other departments in the Westminster
system,[9] was a central player as Ontario worked its way into and out of
a 'Keynesian' period towards a more monetarist policy framework. It
was a dance between the poles of progressivism and conservatism that

were planted by the founding spirit of the new modern 'treasury.' How those values were expressed in terms of budget allocations became the central focus of budget making as year after year, bureaucratic staff negotiated with (some would scoff and simply say 'dictated to') line ministries to determine the fault lines of what was financially possible. The chapter by Dutil, Peter Ryan, and André Gossignac examined how words gave spirit to those negotiations through the compromise documents that budgets are. They showed a remarkable consistency in style through thirty-four years of budget making that conveys mathematically a consistent approach to budget-making, but within which can be perceived the hand of each individual treasurer/minister.

The guardian was also mobilized to the front lines in the intergovernmental battles with Ottawa. Throughout this period, the government of Canada moved or threatened to move vigorously into areas of provincial jurisdiction or, through its policies, to undo or minimize the impact of Ontario's fiscal plans. The treasury building sensed the threat, and, as Penny Bryden describes in her chapter focused on the 1960s, it was treasury that was marshalled as 'guardian' of the interests of the province. It played the major role on the national stage in the area of pensions and at the Confederation of Tomorrow Conference, and would continue to tailgate Ottawa, on both the financial and constitutional fronts, until a separate Ministry of Intergovernmental Affairs was created to focus exclusively on the Trudeau proposals to renew the constitution in the late 1970s.

The third factor was political: Treasury remained strong because political rainmakers held its portfolio in Cabinet. As JP Lewis's chapter demonstrated, Ontario has had a strong tradition of harmony between premier and minister of finance which has endured from George Drew right through to this day. With the 1970s, as spending continued to grow and the economy became unpredictable in producing both high inflation and high unemployment, government built up strengths of other kinds to get a better handle on the budget. The premier wanted better knowledge about both politics and policy and built up an office of bright and energetic young people.

Indeed, new ministries were even created to cope with emerging complexities, and in the 1970s central agencies such as Cabinet Office and the Premier's Office assumed a good part of the coordinating role once played by a handful under the guidance of the likes of Gathercole and Macdonald. As Caroline Dufour portrayed it, the Management Board Secretariat took up some of the tasks in deciding how the spending

budget would be determined and in laying down conditions for spending the moneys. The demands for a more rigorous budgeting approach
did not weaken Treasury, but it did challenge its hegemony in the bargaining process to determine spending ceilings with the line ministries.

The department's structure was affected. Revenue, for instance, was
hived off as a separate department in a way that some would say was
the consecration of a divorce long understood. Municipal Affairs was
carved out of Treasury to manage the growing demands of municipalities and the complex relations the province insisted on having with
this tier of government. The more diplomatic pursuits of federal–
provincial relations were given to a new Ministry of Intergovernmental
Affairs. But throughout the years, the department maintained itself as a
pillar of influence in the premier's office. Perhaps this is not surprising:
The Treasury building faces the office of the premier at Queen's Park:
he (or she, eventually) cannot look outside the window without being
reminded that people at Finance are undoubtedly returning the gaze.

The authority of the Treasury mandarins has been challenged from
the outside. It is important not to lose sight of the fact that – for good
reasons and bad – many in line ministries have perceived Treasury/
Finance staff as arrogant, self-centred, and out of touch with the realities of delivering programs and services to the people of Ontario on a
day-to-day basis. Many of the various management fads promoted by
Finance over the years were viewed by many outside the central agencies as useless make-work projects which required them to waste time
completing endless forms that no one at the centre looked at seriously
and which provided no useful advice or assistance.[10] Demands for more
transparency in the budgeting process, documented here by Ken Ogata
and Gary Spraakman, opened up the process to more consultation in
the legislative assembly and in society. As the chapters by Gervan
Fearon on infrastructure spending and Patrice Dutil on heath care's
impact documented, Treasury/Finance was a (sometimes reluctant)
facilitator of spending – crafting funding formulas and programs for
infrastructure building and for medicare, to say nothing of the tax exemptions it created over the years (which were not systematically documented by the province and which requires a separate study of its own).
There was a difference, however. Where treasurers and ministers of finance trumpeted infrastructure spending as 'investments' and were
understandably pleased to see themselves as 'builders,' they tended to
issue darker warnings about medicare's impact on the provincial budget.
These two case studies of budget priorities – one ascending, the other

descending – reveal how differently the department could manage files. Infrastructure was dominated by agencies, boards, commissions, and numerous inquiries. Health care, by contrast, was never the subject of a thorough inquiry and its funding structures remained static.

Regardless of its limited success as a guardian of the public purse when it came to health care, Treasury/Finance was an organizer, often taking on the delivery of programs itself simply because no other department had the creativity, capacity, and talent to take them on. This is evident in the accordion charts of the department over the past forty years. On many occasions, outside pressures on the government to spend sometimes compelled the guardian to work against its instinct. It did so, nevertheless, because it had the internal capacity to do so, and because its political sensitivity required it to do so.

The pressure to respond to change was illustrated after the defeat of the Progressive Conservatives in 2003 (beyond the scope of this book). In 2004, new measures were introduced by the Liberal government led by Dalton McGuinty. The Fiscal Transparency and Accountability Act, 2004 declared that Ontario's fiscal policy was subject to four overriding principles: first, that this policy should be based on cautious assumptions; second, that it should recognize the need to respond to changing circumstances; third, that its impact on different groups within the population and on future generations should be considered. Finally, it emphasized transparency: it should be clearly articulated and information about it should be readily available for inspection by the public without charge.[11]

The new act compelled Ontario's fiscal policy to 'seek to maintain a prudent ratio of provincial debt to Ontario's gross domestic product' and obliged the government to plan for a balanced budget 'unless, as a result of extraordinary circumstances, the Executive Council determines that it is consistent with prudent fiscal policy for the Province to have a deficit for a fiscal year.' If deficits were to be incurred, the government was required to develop a 'recovery plan.' The law required that the Ministry of Finance produce a multi-year fiscal plan that would include at least the following two years. It also required an extended discussion of the risks and impacts of the plan and provided a reserve to address unforeseen circumstances that would have an important impact on the province's finances. The law also directed the minister to establish an Ontario Economic Forecast Council to advise the department. In a related matter, a Ministry of Revenue was again revived. The law also institutionalized the semi-annual review of the fiscal plan and dictated a number of information items that had to be released for pre-budget consultations with the public as well as quarterly information about Ontario's economic accounts. None of this was new in terms of practice, but it did require the department to ensure that its public profile was maintained. The key feature of the act was its stipulation that the Ministry of Finance release a report on the province's finances before an election, and that the report be reviewed by the auditor general of the province. Time will tell if these measures have any impact on the budget-making processes of the ministry or on its influence. If anything, there may be room to speculate that the demand for clearer transparency will strengthen the hand of Finance even more.

The impact of an institution like a department of finance remains open to question. This book could not hope to examine each and every aspect of the evolution of the Department of Treasury/Ministry of Finance of Ontario. It has lifted the veil to show that the department played a number of 'guardian roles' – as a budget maker, for sure, but also as a spender, regional planner, auditor, and de facto central-agency policy maker – and sought to explain both the sources of its power and the scope of its authority. In that sense, to follow Luc Bernier and Joseph Facal, Ontario's experience was exceptional. No other department in Canada is known to have held as much influence over such a long period of time, both in formulating and in articulating the key messages of the government. As such, this book sheds light on the institutional history of the state and offers a prism through which its politics can be interpreted. The hope of the contributors to this volume is that their efforts will inspire many more into joining them to demystify how this critical feature of government serves the public good.

NOTES

1 J.E. Hodgetts, *The Canadian Public Service: A Physiology of Government, 1867–1970* (Toronto: University of Toronto Press, 1973), 341.
2 Archives of Ontario (AO), Gathercole Papers, box MU5311, 'Interprovincial and Dominion-provincial conferences since confederation, Ontario bureau of statistics and research, 24 October 1946.'
3 Ibid., 4.
4 See, for example, 'Population Projections for the Economic Regions, Counties and Urban Areas of Ontario, Department of Economics, September 1957,' in AO, Gathercole Papers, box MU5363.
5 AO, Gathercole Papers, 'Some Observations on Regional Planning,' 27 May 1954, box MU5311.
6 Ibid., 15.

7 AO, Gathercole Papers, box MU5463, Department of Economics and Development, 'An outline of the government of Ontario's post-World War II trends in revenues, expenditure and net capital debt and the outlook for the next five years,' June 1962, p. 37.

8 Tim Reid, who later became a Liberal MPP, worked in the department in the summer of 1960. John Oostrom, who also worked briefly in the department in the early 1960s after he graduated from the University of Toronto, served as MP for Willowdale in 1984–8 under the PC banner. Ron Atkey, who later became a PC MP and minister of consumer and corporate affairs, worked in the Federal-Provincial Affairs Secretariat in the summer of 1968. Stephen Langdon worked as a summer student in the early 1970s and eventually was elected to the House of Commons for Windsor and served as the NDP Finance critic. Janet Ecker, who eventually became minister of finance in 2002, worked in the Treasury communications branch in the 1970s. Aileen Carroll, former federal minister for CIDA and currently Ontario's minister of culture, was in the Federal-Provincial Secretariat in the late 1960s early 1970s.

Two future judges, John Laskin and Steve Gouge, worked in the federal-provincial affairs secretariat as summer students. Employees eventually promoted to deputy minister ranks are, in alphabetical order: Duncan Allan, Fareed Amin, Colin Andersen, Don Black, Eleanor Clitheroe, Kevin Costante, Bob Christie, Bryan Davies, Mike Gourley, Phil Howell, Jay Kaufman, Carol Layton, David Lindsay, Angela Longo, Steve Orsini, Gary Posen, Bryne Purchase, Saad Raffi, Terry Russell, Brock Smith, Nalini Stewart, Don Stevenson, Elaine Todres, Peter Wallace, and George Zegarac. Some were spectacularly successful in the private sector, such as David Beattie, who became president of the Weston Group. I am indebted to Don Stevenson, Tom Sweeting, and Len Roozen for their phenomenal memory.

9 See Peter A. Hall, 'The Movement from Keynesianism to Monetarism: Institutional Analysis and British Economic Policy in the 1970s,' in Sven Steinmo, Kathleen Thelen, and Frank Longstreth, eds, *Structuring Politics: Historical Institutionalism in Comparative Analysis* (Cambridge: Cambridge University Press, 1992), 90–113.

10 I am indebted to one of the anonymous evaluators of the manuscript for pointing this out.

11 Fiscal Transparency and Accountability Act, 2004, c. 27, s. 2.

Contributors

Luc Bernier is Professor at the École nationale d'administration publique. A former president of the Institute of Public Administration of Canada, his publications include (with Guy Lachapelle and Pierre Tremblay [eds]) *Le processus budgétaire au Québec* (Presses de l'Université du Québec), *De Paris à Washington: La politique internationale du Québec* (Presses de l'Université du Québec), and (with Keith Brownsey and Michael Howlett) *Executive Styles in Canada: Cabinet Structures and Leadership Practices in Canadian Government* (University of Toronto Press). He received his PhD in political science from Northwestern University.

Keith Brownsey is Professor of Public Policy at Mount Royal University in Calgary. His recent publications include (with Luc Bernier and Michael Howlett) *Executive Styles in Canada: Cabinet Structures and Leadership Practices in Canadian Government* (University of Toronto Press) and (with Michael Howlett) *The Provincial State in Canada* (Broadview Press). He has a PhD in political science from Queen's University.

P.E. Bryden is Associate Professor in the Department of History at the University of Victoria. She is the author of *Planners and Politicians: Liberal Politics and Social Policy, 1957–1968* (McGill-Queen's University Press), and co-editor (with Michael J. Tucker and Raymond B. Blake) of *Canada and the New World Order: Facing the New Millennium* (Irwin Publishers). She recently edited (with Dimitry Anastakis) *Framing Canadian Federalism* (University of Toronto Press). She received her PhD in history from York University.

Caroline Dufour is Assistant Professor in the School of Public Policy and Administration at York University, with an appointment to the Graduate Public Policy, Administration and Law Program. She has published works in the areas of public administration education and administrative history. She also has an interest in studying how public administration is portrayed in cultural works. She earned her PhD in political science at the Université de Montréal.

Patrice Dutil is Associate Professor in the Department of Politics and Public Administration at Ryerson University in Toronto. He began his career as a policy officer in the Ministry of Intergovernmental Affairs of Ontario and also worked in a variety of capacities at TVOntario. He was Director of Research at the Institute of Public Administration of Canada from 1999 to 2006. The founder of the *Literary Review of Canada*, he is the author of *The Politics of Liberal Progressivism: Godfroy Langlois and the Liberal Party of Quebec* (Robert Davies Publishing) and the editor of *Searching for Leadership: Secretaries to Cabinet in Canada* (University of Toronto Press). He received his PhD in history from York University.

Bryan Evans is Associate Professor in the Department of Politics and Public Administration at Ryerson University in Toronto. He began his career as a researcher at the Ontario Legislature before joining the Ontario Public Service, where he served in a variety of policy advisory and management roles. He joined academia after working as manager of corporate planning and policy with the Ontario Workplace Safety and Insurance Board. He has published in a number of scholarly journals, and is the author (with John Shields) of *Shrinking the State: Globalization and Public Administration 'Reform'* (Fernwood). He has a PhD in political science from York University.

Joseph Facal is Professor at the Hautes Études Commerciales of the Université de Montréal. From 1994 to 2003 he was a member of the National Assembly of Quebec and served in the Parti québécois government as Président du Conseil du trésor, Ministre d'État à l'Administration et à la Fonction publique, Ministre des Relations avec les citoyens et de l'Immigration, and Ministre délégué aux Affaires intergouvernementales canadiennes. He is the author of *Volonté politique et pouvoir médical: La naissance de l'assurance maladie au Québec et aux États-Unis* (Boréal), *Le déclin du fédéralisme canadien* (VLB), *Qui a raison?*

Lettres sur l'avenir du Québec (with André Pratte) (Boréal) and *Quelque chose comme un grand peuple* (Boréal). He has a PhD in Sociology from the Université de Paris (Sorbonne).

Gervan Fearon is Dean of the Chang School of Continuing Studies at Ryerson University. After many years in various departments of the Ontario Government, he completed a PhD in economics at the University of Western Ontario. He has published many articles in the fields of public finance, labour, and health economics, and on various aspects of microeconomics.

André Gossignac, a graduate of the École nationale d'administration, is currently a policy analyst in the Department of Indian and Northern Affairs of the Government of Canada.

Devyn Leonard is a senior policy adviser in the government of Ontario. She received her MA in Public Policy and Administration from Ryerson University in 2008.

JP Lewis is completing his doctorate in Political Science from Carleton University and is teaching at the University of Guelph.

Ken Ogata is Assistant Professor in the School of Administrative Studies at York University, with a cross appointment to the School of Public Policy and Administration. He worked for several years with the Alberta Treasury Department as a Senior Budget Analyst, and as a Senior Adviser on Performance Measurement. He is completing his PhD at the University of Alberta.

Peter Ryan is completing his doctorate at Ryerson University.

John Shields is Professor in the Department of Politics and Public Administration at Ryerson University. The author of numerous studies and academic articles, he is the co-author (with Bryan Evans) of *Shrinking the State: Globalization and Public Administration 'Reform'* (Fernwood) and, with Stephen McBride, of *Dismantling a Nation* (Fernwood). He is the editor of the *Journal of International Migration and Integration*. He received his PhD in political science from the University of British Columbia.

Gary Spraakman is Associate Professor of Accounting in the School of Administrative Studies at York University and a professional accountant. In addition to being a Chartered Management Accountant, in 2007 he was made a Fellow of the Society of Management Accountants of Canada and awarded the FMCA. Prior to his academic career he worked as a senior consultant at Coopers and Lybrand, as a manager at Molson's, and as a director at Alberta Social Services. He is the author and co-author of *Managerial Accounting: First Canadian Edition* (Nelson) and *Current Trends and Traditions in Management Accounting Case Analysis* (Captus). He received his PhD in accounting from Concordia University.

**The Institute of Public Administration of Canada Series
in Public Management and Governance**

Networks of Knowledge: Collaborative Innovation in International Learning, Janice
    Stein, Richard Stren, Joy Fitzgibbon, and Melissa Maclean
*The National Research Council in the Innovative Policy Era: Changing Hierarchies,
    Networks, and Markets,* G. Bruce Doern and Richard Levesque
*Beyond Service: State Workers, Public Policy, and the Prospects for Democratic
    Administration,* Greg McElligott
*A Law unto Itself: How the Ontario Municipal Board Has Developed and Applied
    Land Use Planning Policy,* John G. Chipman
Health Care, Entitlement, and Citizenship, Candace Redden
*Between Colliding Worlds: The Ambiguous Existence of Government Agencies for
    Aboriginal and Women's Policy,* Jonathan Malloy
The Politics of Public Management: The HRDC Audit of Grants and Contributions,
    David A. Good
*Dream No Little Dreams: A Biography of the Douglas Government of Saskatchewan,
    1944–1961,* Albert W. Johnson
Governing Education, Ben Levin
*Executive Styles in Canada: Cabinet Structures and Leadership Practices in Canadian
    Government,* edited by Luc Bernier, Keith Brownsey, and Michael Howlett
The Roles of Public Opinion Research in Canadian Government, Christopher Page
The Politics of CANDU Exports, Duane Bratt
Policy Analysis in Canada: The State of the Art, edited by Laurent Dobuzinskis,
    Michael Howlett, and David Laycock
Digital State at the Leading Edge: Lessons from Canada, Sanford Borins, Kenneth
    Kernaghan, David Brown, Nick Bontis, Perri 6, and Fred Thompson
*The Politics of Public Money: Spenders, Guardians, Priority Setters, and Financial
    Watchdogs inside the Canadian Government,* David A. Good
*Court Government and the Collapse of Accountability in Canada and the United
    Kingdom,* Donald Savoie
Professionalism and Public Service: Essays in Honour of Kenneth Kernaghan, edited
    by David Siegel and Ken Rasmussen
Searching for Leadership: Secretaries to Cabinet in Canada, edited by Patrice Dutil
Foundations of Governance: Municipal Government in Canada's Provinces, edited
    by Andrew Sancton and Robert Young
Provincial and Territorial Ombudsman Offices in Canada, edited by Stewart Hyson
*Local Government in a Global World: Australia and Canada in Comparative
    Perspective,* edited by Emmanuel Brunet-Jailly and John Martin
Behind the Scenes: The Life and Work of William Clifford Clark, Robert A.Wardhaugh
The Guardian: Perspectives on the Ministry of Finance of Ontario, edited by Patrice
    Dutil